Textbook Gods

Genre, Text and Teaching Religious Studies

Edited by Bengt-Ove Andreassen and James R. Lewis

SHEFFIELD UK   BRISTOL CT

Published by Equinox Publishing Ltd.

UK: Office 415, The Workstation, 15 Paternoster Row, Sheffield, South Yorkshire S1 2BX
USA: ISD, 70 Enterprise Drive, Bristol, CT 06010

www.equinoxpub.com

First published 2014

British Library Cataloguing-in-Publication Data
A catalogue record for this book is available from the British Library.

Library of Congress Cataloging-in-Publication Data
Textbook gods : genre, text, and teaching religious studies / edited by
Bengt-Ove Andreassen and James R. Lewis.
       pages cm
 Includes bibliographical references and index.
 ISBN 978-1-78179-054-0 (hb) -- ISBN 978-1-78179-055-7 (pb)
 1. Religion--Textbooks. 2. Religion--Study and teaching. I. Andreassen,
Bengt-Ove, editor of compilation.
 BL48.T365 2014
 200.71--dc23
                               2013039804

ISBN: 978 1 78179 054 0 (hardback)
ISBN: 978 1 78179 055 7 (paperback)

Typeset by CA Typesetting Ltd, www.publisherservices.co.uk
Printed and bound in the UK by Lightning Source UK Ltd., Milton Keynes and
Lightning Source Inc., La Vergne, TN

TEXTBOOK GODS

CONTENTS

INTRODUCTION: THEORETICAL PERSPECTIVES ON TEXTBOOKS/ TEXTBOOKS IN RELIGIOUS STUDIES RESEARCH

Bengt-Ove Andreassen

In recent years there has been a renewed interest in textbooks, partly because they have maintained their position as an important genre. Not too many years ago—and perhaps currently as well—many considered textbooks outdated or archaic compared with technological advances such as the Internet and different kinds of educational software. Despite these changes, textbooks for school subjects and for academic studies continue to be in demand.

What is a textbook and why focus on textbooks in religious studies research? These two questions are closely linked. If we first try to characterize the textbook genre, it becomes clearer how and why textbooks should be an interesting subject for research in religious studies. Textbooks constitute a genre in which established truths are conveyed, and may thus represent stable forces in a world of flux and rapid changes. This introduction aims to provide some theoretical perspectives and to characterize textbooks in order to explain what type of texts we are dealing with. Arguments for why the textbook should be a genre of interest for research in religious studies will also be presented. Additionally, some challenges regarding methodology will be addressed.

The title *Textbook Gods* indicates that this anthology is about textbooks in religious studies or in religious education, but it also signals that a textbook is a powerful medium which might provide authors with an almost sacred character. Textbooks have multiple different facets that can be researched. As the English textbook researcher John Issitt (2004: 688) has so nicely pointed out: "When the research focus is on the construction, manipulation and reproduction of power and ideology, textbooks offer rich pickings."

TEXTBOOKS—EDUCATIONAL TEXTS

Textbooks are primarily developed as educational texts. A textbook typically has educational purposes and is usually written by an expert in the field. Textbooks can appear in various forms, depending on for whom they are written. An imagined audience will therefore also influence how a textbook is developed. The

English term "textbook" cover books written for the school system, for university studies but also books addressed to a more general public. No matter which audience the textbook is designed to address, the intention of the textbook is to inform the reader of "key knowledge" and to present established truths within a field of research or a specific subject.

In a school context, textbooks often have a deep influence on the actual teaching. At universities, they are often the important first presentation in an academic area for students. Students (and parents) in every part of the educational system often expect the existence of a specific textbook which will be reflected in teaching and lectures. Even in the age of the Internet—with Wikipedia and similar sites—many students in schools or universities expect to be reading a textbook which provides well-established information and insights (overviews, key terms and so on) in the subject which they are studying. The Internet might even have provided authority to textbooks. Textbooks are regarded as trustworthy sources of approved knowledge and information. In addition to a textbook, university students are often given reading lists and compendiums with articles, which provide insights from different—and sometimes conflicting—perspectives. Still, many prefer a textbook (with a capital T) which provides a general (and authorized) introduction to whatever they are studying.

As educational texts, textbooks are regarded as sources for educational research. However, it is rather a question of the focus of the researcher when approaching textbooks as research material. In educational research, one is more concerned or focused on pedagogical/educational qualities—in terms of adaptation to different age groups and contexts (as Pingel 1999). In religious studies one asks different questions about textbooks, and there are different expectations about what a textbook should offer as a textual source. A textbook is not a good source for obtaining insights into how children experience or explain religion. Nor can a textbook say anything about how students are experiencing teaching in school. Textbooks are instead an interesting source for investigating how religions are presented and in what way textbooks produce representations: How are religion and different religions presented? What kind of representation is at play here? What values or perspectives does this particular representation reflect? What might be the reasons for this kind of representation? Such questions might uncover major differences between textbooks. Even if they are written for the same age groups or schools, and in reference to the same legislation and curriculum, the way religion and religions are presented might be very different. Textbooks are therefore sources of interest for religious studies research; they provide insight into how religion and religions are treated and presented in an educational context. This is relevant for the religious studies researcher addressing or working within a public sphere[1] because textbooks might also influence how people think of religion in general and of specific religions or religious groups. Textbooks are thus not "just" educational texts, but also products with academic, educational and ideological content (Härenstam 2000b, Johnsen 1993, Johnsen et al. 1999, Issitt 2004, Selander and Skjelbred 2004). The text is embedded in multiple discourses. Textbooks therefore intend to carve out "the right" way, the authorized way, to understand a phenomenon such as religion, or a specific religious group or how religions are related to each other. One might say that textbooks represent concretizations of power.

THE CONTEXT OF TEXTBOOKS

When writing a textbook, authors have to consider several factors and set multiple priorities. These are important for understanding this specific genre. Textbooks are usually written to fit into a specific context—a certain age group or level in school, or to a course at the university. Firstly, one must take into account relevant legislation and centrally issued curricula which provide guidelines for the preparation of textbooks. This is of particular importance for textbooks in primary, secondary and upper-secondary schools in different national school systems. Legislation and curricula for different school subjects exist in broad variety between different countries. They form a context of political values and priorities which are also expected to be parameters or guidelines for what should be included in an educational text. Legislation and curricula are thus relevant both for the development of textbooks as well as for research on textbooks aimed at a specific national educational system. Curricula and legislation likely provide important insights into why a textbook contains what it does.

Knowledge or content in textbooks is also usually adapted to an audience in some way or another. This is one of the greatest challenges for textbook authors. How does one provide an overview of Judaism to twelve-year-olds or to undergraduate university students? One might argue that the presentation should be more or less the same for both groups, because the religion is the same no matter to what age group it is presented. Nevertheless, authors must make choices that will communicate different things about Judaism when it is presented to twelve-year-olds and to university students. It is not uncommon to see that textbooks for primary and secondary schools have a tendency towards a generalization which religious studies scholars might criticize as essentialism. To describe this phenomenon, the Swedish scholar Kjell Härenstam (1993) has used the term "textbook-Islam" to refer to the representation of Islam in Swedish textbooks. He points out that textbook presentations of specific religions never fully match reality. They are presented as "maps" to match a "territory" but have rather restricted value as such. The presentation of Islam is not only influenced by ideological and cultural factors in the West, but also by the textbook genre, which has to take into account the educational system, legislation and curricula.[2]

AESTHETIC FORMATIONS IN THE QUESTION OF REPRESENTATIONS

Almost every textbook has a large variety of illustrations such as pictures, drawings, art, statistics and maps. Together with the written text, such images are a part of the representation of specific religions. Research on textbooks is therefore not just about the written text, but should also be about the aesthetics used in relation to the presentation of a religion.

One might argue that illustrations are the important first images students/ readers get when they skim through the pages. Pictures of Catholics in the Philippines who let themselves be crucified at Easter time, Shia Muslims whipping themselves bloody in remembrance of the death of Imam Hussain at the battle of Kerbala, or extreme Hindu ascetics are powerful images which will be noticed when students first skim through the book. Even if the texts that accompany the pictures try to explain and nuance what is displayed, such powerful images might stick in the student's memory and continue to be a part of his/her image of specific religions. The challenge is that all of the examples mentioned above have something to do with religion. It is not completely wrong to include them. It is rather a question of how the totality of pictures represents a religion that is important. Pictures in a chapter on Christianity which primarily display conflicts will of course push readers in a specific direction.

Maps also create an understanding of where in the world different religions are found. Often marked with different colours, they give an impression of where different religions belong in the world. Maps tend to represent a certain viewpoint, and in a way define centre and periphery, thus also defining "Us" and "the Others." Bearing in mind the wide usage of different illustrations that are common in textbooks, this is also an important part of how something is presented and thus worth paying attention to in textbook analysis.

CAN TEXTBOOKS BE LABELLED POWER TEXTS?

In order to be valid, textbooks must embody authority. The authority of the textbook is particularly manifested in its orientation toward the future and in its normativity: It has educational purposes. The educational text conveys "key knowledge" from someone who knows to someone who does not know and is in search of or in need of this knowledge. One component of all textbooks is thus an attempt to convince the reader that what it says is correct. A goal for every textbook is to be so persuasive that readers will accept what is written as "key knowledge" and a reflection of the truth (Selander and Skjelbred 2004: 36). This is achieved not only by informative prose but also by the presentation of a case so authoritative and so convincing that it appears to be self-evident and can be taken for granted (Berge 2003; Englund and Svensson 2003; Issitt 2004). Textbooks might produce what Jonathan Z. Smith (1982: 5) calls monothetic definitions of religion. Even if they are poorly formulated, such definitions form canons of how religions are understood. Hence, in being persuasive expressions of ideological positions and values, textbooks can also be characterized as power texts. This means that educational texts always strive to convey a particular idea and/or values. Textbooks can therefore be labelled as "push media," in terms of leading the reader in a specific direction which the author intended (cf. Hoover 2008: 32).

Textbooks therefore also have political implications. There is no such thing as a completely neutral book. Readers expect textbooks to provide the most important knowledge—"key knowledge"—in a subject or special topics. The range of "key knowledge" will of course reflect the author's/authors' perspectives and priorities and will always reflect "somebody's knowledge," as Härenstam (2000a) has pointed out. Knowledge about religions and beliefs is not something that is objectively given, nor does everyone perceive in the same way. A choice of perspectives and "key knowledge" will always reflect the values and wisdom of those who choose it. Although textbooks, regardless of the level for which they are written, strive for a good and factual representation, the choices and the way religions and religious groups are presented always communicate and reflect values. A textbook is thus an adaptation or use of academic knowledge, and textbook development is influenced and embedded in various criteria, both professional and educational.

In defining and outlining "key knowledge" other aspects (including contrasting knowledge) are left out. Michel Foucault's (1972b) discussion of "exclusion mechanisms" is relevant to this question, even if he writes about language more generally and not textbooks. The same mechanisms are at work when "key knowledge" is presented in a textbook; the presentation will always exclude something. What is not mentioned or included in the text appears to be secondary and ultimately unimportant—something the reader does not need to know. Associating the text's power with a specific context is not just about who the intended reader is; rather, it goes beyond this level and links to a larger context. A textbook in religion is not just a textbook for students at different stages of their education. As a representation of an ideological position, textbooks could—in a Bakhtinian (2002) perspective—also be considered as striving for dominance and thus reflect an attempt at mono-cataloguing in the discourse on religion. The text's intention is usually to emerge as authoritative by defining what the important and central knowledge is, and not to be open to other (and) competing perspectives.

Similar perspectives are established in English educational research, which has presented different views regarding the perspective that a text can be considered as representing an ideological position (see for example Luke 1988; De Castell, Luke and Luke [eds] 1989; Apple and Christian-Smith [eds] 1991; Issitt 2004; Peled-Elhanan 2012).

EXTERNAL FACTORS UPHOLDING POWER TEXTS

There are several external factors creating and maintaining power in a text. A first obvious external factor is the institutional base that wields power through a text (Englund *et al.* 2003: 161). Textbooks for universities, colleges or secondary education are of course provided with power by the authors themselves working at such institutions. The text's credibility is increased if it is written by a specialist in the field, a scholar at the university, or a teacher with extensive teaching experience. This is substantiated by the fact that most textbooks have "bioblurbs" about the author(s) which confirm and consolidate the institutional basis for the book. Additionally, authors' competence and experience are emphasized. In textbooks for higher education, the authors' previous publications on different topics are usually highlighted. Combined with a mention of the authors' years of experience in researching and teaching, it makes the text stand out with extra credibility and legitimacy. Bioblurbs give the reader an impression that "the authors really know what they are talking about." The intention seems to be to assure readers that the author, working at that particular institution, with special competence and experience in a specific academic area, cannot be wrong. He or she must be trusted in these matters.

For educational texts, schools, colleges or universities as institutions are important for the text's authority. In some countries there have been—and still are—educational boards that approve textbooks. An approved book is thus a book which has authority in the field and can be trusted. For higher education, universities and university-colleges, well-established publishers might also provide textbooks with power. Religious studies handbooks such as *The Routledge Handbook of Research Methods in the Study of Religions* or *The Blackwell Companion to the Bible and Culture* draw on the reputations of their serious and credible publishers by including their names in the title. Employing the combination of a well-established publisher and an experienced academic scholar, a text stands out as a power text.

A widely-distributed text is more likely to be regarded as a text with authority. Books that frequently show up on reading lists and syllabuses in different educational institutions are more likely to be regarded as authorized texts than those which do not. It is a rather simple mechanism—if it is a book "everybody" knows, this helps provide the book with authority. By examining certain books that have been widely read and distributed, Tomoko Masuzawa, in *The Invention of World Religions* (2005), documents how the term "world religions" was established in the 1800s and early 1900s. The same applies to Stephen Prothero and his *Religious Literacy* (2007). Both Masuzawa and Prothero use a number of different textbooks in their argumentation. The criteria for their use—though not made explicit by either of them—is that they regard textbooks as of great importance—especially books with wider distribution—and as texts which have the ability to establish authorized perspectives and knowledge.

Some textbooks are reprinted in multiple editions, but not necessarily with changes or updated information from edition to edition. When such books appear on reading lists, it means that thousands of students—either in schools, colleges or universities—have read the same book, with the same content, reflecting the same perspectives and values. Those perspectives and values then become established as "the correct" or authorized way to understand a religion or a religious group. This means that textbooks can establish "key knowledge" through generations and thus become shared experiences, forms of shared consciousness, or communities that assemble meanings. In representing "Our culture" or "Us," textbooks can display cognitive and aesthetic patterns that construct and maintain definitive boundaries towards "Others." Textbooks can create or construct a picture of who is inside and outside, us and them, centre and periphery, old and new (cf. Olsson 2010). These structures confer fundamental aspects of social identity by mapping out temporal, spatial and imagined terrains in societies.

Facing, or dealing with, well-established textbooks and their authority, it is difficult to present a different book with different and contrasting perspectives. The historian Fernand Braudel used the concept *longue durée* to characterize the enduring and stable power that lies behind and continues, even in the face of and in spite of history's great and dramatic events (Murray 2001: ix–xx). In discourse analysis the term is used to describe how discourses are maintained and difficult to change even in the face of a world in constant flux. The slow-changing structures—maintained by specific textbooks—can nevertheless not only be understood as inertia in the system, but also as active discourse production. To uphold and maintain established teaching in the face of a new curriculum might be a strategy to preserve and maintain established structures. Even if teachers (in schools or universities) try to contrast and provide nuances to the textbooks, the written text is often difficult for students to ignore or criticize.

On the basis of the theoretical perspectives outlined above and attributed to the textbooks analysed in this anthology, textbooks are of great importance regarding the representation of religion and religions. Textbooks have tremendous value in being a medium for the construction of a conceptualization of religion and of knowledge production. To regard textbooks on religion as texts of power and/or authority is an expression of this. They are expressions of ideological positions which make sense as topics of analysis in order to highlight the importance of representations of religions. Textbooks present no objective or neutral knowledge; they are expressions of someone's perspective and knowledge, a fact which affects how their content is described and presented.

ANALYSING TEXTBOOKS—THE METHODOLOGICAL CHALLENGE

As mentioned above, textbooks and textbook analysis are usually regarded as topics for educational research. Hence it is in handbooks in this academic area that one (sometimes) finds information and perspectives on textbook analysis. A much cited text on textbook analysis is Falk Pingel's *UNESCO Guidebook on Textbook Research and Textbook Revision* (Pingel 1999). Pingel is mainly concerned with the pedagogical implications of how textbooks are used by teachers and read by students. A second concern is the analysis of "the text itself," as Pingel says. He makes an important comment regarding how different research questions and methods reflect different purposes. In the literature on textbook analysis, the research questions presented as relevant are usually directed towards an evaluation of whether or not the textbook being analysed is a pedagogically good text or serves educational purposes, for example, in terms of being adapted to specific age groups, layout, going from easy to more complex topics, and how the text-book is adapted to specific legislation and curricula.

In religious studies, research questions would focus more on how textbooks present religion and religions, and what values, perspectives and patterns of power these presentations reflect. Focusing on such research questions, multiple research methods can be applied. A crucial point, nevertheless, is to decide what kind of source or text the textbook is. A reliable and valuable analysis takes into account the framework that authors have been obliged to follow. When this is done, handbooks for research in religious studies present a range of research methods which can also be applied to textbooks (cf. Stausberg and Engler [eds] 2011).

Content analysis and discourse analysis are both well suited to methodological approaches (Hjelm 2011; Nelson and Woods Jr 2011). However, even with a so-called "close reading," as in discourse analysis, the written text in textbooks can often be difficult to penetrate. They are normative texts, often with an official tone, written to persuade the reader that this is the right way to understand things. At a first glance the texts usually seem trustworthy, maybe with one or two slightly strange statements—especially for the reader educated in the specific topic. One therefore needs to keep in mind relevant research questions when starting the analysis. These could, for example, be inspired by Bruce Lincoln's (2000) fourth thesis in his "Thesis on method": "Who speaks here?—that is, what person, group, or institution is responsible for a text, whoever its putative or apparent author may be. Beyond that, To what audience? In what interests? And further, Of what would the speaker(s) persuade the audience? What are the consequences if this project of persuasion should happen to succeed? Who wins what, and how much? Who, conversely, loses?"[3]

Lincoln's questions are also related to questions regarding what is included and what is left out (and for what reason?) (cf. Foucault 1972b). Authors (and publishers) might always defend themselves facing such questions by pointing out that they work within limited space or within such frameworks as legislation and established curricula, and the fact that some choices must be made regarding what should be included or not. However, there is always a point in discussing what is included and what is not, because the choices that are made might also reflect the author's perspectives and values.

To answer questions about representation and what the text is trying to persuade the audience, discourse analysis might be an effective method to map central and surrounding concepts regarding how the different religions are presented. A second step might be to compare chapters in the same book to investigate whether the presentations of different religions are the same or follow the same principles. To map and analyse how textbooks in religious education for teacher education used and understood "religion," I systematically mapped words that were used in the text to give "religion" meaning. Words like "transcendent reality," "faith, hope and love," "the holy," "indefinable," "interpretation of life" and "culture ennobling" were used when the concept of religion was elaborated. Definitions were rarely given. Inspired by Foucault (1972a), I iden-tified discursive statements which were used to provide "religion" with mean-ing. A part of this analysis was to map the counter words or counter statements (Andersen 2003) that also provided "religion" with meaning. Counter state-ments were, for example, "fragmented reality," "postmodern," and "sensible and perceptible reality." This led to a discussion of how the textbooks were norma-tive, as "religion" was presented as something solely positive for culture and human development in reaction to postmodern tendencies in society. I argued that the textbooks were trying to persuade readers to accept that a society with-out religion, or a person without religion, would be in danger of restlessness, lack of identity, and be part of a "cold culture" based only on sensible and per-ceptible reality. The concepts used in the textbooks were also discussed in terms of the long theological tradition in Norwegian teacher education (Andreassen 2008, 2009).

Every close reading should be accompanied by the methodological ques-tion of blindness in the analysis. Danish Philosopher Niels Åkerstøm Andersen has pointed out that any analysis and observation might also lead to blindness. Andersen argues that a specific observation or analysis sees what it sees, but does not necessarily see what it does not see (Andersen 2003: 22). A methodological challenge using focused analysis and a close reading of texts is at risk of being too focused and thus too narrow. Other important factors or content might be missed. Thus, one challenge is to carry out an analysis with awareness that some empirical data cannot be analysed and discussed as thoroughly as others. A clear analytical focus is therefore methodologically challenging. To be aware of such possible blindness, Lincoln's above-mentioned thesis should be supplemented with the question "What is it that I do not see in the analysis? What do I miss?" This is important in order to be methodologically disciplined.

A close reading of a text—whether it is a content analysis or a discourse analysis—should also include reference to intertextuality. What other texts are present in the text, either *in praesentia* or *in absentia*, to use the words of Norman Fairclough (2003)? Are there specific texts that are heavily cited or on which the text heavily relies? In textbooks for primary and secondary education, citations are frequently used but often without specific references, unlike textbooks for higher education where references are more frequent. Thus, intertextuality in textbooks will often be *in absentia* and therefore a challenge for analysis. In some cases intertextuality *in absentia* might be easy to spot. For example, in one of the textbooks for teacher education it is asserted that "Religion is deeply something which thoughts alone cannot perceive."[4] This formulation and perspective is very close to the well-known formulation of the characteristic of religion by Rudolph Otto (*mysterium tremendum et fascinans*) but occurred in the textbook without any references to secondary literature. Nor did the author mention Otto. To identify an intertextual connection between the two statements, one must have knowl-edge of the history of religious studies and especially of the development of the phenomenology of religion. If authors bring in perspectives from different academic disciplines, it makes it difficult—perhaps impossible—to identify intertextuality *in absentia*. This makes the texts even more difficult to penetrate.

THE CONTRIBUTIONS IN THIS BOOK

The 14 contributions in this volume cover different national contexts and their distinctive educational systems, ranging from primary, secondary and upper-secondary school to higher education such as universities and university colleges. The articles display a wide variety of approaches to analysing textbooks. Most of the contributions focus on content analysis.

Each of the contributions related to a specific national educational system also provide insight into national curricula and legislation. This applies to articles referring to RE in primary, secondary and upper-secondary schools in national contexts such as Australia, Canada (Quebec), Denmark, England, Japan, Norway and Switzerland.

The first article addresses the well-known topic of essentialism within religious studies. Writing from a Swedish context, **Torsten Hylén** addresses the challenge of essentialism in religious studies and teacher education. His point of departure is his experience as a teacher of religious studies. He has found that the majority of students unconsciously carry with them an essentialist view of religion, a perception that presumably was socialized into them during their upbringing. Additionally, through discussions with student teachers who have relatively fresh experiences from their own schooling or who have interned in public schools, he argues that many active teachers in Swedish schools have perceptions about religion that are more or less essentialist. Therefore, the present article is oriented primarily towards student teachers who intend to become teachers of religious studies, but also to current religion teachers. Hylén's principal discussion of essentialism is of particular relevance for textbooks. The question about the role of textbooks in the development of attitudes among teachers and student teachers which he describes remains an open question.

Satoko Fujiwara writes about Japanese textbooks in social studies. The educational programme in social studies for secondary education in Japan is divided into three main categories: geography, history and civic studies. "Ethics" is one of the main themes presented in civic studies, and it is in textbooks developed for this subject that religions are presented. Fujiwara shows how Japanese textbooks on ethics, which are supposed to teach about religions neutrally and objectively, not only hierarchize religions but also ask students to follow the teachings of Jesus and Buddha. The original strategy seems to have been to convert religions into moral teachings and, thereby, maintain the separation between church and state (or the secularity of education). However, textbooks do use the word "religion," and it is highly ambiguous whether they are teaching religion or something else. Fujiwara also shows how the national multiple choice exam influences how teachers and students evaluate a good textbook. A good textbook provides answers which can simply be reproduced on an exam.

Katharina Frank offers an in-depth focus on one specific textbook for the subject "Religionskunde" in Switzerland. Frank discusses how it contributes to the typical negative or positive images of religions which can be found in public and media discourses, as well as in the perception of individuals in Switzerland. Frank's article also provides an interesting example of a methodological approach to analysing textbooks.

The establishing of a new religion education subject for primary and secondary schools in Quebec, Canada, in 2008, required new textbooks. Ethics and religious culture (ERC) replaced the earlier faith-based subject in Christianity and its alternative subject, ethics. **Sivane Hirsch** and **Marie McAndrew** write about six textbooks approved by the Quebec Ministry of Education, as well as some additional material. As the new ERC subject was introduced at the same time at all levels, most teachers were not trained to teach it. Textbooks have therefore been quite important for the teachers' planning and teaching of this course. Hirsch and McAndrew focus on how Judaism is presented in these texts, both generally and more specifically in relation to Quebec's cultural and religious heritage.

Based on a research project on teaching materials used in an English RE project at Warwick University, **Barbara Wintersgill** focuses on the representations of religion in English textbooks. She examines not only how those involved in the research project at Warwick praised many of the qualities in the textbooks they viewed, but also the points picked out for concern. Many books, they found, were designed to broaden students' knowledge of religions, promote positive attitudes towards religions, and to support community cohesion by emphasizing the possibilities for peaceful coexistence among religions.

Carole M. Cusack examines the presentation of Indigenous Australian religions in current textbooks used in Australian secondary schools in the New South Wales Higher School Certificate (matriculation) course, Studies of Religion. Cusack argues that the majority of textbooks for this course, and the subject syllabus they reflect, continue to manifest the dominance of the "world religions" paradigm and the normative status of Christianity in defining religion. Aboriginal religion is generally treated cautiously and with respect, reflecting the aura of "political correctness" surrounding discourses about Indigenous Australians in the twenty-first century.

In her article, **Mary Hayward** argues that more attention has been paid to the analysis of the written text than visuals in textbooks, and suggests that image-based research has low status. She argues that scholars in religious education have paid too little attention to the materiality of religion and to images in textbooks. Hayward further argues that interpreting what is seen is a multi-layered task; different images require different kinds of questions and varied pathways of research, and therefore must receive attention in religious education. Her article thus opens with a reflection on religion and materiality in general, before turning to a discussion of images of Christianity and Hinduism in English textbooks for religious education.

Another contribution on images is **Suzanne Anett Thobro's** article about cartographic representation of religions in textbooks. The point of departure for her study is the general tendency in Norwegian textbooks to describe religions as abstract objects, with no relations to time or space. Analysing cartographic representations in Norwegian textbooks for upper-secondary schools in the period from the 1930s to the present, she describes how the use of maps has developed. A basic premise in her analysis is that the moment one visualizes religion(s) cartographically, spatialization occurs, albeit still as abstract object(s). Depending on the map's view and on where the different religions (or adherents) are placed on the map, the different religions are made local, regional or world religions, and more or less affixed to specific areas.

Textbooks for higher education are discussed in contributions by **Bengt-Ove Andreassen** and **James R. Lewis**. Andreassen draws attention to textbooks in teacher education at university colleges and universities in Norway. He argues that religion is presented as something solely good and as a valuable source for human development. The topics of religion and conflict or religious violence are not included. Such topics are most likely regarded as a disruptive force within the broader project of promoting religion as something good, and confessionally-oriented religious education as something positive for children.

James R. Lewis examines the portrayal of indigenous African religions in world religion textbooks. The chapter is an updated version of an article originally published in 1990. In this volume the article is updated by examining the structures of the texts currently available for world religions survey courses. Thus Lewis' article addresses a tendency which has been stable for over 20 years. The most significant criticism levelled in his survey is the implicit evolutionary structure reflected in the order of chapters, so that smaller-scale traditional religions, such as the aboriginal religions of sub-Saharan Africa, are typically placed at the beginning of these texts as if to suggest that such religions represent an earlier level of religious development. Lewis argues that almost all relevant textbooks continue to embody this structure, but not every survey text groups currently-existing peoples together with prehistoric peoples, and not every such book discusses the religions of contemporary indigenous peoples prior to discussing the dead religions of the classical world. Lewis also comments on how textbooks are perpetuated by being reprinted in new editions and gives examples on how outdated misinformation continues to be reproduced in twelfth and thirteenth editions.

Annika Hvithamar presents the work of developing a textbook in religion for Danish primary and secondary schools. Hvithamar discusses, from the author's point of view, the challenges in developing a religious studies-based textbook in a context where established legislation and curricula are strongly influenced by Lutheran Christianity. Although facing several challenges as a textbook author, Hvithamar argues that scholars in the academic study of religion should be engaged in writing textbooks ourselves, rather than simply criticizing the books that others have written.

A rather different kind of "textbook" is discussed by **Jens Andrè Herbener**. In his article he provides a critical and detailed review of the Danish *The School Bible* (*Skolebibelen*) published by the Danish Bible Society in 2011. This is an edition of the Bible directed towards teaching Christian studies in the Danish *Folkeskole* (both primary and secondary school, ages 7-15). This special educational edition of the Bible includes a *Bible Guide*, a *Bible Dictionary* and two different Bible translations, and it is thus tailor-made for teaching in school. Herbener argues that in spite of a number of good elements, *The School Bible* is characterized by a large number of errors, misleading formulations, shortcomings and omissions—and in many cases by a Christian, usually Protestant, bias. His conclusion is that it is therefore not suitable for a subject such as Christian studies in a public and secular school. In the conclusion, the article also questions the use in the educational system of textbooks and translations for which religious organizations are responsible.

Together the chapters in this volume confirm Issitt's statements cited above: Textbooks do indeed "offer rich pickings." Hopefully, this volume might contribute to an increasing interest in the study of textbooks among scholars of religious studies.

REFERENCES

Andersen, N. Å. 2003. *Borgerens kontraktliggørelse*. København: Hans Reitzels forlag.

Andreassen, B.-O. 2008. "Et ordinært fag i særklasse. En analyse av fagdidaktiske perspektiver i innføringsbøker i religionsdidaktikk." PhD thesis. Tromsø: University of Tromsø.

Andreassen, B.-O. 2009. "Seige strukturer. Perspektiver på endring og diskursivt arbeid i norsk religionsdidaktikk." *DIN. Tidsskrift for religion og kultur* 1: 5-29.

Apple, M. W., and L. K. Christian-Smith, eds. 1991. *The Politics of the Textbook*. London: Routledge.

Bakhtin, M. 2002. *Speech Genres and other Late Essays*. 8th edn. Austin: University of Texas Press.

Berge, K. L. 2003. "Hvor er makten i teksten?" In *Maktens tekster*, ed. K. L. Berge, S. Meyer and T. M. Trippestad, 24-41. Oslo: Gyldendal akademisk.

DeCastell, S., A. Luke and C. Luke, eds. 1988. *Language, Authority and Criticism: Readings on the School Textbook*. London: Falmer Press.

Englund, B., and J. Svensson. 2003. "Sakprosa och samhälle." In *Teoretiska perspektiv på sakprosa*, ed. B. Englund and P. Ledin, 61-89. Lund: Studenlitteratur.

Englund, B., *et al.* 2003. "Texters auktoritet." In *Teoretiska perspektiv på sakprosa*, ed. B. Englund and P. Ledin, 161-80. Lund: Studenlitteratur.

Fairclough, N. 2003. *Analysing Discourse: Textual Discourse Analysis for Social Research*. London: Routledge.

Foucault, M. 1972a. *The Archeology of Knowledge*. London and New York: Routledge.

Foucault, M. 1972b. "The Discourse on Language." Appendix to the *Archaeology of Knowledge*, 215-37. New York: Pantheon.

Hjelm, T. 2011. "Discourse Analysis." In *The Routledge Handbook of Research Methods in the Study of Religions*, ed. M. Stausberg and S. Engler, 134-50. New York: Routledge.

Hoover, S. H. 2008. "Audiences." In *Keywords in Religion, Media and Culture*, ed. D. Morgan, 31–43. New York: Routledge.

Hvithamar, A. 2011. "Uden for murene—når religionsvidenskaben møder fagtraditionen." In *At kortlægge religion. Grundlagsdiskussioner i religionsforskningen*, ed. T. Hammersholt and C. S. de Muckadell, 207–22. Højbjerg: Forlaget Univers.

Härenstam, K. 1993. *Skolboks-islam. Analys av bilden av islam i läroböcker i religionskunskap*. Göteborg: Acta Universitatis Gothoburgensis, Universitetet i Göteborg.

Härenstam, K. 2000a. *Kan du höra vindhästen? Religionsdidaktik—om konsten att välja kunskap*. Lund: Studentlitteratur.

Härenstam, K. 2000b. "How to Choose Knowledge for Swedish Schools and Textbooks in RE?" *Panorama. International Journal of Comparative Religious Education and Values* 12(1): 27–42.

Issitt, J. 2004. "Reflections on the Study of Textbooks." *History of Education. Journal of the History of Education Society* 33(6): 683–96.

Jackson, R. 1997. *Religious Education: An Interpretative Approach*. Norfolk: Hodder & Stoughton.

Johnsen, E. B. 1993. *Textbooks in the Kaleidoscope*. Oslo: Scandinavian University Press.

Johnsen, E. B., ed. 1999. *Lærebokkunnskap. Innføring i sjanger og bruk*. Oslo: Tano Aschehoug forlag.

Lincoln, B. 2000. "Reflections on 'Theses on Method.'" In *Secular Theories on Religion: Current Perspectives*, ed. T. Jensen and M. Rothstein, 117–21. København: Museum Tusculanum Press.

Luke, A. 1988. *Literacy, Textbook and Ideology*. London: Falmer Press.

Masuzawa, T. 2005. *The Invention of World Religions*. Chicago: University of Chicago Press.

McCutcheon, R. T. 2001. *Critics not Caretakers: Redescribing the Public Study of Religion*. Albany, NY: State University of New York City Press.

McCutcheon, R. T. 2006. "A Response to Donald Wiebe from an East-Going Zax." *Temenos* 42(2): 113–29.

Murray, O. 2001. "Introduction." In *Memory and the Mediterranean*, ed. F. Braudel, ix–xx. New York: Vintage Books.

Nelson, C., and R. H. Woods Jr. 2011. "Content Analysis." In *The Routledge Handbook of Research Methods in the Study of Religions*, ed. M. Stausberg and S. Engler, 109–121. New York: Routledge.

Olsson, S. 2010. "*Our* View on the *Other*: Issues Regarding School Textbooks." *British Journal of Religious Education* 32(1): 41–48.

Peled-Elhanan, N. 2012. *Palestine in Israeli School Textbooks*. London and New York: I. B. Tauris.

Pingel, F. 1999. *UNESCO Guidebook on Textbook Research and Textbook Revision*. Hannover: Verlag Hahnsche Buchhandlung.

Prothero, S. 2007. *Religious Literacy*. New York: Harper One.

Selander, S., and D. Skjelbred. 2004. *Pedagogiske tekster for kommunikasjon og læring*. Oslo: Universitetsforlaget.

Smith, J. Z. 1982. *Imagining Religion: From Babylon to Jonestown*. Chicago: University of Chicago Press.

Stausberg, M., and S. Engler, eds. 2011. *The Routledge Handbook of Research Methods in the Study of Religion*. New York: Routledge.

Wiebe, D. 2005. "The Politics of Wishful Thinking? Disentangling the Role of the Scholar-Scientist from that of the Public Intellectual in the Modern Academic Study of Religion." *Temenos* 41(1): 7–38.

Endnotes

1. In recent years there has been an interesting debate among well-established religious studies researchers about the researcher as a public intellectual (cf. McCutcheon 2001, 2006; Wiebe 2005). Writing textbooks, or contributing to textbooks, is not something which is addressed in this debate. However, such can also be regarded as politically controversial. Annika Hvithamar's article in this volume gives a certain insight in this matter (cf. also her article [2011] on the public and political reactions on a book about Christianity in Denmark).

2. In England, a research project at Warwick University has met the challenge of generalization and essentialism by focusing on children's stories about their religion and beliefs. Ethnographic material has been collected and used as a basis to develop educational materials such as textbooks (cf. Jackson 1997). One of the basic ideas has been that children's own stories about different ways to be Christian or Sikh make it easier for other children to relate to the diversity within religions. This might also help students in primary school to reflect that there might be a difference between an individual's religion and a major religious tradition.

3. See also research questions formulated in the different chapters in this volume.

4. This statement is discussed further in my article "A reservoir of symbols" in this book.

1. CLOSED AND OPEN CONCEPTS OF RELIGION: THE PROBLEM OF ESSENTIALISM IN TEACHING ABOUT RELIGION

*Torsten Hylén**

1. INTRODUCTION

Although the concepts "religion" and "religions" have been discussed for decades in other countries—perhaps foremost in the United States and the United Kingdom—debates of this nature have been almost non-existent in Sweden. Few books and articles published in Swedish have seriously addressed the conceptualization of religion. Until relatively recently, a phenomenological approach to religion has prevailed and has seldom been questioned. During the last decade, this approach has in many cases been replaced by more constructivist ways of viewing religion. However, this change has not occurred consistently throughout religious studies in higher education, and what little discussion has emerged has hardly reached beyond academic contexts.[1]

Having spent approximately 15 years as a teacher of religious studies, primarily for prospective religion teachers in public schools, I have reached an increasingly strong conclusion that many students unconsciously carry with them an essentialist view on religion, a perception that they acquired during their childhood. Additionally, through discussions with students in the teachers' education programme who have relatively fresh experiences from their own schooling or who have interned in public schools, I have learned that many active religion teachers in Swedish schools have perceptions about religion that are more or less essentialist.[2] Therefore, the present article is oriented primarily towards students who intend to become teachers of religion, as well as current religion teachers. Of course, I hope others will also find it interesting.

* Torsten Hylén wrote his thesis on the story of Husayn b. Ali's death at Karbala (unpublished 2007). He has also written articles on the early historiography of Islam and on the relation between historiography and myth. At present he is a lecturer in the history of religions at Dalarna University, Sweden.

2. ESSENTIALISM AND THE PROBLEM OF BOUNDARIES

Essentialism is the view that some properties of an object are necessary, whereas others are incidental. Essentialist positions also emerge in contexts other than religion. Common forms of essentialism are racism, sexism, and nationalism; that is, perceptions that human races, genders, or nations compose well-defined entities that have certain specific characteristics necessary for their identity, while other features are temporary. Thus, one could imagine statements such as these: "The black race has a physical constitution that is adapted to physical work" (racism), "Women are by nature more caring than men" (sexism), or "It is important to preserve Swedishness in Sweden, and not allow other cultural elements to come in and destroy it" (nationalism).

These forms of essentialism have been criticized because they have led to contempt for other people, oppression, and sometimes even to genocide. In these cases, essentialism has been combined with a value hierarchy, which entails the idea that certain races or nations or genders are superior to other(s) and have a right to assert their own position at the cost of the other(s). Similar perceptions have been asserted in religious contexts. A number of examples, including the Christian crusades during the Middle Ages, Jewish fundamentalism in today's Israel, ideas of Hinduism and Buddhism on superiority over religious minorities in countries such as India and Sri Lanka, or Islamic terrorism, can all be viewed as expressions of religious essentialism of a sort that creates violence and oppression. However, religious essentialism does not necessarily have these negative consequences. In fact, all forms of religious faith are essentialist. The adherent of Islam, Christianity, Hinduism, or any other religious movement, necessarily has to assert that his or her own belief has certain characteristics that are foundational; for example, that God exists and has revealed himself, or that everything composes a unit and that if we acquire the right knowledge about it, we can avoid the cycle of rebirth. Even the person who has some kind of inclusive perception about the religions—for example that all religions lead to salvation—assumes that religion as such has certain characteristics that make it religion.

In this article, however, I am not primarily interested in religious essentialism, but the kinds of essentialist expressions that emerge within studies, research, and instruction about religion in academia and in school.[3] In these contexts, essentialist perspectives are also very common. Later, I will provide some examples of essentialist positions among scholars of religion, before proposing an alternative way to relate to religion in instruction and research. First, however, I would like to comment briefly on the basic problem and then provide a short background of how the history of religion as a scientific discipline has changed over the last 150 years.

Applying an essentialist position to such a complex phenomenon as religion presents a series of problems. Such an exercise is largely about drawing boundaries between what belongs to the phenomenon and what does not; in other words, to indicate what makes up the essence of religion in general or an individual religion in particular. The difficulty is that, regardless of where one draws the boundary between what is and what is not religion, certain phenomena that are generally viewed as religion will end up outside that boundary, or what is generally not viewed as religion will be included. Of course, anyone has the right to define religion as she or he wishes; however, if the definition deviates too much from the general understanding, it will be difficult to communicate and share this perception with others. Problems can also arise to someone who attempts to study cultures that have an entirely different way of viewing that which we call religion.

The American anthropologist Benson Saler maintains that religion and the designations of the different religions are Western *folk categories*. In other words, they are concepts and categories that have emerged in our societies over the course of several centuries, that generally work very well, and are taken as self-evident by most people who have been raised in Europe or North America (Saler 2000: 21–23). Only when the Western folk category meets other ways of viewing what people in the West call religion, do problems arise. This can happen either through migration of people between cultures or when scholars of religion attempt to study other cultures on site. Somehow, we need to make clear, in a way that works constructively during encounters with other cultures and forms of religion, to ourselves and each other what we mean when we talk about religion and religions. The question is how. Any attempt to provide an essentialist definition of religion will be met with criticism and new definitions.

Scholars of religion sometimes create methodological or stipulated definitions of religion. They are created for specific objectives such as research projects, and are not for general use. Therefore, such definitions do not say what religion is, but only how the concept of religion is used in a specific context. I will not deal with these kinds of definitions here.

3. PERCEPTIONS OF RELIGION WITHIN THE HISTORY OF RELIGIONS

I am a historian of religions, and most of the examples that I will address also come from scholars of the history of religions. Therefore, I want to begin by providing a short overview of how ideas about what religion is and how it should be studied have changed over time within the academic discipline that is now designated as the history of religions.[4] I wish to show that perceptions of religion have not been constant, even within academic research in the West. In the book *Nytt blikk på religion* (*New Views on Religion*), the Norwegian historians of religions Ingvild Saelid Gilhus and Lisbeth Mikaelsson discuss three paradigms within the discipline of the history of religions that have succeeded each other from the late 1800s to the present day (Gilhus and Mikaelsson 2001).[5] The *evolutionist* paradigm was prevalent from the late 1800s to the mid-1900s. The basic notions of this paradigm were taken from Darwin's theory of evolution. The underlying idea was that not only nature, but also society and culture, had undergone a development from lower to higher stages and that cultural development had occurred according to a predetermined pattern. The arrangement of stages of development differed somewhat between different scholars; thus, Edward Tylor (1823–1917), to whom I return below, postulated a development from animism via polytheism to monotheism. James Frazer (1854–1941), on the other hand, discussed development from a stage of magic to a stage of religion, which continues to move closer to the stage at which science prevails in a society. Different cultures develop at various speeds, but always follow the same development scheme. Thus, the evolutionists argued, it is possible to compare various cultures and religions from different historical periods. A common feature of the evolutionists was that they all viewed Christianity as the most developed religion.

In the mid-1900s, the *phenomenological* paradigm replaced the evolutionary one.[6] The designation "phenomenology of religion" is an unclear collective name for an array of different approaches to the study of religion. Here, I will primarily describe the so-called hermeneutic phenomenology that counted individuals such as Gerardus van der Leeuw (1890–1950), William Brede Kristensen (1867–1953), and Mircea Eliade (1907–1986) as its foremost thinkers. An important point of departure for the phenomenological approach, according to Gilhus and Mikaelsson, is the religious person's image of his (less often her) own faith. Therefore, the prototype of the religious person is someone who has the deepest religious experiences, the religious elite (usually men); that is, ascetics, mystics, prophets, and other similar persons. These individuals become the standard for perceptions of the correct interpretation of the religion. Hence, it is possible to talk about, for example, a religion's "core" on the one hand, and its "popular expressions" on the other. Concepts such as "distorted variations" and "syncretism" are common. Since the self-image of religion is the starting point, the perception that the religion is "good" is part of the phenomenological paradigm (Gilhus and Mikaelsson 2001: 31–32). The hermeneutic phenomenology of religion opposed reductionism; that is, the attempt to "reduce" religion to something that can be explained solely by "inner-worldly" factors, such as psychological (e.g., Freud) or socio-economic (e.g., Marx). Instead, it was argued that religion is a *sui generis* category; that is, an entirely unique phenomenon that cannot be explained solely with the help of other sciences. In opposition to reductionist theories, many phenomenologists claimed that "the sacred" actually exists and reveals itself to humankind. Since religion is an entirely unique phenomenon, it is not necessary to study religions in their historical or cultural contexts; they should be studied in the context of each other. In other words, a religion should be studied primarily in relation to other religions, not in relation to the environment.

According to Gilhus and Mikaelsson, the *cultural studies* paradigm is currently replacing the phenomenological one. Within this paradigm, religion is studied as one of several aspects of culture. Here, the emphasis is on the interaction between what we call religion and other cultural phenomena. The communication between actors, both religious and non-religious, becomes important. "The exploration of the subject religion moves...from heaven down to earth" (Gilhus and Mikaelsson 2001: 35, my translation); that is, instead of having gods and the religious elite's religion as a point of departure, the emphasis is on "common" people, both men and women. The existence of "the sacred" is not assumed. Instead, individuals' expressions of faith are studied.

Essentialist attitudes toward religion exist within all three of the above-mentioned paradigms, but are clearly predominant in the first two. Even though the phenomenological paradigm is less common in the academic study of religion today, an essentialist understanding of religion lives on in the consciousness of many, perhaps most individuals in our society outside of the academic sphere. Political debates are conducted on the base of the idea that religion has an essence of some kind, and much of the criticism of religion from the so-called new atheism builds on this assumption. Explanations of religio-political events in different parts of the world, for example, are often based on an essentialist perception of religion. The Swedish scholar of Islam, Jan Hjärpe, discussed this issue in an article on the development of Islamic studies in Sweden. He writes:

> In the debate in Sweden, certain ideas circulate that exist also in the political debate. One is the idea that religious belonging is *determining*, that it decides how people act. Another is the idea that religious traditions are *constants*, unchangeable, recognizable through the centuries. The third is that religious people follow the statements of religious *leaders*, and that what religious leaders say is therefore representative of the entire group. All of these three ideas are demonstrably inaccurate. (Hjärpe 2012: 273, my translation, emphases in original)

Hjärpe continues by showing, firstly that religious people do not always behave as the traditional interpretations of the religion stipulate and that there are several normative systems other than the religious that must be taken into consideration and that are often prevalent. Secondly, religions and norm systems change constantly through new interpretations of rituals, decrees, and other symbols. Thirdly, religious people often do not care what their leader says. In my view, it is even possible to say that most religious people follow their leaders' statements when it suits them; that is, when the social, political, or economic context does not conflict too much with the leaders' decrees.

4. ESSENTIALISM AND RELIGION—AN ATTEMPT AT TYPOLOGY

Several kinds of essentialism are visible in the study of and teaching about religion. In the following pages, I provide a typology of some important forms. My hope is that this typology will help readers discover and identify expressions of essentialism when they appear in different contexts. The model presented below is far from complete. My purpose is to highlight the most common forms of essentialism, including those which a beginner in the field of religious studies is most likely to encounter.

I have avoided using the term "essentialist" to denote the scholars in my examples. Firstly, it is difficult to know to what degree their essentialism is conscious. As some of my examples show, those who express essentialist ideas about religion sometimes do so unconsciously, or at any rate without deeper reflection. Secondly, as the Canadian philosopher Ian Hacking has noted, "essentialist" is a denigrating expression; most people do not readily speak of themselves as essentialists (Hacking 1999: 17). Thus, I will rather speak of essentialist expressions or essentialist formulations.

Furthermore, I occasionally talk of "believers" when referring to adherents of religious traditions. I use this expression merely as an ellipsis for a space-consuming and more complicated designation. It is not my intention to maintain that religion is mainly a matter of belief.

Expressions of essentialism can either concern the religion's *substance* or the religion's *function*. By religion's substance, I mean an expression of essentialism that is about what religion or individual religions *are*, while the religion's function expresses what the religion *does* to people. I have chosen to divide each of these categories into two subdivisions.

Substance of religion
    Theological or transcendental essentialism
    Core essentialism

Function of religion
    Positive essentialism
    Negative essentialism

The designations positive and negative essentialism are short forms of the longer and clumsier positively and negatively *evaluating* essentialism. Of course, it is open to discussion whether the function of a phenomenon can be categorized as its essence. When I refer to positive and negative essentialism, however, I mean statements that assume that religion as such, or individual religions, are good or whether they cause harm to people. If that which is supposed to be religion lacks this quality, it is in fact not religion. Instead, the proponents of this kind of essentialism argue, it is something different, such as politics or culture in a religious disguise. In itself, essentialism concerning the function of religion is a necessary, but not sufficient criterion for what composes religion. In order for a phenomenon to be counted as religion, or an aspect of it, it must have a positive (or a negative) effect on people, but it is not enough that it does this. There are many things in the world that are good (or cause harm) that are not religion. Those who express a positive or negative essentialist position to religion already have an idea of what religion *is*—and therefore about its substance.

In the following section I will illustrate the model with some examples. First, I will discuss expressions of essentialism concerning religion's or an individual religion's substance, then I will address their function.

4.1. *Substance of religion*
4.1.1. *Theological or transcendental essentialism.* By theological or transcendental essentialism, I mean the notion that religion is dependent on a transcendental power of some sort—this power might be called the sacred, divine, or something else—that reveals itself/themselves to people. An excellent example of this is found in the work of the German theologian and historian of religions Rudolf Otto (1869–1937), in his 1917 book *Das Heilige* with an English translation in 1924 called *The Idea of the Holy* (here, I refer to the 1936 edition). At the beginning of the book, Otto writes:

> The reader is invited to direct his mind to a moment of deeply-felt religious experience, as little as possible qualified by other forms of consciousness. Whoever cannot do this, whoever knows no such moments in his experience, is requested to read no farther; for it is not easy to discuss questions of religious psychology with one who can recollect the emotions of his adolescence, the discomforts of indigestion, or, say, social feelings, but cannot recall any intrinsically religious feelings. (Otto 1936: 8)

Otto here says that there is no point for those readers who cannot remember a specific religious experience in reading further, because they will not understand what the book is about. For Otto, religion and the experiences and feelings that constitute it cannot be described with help of other concepts or categories. He talks about the *numinous* feeling[7] that only arises in the meeting with a higher power (Otto 1936: 10–11). This power manifests itself for the person as a *mysterium tremendum*. The feeling of mysterium arises as it is something unutterable and impossible to describe in human terms. It is a mysterium *tremendum* because it inspires feelings of reverence, superiority, and energy. At the same time, however, it is *fascinans*—fascinating and magnetic. This type of experience is unique to religion: "There is no religion in which it does not live as the real innermost core, and without it no religion would be worthy of the name" (Otto 1936: 6).

A more modern representative of this form of essentialism is the above-mentioned Mircea Eliade, who has been tremendously influential. In the book *The Sacred and the Profane*, which has been translated into many languages and published in large editions, Eliade writes: "Man becomes aware of the sacred because it manifests itself, shows itself, as something wholly different from the profane. To designate the *act of manifestation* of the sacred, we have proposed the term *hierophany*" (Eliade 1959: 11, emphases in original).[8] Religions are based on these hierophanies and individuals' reactions to them. Therefore, a starting point here is that "the sacred" exists and manifests itself to people.

This form of essentialism often entails the idea that people have an inherent religious need, a predisposition or instinct to search for "the sacred." Otto and Eliade, as well as the Swiss psychologist Carl Gustav Jung (1875–1961), held this perception.

When scholars of religion use theological or transcendental essentialism, it is almost always applied to religion as a general category. Individual religions constitute historically and culturally determined variants of this manifestation. Understandably, believing people often mean that precisely the manifestation that *they* have experienced is true or genuine. As I have stated above, though, my focus will remain on the secular study of religion.

4.1.2. *Core essentialism*. In the following section, I will examine the form of essentialism that argues for the existence of other fundamental characteristics that determine what religion is, rather than a transcendent or sacred power that reveals itself to humanity.[9] Among such features are, for example, ideas, concepts, actions or feelings that are specific to religion as such or to an individual religion. A core essentialist position in relation to religion as an all-encompassing category differs somewhat from the core essentialism that concerns individual religions, so I will address each position in turn.

The most common form of essentialism within religious studies is based on the idea that religion as such has one or several traits that characterize it and that compose what is and what is not religion. Numerous scholars of religion have attempted to create definitions of religion, and during most of the twentieth century, the absolute majority of these have been of the sort that I have classified as core-essentialist.[10] Below are some examples, with brief comments, of definitions of this type.

One of the simplest and still most influential definitions of religion is that which the British anthropologist Edward B. Tylor (1832–1917) presented in his 1871 book *Primitive Culture*,[11] in which he argues that religion is "the belief in spiritual beings" (quoted in Sharpe 1986: 56). As was the case for most scholars who worked with religion from a comparative perspective at that time, the question that primarily occupied Tylor was the origin of religion. For Tylor, this origin could be found in peoples' questions about death and the difference between the living and the dead, as well as in the observation that dead and sleeping people showed similarities. So arose the belief in the soul as a separate entity, and this idea was furthermore applied to other creatures and natural phenomena. Additionally, the belief arose that these souls could act independently, free from the bodies to which they were normally bound. Tylor called this belief in souls *animism* (from the Latin *anima*, "soul" or "sense"). What distinguished Tylor from many of his contemporaries was his perception that "primitive" religion was something quite rational, and that "savages" were capable of thinking on the same level as his own contemporaries, with the clear exception that "the primitive individual" did not possess the same knowledge as a European at the turn of the twentieth century. For Tylor, religion was primarily an intellectual phenomenon, with faith and philosophy as foundations for other aspects of the religion.

Another influential definition was formulated by the American anthropologist Clifford Geertz (1926–2006) in the article "Religion as a Cultural System."[12] Geertz's definition is longer and more sophisticated than that of Tylor:

> Religion is (1) a system of symbols which acts to (2) establish powerful, pervasive, and long-lasting moods and motivations in men by (3) formulating conceptions of a general order of existence and (4) clothing these conceptions with such an aura of factuality that (5) the moods and motivations seem uniquely realistic. (Geertz 1973: 90)

Here, Geertz is stating that religion is a system of symbols that creates strong and long-term sentiments and motivations in people. By symbols, he is not referring only to that which we might mean by a symbol: for instance a sign, a small image, or a logotype. For Geertz, a symbol is every object, action, event, characteristic, or relationship that functions as a bearer of a concept, and he refers to that concept as the symbol's "meaning." Symbols work as models for people, both as models *of* reality and as models *for* how we should live and act (Geertz 1973: 91–94).

Tylor's and Geertz's definitions have both attracted criticism from various perspectives.[13] The critique that I want to bring out here is that both definitions place religion's real centre in the interior of the human being. Many critics have argued that these definitions present a Western, or even (Protestant) Christian perception of religion. Faith, feelings, sentiments, and motivations are phenomena that occur commonly in Christianity, but often not in the same way in other religious traditions where, for example, actions or the fulfilment of religious law have much greater significance. Neither do all who confess to being Christian possess these mental states, at least not at all times. It is possible to be a passionate believer, and it is possible to exercise religion by force of habit or convention without necessarily placing a great deal of thought or feeling into religious exercise.

Neither Tylor nor Geertz would agree that religion is *only* associated with the inner life. However, by making these aspects into the basis for religion, both accomplish a simplification that causes much of the varied phenomena that we would otherwise call religion to be cut away.

Above, I have discussed that which I call core essentialism concerning religion as a general category. I will now look at some examples of similar positions toward specific religions. Here, the point is that a certain religion contains a core of truths, ideas, or behaviour that are specific to that religion. A person who does not accept or conform to the core does not belong to the religion. In many cases, a certain point in time (often the religion's "formative period," such as the early Christian church or Islam in Medina during Muhammad's time) or the religion's formation in a special geographic area (for example, Islam in the Arab world), is considered to be normative and to indicate the correct formation of the religion.

The varieties of the religion that do not agree with this form can be referred to as "popular religion," "syncretic" or even "distorted forms" of the religion.

This approach is currently not particularly common among scholars of religion. It is generally accepted that there are different expressions of a religious tradition and that the scholar should relate neutrally to all of these. However, an example of the opposite is the book *Islam, the Straight Path* by the American scholar of Islam John L. Esposito (1988). It is an introductory book to Islam that has spread widely and has been translated into numerous languages. In the first three chapters of the book he describes Islam as a religion, its pre-modern history including the Prophet Muhammad's biography, the Qur'an, as well as the early political, theological, and legal development of the Muslim community. Chapters 4–6 address development in modern times. The book is used as course literature on Islam in several universities, both in Sweden and in other countries. The book's popularity is reflected in the fact that it was published in an extended fourth edition in 2011 (Esposito 2011). The interesting point in the context of the present study is the description of Islam in the book's first three chapters. The picture presented there is very traditional and seems to build on an Arabic, "orthodox" Sunni form of Islam that, through the outline of the chapters, appears as more original than other variants (even if Esposito does not expressly say so). Sufism and the religious exercise within the Shiite branch of Islam are placed under the heading "Popular religion" in chapter 3. The outline, which has been maintained in the newest edition, indicates that Esposito regards the more "Shari'a-oriented" interpretation of Islam (either consciously or unconsciously) as the authentic form. Exactly what it is that makes Sufism and Shi'ism more popular variants than the Sunni, non-mystical form of Islam, is not clarified, but by placing these forms of the religion under "Popular religion," Esposito gives them a lower rank than the supposedly authentic Sunni form.

A more explicit expression of core essentialism is found in the book, *Abrahams Barn: Vad förenar och skiljer judendom, kristendom och islam?* (*The Children of Abraham: What Unites and Separates Judaism, Christianity and Islam?*) (1999) by the Swedish historian of religions Christer Hedin. Hedin compares Judaism, Christianity, and Islam, with the primary aim of showing the great similarities that exist between the three religions, rather than the differences that otherwise are so often highlighted. In the introduction of the book, Hedin writes:

> Over the centuries, the three religions have developed in different directions. Many external traits have changed and thereafter become part of the religions. These new features have often been taken from the surrounding culture and have later been incorporated into the religion. These new features have sometimes stood in conflict with the religion's basic principles. When people adhering to different religions have lived in each other's vicinities, they have adopted different external customs, a function of which have often been to create identity and a spirit of community within the group and to separate the supporters of the three religions

from each other. However, these differences do not need to indicate a contradiction between the religious content in the three religions. On the theological and theoretical level, they can well agree. But as soon as a conflict or a competitive relationship arises, the differences come to the forefront. Then, the supporters of one religion highlight their distinctive features in order to differentiate themselves from the competitor or the opponent. It is ironic that the characteristics which are then emphasized, frequently have been taken from outside. The religions are in conflict with each other because of a teaching or a custom that they have borrowed from the surrounding culture. They fight for something that was not originally their own. This alone can be sufficient reason to thoroughly study what separates and unites the children of Abraham. They all have the same god and the same role model in faith. How can it be that they still are perceived as being so different? This is usually because of external factors that can be very important. (Hedin 1999: 10–11, my translation)

The above quotation includes examples of both types of core essentialism discussed above. According to Hedin, Judaism, Christianity, and Islam each have their own core (although Hedin does not use this word in his text) that makes up their original and authentic base. The core consists of the "religious content" on "the theological and theoretical level" in each of the three religions. "External characteristics" have later been added to the religious core, characteristics which have been taken from the surrounding culture and been incorporated within the religions with the purpose of marking the followers' identities with respect to the followers of other religions. It is primarily the external characteristics, rather than the religious content, that cause strife between these religions.

Hedin seems to take for granted both a perception of what constitutes religion as a general category and of what characterizes each of the three religions discussed. As he puts it in the quotation, religion as such belongs to the theological and theoretical level. Consequently, Judaism, Christianity, and Islam also have an original core, which consists of certain theological and theoretical ideas. The external additions did not originally belong to the religions (and probably not to religion as such either) but are taken from the surrounding cultures and later incorporated into the religions. The cores of the three religions do not cause strife. Perhaps it is even possible to talk of the core of religion in the singular. Anyway, it is easy to conclude that religion, in its original, pure form, without any disturbing additions, is peaceful and good. It is the additions that create conflict.

There are several problems with a perception such as that expressed by Hedin. How is it possible to determine what belongs to the core; that is, "religion's basic principles"? Most scholars of religion would agree with Hedin that there are phenomena in religious traditions whose task is to create a sense of community within the group and differentiate them from other, competing groups, and that these are quite common. Thus, for example, it has been proposed that the number of daily prayers within Islam was established at five to contrast them with the three daily prayers in Judaism and the seven within the Syrian church's monastic life (Rippin 2012: 108). However, few scholars would be prepared to refer to such identity-creating elements as "external additions" in contrast to "the religion's basic principles," especially concerning such important aspects of a religion as Islam's five daily prayers.

What we call religion constantly changes, and the drawing of boundaries between what comprises a religion's core and what is an external addition, or religion and culture, becomes quite arbitrary if it is performed by scholars of religion. (Adherents of religious traditions, on the other hand, have the right to interpret their tradition as they wish.) For example, what comprises the religious core of Judaism? The law as it was expressed in the Torah is there, but the interpretations of different aspects of it are totally different today compared to the time when the temple service was performed before the destruction of the temple in 70 ce. In fact, the very concept of law has undergone enormous development since the time of the second temple. It is possible to argue that rabbinic Judaism (the form of Judaism that is by far the most common today) differs from temple Judaism, in that the former hold the oral Torah—that is, the interpretations of the written law codified in the Talmud—to be an expression of God's will (Goldenberg 1992). What, then, are Judaism's "basic principles"? Similar objections can be raised about central ideas within Christianity and Islam.

In fact, precisely the figure that Hedin highlights as the common example in faith—Abraham—also functions as a differentiator within both Christianity and Islam toward the previous traditions. In the New Testament, Paul argues against Judaism by stating that Abraham became righteous through his faith and not through being circumcised and keeping the law (Rom. 4). In the Qur'an, we can read: "Abraham in truth was not a Jew, neither a Christian; but he was a Muslim and one pure of faith" (Qur. 3:67, Arberry's translation).

A particular problem in Hedin's text is found in the first clause of the third last sentence in the quoted text: "They all have the same god..." What does Hedin actually mean by this? Here it seems that Hedin manifests what I call theological or transcendental essentialism. At the same time, it can hardly be viewed as a statement of faith, because Hedin does not express himself as a believing theologian, but as a historian of religions. Now, in a different part of the book where he compares different phenomena of the three religions, he further explains what he means. By saying that the three religions have the same god, Hedin simply means to say that the Hebrew and Arabic words for god are related.

> In Arabic, god is named Allah, with the definite article al and a name of god that in its longer form reads ilah and in its shorter only il. It is the same word as the Hebrew el... The Bible's god is named El, which shows that it is the same god [in Judaism] as in Christianity and Islam. (Hedin 1999: 213, my translation)

How Hedin can draw this conclusion about god's ontological status from similarities between two closely related languages is not apparent.[14]

Hedin shows in several other places in his book that he is fully aware of the fact that religions change and are affected by their contexts. For example, he offers a rationale about Judaic law that is similar to my own above (Hedin 1999: 227). However, his basic thesis—that religions have certain foundational principles that constitute their "religious content," that different "external additions" are subsequently added to these cores, and that the similarities primarily become visible in the key principles of a religion, while the differences are the most clear in the additions—this thesis is still clearly essentialist.

I do not mean to argue against searching for similarities between religions; after all, historians of religion have always worked with comparisons, and it is an important aspect of this discipline (Paden 1994: 1–5). The problem is that scholars and others that search for similarities sometimes do so with the implied premise that, if only the religious adherents understood how similar the religions are, then conflicts between them would be avoided. Below, I argue that this is the purpose of Hedin's book. This notion often entails serious generalizations in order to demonstrate the many similarities between the religions. The religious traditions are not studied in their historical and social contexts; instead, the religions become each other's contexts.

* * *

To summarize the above discussion, I would like to highlight two important arguments against core essentialism. The first is the problem of how to adequately delimit the concept of religion or the essence of an individual religion: Where do you draw the boundary? Who and what is included or left out, and why? In other words, core essentialist concepts of religion indicate unacceptable simplifications of the multi-faceted phenomena that we call religion. The second argument is the difficulty of determining who has the right to create such a boundary. Is it the scholar of religion? In that case, which of all of the scholars' definitions should we accept? Or should we assign the task to the believers? Again, which believers should have the privilege of determining what the core of their religion is?

4.2. The function of religion
I will now move on to a discussion of essentialist perceptions regarding the function of religion or of specific religions in human life and society. As mentioned above, people who express an essentialist position on the function of religion almost always take their point of departure in a perception of the religion's substance that is also essentialist. This is demonstrated in the following examples.

4.2.1. *Positive essentialism.* By positive essentialism I mean the perception that religion in general or a specific religion is characterized by factors such as love, peace, equality, or freedom of opinion; in short, values generally perceived as positive in liberal democracies. If a phenomenon is not what we consider to be "good," then it is simply not an expression of true religion or of a correct interpretation of a certain religion. Interestingly, this type of essentialism is primarily expressed when someone talks about phenomena that are perceived as negative, and thus attempts to alienate religion from these. A common argument is that acts such as violence, war, and oppression take place in the *name* of religion or that religion is *used* for political purposes. By this kind of expression the idea is conveyed that a particular religion is not actually intended to be this way, but that it has been kidnapped by forces that use it for their own purposes.

This form of essentialism is expressed in the American philosopher Martha Nussbaum's book *The Clash Within* (2007), which discusses the violence that ultranationalist Hindu groups have directed toward Muslims in Gujarat and other parts of India. Nussbaum says:

> It would be a serious misreading of this book to see it as an assault on Hindu religion or Hindu traditions. All traditions have good and bad features. On the whole, however, the traditions of Hinduism have been strongly conducive to pluralism, toleration, and peace. What happened in Gujarat was not violence done by Hinduism; it was violence done by people who hijacked a noble tradition for their own political and cultural ends. Piety and spirituality would seem to play little or no role in the choices of Hindu-right politicians; nationalism plays an all-important role, and religious ideas and images are reconstructed for nationalistic purposes (as the loyal yet kindly monkey god Hanuman becomes a ferocious enemy of the Muslims, as even the playful candy-loving Ganesha becomes, at times, a muscled warrior with sword held high). (Nussbaum 2007: 8–9)

Nussbaum argues that even if Hinduism sometimes manifests negative characteristics, it generally promotes pluralism, tolerance, and peace. The violence against Muslims in Gujarat has not been exercised by Hinduism as such, but by people who have distorted it. I will briefly analyse two details of Nussbaum's argument. Firstly, she differentiates between Hinduism as a religion and the people who interpret it. To her, Hinduism as a religious tradition is good on the whole. However, certain contemporary groups that have interpreted Hinduism have distorted the tradition. The second aspect of interest in Nussbaum's argument is that she seems to perceive the core of Hinduism as piety and spirituality, in contrast to nationalistic politics and its effects. Thus, Hinduism is piety, but not politics (at least not of the nationalistic kind). This, I believe, is a clear example of how a form of core essentialism of the sort that I discussed above is behind a positive essentialization of Hinduism. In Nussbaum's statement, the tradition becomes something that is independent of real people. The essence of Hinduism consists of certain values, such as pluralism, tolerance and peace, piety and spirituality, that in Nussbaum's eyes represent what is good. Those whose interpretations of Hinduism do not agree with these values have distorted it—they are not real

Hindus. Of course, it is possible here to pose a series of questions to Nussbaum, such as what Hinduism would be without people who interpret it; whether her own interpretation of Hinduism is not just one of many; and what criteria make it possible to determine whether her interpretation of Hinduism is more correct than that of Hindu Nationalists.

It is important to note that the brief quotation above is the only statement in Nussbaum's 400-page book that can be perceived as essentialism concerning Hinduism as religion and tradition. In many other parts of the book, Nussbaum clearly shows that she does not perceive Hinduism as an essence that is independent of the people who interpret it. I view this paragraph as a carelessly formulated defence in the beginning of the book. The author wants to show that she holds Hinduism in high esteem and that she is not out to criticize the religion as a whole, only a certain form of it. Yet, I have chosen to include this quote because it is a clear example of an essentialist formulation. It also shows that even those who study religion in more reflective ways can express themselves in a careless manner. The fact that Nussbaum is a philosopher and not a scholar of religion might explain this shortcoming.

My second example of positive essentialism is taken from the British author Karen Armstrong, whose popular books about religion have reached a large audience in different countries. Unlike Nussbaum, it is easy to find examples of essentialism in Armstrong's writings, although only one is discussed here. In the book *Islam,* she writes about the emergence of modern Islamism, and about one of its prominent figures, Sayyid Qutb:

> The violent secularism of al-Nasser had led Qutb to espouse a form of Islam that distorted both the message of the Quran and the Prophet's life. Qutb told Muslims to model themselves on Muhammad: to separate themselves from mainstream society (as Muhammad had made the *hijra* from Mecca to Medina), and then engage in a violent *jihad*. But Muhammad had in fact finally achieved victory by an ingenious policy of non-violence; the Quran adamantly opposed force and coercion in religious matters, and its vision— far from preaching exclusion and separation—was tolerant and inclusive. (Armstrong 2002: 169–70)

Armstrong states here that the true interpretation of Islam denies that Muhammad exercised violence against his opponents. Thus, a positive interpretation of Islam (from the perspective of Armstrong's own values) is correct. Armstrong does not reflect on the fact that she, a non-Muslim, claims to present a better and more accurate interpretation of Islam than Sayyid Qutb, who as a believing Muslim for decades studied and attempted to understand God's will with his life and with the society in which he lived. There are certainly many Muslims who share Armstrong's interpretation, and if she had been a Muslim, her statement would have been a statement of faith. In that case, she would have had every right to express herself as she does, and it would have been possible to view her statement as a contribution to an intra-Muslim debate. Instead, Armstrong wants to appear as a scholar of religion and as a scientific authority on the area; therefore, I feel it is necessary to make higher demands on her neutrality in interpreting the religious traditions she presents.

I will return to Christer Hedin for my third example. The purpose of Hedin's book *Abrahams barn (Abraham's Children)* is to show that there are great similarities between Christianity, Judaism, and Islam and that the differences between them have been stressed too strongly (Hedin 1999: 7–9). However, he does not expressly say why it is important to display the similarities. My perception when reading this book is that what Hedin actually argues is that, if the followers of the three religions emphasized the core of their faith rather than the differentiating "external characteristics," they would live in peace and harmony. In a short article in which he compares the three religions, just as he does in *Abrahams barn*, Hedin's text confirms, in my view, this interpretation:

> If the religions will contribute to peace and harmony on earth, it is necessary to first eliminate the idea of having a monopoly on God and the truth. All good powers must co-operate for a better world. The three religions have the same moral message and the same hope for the future. That fellowship must not be obscured by a proclamation characterized by complacency and territorial thinking. (Hedin 2004, my translation)

The core of each of the three religions is good, while the additions often create problems. In this context, Hedin's reasoning about the ethics of the three religions is noteworthy. He states that one must distinguish between the religions' basic morals—in Hedin's terminology their "central ethics"—and the rules and ordinances—"signal ethics"—that are intended to promote inner cohesion and spirit of community as well as mark the boundary with other groups. According to Hedin, the tenets of the central ethics of the three religions could be summarized in four basic principles: stewardship, thirst for knowledge, kindness toward fellow human beings, and righteousness and peace (Hedin 1999: 245–50). Besides the fact that the very distinction between central ethics and signal ethics must be questioned for the same reasons as the division into the religions' cores and external additions, I would argue that the ethical conduct that Hedin highlights as basic in these three religions is in fact rather trivial. One could perhaps agree with Hedin that the principles listed are central (though I highly doubt that a majority of believing Jews, Christians and Muslims would accept that), but the main problem is the content given to these concepts by various representatives of the religious traditions. In other words, religious people have very different ideas of what the central ethical principles that Hedin has listed mean in practice.

Nussbaum, Armstrong, and Hedin all take their point of departure from their own values when assessing what is bad and good. Most of us consider acts of terror, such as the Jewish settler Barukh Goldstein's massacre of praying Muslims in Hebron on 25 February 1994, the extremist Christian pastor Paul Hill's murder of an abortion doctor in the United States on 29 July of the same year, or the attack that followers of al-Qaida directed toward the World Trade Center and the Pentagon on 11 September 2001, terrible deeds and feel that similar actions must be countered. However, the persons who planned and performed these deeds all felt that they were performing God's will. Their actions were a natural consequence of the struggle for the good social order that God wants to establish in the world, *against* true evil. They did not feel that they were *using* religion for political purposes. They believed that their actions had been decreed by God and were performed as a religious ritual.[15]

4.2.2. *Negative essentialism.* The antithesis of positive essentialism is negative essentialism, by which I mean the perception that religion or (less frequently among scholars of religion) a specific religion is irrational, oppressive, violent, and so on; in short, represents values usually perceived as negative in liberal democracies. If something is not bad or causing harm, then it is simply not an expression of true religion or the correct interpretation of a certain religion.

As an example of negative essentialism, I use the well-known biologist and atheist Richard Dawkins' bestselling book *The God Delusion* (2006), in which he sharply criticizes all forms of religion. Dawkins' basic thesis is that all religion is built on the assumption that a god exists.[16] Here, then, is the core-essentialist point of departure in his reasoning. According to Dawkins, belief in God does not build on any empirically verifiable facts. This belief has arisen as the result of a number of evolutionary side-effects; that is, characteristics that originally developed in humanity in order to give us better opportunities to survive in the world, but which have also been put to other uses (Dawkins 2006: 172–90). An example of such side-effects is our ability to ascribe intention and meaning to countless different phenomena. This behaviour is especially common in children. "Clouds are 'for raining.' Pointy rocks are 'so that animals could scratch on them when they get itchy'" (Dawkins 2006: 181). Evolutionary biologists often argue that this characteristic has developed in order to give humans better conditions for survival, for example through the capability to communicate with each other, or to be able to quickly interpret the behaviour of dangerous animals. A side-effect of this important characteristic is that we ascribe will and intention to all types of natural phenomena. Thus, for example, falling blocks of stone and thunder can be interpreted as having the intention to hurt humans because they are angry at us. From that point, the step to fully developed religion is very short.

The notion of evolutionary side-effects as the origin of religion is significantly more complex and sophisticated than what I have described here, and many scholars who work with evolutionary studies of religion (and who do not have the same negative positions towards it as Dawkins) work on the basis of this theory. Specific to Dawkins, however, is the idea that religion is carried on from generation to generation as *memes*. Dawkins has coined the concept of memes as a cultural equivalent to genes in biology, as details in the cultural heritage, such as ideas, actions, and symbols. Dawkins maintains that, just as genes are copied and biologically carried on from generation to generation, memes are copied between generations in the process by which a person is socialized into a certain culture. Religious memes—that is, thoughts, ideas, and behaviours that are connected to God and the supernatural—are spread in the same way from generation to generation in that authorities, such as parents, teachers, and religious officials such as priests and imams, pass them on to children and even to adults who are dependent upon these authorities. Through myths and rituals, the authorities convey ideas about the world, why it is shaped in this way, how a person should behave and act, what is right and wrong, and so on.

Therefore, religion is irrational in its very nature. It is not built on a person's independent search for the truth, but on authorities prescribing what is the truth. This entails negative consequences, such as intellectual narrowness, discrimination against dissidents and dissent, and often also leads to violence. Dawkins is careful to point out that all religion, not just the extreme kinds, potentially can give rise to such unacceptable phenomena, and he quotes, Voltaire, who supposedly said: "Those who can make you believe absurdities, can make you commit atrocities" (Dawkins 2006: 306). Dawkins continues, saying:

As long as we accept the principle that religious faith must be respected simply because it is religious faith, it is hard to withhold respect from the faith of Osama bin Laden and the suicide bombers. The alternative, so transparent that it should need no urging, is to abandon the principle of automatic respect for religious faith. This is one reason why I do everything in my power to warn people against faith itself, not just against so-called "extremist" faith. The teachings of "moderate" religion, though not extremist in themselves, are an open invitation to extremism. (Dawkins 2006: 306)

Regardless of whether a person accepts the theory about the origin of religion in evolutionary side-effects, there are problems with Dawkins' view of religion. Both evolutionary biologists and scholars in various cultural disciplines have criticized Dawkins' theory about memes (Wilson 2007; Deacon 1999). Without going further into this discussion, it is enough to recall Hjärpe's comment that religious people do not unconditionally follow their leader's decrees. Furthermore, the connection between religion and extremism is by no means necessary, as Dawkins claims. "Moderate" religion cannot be viewed as an open invitation to extremism. Under certain circumstances, moderate religion can lead to extremism, as much of the rich flora of literature about "religious fundamentalism" shows, but it is also undoubtedly the case that non-extreme forms of religion often work to dampen extremist tendencies and help its followers interpret their faith in a manner that is less destructive for society. Moreover, non-religious ideologies have the same range of interpretations. One example is the plethora of political ideas inspired by the teachings of Karl Marx, where we encounter everything from parliamentary social democracy to communist dictatorship and extremist left-wing terrorism. However, I totally agree with Dawkins that we must be able to criticize forms of religious behaviour that we feel do harm. Instead we should support and encourage those that are positive for society. All societies must do this. Here, a discussion about the concept of religion and religion's nature that takes into consideration all of its complexity and does not over-generalize, plays an important role. It is to such a discussion that I hope to contribute through this chapter.

Negative essentialism concerning individual religions is not common among scholars of religion. It is found mostly among believers who argue against other religious groups, or among groups who, for political reasons, want to condemn a certain religion. One example of the latter variant is the description of Islam from right-wing extremists.

* * *

Like core-essentialism, negative and positive essentialism represent broad generalizations and simplifications. What we call religion or individual religions consist of phenomena that are too complex to be explained as good or as causing harm. Religions can be interpreted in different ways, and different aspects of the same religion can have varying functions in society and for individuals.

5. AN ALTERNATIVE TO ESSENTIALISM: FAMILY RESEMBLANCE AND PROTOTYPE

The American anthropologist Benson Saler argues for a way of viewing religion and individual religions that differs from the essentialist view. He states that, just like many other concepts we use without problem in daily life, "religion" is so ambiguous and amorphous that it is impossible to draw boundaries using a strict definition. Saler argues that the most natural starting point for a discussion about the concept of religion is the folk category religion, because we cannot get away from it no matter how much we might want to. When scholars of religion begin to study a culture with which they are unfamiliar, they have a starting point, which is their perception about religion with which they were raised. The researchers identify different phenomena in the new culture that are religious when these fit in with their inherited perception of religion. Saler argues: "In large measure, indeed, their scholarly efforts to define and characterize religion are efforts to refine and deepen the folk category they began to use as children, and to foreground what they deem most salient or important about religion" (Saler 2009: 173). Problems arise, however, when the folk category religion does not work, when it conflicts with other perceptions of religion; for example, ideas which assert that things that are not self-evidently included in the folk category are actually closely bound up with what we perceive as religion. In such situations the folk category must be questioned and discussed. In order for people with different understandings about what religion is and its role in society to be able to meet and co-operate, the analytical category of religion cannot be built solely on the Western folk category. Accordingly, Saler starts his book with the question of how we can transform a folk category into an analytical category that can facilitate cross-cultural research and understanding (Saler 2000: 1).

In contrast to a folk category, an analytic category is said to be one that can be used with greater precision to investigate, study, and assess different phenomena that are considered to fall into that category. As noted earlier, the greatest difficulty in creating analytic categories of such complicated phenomena as religion is that we can easily make them too small; we essentialize, or as Saler also puts it, *digitize* the concept of religion. By that, Saler means that we treat the category religion as if it were a binary category: either religion or non-religion; yes or no; 0 or 1 (Saler 2000: 12–13). The difficulty in essentializing religion is how to delimit the category. Saler writes:

> The question of boundaries plagues all efforts to establish universal categories by monothetic definitions, whether the definitions be weighted toward functional considerations...or towards substantive ones. Ideal essentialist definitions would supply unambiguous, un-vague boundary-creating and boundary-maintaining statements so that phenomena could be confidently sorted (digitized) into those that are covered by the definition and those that are not. (Saler 2000: 120)[17]

Saler suggests that, instead of essentialist definitions, we should work with religion as an *open* category that is defined by its centre rather than its boundaries. Where phenomena are located closer to the centre, they are deemed to be religion to a higher degree than phenomena that are far from the centre. One way of doing this, Saler says, is to proceed from the thought of *family resemblances* in combination with *prototype theory* when working with the concept of religion. The idea about family resemblances is especially associated with the Austrian-British philosopher Ludwig Wittgenstein (1889–1951). Wittgenstein stated that there are many concepts in our languages that designate phenomena in society which are so multi-faceted that they cannot be defined in a clear-cut way. He uses the concept of *games* as an example:

> Consider, for example, the activities that we call "games." I mean board-games, card-games, ball-games, athletic games, and so on. What is common to them all?—Don't say: "They *must* have something in common, or they would not be called 'games'"—but *look and see* whether there is anything common to all.—For if you look at them, you won't see something that is common to *all*, but similarities, affinities, and a whole series of them at that. To repeat: don't think, but look!... And the upshot of these considerations is: we see a complicated network of similarities overlapping and criss-crossing: similarities in the large and in the small. (Wittgenstein 2009, I: 66)

Wittgenstein goes on to state that the best way to characterize this sort of relationship between different elements is the concept of family resemblances. In the same way as games are different, no two members of a family are exactly the same as each other, although they often share certain traits: "build, features, colour of eyes, gait, temperament, and so on and so forth—overlap and crisscross in the same way.—And I shall say: 'games' form a family" (Wittgenstein 2009, I: 67).

Saler suggests that when working analytically with the overall category of religion, we should view it as a pool of elements composed of such phenomena that we generally associate with religion, such as faith in transcendental beings, a moral code that is sanctioned by this faith, mythologies that describe origin and end of the world, rituals that refer to these mythologies, and so on. The specific examples we call religions (Christianity, Hinduism, Taoism, etc.) take, to different extents, part of the elements in this pool. The religions are bound to each other through family similarities. This means that not every one of them needs to take part in every element of the pool, and no element needs to be present in all religions. However, they belong together through the complicated net of similarities that overlap and "crisscross," as Wittgenstein put it. This way of reasoning can, of course, be applied to traditions within specific religions as well. Eva Hellman has provided an example of how Hinduism can be viewed as a family of traditions in this way (Hellman 2011: 125), and Saler argues that the idea that each individual religion composes a family of traditions can apply to all religions (Saler 2000: 208–209).

The question, then, is from where we get the elements in "the religion pool." Saler was not the first to apply the theory of family similarities to religion, but he was the first to combine it with the so-called prototype theory, as it has been articulated within cognitive psychology and cognitive linguistics (Saler 2000: ch. 6). According to this theory, a prototype is the best or clearest example of members in a certain category. In order to illustrate what this means, when I teach, I often ask my students to come forward to the white board in the classroom and draw a bird or a fish. Almost every time I ask them to draw a bird, they draw something that looks very much like a sparrow or a warbler. I have never seen anyone draw an ostrich or a penguin. The same occurs if I ask them to draw a fish—what they draw is mostly similar to a dace or a perch, not an eel or a seahorse. The students know that ostriches and penguins are birds and that eels and seahorses are fish, but they are not equally *good examples* of the category to which they belong. A warbler or a house sparrow is among the most prototypical examples of the category bird for someone who grew up in Sweden, and a fish similar to a perch or dace is the most prototypical example of the category fish.

Within cognitive research, it is often argued that a large part of our thinking is based on prototypes, and that we are entirely dependent on them in order to be able to operate as rational beings (Lakoff and Johnson 1999: 19). Our categories are formed through experiences we have during childhood and adolescence, and what counts as the most prototypical examples in a category are generally the most commonly occurring examples within that category—those that we have encountered most often during our lifetime. This also concerns the category of religion, and this is where the idea of folk categories comes into the picture. The folk category religion as it appears in Western Europe and North America has been built around the most prototypical examples in this category—those instances of religion that most people in these parts of the world have had the most experience with: Judaism, Christianity, and perhaps also Islam (even though each of these can show very different faces).[18] It is in this prototypical religion that we find the elements that we include in the overall category religion (Saler 2000: 225–26). In prototype theory, together with the idea of family similarities, Saler asserts that we have the tools with which to transform a folk category into an analytical category.

The categories "birds" and "fish" are *bounded* categories; that is, we can, with relative certainty, delimit them by indicating which conditions should be fulfilled in order to belong to them. *Open* categories, on the other hand, have unclear boundaries and are not distinct from other categories. Many open categories are also graded; they have a centre of clear examples, while examples that are found further from the centre are not such good examples of members of the category. Saler states that we should view the category of religion as an open and graded category where, for example, Judaism composes a *more* prototypical example and where classic Theravada Buddhism, which in certain perspectives can be viewed as entirely free from transcendental elements, is a *less* prototypical example and sometimes is viewed as a life philosophy rather than a religion. An even more unclear case is Soviet communism, which in itself had many elements from the pool of religion but which lacked others. Was it a religion or not? For example, Soviet communism had rituals that in many ways were reminiscent of the Orthodox Church and historical writings that could be perceived as mythical. Where, in cases like this, is the boundary drawn between religion and other aspects of the culture, such as politics, economy, art, and sports? In a similar way this argument can be applied to boundaries between specific religions. When and where was a sect within the tradition we call Judaism transferred into what we call Christianity? Is the form of religion that we see evidence of in the epistle of James in the New Testament closer to Judaism than the Christianity that Paul represents? Or, to consider contemporary examples, are Jehovah's Witnesses and the Jesus Christ's Church of Latter Day Saints' (the Mormons) movements within Christianity, or are they religions in their own right? According to Saler's way of reasoning, it is not possible to give a clear answer to these questions. They must be discussed, and scholars of religion will probably not reach common positions on them. However, by presenting arguments and conclusions, it is possible in each context to show how the discussion has been conducted.

Saler is careful to point out that Judaism, Christianity, and Islam are not in themselves sufficient representatives of the analytical category of religion. They can, at best, represent a point of departure for reflection around what religion is. "As the most prototypical exemplars, the Western monotheisms are useful for purposes of reference, illustration and comparison. They do not, however, define our model" (Saler 2009: 179). With these three religions as a point of departure, the model, the religion pool, can be expanded and redefined. An example of such a change is the study of so-called new religious movements. Not so long ago, it was considered inappropriate for a scholar of religion to study them. Today, the study of such movements provides important insights into how religions originate and develop. Furthermore, it is not possible, from a perspective of secular research about religion, to view prototypical Western religions as superior or more developed than others. They comprise the best starting point because the emergence of the Western concept of religion is, to a high degree, linked to them, and they therefore compose the most prototypical examples of religion.

6. THE PROTOTYPE AS POINT OF DEPARTURE IN INSTRUCTION ABOUT RELIGION

Doesn't the use of "our own" religions and "our" image of what religion is as a point of departure amount to a form of ethnocentrism? Saler admits that this is in fact the case, but he also states that it must be this way. When we attempt to learn something new, all we can do is to proceed from what is familiar to us. He writes, somewhat ironically:

> In English—to indulge in a bit of ethnocentrism—we commonly say that we wish "to arrive at" understanding and knowledge, a phrasing that implies a journey. And journey, as I ethnocentrically understand it, involves a starting point. Ethnocentrism is not necessarily a fatal contaminant when we constitute a starting point, for it enables us initially to identify problems that we deem interesting, and it furnishes us start-up categories with which to embark on a journey towards greater understandings. (Saler 2000: 9)

The journey is a metaphor for learning, and a journey must have a starting point—in this case, our often rather ethnocentrically formed prototypical perception of religion. In the last chapter of his book *Conceptualizing Religion*, Saler discusses the French philosopher Paul Ricoeur's concept of "distanciation" in relation to the ethnocentric starting points of scholars of religion. Saler discusses how distanciation from the familiar categories and the surroundings as well as from the "foreign" environments that are studied, becomes a tool with which to better understand and, in its academic context, be able to explain the worlds that have been investigated (Saler 2000: ch. 7). This requires us to be conscious of the context from which we come and the pre-understanding we carry with us.

The Swedish pedagogue and historian of ideas Bernt Gustavsson offered a similar reasoning in his discussion of education in the book *Bildning i vår tid* (*Education in our Time: About the Possibilities and Conditions of Education in Modern Society*) (Gustavsson 1996: 39–58).[19] Gustavsson proceeds from the idea that education is a journey, a departure from the familiar, out into the world where the traveller has new experiences and makes new discoveries, and returns, changed but still the same. "The journey, the adventure, the departure and the homecoming are the most common metaphors of the idea of education [Sw. *bildning*]" (Gustavsson 1996: 39, my translation). We interpret the new and the foreign with the help of the ingrained and familiar and, in so doing, incorporate the unknown into our image of the world and transform it into something well-known. According to Gustavsson, the very rationale for education is this movement between the familiar and the unfamiliar; through becoming acquainted with the world, we get to know ourselves. The movement between the well-known and the unfamiliar is both individual and shared. "We interpret with the help of others through comparing and giving resistance to each other's interpretations. Therefore, the dialogue, the conversation, is natural and foundational when it comes to education, knowledge and learning" (Gustavsson 1996: 43, my translation).

In Gustavsson's book, education (Sw. *bildning*) in general stands at the centre, not instruction and the learning of individual subjects. The point of discussing Gustavsson here is that even instruction of specific subjects, such as religious education in school and religious studies in higher education, follows the same patterns. I do not mean that all instruction about religion must begin with Judaism, Christianity and Islam, but that we who teach must proceed from the concepts of religion that most of our students have been socialized into, and that they generally use as the basis for their images of these religions. When we become conscious about our own pre-understandings, including essentialist approaches to religion that we might carry, we are given the opportunity to continue the journey that involves studying the complexity of ideas and behaviours that we call religion. Furthermore we will be able to provide our students with the map they need to embark on that journey themselves.

Finally, as I have indicated above, a non-essentialist perception of religion does not automatically involve ethical relativism. Maintaining that religion in general or a certain religion can be interpreted and expressed in different ways, is not the same thing as arguing that all of these interpretations and forms of expression are equally good for individuals or for society. Certain forms (such as authoritarian and oppressive forms) can be perceived as causing harm to individuals, and others (such as extreme and militant forms of Islam or Christianity) can even be dangerous. Of course, we have the right to dissociate ourselves from such kinds of religious expression. Such a position culminates in the question about which forms of religion we are prepared to allow in society today, and therefore in a discussion about the concept of freedom of religion. This, however, is a subject that extends far beyond the scope of the present chapter.

REFERENCES

Andersson, Daniel, and Åke Sander. 2009. "Religion och religiositet i en pluralistisk och föränderlig värld." In *Det mångreligiösa Sverige—ett landskap i förändring*, ed. Daniel Andersson and Åke Sander, 37–148. 2nd edn. Lund: Studentlitteratur.

Armstrong, Karen. 2002. *Islam: A Short History*. Modern Library edn. New York: Modern Library.

Arvidsson, Stefan. 2004. "Gud är en pseudonym." In *Med gudomlig auktoritet. Om religionens kraft i politiken*, ed. Catharina Raudvere and Olav Hammer, 9–31. Göteborg: Makadam.

Arvidsson, Stefan. 2012. *Varför religionsvetenskap? En ämnesintroduktion för nya studenter*. Lund: Studentlitteratur.

Blomkvist, Torsten. 2002. *Från ritualiserad tradition till institutionaliserad religion. Strategier för maktlegitimering på Gotland under järnålder och medeltid*. Teologiska institutionen, Univ. [distribution], Uppsala.

Dawkins, Richard. 2006. *The God Delusion*. London: Bantam.

Deacon, Terrence W. 1999. "Editorial: Memes as Signs." *Semiotic Review of Books* 10(2): 1–3.

Eliade, Mircea. 1959. *The Sacred and the Profane: The Nature of Religion*. New York: Harcourt Brace Jovanovich.

Esposito, John L. 1988. *Islam: The Straight Path*. New York: Oxford University Press.

Esposito, John L. 2011. *Islam: The Straight Path*. 4th edn. New York: Oxford University Press.

Geertz, Clifford. 1973. *The Interpretation of Cultures: Selected Essays*. New York: Basic Books.

Gilhus, Ingvild Sælid, and Lisbeth Mikaelsson. 2001. *Nytt blikk på religion. Studiet av religion i dag*. Oslo: Pax.

Gilhus, Ingvild Sælid, and Lisbeth Mikaelsson. 2003. *Nya perspektiv på religion*. Stockholm: Natur och kultur.

Goldenberg, Robert. 1992. "Talmud." In *Back to the Sources: Reading the Classic Jewish Texts*, ed. Barry W. Holtz, 129–75. New York: Touchstone.

Gustavsson, Bernt. 1996. *Bildning i vår tid. Om bildningens möjligheter och villkor i det moderna samhället*. Stockholm: Wahlström & Widstrand.

Hacking, Ian. 1999. *The Social Construction of What?* Cambridge, MA: Harvard University Press.

Hedin, Christer. 1999. *Abrahams barn. Vad skiljer och förenar judendom, kristendom och islam?* Stockholm: Arena.

Hedin, Christer. 2004. "Olika tro på samma Gud." *Pedagogiska magasinet* (4), http://www.lararnasnyheter.se/tema/religionens-namn.

Hellman, Eva. 2011. *Vad är religion? En disciplinteoretisk metastudie*. Nora: Nya Doxa.

Hjärpe, Jan. 2012. "Perspektiv på islamologin. Essentialism eller religionsantropologi?" In *Islamologi. Studiet av en religion*, ed. Jonas Otterbeck and Leif Stenberg, 265–79. Stockholm: Carlsson.

Juergensmeyer, Mark. 2003. *Terror in the Mind of God: The Global Rise of Religious Violence*. 3rd edn. Berkeley, CA: University of California Press.

Lakoff, George, and Mark Johnson. 1999. *Philosophy in the Flesh: The Embodied Mind and its Challenges to Western Thought*. New York: Basic Books.

Lincoln, Bruce. 2006. *Holy Terrors: Thinking about Religion after September 11*. 2nd edn. Chicago: University of Chicago Press.

Morris, Brian. 1987. *Anthropological Studies of Religion: An Introductory Text*. Cambridge: Cambridge University Press.

Nussbaum, Martha C. 2007. *The Clash Within: Democracy, Religious Violence, and India's Future*. Cambridge, MA: Belknap Press.

Otterbeck, Jonas. 2000. *Islam, muslimer och den svenska skolan*. Lund: Studentlitteratur.

Otto, Rudolf. 1936. *The Idea of the Holy: An Inquiry into the Non-rational Factor in the Idea of the Divine and its Relation to the Rational*. London: Oxford University Press.

Paden, William E. 1994. *Religious Worlds: The Comparative Study of Religion*. 2nd edn. Boston: Beacon Press.

Rippin, Andrew. 2012. *Muslims: Their Religious Beliefs and Practices*. 4th edn. New York: Routledge.

Roald, Anne Sofie. 2005. *Islam. Historia, tro, nytolkning*. Stockholm: Natur och kultur.

Saler, Benson. 2000. *Conceptualizing Religion: Immanent Anthropologists, Transcendent Natives, and Unbounded Categories*. New York: Berghahn.

Saler, Benson. 2009. *Understanding Religion: Selected Essays*. Berlin: W. de Gruyter.

Shahak, Israel, and Norton Mezvinsky. 2004. *Jewish Fundamentalism in Israel*. New edn. London: Pluto.

Sharpe, Eric J. 1986. *Comparative Religion: A History*. 2nd edn. London: Duckworth.

Wilson, David Sloan. 2007. "Beyond Demonic Memes: Why Richard Dawkins is Wrong about Religion." *Skeptic* 13(4): 42–51.

Wittgenstein, Ludwig. 2009. *Philosophical Investigations*. Rev. 4th edn. Chichester: Wiley-Blackwell.

Endnotes

1. Perhaps the first general discussion in Swedish about the concept of religion that took a critical position toward essentialist perceptions was Gilhus and Mikaelsson (2003, originally published in Norwegian). A recently published book that includes a discussion about the Western and Christian basis for the concept of religion is Hellman (2011). Also new is Hjärpe (2012) which examines the conceptualization of religion in terms of the study of Islam in Sweden. Other scholars who critically discuss the concept and the study of religion are Andersson and Sander (2009) and Arvidsson (2004; 2012). Brief discussions about the concept of religion are included in books on Islam published by islamologists from Lund, such as Otterbeck (2000: ch. 2) and Roald (2005: 14–29). In his doctoral thesis, Torsten Blomkvist (2002) discussed a traditional conceptualization of religion that can be applied in the study of ancient Scandinavian religion.

2. However, I have not performed a formal investigation about teachers' perceptions of religion.

3. This does not mean, of course, that all students, scholars, and teachers would lack personal faith. On the contrary, some of the examples that I present below demonstrate the opposite. The idea that I want to convey is rather that in a secularized Western context of research and teaching, personal faith is normally kept in the background in order to avoid it affecting the results.

4. In her book, Hellman (2011) provides a broader overview of this subject.

5. Some of the scholars treated in this paragraph belonged to the discipline of anthropology rather than history of religions. These two disciplines have always been close.

6. Gilhus and Mikaelsson discuss the phenomenological paradigm in several places, e.g., (2001: 31–34, 44–55).

7. From the Latin *numen*, which designates a transcendent power.

8. The term *hierophany* comes from the Greek *hieros* (holy) and *phainomai* (appear).

9. The designation "Core essentialism" is of course a tautology that I have used for want of a better name.

10. In chapters 3 and 4 of the book *Conceptualizing Religion*, Benson Saler (2000) lines up a long series of such definitions and discusses and criticizes each of them.

11. This presentation of Tylor's perception of religion builds on Sharpe (1986: 53–58) and Morris (1987: 98–103).

12. The article was first published in 1966, but was later reprinted in Geertz (1973).

13. The best comprehensive critical discussion that I have found of these two definitions, with many references to other works, is Saler (2000: 88–104).

14. If the same reasoning is applied to Indo-European languages, for example, it would be possible to argue that Hindus and the French believe in the same God because the Sanskrit word *deva* ("divine being") is related to the French word *dieu* ("God").

15. For discussions about these events, see, e.g., Lincoln (2006: 1–18); Juergensmeyer (2003: 19–30); and Shahak and Mezvinsky (2004: 96–112).

16. Dawkins is conscious that there are a number of different types of supernatural beings, but he simplifies the discussion through talking about god, primarily the monotheistic God in which Jews, Christians and Muslims believe (Dawkins 2006: 35).

17. Saler uses the concept of "monothetic definitions" more or less synonymously with "essentialist definitions."

18. As, for instance, Eva Hellman shows, the concept of religion, as it is used today, is a typical Western phenomenon with strong ties to these religions, perhaps primarily to Christianity (Hellman 2011).

19. Gustavsson has, however, a more pronounced hermeneutic perspective than Saler. The Swedish word "*bildning*" (German *Bildung*) is difficult to translate into English. It is more than just "education" and involves a moment of self-development as well as acquiring knowledge.

2. ESTABLISHING RELIGION THROUGH TEXTBOOKS: RELIGIONS IN JAPAN'S "ETHICS" PROGRAMME

*Satoko Fujiwara**

In Japan, all school textbooks for regular subjects are required to be authorized by the Ministry of Education.[1] This fact suggests that what is at stake about the images of religion(s) in Japanese textbooks is not simply a matter of right/ wrong, biased/unbiased, or confessional/non-confessional. If the textbooks promote a particular view of religion or arrange religions into a hierarchy, it can be said that they are virtually "establishing religion" by themselves.[2] There are many other countries where textbooks are authorized by the state,[3] but it is particularly problematic in Japan because its Constitution requires the strict separation of church and state. It would also be especially interesting to examine the Japanese case from this perspective, since a major task for Japan's postwar (WWII) education has been how it can be detached from prewar state religion, namely, so-called State Shinto. Textbooks mixing history with the myth of the divine origin of the imperial family were completely abandoned at the end of the war. Thus, establishing religion through textbooks is the last thing postwar textbook writers and publishers (all in the private sector) imagine they are doing.

In this chapter I will illustrate how Japanese textbooks are "establishing religion" by imposing demarcations and rankings among religions. Remarkably, the religion they are establishing is *not* State Shinto. The factors shaping the establishment of religion are quite complex and cannot be reduced to the single factor of the legacy of State Shinto. I will sort out pedagogical, ideological and business factors.

* Satoko Fujiwara is Associate Professor, Department of Religious Studies, Faculty of Letters, at the University of Tokyo. Her related publications include "Problems of Teaching about Religion in Japan: Another Textbook Controversy against Peace?" in R. Jackson and S. Fujiwara (eds), *Peace Education and Religious Plurality: International Perspectives* (Routledge, 2008), and *Religions in Textbooks: Religious Education that is Not Supposed to Exist in Japan* (in Japanese, Iwanami, 2011).

Readers of this chapter who are familiar with the general religious outlook of the Japanese may wonder whether textbooks have any substantial influence on students, even if they can be viewed as establishing religion. The majority of Japanese people, who are supposed to have been educated by such textbooks, do not have much interest in religion in the first place. Various international statistics show that Japan is one of the nations with the lowest ratio of conscious religious affiliation. According to a poll taken by the Asahi newspaper in 2003, only 13% of respondents said "I have an interest in religion," 10% said "I have some interest in religion," 76% said "No interest." Although many of the 76% respondents keep certain religious customs, such as visiting shrines and temples on New Year's Day, they do not consider such practice to be "religious." To them, being religious is an anomaly, or even dangerous, as seen in the case of Aum Shinrikyō's terrorism. If that is the case, it is unlikely that textbooks have been establishing state religion with nationwide adherents.

It is true that Japan is not as religious a country as, for example, the United States is often said to be. However, try asking students, who have just taken a college entrance exam after months of hard study, what Christianity is, and they will unanimously answer, "Love!" If asked, "What is Buddhism?" they will answer, "Compassion!" And they may add, "Islam is Obedience!" These are exactly what Jonathan Z. Smith calls monothetic definitions of religion, the results of which "have been poorly formulated and violate the ordinary canons of definition. But this is less disturbing than the fact that the presuppositions of the monothetic enterprise have been deliberately tampered with for apologetic reasons" (Smith 1982: 5). This is the kind of established religion that I attempt to problematize in this chapter.

1. RELIGIOUS/RELIGION EDUCATION IN JAPAN

Before turning to textbooks, let me explain the general context of religious education in postwar Japan. The idea of the separation of church and state shaping the current (postwar) Japanese Constitution was influenced by the American model. There has been no religious education as a subject in public schools, while private religious schools are permitted to give confessional RE classes.

In order to clarify how and how far public school teachers can touch on religious issues, Japanese scholars of religion have coined the trichotomy of "*shūkyō chisiki kyōiku* (education about religions, or 'religion' education)," "*shūkyōteki jōsō kyōiku* (cultivation of religious sentiments)," and "*shūha kyōiku* (sectarian, or confessional religious education)." There has been a wide consensus that, under the Constitution and the Fundamental Law of Education, *shūha kyōiku* (confessional RE) is not allowed in public schools, whereas *shūkyō chisiki kyōiku* (education about religions) can be given in any school. *Shūkyō chisiki kyōiku* has actually been offered mostly in social studies subjects. Opinions have been divided as to whether *shūkyōteki jōsō kyōiku* can be introduced to public schools. *Shūkyōteki jōsō* is most commonly described as "a feeling of awe for some being(s) beyond human knowl-edge" or "a feeling of awe for the source of life." In other words, it is considered to be a basic, embryonic religious inclination. *Shūkyōteki jōsō kyōiku*, therefore, stands in the middle of education about religions and confessional RE, more reli-gious than the former, less religious than the latter.

Shūkyōteki jōsō kyōiku (cultivation of religious sentiments), as defined above, has been considered to function as moral education. Some in the religious sector have been opposed to the total secularization of public education, fearing that it would lead to moral decay among young Japanese people. They have been lobby-ing the government to introduce *shūkyōteki jōsō kyōiku* into public schools.[4] Pro-ponents of *shūkyōteki jōsō kyōiku* argue that such religious sentiment is beyond sectarianism, and, hence, its cultivation can be conducted in public schools without violating the separation of church and state. Its opponents regard it as imposing religious faith on students. In addition, they are concerned that the cul-tivation of awe for higher being(s) at public schools may lead to a resurgence of the authoritarian State Shinto educational system.

Fear of moral decay has been shared by a number of conservative politi-cians, who often do not hesitate to show nostalgia for prewar Japan society in which youngsters were obedient to their elders. Their concerns culminated in the revision of the Fundamental Law of Education in 2006, which emphasized the importance of morals, tradition and patriotism. The revision was forced through in the face of opposition from many citizens—above all, from school teachers represented by the Japan Teachers Union, the protagonists of postwar democratic education.

However, the revision did not result in official approval of *shūkyōteki jōsō kyōiku*. Although the new "Course of Study" official guidelines for school teach-ing, based upon the reformed Fundamental Law of Education, has introduced the phrase "feeling of awe for life" in emphasizing the necessity of moral education, it is devoid of the term "*shūkyōteki jōsō*."[5] Therefore, at the moment, there are no remarkably active movements in the public sphere for protecting public educa-tion from top-down religious education. Both liberals and conservatives believe that only *shūkyō chisiki kyōiku* (education about religions) remains available and is actually given at public schools. Moreover, they assume that such *shūkyō chisiki kyōiku* has been neutral enough to be authorized by the secular state.

Despite such assumptions, as will be demonstrated below, textbooks used in public schools are far from being confined to neutral *shūkyō chisiki kyōiku*. Both liberals and conservatives, including academics, educators and the government, have hardly been aware of this fact.[6]

2. "ETHICS" AS A SOCIAL STUDIES SUBJECT

Visible references to religions in textbooks start with secondary education, which covers ages 13-18 (ages 13-15 for lower secondary schools; 16-18 for upper secondary schools). Whereas it is possible to search for implicit religious themes in any subject of any level of education, I will here focus upon social studies and social studies textbooks since, unlike other subjects, they intentionally teach religious topics in accordance with the "Course of Study." Social studies subjects for secondary education consist of three main categories, geography, history and civic studies.

Among them, the programme that most explicitly deals with religious issues is referred to as "Ethics," one of several civic studies subjects designed for upper secondary school students. Other civic studies programmes are "Politics and Economy" and the "Contemporary World" (a sort of comprehensive subject with an emphasis on the present).

Some readers may think it strange that "Ethics" is categorized as a social studies topic. The subject has developed as follows: at the end of World War II, moral education, which was called "*shūshin*" in prewar Japan, was abolished because "*shūshin*" promoted ultranationalism—bluntly, emperor worship. However, moral education was resumed in the late 1950s, despite the resistance of teachers, academics and citizens, who called the reinstitution "*gyaku kōsu* (literally, 'reverse course')." The new moral education for primary and lower secondary schools was called "*dōtoku*" (morals), while for upper secondary schools it was called "*rinri shakai*" (ethics and society). The latter later changed its name to "*rinri*" (ethics).

Although "Ethics" has thus been described as moral education in the official guideline of the "Course of Study," in reality, it has been regarded as intellectual education, both inside and outside of schools. The main reason for this is that it has been one of the elective subjects for the National Center Test, the standardized, multiple-choice style exam for university applicants. That is to say, the learning outcome of "Ethics" is assessed by quantity (how much students have memorized what is written in textbooks), in the same way as history, geography and other social studies subjects. Since children's performances in "*dōtoku*" (morals) classes at primary and lower secondary schools have never been assessed by test scores, it is natural that people do not consider "Ethics" to be moral education.

Ethics is elective and not offered at every school, yet the number of Ethics textbooks adopted in 2009 was substantial: 213,415 copies were distributed in total. Additionally, Japanese schools have a tendency to depend heavily upon textbooks. Textbooks are believed to offer the highest standard of reliable knowledge. Therefore, it can be said that Ethics textbooks represent what Japanese, both inside and outside schools, take as the most valid understandings of religions.

Ethics textbooks are divided into three sections:

1. History of philosophy, both western and eastern (Japanese in particular), from ancient Greek philosophy to contemporary philosophy
2. History of religions, with a focus on the life and the teaching of Jesus,

Muhammad, Buddha and other major religious leaders in the world and in Japan.

3. Contemporary issues of ethics, such as bioethics, environmental ethics, information ethics, conflicts and dialogue.

Religions thus mostly appear in the second section of Ethics textbooks and a little in the third. Descriptions of religions account for about 30% of an entire textbook.

3. MAJOR PROBLEMATIC DESCRIPTIONS OF RELIGIONS IN ETHICS TEXTBOOKS

While Japanese history textbooks have often been the foci of controversy for political reasons (especially regarding the descriptions of WWII), textbooks for the Ethics program have scarcely been criticized, and have mostly adhered to the same style for decades. However, these textbooks are no less problematic than history textbooks. Indeed, it could be said that they are even more problematic because it is less clear what purpose or agenda is behind such descriptions.

3.1. World religions over ethnic religions
Ethics textbooks give high priority to Christianity and Buddhism over Judaism and Hinduism, apparently because of a dichotomy between world religions and ethnic religions utilized in older Western treatments of world religions. The number of pages allotted to each religion alone reflects such a hierarchy, though, among ethnic religions, Shinto and Chinese religions, which are considered to have been dominant in Japan (for the reasons given later, Shinto appears by the name of "traditional Japanese thought"), are exceptions. When I showed my undergraduate students Encyclopedia Britannica's statistics of the religious population of the world, one of them, who had taken Ethics at high school, did not hesitate to show how shocked she was and said, "Why is it that I learned nothing about Hinduism, the third largest religion in the world, in high school!"

The truth is that she had learned something about Hinduism, but in her textbook it was called Brahmanism and was included in the chapter entitled Buddhism. In other words, she only learned about ancient Hinduism prior to the emergence of Buddhism. This fact suggests that the problem is not merely the imbalance of quantity. Both Judaism and Hinduism only appear as the historical pre-stages of Christianity and Buddhism. The underlying logic is that religions which have spread beyond a particular ethnic group have teachings with universal validity, and are therefore superior to religions which have not. There is no demonstration of this logic in textbooks. It is regarded as self-evident that Judaism and Hinduism can be dismissed.

Table 1.

Pages allotted to each religion in Ethics textbooks with the highest and the
second highest market share
 (All textbooks have exactly the same number of pages in total.)
 The order is that of appearance in the textbook.

New Ethics (Shimizu Shoin Publisher)

Judaism 2 pages
Christianity 5
Islam 2
Brahmanism 2
Buddhism 7
Confucianism 4
Daoism 5
Traditional Japanese ways of thinking 6
Japanese Buddhism 11
Japanese Confucianism 7

Ethics (Tokyo Shoseki Publisher)

Confucianism 4 pages
Daoism 3
Judaism 2
Christianity 6
Islam 2
Brahmanism 2
Buddhism 5
Traditional Japanese mind 7
Japanese Buddhism 12
Japanese Confucianism 5

3.2 Christianity is the religion of love
In order to convince readers of the superiority of Christianity, the textbooks
emphasize that Christianity is a religion of love, in sharp contrast with Judaism as
a religion of law. Moreover, all of them apply judgmental, discriminatory terms,
such as "legalism" and "the ideology of a chosen people," strictly to Judaism. It is
noteworthy that Japanese in general do not place importance on the observation
of religious law. They tolerate Buddhist priests getting married and not restricting their diets. Additionally, in postwar liberal education, rules have often been
negatively perceived as freedom-restricting. On the other hand, the word "love"
sounds not only positive but also very Western (hence, advanced, or civilized) to
contemporary Japanese.

The textbooks praise Jesus to the point of acquiring a confessional overtone. A quote from one textbook:

> Jesus says "Love your enemies and pray for those who persecute you." For what purpose? In order to be one with God's love. Since God loves even a sinful person, we should pray for those who persecute us. Our love for neighbors that has become one with God's love should reach universal philanthropy, beyond families and ethnic groups. (Furuta *et al.* 2009: 35)

The textbook asks students in public and private schools alike—both of which have few, if any, Christian students—to follow Jesus and feel united with God. Christians do not exceed 2% of the entire population of Japan.

Furthermore, some textbooks go as far as to argue that love, the essence of Christianity, should be the essence of any authentic religion. The table below appears in one such textbook. The purpose of the table is to compare three world religions (which it calls "the three biggest religions").

Table 2.

	Christianity	Islam	Buddhism
Founder	Jesus	Muhammad	Gautama Buddha
Sacred text	Old and New Testament	Qur'an	Sutras (e.g., Suttanipāta)
Teaching	love for God,	5 pillars, 6 articles of faith	4 truths,
	love for neighbors	total obedience to God	dependent arising
	idolatry forbidden		
Love	agape	love for neighbors (zakat)	compassion

(Sakagami *et al.* 2009: 231)[7]

To my readers of this chapter, it must look strange that only four items are used to compare the religions, and one of them is "love." "Rituals," "festivals," "special days," "special cities/sites" or "schisms, sects" are not used. However, to Japanese readers, including teachers, who believe that love is the essence of all religions, this table does not seem to be odd.

3.3. Buddhism is good for the environment
On the other hand, all the textbooks praise Buddhism as an eco-friendly religion.

> Modern western civilization has been controlling and making use of nature for the profit of human beings. Today, when the civilization is destroying the natural environment for the sake of material wealth, the Buddhist spirit of compassion gives us a valuable instruction. (Sato *et al.* 2009: 45)

The idea of compassion, which makes people appreciate all beings, including all animals, plants and weeds, gives various valuable instructions to us who need to overcome environmental destruction and seek a way to coexist with nature. (Takahashi *et al.* 2006: 29)

Although there are many more students whose family religion is Buddhism rather than Christianity, it is, nonetheless, undesirable for textbooks to promote a particular religion in this manner. More so because none of the textbooks speaks highly of Islam nor suggests learning from it.

It is also remarkable that, in many other Buddhist countries, environmental preservation is not highlighted as the top Buddhist value. For instance, it seems that, in Thai RE textbooks, Buddhism is described as a religion that advances civilization. A quote from a Thai RE (Buddhist) textbook for secondary school students:

The importance of Buddhism is not solely spiritual influence on the minds of Buddhists. Buddhism has various crucial roles in overall society. We are going to learn Buddhism's important role in building civilization and establishing peace in society. (Phayakkharachasak and Isiriwan 2005: 28, originally in Thai)

Clearly, this Thai textbook associates Buddhism with social prosperity whereas the Japanese textbooks describe Buddhism as a counter-cultural environmentalist thought. The Thai textbook numbers 184 pages (all about Buddhism), but it mentions the word "nature" only once, which is a key term of the unit of Buddhism in Japanese textbooks. Towards the end of the book, the Thai textbook does point out that the Thai government has recently been promoting a self-sufficient economy, which puts the brakes on environment destruction. Nonetheless, it relates the policy with the Buddhist idea of the Middle Path rather than compassion.

It is understandable that different societies give Buddhism different roles, according to the kind of problems they are facing. However, the Japanese textbooks are problematic because, in so doing, they essentialize Buddhism. They ascribe the idea of compassion (*jihi*, in Japanese), which is prominently a Mahayana term, to the essence of all Buddhism. They stress compassion, a Buddhist equivalent of love, far more than the Buddhist idea of wisdom.

3.4. Christianity versus Buddhism favoured

Another major characteristic of Japanese Ethics textbooks is that many of them favour confronting Buddhism with Christianity. It would be reasonable and fair if they explain both similarities and differences between the two religions, or better yet, among various religions, but they persist in only exclusively contrasting the two. To take some examples,

> Due to the influence of Judaism and Christianity, Westerners think that only human beings are special. In contrast, Buddhism teaches that not only human beings but also any living being can equally, by nature, be delivered from samsara. (Ochi *et al.* 2009: 57)

> The basic teaching of Buddhism does not discriminate between living beings. In this regard, Buddhism is different from the human-centered teaching of Judaism and Christianity, which tells humans, who are the images of God, to "have dominion over the fish of the sea and over the birds of the air and over every living thing that moves upon the earth." (Sato *et al.* 2009: 45)

> Compassion is different from Christian love (*agapē*). Compassion is to be extended to all living things, beyond human beings. (Furuta *et al.* 2009: 48)

Clearly, the textbooks are not merely contrasting Buddhism with Christianity but, rather, placing the former over the latter. If these statements are well grounded, it can be said they are expressing the truth/fact even though accompanied by value judgment. But they are not. These statements are based not upon the core teaching of Buddhism encompassing most of its branches and schools, but upon uniquely Mahayana, especially Tendai sect's idea of "All sentient beings, including trees and grasses, have Buddha-nature[8] (*issai-shujō sitsuu busshō*)." Again, they regard a characteristic of a part of Mahayana Buddhism as the essence of the entire Buddhism. Further, they completely ignore the more popular Buddhist idea of "six realms of samsara, or transmigration in the six lower worlds," according to which life as an animal is much lower and more disgraceful than life as a human being. They only select the relatively minor Buddhist idea of the omnipresence of Buddha-nature, which they think to be able to contrast sharply with Christian ideas. The underlying logic is the civilized West versus the "green" East: Christianity representing the West, Buddhism the East.

There is also a textbook which contrasts Buddhism as being an active, intellectual religion with Christianity as being passive and devotional.

> Buddhism can be said to be a very intellectual religion. Whereas in Christianity, the importance of prayer tends to be emphasized, in Buddhism the importance of meditation tends to be stressed. This is one of their characteristic differences. (Hiraki *et al.* 2009: 65)

If these sentences had been placed after the textbook had explained the similarities between the two religions, they would appear neutral. However, the text does not even touch upon similarities. It applies one whole page to the discussion of differences. Additionally, the pictures attached to this page are quite suggestive. As a representative of Buddhism, the textbook has chosen a picture of *Rakan* (*arhat*), a thoughtful monk in a powerful bright red robe in meditation. For Christianity, it has chosen Philippe de Champaigne's picture of Mary Magdalene, who looks helpless praying in darkness. The pictures appear to say: "If you are a man, go for Buddhism!" It is ironic that, in a different chapter, the textbook includes a page on feminism and gender issues, which most textbooks do not discuss at all. The writers are predominantly male, and the gender ratio of high school teachers who teach civic studies, including Ethics, is 3.5:1 (that of math teachers is 2.5:1), according to 2008 governmental statistics.

3.5. Islam is put outside the battle

As seen in this Christianity-West/Buddhism-East dichotomy, most Japanese associate the word "Orient" with the Far East rather than with the Middle East. This implies that, for the Japanese, Islam is *not even* "the Other." It is a religion that the Ethics textbooks do not seem to know how to deal with. Whereas they vigorously argue that Japanese students should learn how to love their neighbours from Christianity and how to show compassion to nature from Buddhism, they do not present anything to learn from Islam. It appears as if there is nothing comparable to Christian/Buddhist thought in Islam.

What they cram into a mere two pages for Islam are the etymological meaning of Islam, the life of Muhammad, the development of Islam, the Qur'an, the five pillars and the six articles of faith. Muhammad's teachings are described so briefly that students would not be able to understand why he had many followers, or what was so attractive about his teachings. To quote a passage regarding how Muhammad is described in a popular textbook:

> Muhammad was born in Mecca, a commercial city on the Arabic peninsula. After growing up, he earned his living as a merchant. Around the age of 40, while he secluded himself from the city in a cave of Mt. Hira, he heard a divine voice saying "Wake up and warn," and came to realize that he was an apostle of God. He gradually spread God's teachings to the people of Mecca, but, as he was opposed to their polytheism, which had been their familial traditional religion, and criticized their practice of idolatry, he was persecuted by major merchants, the ruling people of the city. In 622, to escape persecution, he emigrated to Medina (*hijra*), where many people regarded him as God's prophet. However, he then started to be successful militarily and diplomatically, so that he established both political power and religious authority, and eventually recovered Mecca. Later he died of disease. (Hiraki 2009: 56)

This condensed explanation may make some sense to people in Judeo-Christian traditions, but not to people in Japan, whose traditional religion has largely been polytheistic and centred upon ancestor worship. Japanese students would be puzzled to read why Muhammad denied ancestral traditions, why he disliked statues, or what he had to "warn" the people about. Moreover, to students familiar with the legal separation of religion and politics, it would appear strange that a religious leader sought military/political success. In short, nearly everything that needs to be carefully explicated to avoid misunderstanding is not explained.

The only positive reference to Islam is that the Islamic culture of its Golden Age influenced the Western world. That is to say, the textbooks argue that the historical significance of Islamic culture is that it played a role in giving rise to the Renaissance.

3.6. Where is Shinto?

On the other hand, what may most puzzle my readers of this chapter is the fact that none of the textbooks has a unit entitled "Shinto." As seen in Table 1, they have units on Judaism, Christianity, Islam, Brahmanism, Buddhism, Chinese religions, Japanese Buddhism, Japanese Confucianism, but not on Shinto, the indigenous religious tradition of Japan. Shinto does have a visible presence in contemporary Japan. The number of Shinto organizations (registered Shinto shrines) is over 88,000, which outnumbers Buddhist organizations (temples), 86,000 and Christian organizations (churches), 9,300.

Upon closer examination, it appears that the textbooks are not totally lacking elements of Shinto. It is rather that word "Shinto" is taboo. What scholars of religion usually classify as Shinto beliefs and practices, such as various *kami* (gods) in ancient myths or immanent in nature, the idea of purity/impurity and *misogi* (ritual purification), festivals related to agriculture, are described as "the traditional Japanese ways of thinking" or "the traditional Japanese mind." Another word that is employed to replace the word "Shinto" is "animism," defined as "belief that souls and spirits exist not only in human beings or even only in living beings but also in natural objects (such as rocks) and manufactured objects (such as mirrors) and the like." For Japanese textbook writers and publishers, "animism" is a safer word to use than "Shinto." They are so meticulous in avoiding the word that the technical term "*shinbutsu shūgō*," which is usually described as "syncretic fusion of Shinto and Buddhism" in normal (commercial) dictionaries of religions edited by the scholars of religions, is explained either as "fusion of *kami* (gods) and *hotoke* (buddhas)" or as "fusion of kami-worshipping and Buddhism" in the Ethics textbooks.

The textbooks illustrate the elements of "the traditional Japanese ways of thinking" quite positively, but they refrain from arguing for its superiority over the Western ways of thinking, at least explicitly. Instead, they emphasize the uniqueness of the Japanese way. Again, rather than presenting both similarities and differences, they only discuss how the Japanese way is different from the Western way. For example, they argue that the symbolic idea of pure/impure or clean/unclean is central to the traditional Japanese mind. One of them begins the relevant section by saying:

> Even now, Japanese sometimes express something morally bad as "unclean" and morally good as "clean." From ancient times, Japanese people have valued purity and cleanliness of mind... (Hiraki *et al.* 2009: 74)

What is implied in this passage is that Westerners distinguish between the moral good and ritual purity, while Japanese do not. It is a typical example of Orientalism, though the textbook does not argue which is a better way of thinking. Seemingly, the textbook writers have no knowledge of the English phrase "clean politics" or "clean life." The uniqueness of Japanese religious tradition is over-stressed without firm grounds for doing so.

4. FACTORS SHAPING THE PROBLEMATIC DESCRIPTIONS

Textbooks writers are listed at the end of each textbook, and it is clear that most of them are university professors, who are supposed to know about the problem of Orientalism as well as about what kind of religious education is appropriate for public schools. Then why is it that the textbooks are so naively discriminatory and confessional?

4.1. Pedagogical factors
The first factor is a pedagogical one which shapes the outline of the subject of Ethics. Both textbook writers and the advisory board of the Ministry of Education who compose the "Course of Study" are scholars specializing in philosophy or ethics, rarely in the study of religions. Accordingly, Jesus and Buddha end up being treated more like philosophers than as religious figures. The general conception shaping the textbook is sketching out the history of (philosophical/ethical) thoughts that influence the contemporary world, Japan in particular. The textbooks attempt to convince young Japanese readers that ancient Greek philosophy is worth learning because Socrates and Plato were such great, influential thinkers. In the same way, they admire Jesus and Buddha, and recommend students accept their thoughts and cultivate themselves. They do not treat Muhammad in a similar way because Islam is not considered to have anything to do with the formation of Japanese philosophical thinking.

This style derives from the Japanese kyōyōshugi, which is close to and was influenced by the German concept of Bildung. The kyōyōshugi movement, which was popular among university students from the late nineteenth to the first half of the twentieth century, aimed at building one's character by reading great philosophical classics. Though the movement had a certain role in the development of modern Japanese education, in the twenty-first century such pedagogy may contradict the ideal of intercultural education—that is, education which respects cultural and religious diversity. In the context of this new ideal, it now appears very strange that official textbooks recommend Jesus' and Buddha's teachings to all students equally, while dismissing Judaism, Hinduism and Islam.

They also duplicate the holy traditional account of the lives of Jesus and Buddha, including Jesus' crucifixion, as if they were historical facts. For public education, the writers should add "It has been believed by followers that Buddha..." However, since they write in the chapter on ancient Greek philosophy (which precedes the chapter on Christianity) that "Plato wrote so and so" or "Aristotle said so and so" instead of "Plato is believed to have written so and so" or "Aristotle is believed to have said so and so," they apply the same style to the chapters on Christianity and Buddhism.

Additionally, due to *kyōyōshugi*, the textbooks tend to circumscribe religion within the limits of ethics. They shed light upon only those elements of religious traditions that directly serve to enhance contemporary ethics. This is a primary reason they emphasize the importance of love for one's neighbours as written in the teachings of Jesus. They expect that the Christian idea of love will assist Japanese children to live in harmony and peace with each other and with people around the world. On the other hand, they hardly mention the coming judgment of God, miracles performed by Jesus, or the devaluation of this-worldly values and so forth, apparently because such aspects of Christianity are not useful for well-being in this world, at least from a secular perspective. Likewise, the textbooks promote the insufficiently-grounded idea that Buddhism is a religion of environmental ethics because it helps teachers convince students of the usefulness of Buddhist teachings in this highly industrial society. They entirely ignore famous legends of Buddha (e.g., how he was born), the idea of an afterlife, not to mention gender inequality in Buddhist traditions.

Since it is impossible to describe everything about Christianity or Buddhism in a small textbook, it should be permissible that textbooks focus on limited aspects of (a) religion. The problem arises, however, when both textbook producers and teachers forget the particular perspective from which religions are described in textbooks, believing they are offering a standard and basic, hence, universal explanation of religions.

The second pedagogical factor is the exam system. As mentioned, Ethics is one of the subjects for the National Center Test, the standardized preliminary exam for university applicants. The exam consists of multiple-choice questions, regardless of the diverse natures of subjects. Because of the exam, Japanese Ethics teachers are more inclined to transmit rote knowledge effectively than making their students think about ethical questions by themselves. And students assume that there is always a single, right answer for anything and expect that textbooks offer such right answers for them to memorize. This is a major reason why textbooks provide a monothetic taxonomy of religions. They present only one interpretation to all religious matters including highly controversial ones—for instance, whether Christianity is pacifist or militant, whether Buddhism is non-discriminatory or discriminatory.

4.2. Ideological factors

The ideologies shaping textbooks are mixed and also multi-layered. At the top, the Ministry of Education, being more conservative than educators, expects Ethics to function as moral education with patriotism. At the bottom, teachers are generally more liberal. Many teachers, especially those in their 40s and over, are sceptical of moral education, and critical of the compulsion to sing the national anthem at school ceremonies (they reject the national anthem and the flag, both of which evoke prewar emperor worship). The "Course of Study" and textbooks stand in the middle. The Course of Study is statutory, and a textbook does not receive authorization unless it follows this guideline, though it is not predetermined exactly how it should be followed.

That is to say, Ethics textbooks are fields of ideological negotiation. Though many textbooks are targeted at the college entrance exam, they do not simply describe facts. As explained above, they promote certain values embodied in the teachings of Jesus and Buddha so naively that they acquire confessional overtones. At the same time, it should be noted that the values thus promoted can be classified as liberal or even left-wing. Love for one's neighbours is a value of peace education. Compassion for animals and plants in nature is an ecological value. If the values the textbooks were pushing were conservative, such as respect for elders or naked patriotism, teachers would resist. (If the "Course of Study" had required textbooks to include such values, textbook writers, largely liberal university professors, would have resisted.) On the contrary, as they are all liberal values, liberal writers and teachers feel safe and fail to realize that the textbooks have become confessional as a result of attempting to instil such values into students via Jesus and Buddha.

Liberal or left-wing values are not confined to the counter-cultural preference for peace and ecology. As mentioned, the textbooks place Christianity over Judaism and Buddhism over Brahmanism. Many of them justify such favouritism by adopting the Marxist view of history as class struggle: the rich versus the poor, Jesus and Buddha as social revolutionary heroes who saved the poor. To quote such a view from one textbook:

At that time [the time of Jesus], in Jewish society Sadducean priests and Pharisee lawyers were dominant and people were required to observe Jewish religious laws which covered every aspect of daily life. However, people who could observe the laws were limited either to those who were entirely devoted to religious life or to those who were rich. Therefore, those who were poor and could not observe the laws, as well as prostitutes and tax collectors, were condemned as "sinners" and despised. Gentiles, who worshipped idols, were also discriminated against. In addition, diseases and physical disabilities were abhorred because they were believed to be the results of divine punishments of the sins committed either by the sick, the disabled or their ancestors. The original Judaism had been distorted by the ruling class and had turned into mere formalism: one would be saved just by observing laws. It was Jesus who criticized such legalism and embraced those discriminated against. (Takahashi *et al.* 2006: 21)

A similar logic is applied to the historical context of the life of Buddha.

When the founder of Buddhism, Gautama Siddhartha was born, the authority of Brahmans had been shaken, and Warriors and the common people had started to gain power. Born as a Kshatriya, he criticized the caste system and argued that everyone was equal in the face of the truth. He pursued the practice of the right laws called dharma. (Ochi *et al.* 2009: 51–52)

Buddha is also a hero who rescued the suppressed underclass. The same is applied to the historical context of the emergence of Mahayana Buddhism or that of Kamakura Japanese Buddhism.[9] They argue that Mahayana Buddhism is better than its predecessor (Theravada Buddhism) or that Kamakura Japanese Buddhism is better than Nara Japanese Buddhism because it is non-authoritarian (lay-centred), and therefore, spread among the common people.

It should be noted that, with respect to these remarks, textbook writers do not really mean to favour Christianity, Buddhism, or Mahayana Buddhism. What they favour are revolutionary movements standing up for the poor. It can be said that the teachings of Jesus and Buddha are, for them, the "means" to spread their political ideology. Most of them seem to be neither Christians nor practising Buddhists.

Then, why do the textbooks admire Buddhism by contrasting it with Christianity, if the writers are liberal and are supposedly the least ethnocentric? As mentioned, there are two major points textbooks raise as an argument for the superiority of Buddhism: first, it is non-discriminatory (not human-centred) and, hence, eco-friendly; second, it is intellectual.

The first point derives from 1970s–80s academic/popular discourses in Japan, following the publication of Lynn White Jr's *Machina ex Deo* (1968), which ascribed modern environmental destruction to Christianity. Ironically, counter-cultural arguments in the West, when imported to Japan, often embody a tone of naïve ethnocentrism or counter Orientalism (the East over the West). Textbooks have increasingly become part of the problem by presenting the Whitean thesis as the one and the only truth instead of an interpretation from a particular perspective.

The second point derives from academic discourses during the Meiji era (1868–1912). In the process of modernization, a number of Japanese scholars attempted to prove Buddhism's superiority over Christianity, fearing the total Westernization of the country. They argued that Buddhism was more philosophical and less religious than Christianity, and therefore, more rational and fitted to modern society. This is sheer counter Orientalism, which has been handed down by Buddhist scholars up to this very day. Some ethics textbooks seem to be under the influence of such Buddhist schools.

On the other hand, the legacy of State Shinto on the textbooks is negative rather than positive. The word "Shinto" is neurotically avoided, probably because the word evokes State Shinto. Writers are also attentive to not mentioning the superiority of the Japanese traditional way, also known as Shinto, though they take its uniqueness for granted. This taboo is shared by textbooks on other subjects as well, such as history and geography. In history textbooks, the word Shinto appears only in the context of the Edo-period revival of Shinto and in that of prewar State Shinto. Shinto tradition prior to the early modern period is described without using the word. The textbooks introduce Shinto shrines and Shinto customs, but never with the word "Shinto." The word is missing not only in textbooks but also in the "Course of Study," both Ethics and History/Geography. However, the Course of Study does not ban the use of the word. It is, rather, self-censorship by textbook writers and publishers.

By replacing the word Shinto with "the traditional Japanese ways of thinking" or "the traditional Japanese mind," Ethics textbooks have also converted Shinto practices to a set of beliefs. Apparently, the textbooks are attempting to present Shinto as a system of thought, comparable to philosophy, rather than as a religion. The word "animism" fits this agenda, since, as implied in E. B. Tylor's original definition, it denotes a distinctive belief, rather than rituals and other practices. With this conversion, the textbooks have also managed not to bring up the political aspect of Shinto.

4.3. Business factors

As mentioned, all Ethics textbooks are authorized by the Ministry of Education before they can be distributed. The committee which has this role is composed of university professors and high school teachers appointed by the Ministry. What kind of check lists they have is not disclosed, except for a general statement that they examine whether textbooks follow the "Course of Study" or not. As far as Ethics textbooks are concerned, the authorization process is relatively loose, at least ideologically.

For instance, the "Course of Study" sets forth a heading "Having an identity as being a Japanese in international society" in the chapter on Japanese religions and thoughts. Most textbooks have simply adopted this heading for the relevant chapter. One of them, edited by well-known, left-wing scholars, has apparently refused the heading, which can be taken as forcing national identity on all students, and used an original heading, "The beginning of Japanese thought" (Takahashi et al. 2006). The textbook passed, which implies that the ideological controlling power of the committee (or of the Ministry) is not strong.

However, the textbook suffered from poor sales. It did receive positive reviews from school teachers. Nevertheless, it was never reprinted and its publisher was soon merged with a larger textbook publisher. This incident suggests that marketing is another large factor that shapes textbooks. It is not sufficient to invite well-known scholars to join a textbook's editorial board. It should be tailored directly to college entrance exams, represented by the National Center Test.

There are teachers and textbook writers who are not satisfied with memorization-centred pedagogy. They think it improper, not only for teaching the history of religions but also for philosophy. It is indeed pathetic that philosophy classes end in memorizing philosophers' names and key terms of their thoughts, instead of improving one's logical thinking or dialogical skills. However, as long as the National Center Test continues giving the same kind of multiple-choice exam, textbooks directly targeted at the exam, that is, textbooks with as many key words as possible that might be asked on the exam, will sell best. The aforementioned textbook, which received a good review but did not sell well, is an example of a textbook that is weak for exam preparation.

CONCLUSION

In sum, current Japanese Ethics textbooks, which are supposed to teach about religions neutrally and objectively, not only arrange religions in a hierarchy but also ask students to follow the teachings of Jesus and Buddha. The original strategy seems to have been to convert religions into moral teachings and, thereby, maintain the separation between church and state (or the secularity of education). However, such textbooks do use the word "religion," and it becomes highly ambiguous whether they are teaching religion or something else. I have examined factors behind this paradox.

Pedagogically, the Ethics programme was designed by scholars of philosophy and ethics who wanted to outline the western history of philosophy and the eastern/Japanese history of philosophy in the style of *kyōyōshugi*. This approach has resulted in privileging of Christianity and Buddhism, and at the same time reducing them into partial moral values easily accessible by contemporary Japanese. As a consequence, it appears that the religions worthwhile teaching in schools are only rational religions that contribute to world peace and environment preservation. Thus textbooks are establishing religions which do not exist in the real world.

Ideologically, it is liberal scholars rather than conservatives who have been making the descriptions of religions appear to be confessional and ethnocentric. They have not been under the influence of any particular religious interest groups. They also chose to conceal the word "Shinto," instead of cultivating critical literacy about Shinto, including State Shinto. Marketing forces also shaped these textbooks. Simplistic contrasts between religions and essentialized views of religions, which lead to exaggerated descriptions in textbooks, have been favoured by teachers who are conscious of the multiple-choice college entrance exam.

One might think it impossible or naïve to expect school textbooks to be completely neutral because school education is a national enterprise. It is almost inevitable that textbook images of religions are manipulated in one way or other for the purpose of developing ideal citizens. Accordingly, the real problem of Japanese Ethics textbooks is that writers and teachers are unaware, not only that their textbooks are promoting certain religions, but also what interests are usually behind their value-laden descriptions of religions.

Needless to say, it is also true that there used to be too few Jews, Hindus, and Muslims in Japan to have a voice over the descriptions of their religions in Japanese textbooks. Vice versa, textbook authors seem to have never considered that some of the students in Ethics classes might be people of such faiths and feel embarrassed by the textbook descriptions of the religions, or feel uncomfortable being asked to accept Christian and Buddhist teachings. However, Japanese society is now changing quickly and becoming more religiously diverse. Even the description of Buddhism in the Ethics textbooks is now turning out to be inappropriate to students from Theravada Buddhist countries, because textbook authors took it for granted that they could represent the entirety of Buddhism with Mahayana Buddhism.

The biggest irony is that liberal intellectuals who are supposed to be the promoters of intercultural education have been arranging religions into hierarchies and discriminating against certain religions by manipulating the images of religions to make them serve their educational purposes. *Kyōyōshugi* used to play a certain role in Japanese education, but it has clearly become outdated as far as teaching about religions is concerned.[10]

REFERENCES

Alberts, Wanda. 2008. "The Challenge of Religious Education for the History of Religions." *Numen* 55: 121–22.

Ishihara, Chiaki. 2005. *Kokugo Kyōkasho No Shisō* (Ideologies of Japanese Textbooks). Tokyo: Chikuma Shobō.

Jensen, Tim. 2008. "RS Based RE in Public Schools: A Must for a Secular State." *Numen* 55: 123–50.

Smith, Jonathan Z. 1982. *Imagining Religion: From Babylon to Jonestown*. Chicago: University of Chicago Press.

Sullivan, Winnifred F. 2005. *The Impossibility of Religious Freedom*. Princeton and Oxford: Princeton University Press.

White, Lynn Townsend. 1968. *Machina Ex Deo: Essays in the Dynamism of Western Culture*. Cambridge, MA: The M.I.T. Press.

Textbooks

Kanno, Kakumyo, *et al.* 2009. *Shinrinri* (New Ethics). Tokyo: Shimizu Shoin. (No. 1 market share.)

Hiraki, Kojiro, *et al.* 2009. *Rinri* (Ethics). Tokyo: Tokyo Shoseki. (No. 2.)

Ochi, Mitsugu, *et al.* 2009. *Rinri* (Ethics). Tokyo: Daiichi Gakushūsha. (No. 3.)

Sato, Masahide, *et al.* 2009. *Rinri* (Ethics). Tokyo: Sūken Shuppan. (No. 4.)

Furuta, Hikaru *et al.* 2009. *Kōkō Rinri* (Highschool Ethics). Tokyo: Jikkyō Shuppan. (No. 5.)

Takahashi, Tetsuya, *et al.* 2006. *Rinri* (Ethics). Tokyo: Hitotsubashi Shuppan.

Sakagami, Nobuo, *et al.* 2009. *Gendai Shakai* (Contemporary World). Tokyo: Daiichi Gakushūsha.

Phayakkharachasak, Carat, and Kawi Isiriwan. 2005. *Nangsu'riang Sarakanrianru Phu'nthan Phraputthasasana Mo 3*. Watana Panich (a Thai Buddhist RE textbook).

Endnotes

1. Precisely, the Ministry of Education, Culture, Sports, Science and Technology.
2. In *The Impossibility of Religious Freedom*, Winnifred F. Sullivan argues, "This book is intend-ed, at the simplest level, to show that 'religion' can no longer be coherently defined for purposes of American law" (Sullivan 2005: 150). If, as she demonstrates, lawsuits have the potential for establishing religion, by dividing between religion and non-religion, then the same problem applies to state-authorized textbooks.
3. Strictly, there are three types of textbook authorization. There are countries where the gov-ernment produces state-approved textbooks (e.g., Russia, South Korea, Thailand, Malaysia, Iran), countries where private publishers produce textbooks which are to be "authorized" by the government (e.g., Germany, Norway, Canada, Japan), and countries where educa-tional boards adopt textbooks respectively, without governmental intervention (e.g., USA). There are also countries which have no textbook authorization system, that is to say, teach-ers/schools are free to choose textbooks (e.g., UK, France).
4. Not all religious organizations are involved. Sōka Gakkai, a new religious group that was the original founding body of the Kōmeitō Party, has been against the idea of introducing *shūkyōteki jōsō kyōiku* into public schools, fearing that the government-led RE might cause the persecution of new religious groups. Christian groups are also generally sceptical of the idea, since, like Sōka Gakkai, it experienced persecution during the prewar period.
5. When the Fundamental Law of Education was revised, the Government party at that time, the Liberal Democratic Party, formed a coalition with the Kōmeitō Party. The LDP failed to add the word "*shūkyōteki jōsō*" to the Law because the Kōmeitō Party (Sōka Gakkai) was opposed to it.
6. Some scholars of education have revealed the hidden ideology of Japanese textbooks. One of the recent studies which is closest to the theme of this chapter is Chiaki Ishihara's analysis of Japanese (language/literature) textbooks. He argues that Japanese textbooks are aiming at moral education rather than logical comprehension, telling readers to serve communal benefits sacrificing individual rights (Ishihara 2005). He does not dis-cuss the issue of religious education, however.
7. This is a quote from a textbook about the "Contemporary World" in civic studies. Due to its nature as a comprehensive subject, Contemporary World textbooks are a condensed version of other civic studies subjects. In other words, this table is a summary of what the Ethics textbook published by the same publisher writes about the religions.
8. "Buddha-nature" means the potentiality to attain enlightenment.
9. Kamakura Buddhism means Buddhist sects (e.g., Sōtōshū, Rinzaishū, Jōdo-Shinshū) that originated in the Kamakura period (1185–1333). Nara Buddhism means sects (e.g., Tendaishū, Shingonshū) from the Nara period (710–794).
10. European scholars of religion have recently rephrased "teaching about religion" or "non-confessional, multifaith RE" as "RS based RE" as opposed to traditional "theology based RE" (Alberts 2008; Jensen 2008). In this chapter I have shown that the Japanese equivalent of "theology based RE" has been the Ethics programme designed by scholars of philosophy and religion, who are self-consciously secular.

3. BAD RELIGIONS AND GOOD RELIGIONS: THE REPRESENTATION OF RELIGION AND RELIGIOUS TRADITIONS IN A NEW SWISS TEXTBOOK[1]

Katharina Frank*

Over the last couple of years, the religion education of all pupils in Swiss public schools has been more and more institutionalized. This situation has led to a growing market of teaching materials, which all claim to serve as guides for the compulsory new school subject, which has to be a "Religionskunde." One of these recently published textbooks is the "Sachbuch Religionen. Hinduismus, Buddhismus, Judentum, Christentum, Islam," which was developed by a team of Christian theologians and scholars of the study of religions. This chapter focuses on the question of how religion and religious traditions are conveyed in this book. Who is speaking? Which fictive readers are addressed? What are the general aims of the texts? Which implicit valuations shape the representations of the different religions? The chapter argues that the images of religions conveyed by this textbook promote similar stereotypes as were recently identified for Swiss media and public discourse.

1. OUTLINE OF THE PROBLEM: CONTEXT OF THE NEW TEXTBOOK "SACHBUCH RELIGIONEN"

There are two recent political developments in Switzerland that concern religion education at public schools and influence the production of teaching material:

*   Katharina Frank is a lecturer in teacher education and senior researcher at the Departments of Religious Studies at Zurich University and Lausanne University. She is interested in the representations of religions in the public sphere and in the research on religion education. Her dissertation, "Schulischer Religionsunterricht—eine religionswissenschaftlich-soziologische Untersuchung," examines religion education at public schools and develops an empirically-based instrument to identify teaching aims. She is currently working on a study of religions-based didactics and in a synthesis project of the National Research Programme "Religionsgemeinschaften, Staat and Gesellschaft" of the Swiss National Research Foundation.

On the one hand, many cantons[2] started to organize *a compulsory religion educa-tion*[3] *for all pupils*. Besides this new school subject, some cantons maintain their voluntary Christian religion classes and also started to establish an Islamic reli-gion class (e.g., the canton of Lucerne). Therefore the pupils with a Christian or an Islamic background may have two different kinds of religion education where-as the pupils without any religious background can only attend the compulsory religion class, which is taught according to the state's regulations. On the other hand, it was decided to harmonize the syllabuses and curricula of different can-tons in the future. The French, the Italian speaking, as well as the German and the Rhaeto-Romanic speaking regions will each have a unified syllabus.[4] This devel-opment also affects the orientation of compulsory religion education. New text-books for religion education take these two tendencies into account and claim to be either for a religion education for all pupils or for a Christian or an Islamic religion education.

The *Sachbuch Religionen. Hinduismus, Buddhismus, Judentum, Christentum, Islam*[5] is one of these new textbooks developed for a religion education for all pupils at secondary school level I and II (grammar school, 7th–12th school year). It was composed by a team of Christian theologians and scholars of religion, who are presently working at the University of Lucerne and in the teacher education departments of the cantons of Lucerne and Berne. The three theologians in this team initiated the publication, which addresses pupils and students of different religious or non-religious socializations in the compulsory grammar school sub-ject. Following the Swiss constitution, this has to be a "Religionskunde."[6]

2. RESEARCH QUESTIONS AND THE RELIGIOUS STUDIES APPROACH

In this chapter, I will analyse the new textbook *Sachbuch Religionen* with respect to how "religion" generally and the religious traditions of Hinduism, Buddhism, Judaism, Christianity and Islam specifically are represented and what images of these religions are conveyed.

I would like to do this via the following research questions: What comprehen-sion of the school subject does the book represent? How is "religion" introduced, defined and established in the book? Is it a matter solely about "religion" or also about how religions are perceived and presented in society, the media, politics, economy and so on? Which religions and which topics are included? How are these constructed? Who is the audience? What societal significance do the presented objects have for pupils of different religious backgrounds and worldviews, now and in the future? What goals do the authors try to achieve? Are the five religions pre-sented in the same way with respect to their aims? How far (implicitly or explicitly) do the chapters about the separate religions reflect the aspiration mentioned at the beginning of the book to convey knowledge about religions in the surrounding world or "before our own door"[7] as the authors call it? Do the representations of religions in the book correspond with the empirical reality in Switzerland?

In order to answer these questions I will refer to several theories and empirical studies.

As a first step general approach I will use the didactic model of Wolfgang Klafki. His critical-constructive didactics is one of the basic models used in the academic discipline of education. Klafki analyses three possible justification criteria for educational offerings: the present significance, the future significance and the exemplary significance for pupils of a certain school level.[8] However, when adopting Klafki, it is important to bring to mind that the *Sachbuch Religionen* is a textbook for all pupils, not just for religious pupils. Therefore the justifications of the educational offering do not depend on religious significance, but on cultural and societal significance.

In a second step I will concentrate on the general goals of the textbook,[9] which are often not formulated explicitly. In order to do so I will refer to categories I have generated through my research on religion education at public schools in Switzerland. The analysis shows that the education sequences can be divided into "object" and "frame." According to Erving Goffman's communication theory,[10] the frame reveals what aim a teacher pursues when dealing a certain object: Does he intend identification with the religious object or does he rather encourage a more distant attitude towards the object? By analysing the teaching sequences I have defined four main object-frame combinations:

- The first variant is the presentation of an object *without any frame*; the presentation remains purely *narrative*. The teacher leaves the framing to the pupils, which will probably lead to them framing the religious object in the way they are used to (usually in a dogma-related or life-world-related way; see below).
- In the second variant the teacher establishes a frame that can be called dogmatic. A *dogma-related frame* leads the pupils to adopt a fixed religious idiom and doctrine. They therefore participate in a certain religious symbol system.
- The third variant is a *life-world-related frame* of the religious object. Life-world-related religious education also invites the pupils to communicate in religious codes, but it allows them to use these codes in an individual way so that they can express their religiosity through individual or anthropogenic life-world codes. The pupils also participate in a religious symbol system — which is transformed into an individual or anthropogenic form.
- The fourth variant is a *cultural-studies-related frame* of the religious object. Teachers and pupils communicate in codes borrowed from cultural studies, as for instance codes derived from history or the social sciences. Participation is restricted to the observation of religious symbol systems, religious communities and their members. The mode of their participation is therefore passive, purely intellectual and temporary.

In a third step of the analysis of the book I would like to draw on empirical studies about religions and religiosity in Switzerland in order to reflect on whether the authors of the textbook fulfil their promise of representing the religions that are "before our own door" (p. 7). These surveys about religion in Switzerland cover a time span of more than 20 years:

- Roland Campiche and Alfred Dubach: survey conducted in 1989, published in 1993;[11]
- Roland Campiche, survey conducted in 1999, published in 2004;[12]
- Jörg Stolz, Judith Könemann, Mallory Schneuwly Purdie, Thomas Engelberger and Michael Krüggeler: survey conducted in 2009; short report published in 2011.[13]

In addition to this quantitative research, I will refer to the book "Eine Schweiz—viele Religionen"[14] which describes religions and religious communities in Switzerland in different social contexts, as well as several empirical findings from the National Research Programme NRP58 "Religions, the State, and Society."[15]

3. ANALYSIS, RESULTS AND INTERPRETATION

The book begins with a quote from Hermann Hesse:

"Die Religionen und Mythen sind, ebenso wie die Dichtung, ein Versuch der Menschheit, eben jene Unsagbarkeiten in Bildern auszudrücken, die Ihr vergeblich ins flach Rationale zu übersetzen versucht."

In Hesse's view, each approach to the "inexpressible things of the world" remains deficient, especially the rational or intellectual approach (e.g., a natural sciences' or cultural studies' approach) which is a vain attempt to comprehend them. Religions, myths and poetry are worthwhile because they try to convey these inexpressible things in images.

Such a statement at the beginning of a textbook has far-reaching consequences: It points to the fact that the authors of the book do not see a rational or intellectual approach to religions as an adequate manner of dealing with them. Rather, the best way of acting in this situation seems to reflect an insider's view of or an insider's feelings about religion. In other words, the editors signal that emic religious knowledge is more valuable than scientific etic knowledge about religions.

3.1. "What is religion?" The representation of religion (Andreas Kessler: 13–51)
In the first part of the *Sachbuch Religionen*, Kessler problematizes the term "religion" and decides on a certain definition in order to establish the perspective from which the book should be read.

3.1.1. *Exposition of definitions and positions towards "Religion."* The introduction to chapter 1 "Was ist Religion?" (What is religion?) describes Switzerland as a society that is becoming more and more religiously diverse (p. 13, ch. 1.1). However, the picture that is presented of religion in Switzerland is not just one of a generally increasing plurality of religions in the country, but one of an altogether religious society: on Fridays Muslims go to mosques, Tamils go to their temple, on Saturdays Jews go to synagogues, on Sundays Catholics go to the mass and Protestants to prayer services (p. 13). The reader gets the impression that Switzerland is still—or again—a very religious country where people of different religious backgrounds follow their corresponding traditions and go to common rituals weekly. However, this idea does not correlate with reality in two ways: Stolz *et al.*'s newest study about religion in Switzerland shows that the number of people who visit religious services is decreasing.[16] Furthermore, the same survey shows that a large proportion of Swiss do not belong to any religious community.[17] Even if individuals were socialized in a Christian manner, most of them have a very distant attitude[18] towards the churches.

Through this introduction to the *Sachbuch Religionen*, readers who do not know Switzerland get the impression of a very religious and religiously plural country. Readers who know that Switzerland is not a religious country, automatically identify this introduction as being written from a religious normative perspective. In subsequent sections (1.1–1.3) Kessler discusses the etymology and several definitions of the term "religion." The following authors' definitions of religion are presented in separate text boxes: Hans G. Kippenberg and Kocku von Stuckrad, Jonathan Z. Smith, Cicero, Laktanz, Roger Callois, Rudolf Otto, Friedrich Schleiermacher, Helmuth von Glasenapp, Gustav Mensching, Paul Tillich, Hermann Hesse, Fritz Stolz, Hermann Lübbe (pp. 15, 16 and 19). With the exception of Rudolph Otto's definition (ch. 1.3, p. 14), Kessler does not explain either the choice of definitions or the definitions themselves. Therefore the propositions remain objects; there is no frame provided.[19] The teacher or the pupil has to deal with this non-contextualized information her- or himself. It is merely a collection of material; there is no additional information provided to organize the material.

The next sections reflect the diverse aspects of "religion" (ch. 1.4–1.7: 20, 22 and 26, the longer text passages are interrupted by pages with pictures and text boxes): "Was leistet Religion?" (What does religion achieve?) (1.4), "Wie wirkt Religion?" (How is religion taking effect?) (1.5), "Wie zeigt sich Religion?" (How does religion reveal itself?) (1.6) and "Woher kommt Religion?" (Where does religion come from?) (1.7). In these paragraphs, current perspectives on religion are presented: functionalist, dimensional, evolutionary, neurological and so on. The statements in this section are again either not or only barely contextualized. For example, Kessler describes dimensions of religion and religiosity without mentioning the authors of these recent approaches: Ninian Smart, Charles Glock and Rodney Stark, Stefan Huber. Nor does he mention where these approaches were published or in which disciplinary context.

3.1.2. A universally valid definition of religion. The title of the next chapter (ch. 2) reads "Nochmals: Was ist Religion?" (Again: What is religion?). This title promises a clear position about what religion is. At the beginning Kessler admits that it is problematic to provide a fixed definition of religion. However, Kessler asserts that the representation of "religions" in the textbook requires such a definition.

He decides on a definition of religion, which is a modification of Clifford Geertz's definition. It is the definition of Gerd Theissen, a German protestant theologian of the New Testament:

> "Religion ist ein Zeichensystem, das Lebensgewinn durch Entsprechung zu einer letzten Wirklichkeit verheisst." (p. 38)[20]

Geertz's definition[21] is also reprinted in one of the text boxes, but without any comment. Theissen's definition, on the other hand, is outlined very precisely (ch. 2.1–2.6 and text boxes number 14: 38–40, 43, 44). Theissen's modifications of Geertz' definition are distinctive: in contrast to Geertz's definition, Theissen does not use a scholarly terminology but a terminology which could be called poetic and theological: "Lebensgewinn" (benefit for someone's life), "verheissen" (augur), "Entsprechung zu einer letzten Wirklichkeit" (correlation to an ultimate reality). Saying that religion promises a benefit for someone's life means to adopt and promote the manner of speech of religious actors.

This religious manner of speaking is also visible in the explanations of the definition's constituent parts. When Kessler outlines that religion is a "kulturelles Zeichensystem" (cultural symbol system) (ch. 2.2, p. 38), he uses a scholarly language influenced by religious studies. However, when he focuses on the parts "Lebensgewinn verheissen" (augur a benefit for someone's life) and "Entsprechung zu einer letzten Wirklichkeit" (correlation to an ultimate reality) (ch. 2.5. and 2.6, pp. 43–44), Kessler switches to a personalized manner of speaking about religion. Religions are presented as agents in the political field, but it is not mentioned that human beings, stakeholders, politicians, journalists, religious people and so on are the real agents. This personalized manner of speaking about religions implies a generally problematic image of religions. Instead of certain people relating to a specific religious community, a religion as a whole is seen as a social agent.

In some places Kessler intervenes in a judgmental manner and conveys his view of a "good" and a "bad" religion or religious community:

> Bei individuellen Krisen hilft die Religionsgemeinschaft, diese so zu überwinden oder auszuhalten, sodass der Welt weiterhin vertraut werden kann. Wird aber eine rigide religiöse Erziehung eingesetzt, um die Spontaneität einzuschränken und den freien Willen zu brechen, dann kann auch eine Abkehr von der Religion die Folge sein.[22] (p. 44)

In a separate part of the text, two sociologists of religion—Jörg Stolz of the University of Lausanne and Gaetano Romano of the University of Lucerne—present two current and important topics: Stolz presents information about "religions and religious affiliations in Switzerland" (4 pages). Romano gives an interview about the idea that religion is becoming more important again, including in Switzerland (2 pages). These two parts of the text are concerned with problems, approaches and knowledge that are very important for the pupils in Switzerland—now and in the future.

3.2. The representation of different religions (pp. 52–285)
In the second part of the book, authors of different disciplines introduce five religious traditions: Hinduism, Buddhism, Judaism, Christianity and Islam.[23] These are the religious traditions that are currently represented in the Swiss society by different associations. However, there are some religious traditions (e.g., Chinese religions), atheistic associations and also differences between movements within a specific "religion" that are not mentioned—though they would be very important for a better understanding of the religious landscape in Switzerland. The selection of these five religions is not explained. Perhaps the editors followed some of the various cantonal syllabuses for the secondary school level which request that a textbook on religion should convey knowledge about these five "world religions."

At first sight, the chapters seem to be organized clearly and in a logical way: The chapters are highlighted in different colours: Hinduism in orange, Buddhism in yellow, Judaism in blue, Christianity in purple, and Islam in green. There is a short introduction at the beginning and a glossary as well as sources for further information at the end of each chapter. For each religion, chapters focus on the same themes:

- plurality and unity;
- important figures and founders;
- principles and doctrine;
- community;
- affiliated people's way of life.

Corresponding texts and pictures, interviews and reports are integrated in the chapters.

At a second sight, however, this attractive presentation leads to increasing confusion: Looking more closely and reading the texts more carefully, the reader gets the impression that the five religions are not presented in the same way at all and the main text is constantly disrupted by pictures that seem to have nothing to do with the content of the text. To verify this impression, a more precise analysis is required.

As a first step, I will consider each chapter in itself (3.2.1–3.2.5). As a second step, I will examine conclusions, comparing the representations of these five religions (4).

3.2.1. Chapter 2 "Hinduismus" (text: Frank Neubert; text boxes: Benno Bühlmann; 40 pages). The Hindu family of related religions is portrayed the way they are lived in South Asia today. The author presents the Hindu tradition for a European reader who is geographically and culturally far away from this religion and also distant from being religiously affected by Hindu narratives, deities and lifestyles. He writes, for example, "Die Veden gelten als heilige Texte Indiens" (The Vedas are considered the holy texts of India) (p. 55) or "Das 'grosse indische' Epos (Mahabharata) und die Erzählung von der 'Reise Ramas' (Ramayana) erfreuen sich bis heute grosser Beliebtheit" (The "great Indian" epic [Mahabharata] and the narrative of "Rama's journey" [Ramayana] are still very popular today) (p. 57); "Den meisten Europäern gilt das so genannte Kastensystem als das wichtigste Merkmal der indischen Gesellschaft" (Most Europeans consider the caste system to be the most important feature of Indian society) (p. 68); "Wer einmal in Asien unterwegs ist, trifft vor allem auf dem Land überall Asketen" (When travelling in Asia, particularly in the countryside, one meets ascetics everywhere) (p. 68). These passages state that Hinduism is practised on the Indian subcontinent. The author meets the pupils in order to take them to the foreign and strange country of India as European observers of a non-European culture. Except for a few casual remarks (one side remark even with a negative tone about yoga in Europe, p. 66), Hinduism in Switzerland (or Europe) is not mentioned until the very end of the chapter. It closes with a paragraph about "Tamilen in der Schweiz" (Tamils in Switzerland) with two sub-sections "Festhalten an den Traditionen" (Holding on to the traditions) and "Die Tamil Tigers (LTTE)" (The Tamil Tigers [LTTE]). In these passages, the pupil learns that Tamils constitute the largest group of Hindus in Switzerland and that they mostly retain their religious traditions.

The author tries to avoid the term "Hinduismus" because of its unifying and exonym character. At the beginning, he explains why he likes to speak of "Hindu-Religionen" (Hindu religions) instead. This is also the term which he uses throughout the text. It is unclear why the chapter's title is "Hinduismus" nevertheless and has not been changed to "Hindu-Religionen" (Hindu religions).

Neubert writes mostly from an emic perspective, but he often contextualizes religious objects in an etic scientific way. In this manner, the text always preserves a certain distance between the pupil and Hindu religions. As noted earlier, the passages about Hindu religions in Switzerland are very short and neither match with the reality nor with the claim of the book to present the religions "before the reader's own door" (p. 7). In Switzerland, 0.4% of the people are Hindus (28,000 inhabitants)—which means that there are almost twice as many Hindus in Switzerland as Jews (18,000). Hindu temples and Krishna adherents belong to the daily life of big Swiss cities. Yoga practices are widely spread throughout Switzerland. Arranged Hindu marriages—a problem for many young Hindus as well as the state, are not problematized.[24]

There are major gaps in the representation of Hindu life in Switzerland in the main text. However, there is additional information about it in the text boxes. Bühlmann comments, for example, on the temple celebration in Adliswil, a village near Zurich. Still, the description of rituals without any further explanation, pictures of men pierced by hooks (p. 84) and hanging on hooks in the air during a Hindu procession (p. 85), or treating statues of deities like human beings (p. 83) are irritating. The effect of these pictures is perhaps not necessarily the image of a cruel religion, but certainly that of a very strange, incomprehensible, exotic religion.

3.2.2. Chapter 3 "Buddhismus" (text: Martin Baumann; text boxes: Benno Bühlmann; 40 pages). The introduction to this chapter brings to mind the great popularity of Buddhism in Switzerland and Europe generally. Subsequent paragraphs, however, depict the life of Buddha, present the doctrine of Buddhism (Dharma) and the Buddhist community (Sangha) without any reference to Swiss Buddhists.

The paragraph about Siddharta Gautama—in opposition to the rather narrative description of Jesus' life in the chapter about Christianity—is written in a sober language. The author denotes the story of Buddha's life as "legend" (p. 95), which makes it clear that he relies on a framing based on concepts from the cultural studies. However, the next paragraphs about Dharma are clearly written from an emic perspective and a dogmatic normative language. The doctrine is described but not contextualized. When the author presents the Sangha, he describes, for the first time, different denominations which have developed over the centuries: the Theravada, Mahayana and the Vajrayana Buddhism. At this point in the text, the topic of Buddhism in Switzerland is also addressed (22,000 adherents), but the special significance of the Tibetan Buddhism in Switzerland is not mentioned.[25]

When the author describes the everyday life of professional and lay Buddhists, he draws on an ideal representation of Buddhists: they are good, peaceful, responsible, and so on. An individually-lived religiosity is not thematized and, except for some minor conflicts between the generations, no problems are mentioned (p. 119). This image does not coincide with empirical reality. Buddhists had and have problems establishing themselves in Switzerland.[26] Or thinking in a different direction: The author could have mentioned the relatively problem-free integration of Tibetan, Vietnamese and Thai-Buddhists into Switzerland in comparison with migrants of other religious an national origins.[27]

3.2.3. Chapter 3 "Judentum" (text: Simone Rosenzweig and Simon Erlanger; text boxes: Benno Bühlmann; 46 pages). At the very beginning of the chapter about Judaism, the authors explain how plural the lives and beliefs of Jewish people are. This argument makes sense, because Jews themselves are aware of the rough classification of Orthodox, Conservative and Reformed Judaism. The plurality within Judaism is not only mentioned in the introduction, but referred to almost throughout the whole chapter. This helps pupils understand that there is not one unified "Judaism," but, rather, to understand how diverse this religion is.

In one section, the authors present the "history of Judaism" and a timetable of this history, beginning with the era of the patriarchs to the pogroms during the Second World War, ending with the foundation of the State of Israel. Historical information and legends are presented in the same table, without any comments about which information is scientifically reliable and which information belongs to the "cultural memory" (Assmann) of Judaism. This mixture of cultural and scientific knowledge leaves the impression that non-believers have to accept Jewish myths and religious conceptions as science-based knowledge. There is no larger contextualization; the authors do not explicitly say that the timetable and the stories reflect mythic narratives that have been passed on from one generation to the next.

A paragraph about Judaism in Switzerland is followed by longer discussions about the Holocaust and the State of Israel, which take up a large part of the chapter. The term "Holocaust" is problematized immediately after it is introduced and the authors suggest using the term "Schoa" instead. The authors use this term throughout the subsequent discussion, though the title "Holocaust" for the subsection is maintained.

3.2.4. Chapter 4 "Christentum" (text: Willi Bühler and Andreas Kessler; text boxes: Benno Bühlmann; 56 pages). The chapter about Christianity probably bears the greatest challenge for a textbook on religion education in Switzerland. It has to demonstrate that the paradigm change from a Christian religion education to *Religionskunde* will be successful. Therefore it might have been a good idea to have let a study of religions' scholar write this chapter. However, it was written by theologically-trained authors instead.

The choice of the objects as well as the approaches to these objects are dominated by an emic perspective, above all a catholic perspective. In many chapters, particularly in the chapters about Jesus and Jesus' life, the writing style is highly narrativized and religious. The target audience for this chapter seems to be younger generations of Christians. To illustrate, some sentences from the chapter: (p. 183) "Vom historischen Jesus zum Christus des Glaubens" (From the historical Jesus to the Christ of belief); "Johannes der Täufer [...] verhiess ihnen [d.h. den Menschen] Rettung" (John the Baptist augured them [men] salvation); "Jesus glaubte, dass das Böse in der Welt überwunden sei und die Herrschaft des barmherzigen Gottes begonnen habe" (Jesus believed that the evil in the world was overcome and the reign of the compassionate god had begun). One might doubt whether a pupil who is not religiously educated knows religious terms like "verheissen" (augur) or "barmherzig" (compassionate). The pupil will inevitably feel excluded by this style of communication.[28] The chapters about the historical development of Christianity (pp. 194–200) and its doctrine (pp. 202–208) are coined in theological language as well. In contrast to the chapter about Judaism, the one about Christianity is written as if there was only one way of believing in God and only one way to practise Christianity. Of course, the (Catholic) Christian theologians have a certain normative ideal of a Christian in mind when writing about Christians, but the authors do not explain this. On the contrary, the text conveys the impression that we are dealing with an empirical fact (p. 202):

Christinnen und Christen glauben an Gott als Urheber allen Seins... Christen vertrauen darauf, dass Gott mit seinen Geschöpfen in Beziehung steht... So ist der eigentliche Ausdruck christlicher Religiosität Gebet und Gottesdienst. Es geht dem Christen nicht in erster Linie darum, über Gott zu sprechen, sondern mit ihm in Beziehung zu treten etc.[29]

As we know from qualitative research[30] as well as from quantitative research,[31] most Christians in Switzerland and Europe do not live their religion in this way. However, the authors do not mention this fact and neither do they contrast this ideal of a Christian's everyday life with empirical representations of how the majority of Christians live Christianity in Switzerland (or elsewhere in Europe) today. Though the Orthodox and especially the Protestant denominations are mentioned, Catholicism dominates the representation of Christianity in this chapter.

In a new paragraph, free churches are described as "Fundamentalisten und Charismatiker" (Fundamentalists and charismatic persons). In German, "Fundamentalist" is a rather negative term and would never be used by Swiss Evangelicals themselves. The Anglican Church, African Churches and many other congregations are not mentioned. But most aggravating of all is the fact that no results from qualitative and quantitative research on religion are referred to. This knowledge would be relevant for the pupil's present and future.

The text boxes (by Bühlmann) impart a similar image of Christianity: more than ten pictures of divine services with many young Swiss people attending are shown, but no Christmas trees and no Easter eggs, which are very present in the public space, whereas the chapters about the other religions include many pictures of religious festivals.

The authors present Christianity as "our religion," but a Christianity as it should be in a theological perspective and not as it is in reality with all of its problematic aspects.

3.2.5. *Chapter 5 "Islam" (text: Samuel Behloul; text boxes: Benno Bühlmann; 48 pages).* Similar to the chapter on Christianity, the representation of Islam in this chapter is written from an insider's perspective—an Islamic insider's perspective on the one hand and a Christian perspective on the other.

After a short introduction, the chapter begins with a description of Muhammad and his life. This does not agree with the insider's understanding that the Qur'an is the most important component of this religion rather than Muhammad. Narrating first and prominently the life of Muhammad, "Muhammad—das 'schöne Vorbild'" (Muhammad—the "true role model") (p. 239) the chapter appears to follow the model of the chapter about Christianity where the life of Jesus occupies a considerable part of the text. Contrary to the life of Muhammad, the Qur'an is presented in a short paragraph entitled "Die Quellen des Islam" (The Sources of Islam) (p. 244)." While the section about Muhammad takes up one and a half pages, the exposition of the Quran is given only a quarter of a page.

Many statements in the text reproduce widespread stereotypes about Islam: "Das Selbstverständnis und der Anspruch des Islam als Offenbarungsreligion" (Islam's self-understanding and the claim as a revealed religion) (title, p. 246), "Islam als die vollkommene und endgültige Form des Eingottglaubens" (Islam as the complete and final form of the believe in one god) (subtitle, p. 250), "Das Selbstverständnis und der Wahrheitsanspruch des Islam gegenüber anderen Religionen manifestiert sich bereits in seinem Namen" (The self-understanding of Islam and its truth claim against other religions already manifests itself in its name) (p. 250). It is especially striking that formulations with similar claims for exclusivity were not used for other religious traditions such as Christianity and Judaism in the preceding chapters.

In the paragraph "Lebensgestaltung" (way of life) (pp. 252, 259, 266, 268), the author often uses the terms "die Gläubigen" (the believers), "der gläubige Muslim" (the believing Muslim) as well as terms of obligation and responsibility: "Der Islam verpflichtet alle erwachsenen Muslime..." (All adult Muslims are required by the religion to...), "Beim Gebet muss der Muslim neben den korrekten Zeiten noch zwei weitere Vorschriften beachten" (Besides the correct times, the Muslim has to observe two more rules when praying) (p. 252) and so on. These statements are not relativized by juxtaposing them with empirical representations of Islam according the requirements of religious studies.

Even the portraits in the text boxes signal a theologically normative Islam. All women in the photographs wear headscarves, which gives the impression that the everyday life of all young Muslim people is greatly affected by Islamic law.

An interesting detail: In one of the text boxes bearing the title "Gut integriert—trotz Kopftuch" (Well integrated—in spite of the headscarf) a young woman is portrayed. The reader learns that the woman is wearing her headscarf while playing basketball without any problems. However, this representation of successful integration is no longer accurate. In summer 2009, the Swiss union for basketball forbade a 19-year-old woman from wearing a headscarf during matches.[32] It was same woman portrayed in the *Sachbuch Religionen*, which was published in 2009 as well. In January 2010, the district court of Lucerne confirmed the decision of the basketball union.[33] The reality of Islam in Switzerland looks different from its representation in this chapter:

- not all Muslims lead a life like the authors present it;[34]
- not all Muslims see themselves as non-believing or non-religious if they do not lead their lives as presented by the author;
- the integration of Muslims in Switzerland is highly dependent on the incorporation regime of Switzerland,[35] a fact that is not mentioned.

All of these empirical matters remain unspoken. The objects presented in this chapter are not empirically contextualized enough—neither the Islamic principles nor the integration of Muslim people in Switzerland.

The description of Islamic plurality in Switzerland is limited to Shiites, Sunnis, Alevi and Sufi. The Ahmadiyya, a small community which has been located in

Switzerland for a long time, is not mentioned, though they are quite present in the public sphere.[36] The differences between the Islamic groups in Switzerland manifest themselves along the lines of several different national and ethnic groups. Bosnian and Albanian speaking Muslims, for example, have a specific concept of what Islam is and how to live and establish Islam in Switzerland. The Turkish and Maghreb Muslims, on the other hand, have different ideas about Islam.[37] However, the many differences in the interpretation of Islam and Muslim life in Switzerland are never mentioned.

4. RESULTS AND DISCUSSION: THE IMAGES OF RELIGIONS IN THE *SACHBUCH RELIGIONEN* AND IN THE SWISS SOCIETY

4.1. Main thesis and comments

Looking at the chapters about the five religions from a comparative perspective, one can say that the representations of the religions mirror to a large extent the representation of religions as "cultural memory" (Assmann) and the representation of a theological and not an empirical religiosity without making explicit these perspectives.[38] The contextualization of the information from a cultural studies' point of view is often missing. The authors do not impart the empirical fact that a quarter of the Swiss people do not join any religious associations and that three-quarters of the Swiss people are secular or feel distant towards religion(s).

Except for the sections which were written by the two sociologists Gaetano Romano and Jörg Stolz, religions are conveyed in an essentializing manner and hardly as social constructs and empirical findings in Swiss or World society and history. The portraits of religiously-affiliated people (in the text boxes and pictures) which show religious activities in temples, churches, mosques or at home do not overturn this impression—quite the contrary. However, to present religions in a narrative way without or only very sparse empirical framing and without contextualization based on the findings of the cultural studies means to portray religion as resource or "Lebensgewinn" as the definition of religion in the first part of the book asserts (p. 38). The authors convey much more religious knowledge than scientific knowledge based on non-confessional religious studies.

In connection with this, we encounter one of the main problems: Christian teachers often distinguish between an ecclesiastical education and a school education. They do so by teaching religious practices in their religious communities and religious knowledge in the school.[39] For religion education, which all pupils attend at public school, they broaden this Christian insider model to include all religions. Through the logic of this model, pupils should be able to access the religious knowledge of their own tradition as well as the religious knowledge of other religious traditions, that is, they know not only the stories of the Bible, but also the stories of the Qur'an, the Mahabharata and Ramayana; not only the knowledge of the Christian doctrines, but also the Islamic, Jewish and Buddhist doctrines and so on. This way of teaching and testing[40] religions assumes that they will not make the pupils religious. However, this knowledge—generated within a certain religious tradition—remains *religious* knowledge[41] and is not secular scientific knowledge about religions. The contextualization of religious contents is unsatisfactory if agents are only mentioned in the third person. A contextualization as taught in cultural studies requires the presentation of religious objects as a summarized description and with an emphasis on scientific framing. The pupil has to adopt study of religions or *religionskundliches* knowledge and not religious knowledge.

Next to the observation that the self-conceptions of the religions in each chapter occupy much of the given space and that the knowledge is not or is hardly ever denoted as self-representation, the textbook fails to show how religions and religious people are represented *in* the public space, within medias, political contexts and in society more generally.

4.2. The representations of religions in the Sachbuch Religionen and in different discourses in Switzerland

When we focus on the detailed representations of the five religions in the *Sachbuch Religionen,* we can state that besides the primary results described above, there are also important differences between the presentations of the different religions:

- Hinduism is represented as a foreign religion from India with a strange and exotic touch. The pictures in the boxes especially contribute to this image.
- Buddhism is also represented as a foreign religion, but as a good, peaceful and politically unproblematic tradition.
- Judaism is represented as the religion of the other Swiss people, an inaccessible but respected and also a suffering religion.
- Christianity is represented as "our religion" and the knowledge of a Christian vocabulary is taken for granted. However, it is not represented as the neglected and shrinking religion it actually is (i.e., as empirical studies show) but as an actively practised religion in Switzerland.
- Islam is represented as a religion which seems to be the worst, most violent and most politically dangerous religion. Although the authors seem to be willing to correct this negative image, by adopting all the clichés about Islam without doing the same in the representations of the other religions, negative stereotyping of Islam is amplified.

When we look at representations of these religions in Swiss society, we find that the images conveyed by the textbook *Sachbuch Religionen* are similar to the images we find in different analyses of the Swiss media and in surveys about the perception of religions by European people.

In a study about Swiss print media and the first channel of Swiss television,[42] Carmen Koch analysed the broadcasts and texts in terms of different encoding paradigms.[43] She came to the conclusion that each religion is constructed in the same typical way in each media. Her analysis of the narrative patterns of these representations is particularly revealing: Muslims are represented as the bad guys and the guilty ones; Buddhists, especially the Dalai Lama, as trickster, hero, good mother; Jews as victims; Christians and the Christian church on the one hand as guilty, on the other as the good mother.

In their quantitative study of Swiss people's attitudes toward religions, Jörg Stolz *et al.* asked their respondents about their personal perceptions of different religions. On the one hand, the respondents distinguished between their "own" and other "foreign" religions, on the other hand, between "good" and "bad" religions. Christianity was seen as their "own" religion, which was criticized, but generally still seen as being "good." All other religions were classified as "foreign religions." While Buddhism was seen as a "positive" foreign religion, nonviolent, peaceful, welcoming and undogmatic, Islam was clearly a negatively evaluated, foreign religion, violent, producing conflicts, repressive and intolerant.[44]

These representations of religions in the Swiss media and the perceptions of Swiss people about the different religions have an effect on political decisions (e.g., the federal popular initiative for the banning of minarets)[45] and also on the discourse of young people. In their quantitative as well as qualitative research,[46] Janine Dahinden *et al.* inquired how young people deal with religion and ethnicity. They state that adolescents are not very religious, but use religions and ethnicity for boundary work between the own (Christian or Swiss) group and other (Muslim or Albanian) groups. In doing so, they often draw on gender arguments. Typical topoi are "the Kosovar girl who is forced to marry" or "the suppressed Muslim girl who is wearing a headscarf."[47] By emphasizing "Islamic problems," the *Sachbuch Religionen* offers a big range of material for this kind of boundary work.

This new function of religions as categories of boundary work has recently been used by the Swiss People's Party SVP. In the programme of the party, the adherents distance themselves from Islam and the Muslims by emphasizing "the Christian culture" of Switzerland.[48]

In summary, we can say that the *Sachbuch Religionen* contributes to the typical negative or positive images of religions as we can find them in the public and medial discourses as well as in the perception of individuals in Switzerland. The stereotypical images of Islam and Christianity are used for boundary work and identity formation in conversations between young Swiss people and recently also in the programme of the Swiss People's Party (SVP).

The editors of the book contribute to these images by presenting the religions alongside the doctrines of the respective religion without any empirical framing, and also by including pictures which are hardly or not explained in a religious studies manner. This approach facilitates an essentialized and theological understanding of religions, the uncritical adoption of the problematic representations of these religions and the application of these representations for boundary work between Swiss Christian groups and foreign Muslim groups. Furthermore, the valuations of what is a good and what is a bad religion contribute to the unreflecting construction of criteria for the quality of a religion.

5. DIDACTICAL BENEFIT OF THE ANALYSIS AND FURTHER REFLECTIONS ON A "RELIGIONSKUNDE" TEXTBOOK

Considering all the results of this analysis, the profit of the *Sachbuch Religionen* for a *Religionskunde* teacher is small. Although the textbook provides much religious knowledge and is rich in visual material, it fails to provide any information about how to use this knowledge in a teaching situation. However, the challenge for a *Religionskunde* teacher today is not a shortage of religious material, but the lack of an approach to teach religions and religiosities in a way that can be called *religionskundlich*. The teacher who uses the *Sachbuch Religionen* is, in the absence of a satisfactory approach to teach *Religionskunde*, forced to use existing books on teaching, which focus on religious or interreligious competences[49] and not *religionskundliche* competencies.

However, as a constructive result of the analysis of this textbook, we can formulate some outlines of an approach to teach *Religionskunde*.[50]

The guiding question is: What knowledge and skills are necessary for all students (whether they are religious or not) in order to communicate in a responsible manner about religions and the adherents of religions in different nonreligious societal contexts?

The requirements for a *Religionskunde* differ very much from a religious education as is demonstrated several times implicitly or explicitly in the *Sachbuch Religionen*:

- The definition of "religion" should orientate itself by an empirically developed definition of "religion" and not by a theological definition.
- Religiosity should not be considered an anthropological constant.
- Religions are not considered a free choice. Pupils cannot choose or change their religion, they cannot create their own religion from different traditions, but usually have to follow the religion of their parents. Most religious doctrines and communities exclude other religious affiliations.
- In each lesson, the teacher should explicitly mention what the societal relevance of the lesson for the pupils is, now and in the future.[51]

Aims are the following:

- The pupils have a *basic knowledge* about religions. Which religions (including atheism) and elements a pupil has to know about depends on the empirical evidence regarding which religions are most common in the specific society. All knowledge about religions is deduced from empirical observations and the findings of religious studies and not from the curricula of the corresponding religious communities.

– The pupils learn to identify and distinguish between a religious language and a secular language (which is based on concepts borrowed from the cultural studies and social sciences). They know which kind of language is used in which contexts (religious, interreligious dialogue vs. secular social contexts and *Religionskunde*). The pupils learn how to speak about religions, possibly also about their own religion, in a cultural studies-based language.

– The pupils should be able to recognize the societal dimensions of the religious discourse in the public sphere, in art, media and politics. They should be able to formulate appropriate questions as well as discuss and judge the public discourse about religions in accordance with the ethical consensus in Switzerland.

– The teaching method used should be the Inquiring Learning (forschendes Lernen).[52]

The analysis of the textbook *Sachbuch Religionen* has shown that the book was not written with an explicit attitude of regret about the loss of an education in Christian religion and values in Swiss public school or as a defence of Christian tradition.[53] The publisher's aim seems to be to demonstrate the benefits of religion as well as to encourage religious pluralism. However, a closer analysis leads to the conclusion that such a pluralistic attitude can have the opposite effect. It is *not religious pluralism* that should matter to the authors of future books for religion education, but—as the scholar of the study of education, Cristina Allemann-Ghionda, says—*the acceptance of religious and cultural plurality*,[54] and the attempt to analyse this plurality in a scientific religious studies manner and to convey the empirical results.

BIBLIOGRAPHY

Aepkers, Michael, and Sabine Liebig. *Entdeckendes forschendes genetisches Lernen, Basiswissen Pädagogik, Unterrichtskonzepte und Techniken*. Hohengehren: Schneider Verlag, 2002.

Alberts, Wanda. *Integrative Religious Education in Europe: A Study of Religions Approach*. Berlin/New York: De Gruyter, 2007.

Allemann-Ghionda, Cristina. *Schule, Bildung und Pluralität. Sechs Fallstudien im europäischen Vergleich*. Frankfurt a.M./Bern u. a.: Peter Lang, 1999.

Baumann, Martin, and Jörg Stolz, eds. *Eine Schweiz—viele Religionen*. Bielefeld: transcript, 2007. [French: *La nouvelle Suisse religieuse. Risques et chances de sa diversité*. Genève: Labor et fides, 2009].

Baumann, Martin, Frank Weigelt and Rafaela Eulberg. *Tamil Hindus and Vietnamese Buddhists in Switzerland*. PNR58, final report, 2007. online: http://www.nfp58.ch/files/downloads/Schlussbericht_Baumann.pdf

Behloul, Samuel M. *How Bosnian and Albanian Muslims in Switzerland are Reacting to the Islam Discourse.* NRP58, final report, 2011. Available online: http://www.nfp58.ch/files/downloads/Schlussbericht_Behloul.pdf

Beyeler, Sarah, and Virginia Suter Reich. "Sichtbarkeit von Inkorporationsbedingungen. Ein Vergleich muslimischer Bauvorhaben in der Schweiz." *TSANTSA* 14, 2009, 141–46.

Bochinger, Christoph, Winfried Gebhardt and Martin Engelbrecht. *Die unsichtbare Religion in der sichtbaren Religion—Formen spiritueller Orientierung in der religiösen Gegenwartskultur.* Stuttgart: Kohlhammer, 2009.

Bühler, Willi, Benno Bühlmann and Andreas Kessler, eds. *Sachbuch Religionen.* Horw/Luzern: db-Verlag, 2009.

Campiche, Roland. *Die zwei Gesichter der Religion. Faszination und Entzauberung.* Zürich: TVZ, 2004.

Campiche, Roland, and Alfred Dubach. *Jeder ein Sonderfall. Religion in der Schweiz.* Zürich: NZN Buchverlag, 1993.

Chidester, David. "Unity in Diversity: Religion Education and Public Pedagogy in South Africa." *Numen* 55, 2008, 272–99.

Dahinden, Janine, Kerstin Duemmler and Joëlle Moret. *Religion and Ethnicity—a Survey among Young Adults.* NRP58, final report, 2010. Available online: http://www.nfp58.ch/files/downloads/Schlussbericht_DahindenJanine.pdf

Dahinden, Urs, Vinzenz Wyss, Guido Keel and Carmen Koch. *The Role of the Mass Media in the "Clash of Civilizations."* NRP58, final report, 2010. Available online: http://www.nfp58.ch/files/downloads/NFP58_Schlussbericht_DahindenU.pdf

Frank, Katharina. *Schulischer Religionsunterricht.* Stuttgart: Kohlhammer, 2010.

Frank, Katharina, and Christoph Bochinger. "Religious Education in Switzerland as a Field of Work for the Study of Religions: Empirical Results and Theoretical Reflections." *Numen* 55, 2008, 183–217.

Geertz, Clifford. "Religion als kulturelles System." In *Dichte Beschreibung. Beiträge zum Verstehen kultureller Systeme*, 44–95. Frankfurt a.M.: Suhrkamp, 1987. (English trans., "Thick Description: Toward an Interpretive Theory of Culture." In *The Interpretation of Cultures: Selected Essays*, 3–30. New York: Basic Books, 1973).

Gianni, Matteo, *et al. Muslime in der Schweiz. Identitätsprofile, Erwartungen und Einstellungen. Eine Studie der Forschungsgruppe "Islam in der Schweiz" (GRIS).* Bern: Eidgenössische Kommission für Migrationsfragen, EKM, 2nd edn, 2010, (2005). http://www.ekm.admin.ch/de/dokumentation/doku/mat_muslime_d.pdf

Giugni, Marco, Matteo Gianni and Noëmi Michel. *Muslims in Switzerland between Recognition as Minority and Assimilation.* NPR58, final report, 2010. Available online: http://www.nfp58.ch/files/downloads/Schlussbericht_Giugni.pdf

Goffman, Erving. *Frame Analysis: An Essay on the Organization of Experience.* Cambridge, MA: Harvard University Press, 1974.

Hilger, Georg, Stephan Leimgruber and Hans Georg Ziebertz. *Religionsdidaktik. Ein Leitfaden für Studium, Ausbildung und Beruf.* München: Kösel, 2001.

Jödicke, Ansgar, and Andrea Rota. *Religious Education between the State and Religious Communities.* 2010. Available online: http://www.nfp58.ch/files/downloads/Joedicke_Schule_Schlussbericht_def.pdf

Klafki, Wolfgang. "Die bildungstheoretische Didaktik im Rahmen kritisch-konstruktiver Erziehungswissenschaft." In *Didaktische Theorien*, ed. Herbert Gudjons and Rainer Winkel, 13–34. Hamburg: Bergmann und Helbig, 12th edn, 2006.

Koch, Carmen. "Das Politische dominiert. Wie Schweizer Medien über Religionen berichten." *Communicatio Socialis* 42(4), 2009, 365–81.

Kollmar Paulenz, Karénina, and Eva Funk. *The Perception of Tibetan Buddhism in Public Swiss Institutions.* NRP58, final report, 2010. Available online: http://www.nfp58.ch/files/downloads/Schlussbericht_Kollmar-Paulenz.pdf

Lüddeckens, Dorothea, Rafael Walthert, Christoph Uehlinger *et al. Controversies Concerning Visible Symbols of Religious Identity.* NRP58, final report, 2010. Available online: http://www.nfp58.ch/files/downloads/Schlussbericht_Lueddeckens.pdf

Plüss, David, and Adrian Portmann. *Secularized Christians and Religious Diversity.* NRP58, final report, 2011. Available online: http://www.nfp58.ch/files/downloads/NFP58_Schlussbericht_Pluess.pdf

Riaño, Yvonne, and Janine Dahinden. *Zwangsheirat: Hintergründe, Massnahmen, lokale und transnationale Dynamiken.* Zürich: Seismo, 2010.

Schlieter, Jens, Marietta Kind Furger and Tina Lauer. *Second and Third generation Tibetans in Switzerland.* NRP58, final report, 2010. Available online: http://www.nfp58.ch/files/downloads/Schlussbericht_Schlieter.pdf

Schmid, Kuno. *Religion lernen in der Schule. Didaktische Überlegungen für einen bekenntnisunabhängigen schulischen Religionsunterricht im Kontext einer Didaktik des Sachunterrichts (mit Beiträgen von Monika Jakobs).* Bern: hep, 2011.

Sökefeld, Martin, Sarah Beyeler and Virgina Suter Reich. *Ahmadi and Alevi Diaspora in Switzerland.* NRP58, final report, 2010. Available online: http://www.nfp58.ch/files/downloads/Schlussbericht_Soekefeld.pdf

Soysal, Yasemin Nuhoğlu. *Limits of Citizenship: Migrants and Postnational Membership in Europe.* Chicago: University of Chicago Press, 1994.

Stichweh, Rolf. *Inklusion und Exklusion. Studien zur Gesellschaftstheorie.* Bielefeldt: transcript, 2005.

Stolz, Jörg, Judith Könemann, Mallory Schneuwly Purdie, Thomas Englberger and Michael Krüggeler. *Religiosity in Modern Times.* NRP58, final report, 2011. Available online: http://www.nfp58.ch/files/downloads/Schlussbericht__Stolz.pdf

Vatter, Adrian, ed. *Vom Schächt- zum Minarettverbot. Religiöse Minderheiten in der direkten Demokratie.* Zürich: Verlag Neue Zürcher Zeitung, 2011.

Voas, David. "The Rise and Fall of Fuzzy Fidelity in Europe: European." *Sociological Review* 25, 2009, 155–68.

Endnotes

1. The article represents the status of textbooks and research on religion education in Switzerland in 2011.
2. The schools in Switzerland are up to now organized by cantons.
3. I use the term "religion education" for every form of education in which "religion" or "religions" are taken up as a subject: cf. also the German terms in Katharina Frank, *Schulischer Religionsunterricht* (Stuttgart: Kohlhammer, 2010), ch. 6, 194–211. I will do this in contrast to my former articles in English (Katharina Frank and Christoph Bochinger, "Religious Education in Switzerland as a Field of Work for the Study of Religions: Empirical Results and Theoretical Reflections," *Numen* 55 [2008], 183–217, 203–204) and also in contrast to David Chidester who uses "religion education" for a compulsory education for all pupils in South Africa. (cf. David Chidester, "Unity in Diversity: Religion Education and Public Pedagogy in

South Africa," *Numen* 55 [2008], 272–99). Other authors use the abbreviation RE to avoid the misleading term "religious education."

4. Information on the newest development cf. online: http://www.edk.ch/dyn/11659.php

5. Willi Bühler, Benno Bühlmann and Andreas Kessler (eds), *Sachbuch Religionen* (Horw/ Luzern: db-Verlag, 2009).

6. The Swiss constitution doesn't allow a "religiöser Unterricht" for all pupils of a class. Jurists therefore propose to speak of a "Religionskunde." The authors of the *Sachbuch Religionen* refer to a "bekenntnisfreier Religionsunterricht." Cf. Bühler, *et al.*, *Sachbuch Religionen*, 7. Other authors speak of "bekenntnisfreier schulischer Religionsunterricht," cf. Kuno Schmid, *Religion lernen in der Schule. Didaktische Überlegungen für einen bekenntnisunabhängigen schulischen Religionsunterricht im Kontext einer Didaktik des Sachunterrichts (mit Beiträgen von Monika Jakobs)* (Bern: hep, 2011). The manual used in the courses for "Religion und Kultur" teachers speaks of "religionskundlicher Unterricht." cf. online: http:// stud.phzh.ch/webautor-data/61/Fachwegleitung_ReligionKultur_Sek1.pdf, 6. All authors mean a compulsory religion education when using these terms. Here and in the following text, I will use the term "Religionskunde" or "religionskundlicher Unterricht" in German, because there is no appropriate corresponding term in English. See Frank and Bochinger, "Religious Education in Switzerland as a Field of Work for the Study of Religions: Empirical Results," 183–217, 203–204.

7. Bühler, *et al.*, *Sachbuch Religionen*, 7.

8. Cf. Wolfgang Klafki, "Die bildungstheoretische Didaktik im Rahmen kritisch-konstruktiver Erziehungswissenschaft," in Herbert Gudjons and Rainer Winkel (eds), *Didaktische Theorien* (Hamburg: Bergmann und Helbig, 12th edn, 2006), 13–34 (18).

9. Cf. Frank, *Schulischer Religionsunterricht* and Frank and Bochinger, "Religious Education, 183–217 (195–204).

10. Cf. Erving Goffman, *Frame Analysis: An Essay on the Organization of Experience* (Cambridge, MA: Harvard University Press, 1974).

11. Cf. Roland Campiche and Alfred Dubach, Alfred, *Jeder ein Sonderfall. Religion in der Schweiz* (Zürich: NZN Buchverlag, 1993).

12. Cf. Roland Campiche, *Die zwei Gesichter der Religion. Faszination und Entzauberung* (Zürich: TVZ, 2004).

13. Cf. Jörg Stolz et al., *Religiosity in Modern Times* (NRP58, final report, 2011), online: http:// www.nfp58.ch/files/downloads/Schlussbericht__Stolz.pdf

14. Cf. Martin Baumann and Jörg Stolz (eds), *Eine Schweiz—viele Religionen* (Bielefeld: transcript, 2007) or in French: *La nouvelle Suisse religieuse. Risques et chances de sa diversité* (Genève: Labor et fides, 2009).

15. For further informations about the NRP cf. Online: http://www.nfp58.ch/e_index.cfm

16. Cf. Stolz et al., *Religiosity in Modern Times*, 18: While in 1976, 59% of the people asked still answered they regularly take part in a religious service, in 2009 as much as 85% answered that they attend such services less than once every month or only on special occasions.

17. The percentage of people who are not members of any religious community has increased to 24.8%, see Stolz et al., *Religiosity in Modern Times*, 5–6.

18. Cf. For the term "distant" see Stolz et al., *Religiosity in Modern Times*, 5–6. Stolz refers here also to Voas' concept of "fuzzy fidelity," see David Voas, "The Rise and Fall of Fuzzy Fidelity in Europe," *European Sociological Review* 25 (2009), 155–68.

19. Cf. Frank, *Schulischer Religionsunterricht*, 135–36 and 213–14.
20. Translation in English: "Religion is a system of symbols which augurs a benefit for some-one's life through a correlation to an ultimate reality."
21. As a reminder the definition by Geertz in German: "Religion ist ein Symbolsystem, das darauf abzielt, starke, umfassende und dauerhafte Stimmungen und Motivationen in den Menschen zu schaffen, indem es Vorstellungen einer allgemeinen Seinsordnung formuli-ert und diese Vorstellungen mit einer solchen Aura von Faktizität umgibt, dass die Stim-mungen und Motivationen völlig der Wirklichkeit zu entsprechen scheinen." Cf. Clifford Geertz, "Religion als kulturelles System." In *Dichte Beschreibung. Beiträge zum Verstehen kul-tureller Systeme* (Frankfurt a.M.: Suhrkamp, 1987), 44–95. Translation in English: "Religion is defined as a system of symbols which acts to establish powerful, pervasive, and long-lasting moods and motivations in men by formulating conceptions of a general order of existence and clothing these conceptions with such an aura of factuality that the moods and moti-vations seem uniquely realistic," cf. Clifford Geertz, *Thick Description: Toward an Interpre-tive Theory of Culture*, in: *The Interpretation of Cultures: Selected Essays* (New York: Basic Books, 1973), 3–30.
22. English Translation: "In an individual crisis, the religious community helps to overcome or to endure it, with the effect that one can still trust in the world afterwards. When, however, the religious education of a person is used to restrict his or her spontaneity and to break the person's free will, he or she might renounce religion altogether."
23. The textbook "Sachbuch Religionen" includes the following chapters:

    - "Hinduism" (pp. 52–91) written by Frank Neubert who was educated in the Study of Religions and currently works at the University of Lucerne.
    - "Buddhism" (pp. 92–133): Martin Baumann, *Study of Religions* (University of Lucerne).
    - "Judaism" (pp. 134–79): Simone Rosenzweig and Simon Erlanger, who studied Jewish Studies and other subjects, currently working as a scholar of Jewish-Christian Studies, University of Lucerne.
    - "Christianity" (180–235): Willi Bühler, theologian and teacher of the subject "Religion-skunde und Ethik" at a grammar school in Lucerne; Andreas Kessler, theologian and teacher of "Religionskunde und Ethik" at a grammar school in Lucerne, currently working as a scholar of Religious Pedagogy at the University of Berne and as a lecturer for Didactics of Religions at the University of Teacher Education in Berne.
    - "Islam" (236–283): Samuel Behloul, studied Theology and Islamic Studies, currently working as a scholar of the Study of Religions at the University of Lucerne.
    - The portraits, interviews and reportages for all religious traditions: Benno Bühlmann, theologian and journalist, currently working as journalist and as teacher of "Religion-skunde und Ethik" at a grammar school in Lucerne.

24. See Yvonne Riaño and Janine Dahinden, *Zwangsheirat: Hintergründe, Massnahmen, lokale und transnationale Dynamiken* (Zürich: Seismo, 2010).
25. Tibetan Buddhist groups are the most common Buddhist groups in Switzerland. Cf. Martin Baumann, online: http://www.religionenschweiz.ch/buddhismus.html. The Dalai Lama visits Switzerland regularly. He is well represented in the Swiss media and maintains close contact to Tibetan refugees and his adherents as well as scientists and politicians. Cf. Karénina Kollmar Paulenz and Eva Funk, *The Perception of Tibetan Buddhism in Public Swiss*

Institutions (NRP58, final report, 2010), online: http://www.nfp58.ch/files/downloads/ Schlussbericht_Kollmar-Paulenz.pdf

26. Many Tibetan Buddhists lived in larger separate groups when they first arrived in Switzerland. Those who lived alone or as children in foster families integrated quickly and well, although they later often had health problems. The Tibetan Buddhists who come to Switzerland today and live alone also often have serious problems. See Jens Schlieter, Marietta Kind Furger and Tina Lauer, *Second and Third Generation Tibetans in Switzerland* (NRP58, final report, 2010), online: http://www.nfp58.ch/files/downloads/Schlussbericht_Schlieter.pdf, 12, 16. Similar facts are analysed concerning Vietnamese Buddhists. Cf. Martin Baumann, Frank Weigelt and Rafaela Eulberg, *Tamil Hindus and Vietnamese Buddhists in Switzerland* (PNR58, final report, 2011), online: http://www.nfp58.ch/files/downloads/Schlussbericht_ Baumann.pdf.

27. The Thai-Buddhist temple in Gretzenbach, for example, is an advertised tourist attraction on the website of MySwitzerland, cf. online: http://www.myswitzerland.com/de/infra_ anlagendetail.cfm?rkey=1046&instance=1016783&art=Oeffentliches%20Gebäude. See Dorothea Lüddeckens, Rafael Walthert, Christoph Uehlinger *et al.*, *Controversies Concerning Visible Symbols of Religious Identity* (NRP58, final report, 2011), online: http://www.nfp58.ch/ files/downloads/Schlussbericht_Lueddeckens.pdf.

28. Cf. Frank, *Schulischer Religionsunterricht*, 209. See also Rolf Stichweh, *Inklusion und Exklusion. Studien zur Gesellschaftstheorie* (Bielefeldt: transcript, 2005), 13–44.

29. Christians believe God to be the Creator of all beings... Christians trust their knowledge that God has a relationship with all his creatures... Therefore the actual expression of Christian religiosity is prayer and the attending of the divine services. It is not the foremost goal of a Christian to talk about God, but to create a relationship with him, etc.

30. E.g., Christoph Bochinger, Winfried Gebhardt and Martin Engelbrecht, *Die unsichtbare Religion in der sichtbaren Religion—Formen spiritueller Orientierung in der religiösen Gegenwartskultur* (Stuttgart: Kohlhammer, 2009).

31. Cf. Campiche and Dubach, *Jeder ein Sonderfall*; Campiche, *Die zwei Gesichter*; Jörg Stolz *et al.*, *Religiosity in Modern Times*.

32. Cf. online: http://www.nzz.ch/nachrichten/politik/schweiz/basketball_schweiz_verbot_ kopftuch_luzern_spielerin_1.3378714.html

33. Cf. online: http://www.nzz.ch/nachrichten/panorama/amtsgericht_luzern_stuetzt_kop-ftuchverbot_im_basketball_1.4660222.html

34. Cf. Matteo Gianni *et al.*, *Muslime in der Schweiz. Identitätsprofile, Erwartungen und Einstellungen Eine Studie der Forschungsgruppe "Islam in der Schweiz"* (GRIS) (Bern: Eidgenössische Kommission für Migrationsfragen, EKM, 2nd edn, 2010 [2005]). http://www.ekm.admin.ch/de/ dokumentation/doku/mat_muslime_d.pdf.

35. Cf. Martin Sökefeld, Sarah Beyeler and Virgina Suter Reich, *Ahmadi and Alevi Diaspora in Switzerland* (NRP58, final report, 2010), online: http://www.nfp58.ch/files/downloads/ Schlussbericht_Soekefeld.pdf or Yasemin Nuhoğlu Soysal, *Limits of Citizenship: Migrants and Postnational Membership in Europe* (Chicago: University of Chicago Press, 1994).

36. In 1963, the Ahmadis built a mosque in Zurich which today is still the only one in the canton with a minaret and they are very active in publicizing Islam. Cf. Sarah Beyeler and Virginia Suter Reich, "Sichtbarkeit von Inkorporationsbedingungen. Ein Vergleich muslimischer Bauvorhaben in der Schweiz", *TSANTSA* 14 (2009): 141–46 (143).

37. The author of this chapter himself has done research and written about different Muslim groups, cf. Samuel M. Behloul, *How Bosnian an Albanian Muslims in Switzerland are Reacting to the Islam Discourse*, http://www.nfp58.ch/files/downloads/Schlussbericht_Behloul.pdf, or Marco Giugni, Matteo Gianni and Noëmi Michel, *Muslims in Switzerland between Recognition as Minority and Assimilation* (NPR58, final report, 2010), online: http://www.nfp58.ch/files/downloads/Schlussbericht_Giugni.pdf.

38. The book "Eine Schweiz—viele Religionen" could be seen as a counterexample. The study of religions scholars Martin Baumann and Samuel Behloul as well as the sociologist Jörg Stolz were involved in the making of the book. Cf. Stolz and Baumann, *Eine Schweiz*. What is missing in this book is the perspective of the *Freidenker-Vereinigung* (association of the freethinkers), which is a very present group in the Swiss public space. See Urs Dahinden, Vinzenz Wyss, Guido Keel and Carmen Koch, *The Role of the Mass Media in the "Clash of Civilizations"* (NRP58, final report, 2010), online: http://www.nfp58.ch/files/downloads/NFP58_Schlussbericht_DahindenU.pdf, 3.

39. See the syllabus "Religion und Kultur" of the canton of Zurich, Switzerland. The syllabus forbids the teacher to engage in any religious practice with the children (e.g., praying), demands however much religious knowledge from the pupils (http://www.phzh.ch/webautor-data/669/Lehrplan-Religion-und-Kultur.pdf), 7.

40. The subject, the schoolbook is developed demands marks as with other school subjects.

41. In this context, the dimensions of religions (Ninian Smart) or the dimensions of religiosity (Charles Glock or Stefan Huber) are important. Both models assume that also an intellectual dimension, e.g., the knowledge about myths, belongs to the religion or religiosity itself. In this view, religious knowledge belongs to religiosity as well as the ritual dimension.

42. Cf. Dahinden *et al.*, *The Role of the Mass Media*.

43. Carmen Koch, "Das Politische dominiert. Wie Schweizer Medien über Religionen berichten," *Communicatio Socialis* 42(4) (2009), 365–81.

44. Cf. Stolz *et al.*, *Religiosity in Modern Times*.

45. For further information cf. Adrian Vatter (ed.), *Vom Schächt- zum Minarettverbot. Religiöse Minderheiten in der direkten Demokratie* (Zürich: Verlag Neue Zürcher Zeitung, 2011).

46. Cf. Janine Dahinden, Kerstin Duemmler and Joëlle Moret, *Religion and Ethnicity—a Survey among Young Adults* (NRP58, final report, 2010), http://www.nfp58.ch/files/downloads/Schlussbericht_DahindenJanine.pdf

47. Dahinden *et al.*, *Religion and Ethnicity*, 7.

48. Cf. SVP, *Political Programme 2011-2015* (online: http://www.svp.ch/display.cfm/id/101395), 4, 62–63.

49. Cf. Georg Hilger, Stephan Leimgruber and Hans Georg Ziebertz, *Religionsdidaktik. Ein Leitfaden für Studium, Ausbildung und Beruf* (München: Kösel, 2001) or a didactics, recently published in Switzerland, Schmid, *"Religion" lernen in der Schule*.

50. Important inputs for a study of religions approach gave Wanda Alberts, *Integrative Religious Education in Europe: A Study of Religions Approach* (Berlin and New York: De Gruyter, 2007), 353–87.

51. Cf. Klafki, *Die bildungstheoretische Didaktik*, 13–34.

52. E.g., Michael Aepkers and Sabine Liebig, *Entdeckendes Forschendes Genetisches Lernen, Basiswissen Pädagogik, Unterrichtskonzepte und Techniken* (Hohengehren: Schneider Verlag, 2002).

53. For this problem, see Ansgar Jödicke and Andrea Rota, *Religious Education between the State and Religious Communities* (online: http://www.nfp58.ch/files/downloads/Joedicke_Schule_

Schlussbericht_def.pdf, 2010). See also David Plüss and Adrian Portmann, *Secularized Christians and Religious Diversity* (NRP58, final report, 2011), online: http://www.nfp58.ch/files/downloads/NFP58_Schlussbericht_Pluess.pdf.

54. Cf. Cristina Allemann-Ghionda, *Schule, Bildung und Pluralität. Sechs Fallstudien im europäischen Vergleich* (Frankfurt a.M. / Bern u. a.: Peter Lang, 1999), 484–95.

4. TO LEARN ABOUT THE OTHER AND TO GET TO KNOW HIM: JUDAISM AND THE JEWISH COMMUNITY OF QUEBEC AS REPRESENTED IN ETHICS AND RELIGIOUS CULTURE TEXTBOOKS

Sivane Hirsch and *Marie Mc Andrew***

The "Ethics and Religious Culture" (ERC) program, recently (2008) introduced in all primary and secondary schools in the province of Quebec, has been a subject of numerous analyses and debates (Estivalèzes 2009; Milot 2007; Racine 2008). Its opponents, religious and non-religious alike, dispute the acknowledgement in the classroom of religious pluralism within society. They also emphasize that transmitting beliefs about diverse religions in the classroom is an impossible task for teachers who do not necessarily share them. Even those who support the programme worry that, in order to fulfil its objectives—notably to allow youth to discover the different influences on their society's history as well as on contemporary culture and values—teachers will need to access considerable information and acquire deeper understanding of diverse doctrines, philosophies and beliefs. The immediate and universal establishment of the programme in all classes, without a transitional period, has heightened the role of ERC textbooks in providing that information not only to the children learning from them, but also to the teachers using them. The study of Judaism and the portrayal of Jewish communities in these textbooks will be the subject of this chapter, which is part of a larger

* Sivane Hirsch was responsible, during her postdoctoral fellowship at Canada's Chair on Education and Ethnic Relations at the University de Montréal, for research on the role of education in the relations between the Quebec Jewish community and other Quebecers. She has published a few articles on the treatment of the Holocaust and of the Quebec's Jewish community in history textbooks as well as on the way Montreal's Jewish schools integrate national curriculum in their educative project.

** Marie Mc Andrew is a full professor at the Faculty of Education of the University of Montréal where she carries out an important research programme on the role of education in the transformation of ethnic relations. She has published numerous articles and books on minority education and intercultural education in Quebec, Canada and around the world.

research project focusing on the role of education in intercultural relations, and more specifically between the Jewish community and other Quebecers. In spite of being the oldest religious minority in Quebec, and of having been the largest one for a long time, the understanding and knowledge that other Quebecers have of the Jewish community are still largely deficient (Jedwab 2000; Weinfeld 2001). Can the new textbooks change perceptions of this community by making its social, cultural and religious reality more intelligible?

1. A NEW PROGRAM TO TEACH ABOUT RELIGION: ETHICS AND RELIGIOUS CULTURE (ERC)

The Ethics and Religious Culture programme was introduced in Quebec schools at all levels in 2008, replacing a confessional model for the teaching of religions (Catholicism and Protestantism) that was combined with a more philosophical model of instruction, referred to as "moral" instruction, for those who preferred a secular option. The two models stayed in place even after schools and school boards had been "de-confessionalized" by 2000, and it enjoyed a certain attachment among parents who often liked this last vestige of tradition in their lives.[1] Even before the new programme was introduced to the public, a long and turbulent debate emerged in the media, but also a juridical battle that has yet to arrive at the Supreme Court. On the one hand, Catholic parents and even a Catholic high school, Loyola,[2] claim that the programme is unconstitutional, as it does not allow them to raise their children as Catholics. On the other hand, many people worry that the programme is too religious, treating all beliefs as relevant. In other words, the programme's sociological approach was criticized for being anti-religious at the same time that its relativity was criticized for teaching children that no religion is better than any other—for allowing too great an acceptance of religion as a means of explaining the world and determining one's actions in it.

Since the programme's introduction in schools, new debates have arisen, mostly questioning the system's capacity to integrate such an ambitious programme in such a short period of time. Many question the training of its future teachers and even their capacity to learn enough about different religions in order to teach them without spreading confusion.[3] Others question the dependency of teachers on textbooks—choosing a position not unlike our own in this chapter—and the ways in which textbooks present the different religions.

The programme not only teaches religion, but aims to develop three competencies: ethics, religious culture, and dialogue. The three share the same general goals: the recognition of others and the pursuit of the common good. In other words, this approach tries to help students better understand and behave in a pluralistic society where everyone has the right to their own opinion, within the limits of general values and norms. The competency of dialogue, aimed at helping learners engage in a dialogue about any subject, including those that are a potential source of conflict, is therefore an important condition for the success of the programme. Students learn how to organize their thoughts, interact respectfully with others, and develop a substantiated point of view using specific tools, such as different forms of dialogue (conversation, discussion, deliberation, debate, etc.).

The ethics competency offers to "lead students to reflect on ethical questions" by analysing different situations from an ethical point of view. Students learn how to integrate various sources when reflecting on their possible reactions, regarding themes such as freedom (its different manifestations and its limits), tolerance (when, how and why it is appropriate), justice (different types and dilemmas) and human ambivalence (as opposed to the good/bad dichotomy). Religious texts can be used as sources, much like any other philosophical influence on ethics today. The Ten Commandments are undoubtedly the most popular example in textbooks, used in the discussion of different charters defining human or civil rights.

The Religious Culture competency in which religions are specifically discussed is our main interest here. Its primary objective is to help students "demonstrate an understanding of the phenomenon of religion" and recognize that "various forms of religious expression constitute a significant [part of Quebec's] heritage, which over time, is renewed and evolves as a result of new cultural contributions" MELS (2008: 20). This statement should not be taken lightly in a society that has rejected its own religion over the past 40 years. This programme acknowledges religious pluralism in contemporary Quebec, clearly choosing "open secularism" (Taylor 2011), according to which society should (and can) stay secular while allowing religion to be expressed in public. As the programme explains:

> Living together in our society requires that we gain an understanding of the phenomenon of religion. In this program, the goal is to encourage students to understand the various forms of religious expression, grasp the complexity of the phenomenon and gain perspective on the various dimensions: experiential, historical, doctrinal, moral, ritual, literary, artistic, social or political. MELS (2008: 20)

Every one of these aspects is addressed in the programme's themes and the examples it provides. The secondary level programme, which interests us most in this chapter, covers six units: the "key elements of religious traditions," such as stories, rites and rules; the "representations of the divine and of mythical and supernatural beings," like names, attributes and symbols; the "religions down through time," which even provides space for new religious movements; and "existential questions" that allow students to go beyond each religion's specificities and develop more philosophical questions with which religions deal.

Two themes more specifically cover the place of religion in contemporary society in general, as well as in Quebec in particular. "Religious references in art and culture" presents religious works of art, and also religious references in secular art. Meanwhile, "Quebec's religious heritage" shows the influence of different religions on Quebec culture and society, through the presentation of influential figures and institutions, and their contribution to Quebec's current values and norms. Throughout these themes, students can learn "to associate forms of expression with their respective religion, and to make connections between diverse elements of the social and cultural environment, both here and elsewhere in the world" MELS (2008: 20).

It is therefore not surprising that the programme also determines the place that each religion should occupy in the overall discussion of different themes, according to its role and importance in Quebec society. It recognizes the particular place of Christianity (Catholicism and Protestantism) to be treated through all the themes. Native spirituality and Judaism are to be covered on a number of occasions in each year of the cycle. The latter owes its presence to its influence on Christianity, and also to its relatively long presence in Quebec. Islam, Buddhism and Hinduism, which arrived to Quebec only at the beginning of the twentieth century, should also be covered on a number of occasions over the course of a cycle. Finally, other religions besides those mentioned can also be covered, depending on the situation and needs of the class. This hierarchical organization of the studied religions has an important impact on the treatment of Judaism in the ERC textbooks, which generally respect this requirement, as well as on the methodology used.

2. STUDYING THE ERC TEXTBOOKS: SOME METHODOLOGICAL REMARKS

Only six textbooks approved by the Quebec Ministry of Education (MELS) cover the ERC program for secondary school (Junior and Senior High School).[4] These nevertheless provide a consecutive sample of extracts to analyse, probably because of the specific place assigned to Judaism in the programme (mentioned earlier), obligating textbooks to present it repeatedly. In addition to these sources, we decided to consider an activity book that does not have to be submitted for ministerial approval (only textbooks are submitted). Since it is published by a major Quebec publisher—one that usually publishes textbooks—we believe that this activity book was a deliberate choice in order to speed up publishing, and also to make it more attractive for teachers. Our study also benefits from the examination of more diverse material. In total, we analysed more than 160 extracts for the purpose of this study, which lead us to a study of the representation of Judaism in textbooks rather than a quantitative summary. That is why we present the results as a general portrait and concentrate on some examples that are the most relevant to our question: Can learning about others in this program encourage better relations between groups?

The context in which these textbooks were published should also be mentioned. Since the program was implemented at the same time at all levels, most teachers could not be specifically trained to teach it.[5] They therefore relied heavily on the textbooks for planning and teaching the course. Thus, the authority of the textbooks has been considerably amplified (Lenoir *et al.* 2001). Thus, studying the ERC textbooks gives us concrete access to the programme's teachings in the classroom.

This study is a part of a larger one that examines the role of education in relationship between the Jewish community and other Quebecers, through three aspects of society: the integration of Quebec's official curriculum into the educational projects of Montreal's private Jewish schools; the impact of public activities offered by the Jewish community on the general public's perceptions of the community; and finally the representation of the Jewish community's culture, history and religion in the Quebec curriculum, more particularly History and Civic Education (HEC),[6] as well as Ethics and Religious Culture (ERC).

Indeed, formal education plays a considerable role in society, not only through the transmission of knowledge, but also through socialization (Ballantyne 2001), contributing to the maintenance or transformation of ethnic barriers. By choices made in the curriculum, it can reproduce or, on the contrary, contribute to the disappearance of linguistic, religious and cultural identifications (Juteau 2000; Mc Andrew 2006), as well as intercultural competencies (Banks 2007). More specifically, instructional materials can reflect the image of Quebec society today, or at least the image its members have of it (Choppin 1992), and even more so in a society where it goes through an approval procedure, such as in Quebec.

Our analysis tried, first, to determine the way textbooks cover the specific themes suggested by the programme with regards to Judaism, and second to suggest a meta-analysis that considers the overall image of Judaism. Special attention was given to examples used in the textbooks to explain different themes. Indeed, the images, anecdotes, and even the specific holidays that authors of each textbook have chosen to present can considerably influence the overall image of Judaism projected. Does this presentation enable students to better appreciate Judaism in Quebec today?

3. JUDAISM IN THE ERC TEXTBOOKS

Judaism's general presence in the textbooks is evident, though it is not covered in all the programme's themes. Generally, it is most often present in chapters dedicated to stories and practices, and less to its influences on Quebec's society through art or culture, even though it is clearly covered as a part of Quebec's religious heritage in the chapter dedicated to this topic.

Judaism is first and foremost presented as the first monotheistic religion, often relating it via a comparison with Christianity and Islam. Thus, when the notion of alliance with God is discussed, or when the vision of world's creation is explained, it is always with reference to these two other religious perspectives. Certain rituals and practices are also presented through that approach: the interdiction to create an image of God, as in Islam, or even just to say his name; the Sabbath and the general idea of a resting day that is dedicated to God; and the definition of diet and clothing restrictions. Often, Judaism is presented in the same paragraph with the other two monotheistic religions, or at least next to them. While we will concentrate on Judaism's overall portrait in these textbooks, we should mention that a parallel study is being carried out by another member of our research team regarding the portrayal of Islam in the same textbooks, and will soon be published.

Judaism in practice

When textbooks tell Judaism's stories, explain its beliefs or present its fundamental texts, they generally refer to the same ones: Abraham and his alliance with God; the world's creation; the Hebrews' exodus from Egypt and the Ten Commandments given to Moses. They all explain that the Jewish Bible (and they even name it the Torah) is the main source of these stories, as well as of Jewish practices. These aspects can indeed help students to better understand Judaism. However, it is mostly in the influence that these stories have on practices that their deeper meanings are conveyed, which helps to explain how Judaism is lived today, especially in Quebec. One textbook links, for example, the story of Exodus to the Jewish tradition of Passover, explaining why Jews should not eat leavened food (*Tête-à-tête* [Junior High School], p. 162). Another tells the story of creation, explaining the sacralization of the Sabbath (*Passeport pour la vie*, pp. 179–80). By contrast, the Star of David, which is an important Jewish symbol, is presented in relation to Israel's flag without explaining its origins (except in *Tête-à-tête*). In this case, it is the overt aspect that is presented, without considering the symbol's important significance.

This is why we find it particularly interesting to consider the examples used by the textbooks to illustrate their explanations. Our analysis shows that Jewish practices are often presented as timeless and "anonymous," without signs of a specific place or context. At other moments, they are represented as existing elsewhere, and more specifically in Jerusalem and at the Western Wall. Finally, when Jewish practices are presented in the context of Quebec, it is by referring to this community's most stereotypical representation, namely the Hassidim.

The Sabbath is a good example of this approach. In four textbooks, it is explained as a sacred day of rest and often compared (in three of them) to the Christian Sunday. However, its practice is described in terms of the more orthodox practice: "the meals for Shabbat should be prepared in advance since one cannot cook during the day of the Sabbath... the use of a car, electricity or the telephone is also forbidden" (*Passeport pour la vie*, p. 201). The activity book *Vivre ensemble 2* announces that "Jewish students refuse to present themselves to exams on Saturday" (p. 82) supposedly because of their religious practice. However, while another textbook specifies that the interdiction to work on a Sunday "was abolished for Christians in numerous countries for a few years" (*Être en société*, p. 128), none offers the same nuanced presentation of Judaism, although many levels of practice also exist within this religion.

Another example is the different Jewish holidays that are described in a very general manner, showing timeless rituals without any specific consideration for their practice in Quebec. Thus Passover dinner, the *seder*, is accompanied by a photo of the traditional plate of symbolic dishes, but without any explanation of their symbolism. Meanwhile, a photo of a rabbi blowing the *shofar* (a trumpet) is accompanied by the text for *Rosh hashana* (the New Year). The more "familial" aspects of it, for example eating sweet dishes to have a sweet year, or wearing new cloths to mark the beginning of a new year, are never mentioned.

However, two exceptions should be noted. The holiday of *Soukkot* (traditional cabins) is illustrated in two textbooks with pictures of either the inside of a *Soukkah*, the traditional cabin (*Tête-à-tête* [Junior High School], p. 172), or a *Soukkah* "on a balcony in the middle of a city" (*Être en société*, p. 125). Considering the resentment that these "constructions" have already inspired in Montreal, showing what they look like should, indeed, not be neglected. While Hanukkah is often mentioned, it is presented on only one occasion through the traditional game of spinning tops (*Réflexions*, p. 68), and is included as part of Quebec's religious heritage next to, among other examples, Christmas blessings. These examples show not only how important these are, but also how easy it is to portray Jewish rituals within their local context—presenting Judaism as a living religion and not just a theoretical one.

By contrast, the frequent use of pictures from the Western Wall encourages a sense of a religion that comes from elsewhere. Without denying the symbolic significance of the *Kotel* for today's Judaism, we regret that textbooks accord such an important position to the Wall's rituals. Indeed, there is no religious obligation to celebrate any ritual next to the Wall, even though some celebrate personal events, like a *Bar* or *Bat mitzvah* (which celebrates the child's arrival at the age of reason) or a marriage ceremony, on its premises. Nevertheless, one textbook mistakenly explains that Jews pray there "especially on the occasion of three Jewish celebrations: Passover, Shavuot (the Jewish Pentecost) and Sukkoth" (*Être en société*, p. 132). This was only true while the Temple was standing. Most of the textbooks show photos of Jewish practices at the Western Wall on various occasions. By doing so, the textbooks mislead readers and encourage an image of a religion that should be practised far away, when in truth it can be practised everywhere and does not obligate members to undertake pilgrimages, unlike certain other religions.

Everyday practices

Everyday practices are also described in the textbooks, but while some of these descriptions suffer from similar weaknesses (i.e., not referring to Quebec's specific milieu), others directly address Quebec's situation. Dress codes are a good example, because they are easily visible in the local landscape. Textbooks discuss ritual clothing such as the *kippa* (skullcap worn by orthodox men) or the *tallit* (the prayer shawl), directly relating them to prayer. However, only one textbook makes the distinction between men who wear the *kippa* all the time, and those who use it only for prayer (*Vivre ensemble 1*, p. 156), while another textbook explains that it is not a religious obligation (*Réflexions B*, p. 44). Still, the images accompanying these explanations are as anonymous as possible, and often show only the object itself. All the others were taken at the Western Wall.

Two textbooks also refer to the dress code observed by the Hassidim communities. One source (*Réflexions A*, p. 41) treats this tradition as a "religious expression" not unlike Christmas carols and *pow-wow* dancing (a traditional dance of aboriginal communities). But the other clearly explains that they simply kept their traditional clothing from their lives in Europe, even adding that "the majority of Jews do not wear any distinctive sign and blend into the general population" (*Tête-à-tête* [Junior High School], p. 169). This last remark seems important to us because it allows students to better understand the Jewish reality of Montreal, that the religion is not restricted only to those who wear orthodox clothing.

The difference between these two approaches is also clearly apparent in the way four textbooks cover the *kashrut*, the dietary laws. Two of them explain these laws through comparison with diet restrictions imposed by Islam (*Réflexions B*. p. 43) and even Christianity (*Être en société*, p. 129). They cite the different sources (the Qur'an, the Bible, and the New Testament), and give specific examples. However, they refrain from using the term *Kashrut,* so that their explanation remains theoretical. The other two textbooks not only explain its logic, but also how it is used in daily life; the first speaks of the symbols MK or COR that "mark *kosher* products, sold in almost every supermarket" (*Tête-à-tête*[Junior High School], p. 173), and the second mentions the existence of specialized butcher shops that are "strictly *kosher*" (*Passeport pour la vie*, p. 202).

These examples demonstrate how the same reality can be seen as more or less distant, or more or less a part of the student's own social environment. Another way to integrate religion into the "real life" of students is proposed in one textbook's ethics chapter (*Tête-à-tête* [Senior High School]), discussing various aspects of the Jewish tradition, such as its vision of religious freedom and its limits, and the role played by the Jewish community in the life of its followers. This approach suggests a more philosophical reflection on the daily reality of religious life.

Judaism as part of Quebec's religious heritage
The place of Quebec's Jewish community in the province's religious heritage is covered by the programme's cultural references, including to Abraham de Sola, rabbi of the first Jewish congregation in Montreal who founded its first Jewish school. All textbooks (but not the activities book) tell his story, from his arrival to Montreal, through his various contributions to his community, never neglecting to remind readers of his teaching position at McGill University. However, only two of the four textbooks use this reference to further discuss religious diversity in Quebec today (*Réflexions A.*, p. 54) or even diversity within the community itself, by noting its numerous schools in Montreal (*Tête-à-tête* [Junior High School], p. 178).

Another influential personality, Ezekiel Hart, is introduced in two textbooks and in the activity book. As the first Jew to be elected to the Canadian Assembly in 1807, he was soon thereafter excluded, supposedly because of his religion (as he would not swear on a Christian Bible). Historians agree that it was more of a political issue, of his adversaries wanting to gain political leverage in the famous "prisons quarrel" which disputed how to finance the construction of new prisons (Linteau *et al.* 1989). Nevertheless, in 1834 the Hart sons became allies of the Patriotic Party (which had opposed Harts' election in 1808). Thanks to their collaboration, Canada became the first British colony to accord all civil rights to Jews, and therefore to all religious minorities. It is possible that this story did not find its place in the new programme because it was already referenced in the History and Civic Education (HEC) programme for secondary schools, and thus is treated in all of its textbooks (Hirsch and Mc Andrew 2013a). However, it is also clearly a part of Quebec's religious heritage, and the textbooks that discuss it openly celebrate its legacy.

The material presence of the Jewish community in Montreal's landscape is mostly presented through its synagogues and cemeteries. Although the ERC programme treats religious sites as places to live the religious experience or to discover religious art, textbooks tend to include synagogues (and other worship sites) in their "religious heritage" chapters. This can maybe be explained by their somewhat "sober" architecture of these structures (even more so comparing them to Catholic churches) as one of the texts explains (*Vivre ensemble 1*, p. 111) and the fact they have no architectural specificities (*Tête-à-tête* [Junior High School], p. 177), as explains another text. Recalling their main function in Jewish life, as a place of community gathering and celebration, their presentation becomes the prefect occasion to discuss the community history and its installation in Montreal.

Here again, the pictures of synagogues show mostly old façades, and when their insides are displayed as well, it is with very little explanation—which is clearly insufficient for helping students understand what they see. Instead of placing the Jewish community in contemporary Montreal, it seems to focus on its image as a part of the city's history. The Jewish cemeteries, which according to one of the textbooks represent some of Montreal's "Jewish historical traces" (*Tête-à-tête* [Junior High School], p. 177), are mentioned in two textbooks, but are never shown in photos, even though their difference from the architectural style of Christian cemeteries would have been interesting to consider.

Another kind of contribution of the Jewish community to the city is introduced through the presentation of the Jewish hospital in two textbooks (*Réflexions* and *Vivre ensemble* 1). They explain how the difficulties encountered by Jews in getting good treatment or a job in other Montreal hospitals led the community to found the hospital in 1934, but it is also noted that it accepted patients of all religions. In that sense, the foundation of the Jewish hospital could be considered a moral contribution to Quebec's heritage. Other aspects of Judaism are clearly recognized as having influenced Quebec's cultural heritage, or even ethics: the Ten Commandments are mentioned as having influenced Quebec's Charter of Rights and Freedoms; Jewish commitment to social justice helps explain the community's involvement in Quebec's unionist movement and contributions to the province's different welfare organizations; and even the community's rich cultural life is presented in one of the textbooks (*Tête-à-tête* [Junior High School], p. 180).

The Jewish community and Judaism in general clearly have a place in Quebec's religious heritage, but its image is presented as an historical one. The textbooks speak of its influence on Quebec society and of its contributions to Montreal's landscape, without really showing contemporary consequences, and even less showing "traces" as they appear in contemporary society.

4. CONCLUSION

Judaism's place in the ECR textbooks is safeguarded by the programme's require-ments, which determine to what extent each religion should be covered. Our objective has therefore not been to quantify its appearance in textbooks, but rather to analyse the portrayal found in this treatment of Jewish practice and its presence in Quebec's social landscape. Since theoretical explanations of the reli-gion that are fundamental to beliefs and symbols were not specifically analysed in this discussion, we will not conclude by focusing on the accuracy of textbook representations, or even on the choices of textbook authors regarding which aspects of the religion to present.

What has interested us here more particularly was the question of how a better understanding of Jewish religion and its traditions could facilitate rela-tions between this community and other Quebecers. In that sense, our findings raise some important concerns. While the contribution of Judaism to Quebec's religious and cultural heritage is mentioned, it is rarely considered in its contem-porary forms. Synagogues, for example, are a place of the past.

The presentation of Jewish practice, whether it is important holidays or daily routines, suffers from the same weaknesses. The different rituals are usually described in their most orthodox fashion, neglecting to show diversity within the religion, and when this diversity is discussed (*Tête-à-tête*), it is not really demon-strated through the chosen examples. Moreover, they are presented in a neutral fashion or a distant context, as if relating to another reality entirely.

Judaism is therefore present in the textbooks as a part of Quebec's history, but appears as having much less of a role in Quebec's contemporary reality. Hence, though our study does not show any major problems with the texts, we regret the limited image that emerges of this religion, especially in a society that encoun-ters these same distant portrayals on a daily basis. Indeed, the Hassidic commu-nities that represent 12% of Montreal's Jewish population, attracts most of the general population's attention. While it seems important to explain to students the specificities of such groups as a way of encouraging tolerance toward their practices, it is regrettable that the textbooks do not succeed in expanding Que-bec's image of Judaism.

REFERENCES

Ballantyne, Jeanne H. 2001. *The Sociology of Education: A Systematic Analysis.* Englewood Cliffs, NJ: Prentice Hall.

Banks, James A. 2007. *Educating Citizens in a Multicultural Society.* New York: Teachers College, 2nd edn.

Cherblanc, Jacques, and Dany Rondeau, eds. 2010. *La formation à l'éthique et à la culture religieuse: un modèle d'implantation de programme.* Québec: PUL.

Choppin, Allain L. 1992. *Les manuels scolaires: Histoire et actualité.* Paris: Hachette.

Estivalèzes, Mireille. 2009. "Éducation à la citoyenneté et enseignement sur les religions à l'école, un mariage de raison?" *Diversité urbaine - reconnaissance de la diversité religieuse: débats actuels dans différentes sociétés,* 9(1): 45-57.

Hirsch, Sivane, and Marie Mc Andrew. 2013a. "Le traitement du judaïsme dans les manuels scolaires d'éthique et culture religieuse contribue-t-il à un meilleur vivre ensemble ?" *McGill Journal of Education / Revue des sciences de l'éducation de McGill,* 48(1): 99–114.

Hirsch, Sivane, and Marie Mc Andrew. 2013b. "La représentation de la communauté juive dans les manuels scolaires québécois." *Nouveaux Cahiers de Recherche en Éducation* (NCRE), 15(2): 34–63.

Hirsch, Sivane, and Marie Mc Andrew. Forthcoming 2014. "Teaching the Holocuast in Quebec."

Jedwab, Jack. 2000. "Quebec Jews: A Unique Community in a Distinct Society." In *Juifs et Canadiens français dans la société québécoise,* ed. P. Anctil, I. Robinson and G. Bouchard, 51–73. Québec: Septentrion.

Juteau, Danielle. 2000. *L'ethnicité et ses frontières.* Montréal: Presses de l'Université de Montréal.

Lemieux, Raymon. 1991. "Croyances et incroyances; une économie du sens commun." In *Croyance et incroyances au Québec,* ed. André Charron, Raymond Lemieux and Yvon R. Théroux, 13–86. Rencontres d'aujourd'hui, 18; Montreal: Fides.

Lenoir, Yves, Rey Bernard, Roy Gerard-Raymond and Johanne Lebrun, eds. 2001. *Le manuel scolaire et l'intervention éducative: regards critiques sur ses apports et ses limites.* Sherbrooke: Édition du CRP.

Linteau, Paul-André, René Durocher, Jean-Claude Robert and François Ricard. 1989. *Histoire du Québec contermpoain.* De la Confédération à la crise (1867–1929); Le Québec depuis 1930 (Vol. 2). Montréal: Boréal.

Mc Andrew, Marie. 2006. "The Hijab Controversies in Western Public Schools: Contrasting Conceptions of Ethnicity and Ethnic Relations." In *The Making of the Islamic Diaspora,* ed. S. Rahnema and H. Moghissi. Toronto: University of Toronto Press.

MELS Quebec Ministry of Education. 2008. *Ethics and Religious Culture Program,* Secondary School Cycle One and Two.

Milot, Micheline. 2007. "La dimension religieuse dans l'éducation interculturelle." In *Diversité religieuse et éducation interculturelle / Religious Diversity and Intercultural Education,* 23–36. Stradbourg: Éditions du Conseil de l'Europe.

Racine, Jacques. 2008. "Vers la laïcité scolaire." In *L'accommodement raisonnable et la diversité religieuse à l'école publique. Normes et pratiques,* ed. M. Mc Andrew, M. Milot, J.-S. Imbeaut and P. Eid, 15–26. Montréal: Fides.

Taylor, Charles. 2011. "What Does Secularism Mean?" In idem, *Dilemmas and Connections: Selected Essays.* Cambridge, MA: Belknap Press of Harvard University Press.

Weinfeld, Morton. 2001. *Like Everyone Else, but Different: The Paradoxical Success of Canadian Jews.* Toronto: McClelland & Stewart.

LIST OF TEXTBOOKS STUDIES

Junior High School

Bélanger, D., A. Carrière, P. Després, C. Mainville and A.-C. Vachon. 2008. *Être en société*, manuels A et B, CEC.

Charbonneau, N.-A. 2010. *Passeport pour la vie*. Les éditions de la Pensée.

Grondin, J., S. Lefebvre and D., Weinstock. 2009. *Tête-à-tête*. Éditions Grand Duc.

L'Hérault, B., and C. Sirois. 2011. *Réflexions*, manuels A et B, Chenelière éducation.

Senior High School

Caron, G., and P. Garber (with M-F. Beaulieu). 2009. *Tête-à-tête, 2ᵉ-3ᵉ année du 2ᵉ cycle*. Éditions Grand Duc.

Dansereau, J., (Dir.), with S. Deraspe, P. Després, I. Fournier-Courcy and S. Tardif. 2011. *Tisser des liens, 2ᵉ-3ᵉ année du 2ᵉ cycle*, CEC.

Activity Book

Dubreuil M., and S. Farley (with Jézéquel). 2008. *Vivre ensemble 4 et 5*. Erpi.

Tessier, J., with M. Dubreuil, S. Farley (and M. Gaudreault for 1), *Vivre ensemble 1 et 2*, Erpi, 2008.

Endnotes

1. As Raymon Lemieux shows, most parents kept choosing the religion option even though they could have chosen the "moral" one, explaining that since they did not live religiously, at least their children would learn the "basics" at school (Lemieux 1991: 13–86).

2. The Loyola High School has requested to be permitted to continue teaching the Catholic religion, as it always has, with recognition for other religions.

3. Cherblanc and Rondeau (2010) offer a wide-ranging discussion of this question.

4. Only one edition translated its textbooks into English. We refer to them according to their original French titles, which we will translate to English in the complete list in the references.

5. The Quebec Ministry of Education put in place a continuing education programme throughout networks of teachers in each school board. Some teachers followed the training with specialists and then became resource persons for their colleagues.

6. Two papers are analysing these textbooks, one on the treatment of the Holocaust (Hirsch and Mc Andrew, forthcoming 2014), and the other on the treatment of the Jewish community's history in Quebec (Hirsch and Mc Andrew, 2013).

5. RESEARCHING MATERIALS USED TO TEACH ABOUT WORLD RELIGIONS IN SCHOOLS IN ENGLAND

Barbara Wintersgill*

1. OVERVIEW

This chapter is a report on research into materials used in religious education teaching conducted by the Warwick Religions and Education Research Unit (WRERU) throughout the academic year 2008–2009. The research considered a wide variety of resources but this chapter considers only the findings that relate to textbooks. In relation to books specifically, the research identified both value and concern with respect to accuracy in detail; authenticity, coherence and balance in representations of religions; recognition of the internal diversity in religions and of their numinous and transformative power; the complexity of religions and the relationships between them. Several publications caused concern in these areas.

2. INTRODUCTION

2.1. *The context of the research*
Schools in England[1] are free to choose the resources they wish to use to support teaching and learning in the classroom. For the religious education teacher this involves selecting from a wide array of books, computer software, online and audiovisual materials. The Office for Standards in Education (Ofsted), the government's schools inspection service in England, has frequently been criti-

* Barbara Wintersgill has a BA and MA in theology from the University of Exeter and a PhD from Warwick University. Her varied career includes: teaching RE in London, Advisory Teacher for RE, Chief Examiner RS, Officer for RE at the National Curriculum Council (NCC) and the School Curriculum and Qualifications Authority (SCAA), Her Majesty's Inspector (HMI) and National Adviser for Religious Education, working at the Office for Standards in Education (Ofsted), and author of many NCC, SCAA and Ofsted publications as well as academic articles. Dr Wintersgill is now an independent researcher and education consultant.

cal of the quality of some RE text books and the way in which teachers use them.

In 2007 the Department for Children, Schools and Families (forthwith to be referred to as the Department)[2] commissioned research into the teaching materials used to teach about world religions in English schools. The research was carried out by the Warwick Religions and Education Research Unit (WRERU) at Warwick University following research throughout the academic year 2008–2009. The culminating report was published in 2010.[3]

2.2. Previous research

Prior to the Warwick research there had been some international research on religious education textbooks, particularly on the representation of Islam in European textbooks.[4,5] Although no research had surveyed the use of books and materials on world religions across England or the UK, some UK projects have linked theory, textbooks, and occasionally empirical research. These include the Chichester Project, on Christianity,[6] the Westhill Project,[7] the Religion in the Service of the Child Project,[8] the Warwick RE Project[9] and the Stapleford Project.[10]

2.3. Key research questions

The Department identified five key research questions on which they wished the project to focus. These questions were predominantly factual rather than evaluative. For example, the department wanted to know what materials were available for teaching about and learning from world religions; what materials schools actually used and *how* they were used to promote community cohesion.

The third and fifth questions are of particular interest here because they provide the rationale for the investigation into the quality of textbooks. These questions asked:

- What is the *content/nature* of materials used by schools and how does this relate to current school regulations (in particular the duty on maintained schools to promote community cohesion and the independent school standard to assist their pupils to acquire an appreciation of and respect for their own and other cultures in a way that promotes tolerance and harmony between different cultural traditions)? [11]
- What are *the key factors for schools to consider* when determining which materials should be used to teach world religions?

The report stopped short of recommending or advising against the use of specific materials, as to do so was not regarded as the role of university or government. Instead, the purpose of the report was to identify key issues that would be of value to stakeholders, notably publishers, authors and teachers in writing or making choices.

2.4. Methodology
The research was carried in three inter-related strands:

(i)   a three phase *review of materials*, which drew on an existing audit of text-books.[12] In addition specially appointed academic experts, profession-al RE specialists and faith group consultants conducted a review of a sample of text books. Later in the process, following the visits to schools and the quantitative survey of materials used by teachers, the experts and consultants identified issues raised and made recommendations. During this phase 101 books were reviewed.

(ii)   *qualitative case studies* for which researchers visited ten primary and ten secondary schools[13] to interview teachers and pupils, observe lessons and review RE departmental policy documents.

(iii)   a *quantitative survey of materials* used in a nationwide random sample of 2,723 schools of all types. The response rate was low (23%).

This chapter is particularly concerned with strands (i) and (ii). It should be noted that although this chapter refers to a review of "text books," a wide range of other materials was also reviewed.

3. THE DIVERSE NATURE OF RELIGIOUS EDUCATION IN ENGLAND—A CHALLENGE TO PUBLISHERS

The Warwick report helpfully reflects on the difficulties faced by textbook authors and the implications of their work for a multi-cultural society such as that in the UK. The portrayals of religions in textbooks have the potential to influence atti-tudes between religious and cultural communities and have the potential to give offence.

Publishers for the RE market in England face several challenges, which explain in part the criticisms that have been levelled at their work by Ofsted and others.

3.1. Agreed syllabuses
In 1988 the Education Reform Act[14] created the national curriculum in England. One purpose of the national curriculum was to create consistency in expecta-tions of pupils' learning and in what was taught across the country. Inevitably this reduced the previous autonomy of schools. RE was not one of the ten subjects included in the national curriculum. Instead the act reaffirmed its historic place as a locally determined subject. Religious education is taught in state schools fol-lowing a locally *agreed syllabus*, which has been agreed by an *agreed syllabus con-ference* consisting of representatives of faith communities, local councillors and teachers. Consequently there are 152 agreed syllabuses in England, compared with only one curriculum for subjects such as history and geography.

In the years following 1990, the diversity in what these syllabuses expect-ed schools to teach was matched by their expectations of the standards pupils were expected to attain. From a publisher's point of view this situation created problems that applied to no other subject. A publisher could produce a textbook on Tudor England for upper primary pupils in the confidence that most schools would teach this topic. The only certainty for publishers with regard to religious education was that all students aged from 5-14 would study Christianity in some form. There was no such certainty as to whether Hinduism, for example, would be taught to lower secondary students, since the allocation of specific religions to age groups was a matter for agreed syllabus conferences.

In an attempt to rationalize religious education provision across the country, in 2004 the Department commissioned the Qualifications and Assessment Authority (QCA) to produce a Non-Statutory National Framework for Religious Education (to be known as the Framework).[15] The Framework was not a statutory curriculum but was designed as guidance to those writing agreed syllabuses in the hope that its use would result in greater commonality in what was taught and in the standards expected of students. The Framework has resulted in greater uniformity between local syllabuses but major differences still persist. For example, agreed syllabuses still require schools to teach about different religions or different themes. To compound the issue, schools with a religious character are able to determine their own RE curriculum rather than follow an agreed syllabus.

Publishers face similar problems when producing textbooks for 14-18 year old students. Although technically RE is taught to all age groups according to the agreed syllabus, in reality most teaching to upper secondary students follows an examination syllabus, as many agreed syllabuses direct. Here again there is no consistency. Schools may choose to teach from the syllabuses offered by five different examination boards, each syllabus offering several options.

For publishers, producing cost-effective books to meet all of these requirements creates an insurmountable challenge. Ofsted concludes that in the absence of a statutory national syllabus:

> publishers find it difficult to decide how to focus their publications and other resources, so much of the published material is too general. If the Framework were to become a nationally agreed syllabus, it would provide a secure basis from which publishers could develop materials. The publication of the Framework has helped, but it has not given them the confidence to produce innovative new materials.[16]

3.2. Pedagogies of religious education

The Warwick research concluded that the varying nature of textbooks and the choices made by teachers in selecting them can only be properly understood in the context of the contrasting pedagogies of religious education in England. These pedagogies are occasionally embedded in agreed syllabuses but more particularly are discussed during the influential period of initial teacher training. Teachers may decide to adopt one approach over another or more likely to combine elements of two or more. To give a simple example, some teachers focus is on teaching religions (world religions approach) while others plan their curriculum around key theological, philosophical and ethical questions (philosophy and ethics approach). It is rarely that simple; for example, the same RE department may take a world religions approach with lower secondary students and a philosophy and ethics approach with upper secondary. Different resources are required for each of these approaches.

3.3. Attainment targets for religious education

This chapter will make frequent reference to attainment targets. Attainment targets set out the general defined level of ability that a student is expected to achieve in every subject at each key stage[17] in the National Curriculum. They are set out in eight levels, which indicate the standards that students are expected to achieve at different ages and stages of education; for example, lower primary pupils are generally expected to work at levels 1 and 2. Attainment targets had been introduced in the context of the national curriculum and for national curriculum subjects were ratified by parliament. Attainment targets for religious education were developed by subject experts and have never been statutory, although now they are included in most agreed syllabuses. Teachers should be able to rely on textbooks for specific key stages to be appropriate for the levels that those pupils should be achieving.

The Framework confirmed the two attainment targets for RE that were already in use in some schools and added an eight-level scale. The attainment targets are "learning about religion" and "learning from religion." Learning about religion refers to how pupils develop their knowledge, skills and understanding with reference to beliefs, teachings and sources; practices and ways of life; and forms of religious expression. Learning from religion refers to how pupils, in the light of their learning about religion, express their responses and insights with regard to questions and issues about identity and belonging; meaning, purpose and truth; and values and commitments.

4. THE REPRESENTATION OF RELIGIONS IN TEXT BOOKS

The review of materials, which constituted the first strand of the research, was conducted by two separate groups of reviewers. The first group comprised professional RE experts and the second, faith group consultants. This dual approach to the analysis of materials reflects the creative debate in England over who has ownership of RE—educationalists or the religions themselves. Each group had distinctive perspective and concerns which were reflected in the separate templates designed for them.

4.1. Professional perspectives

The review template used by the professional RE experts was underpinned by five interrelated closed and focused questions, allowing for open comments.

These questions directed the RE experts to consider the ways in which text-books responded to specifically educational issues. The Warwick report summarized their findings following these five questions and in relation to the three key stages and the sixth form.[18] The questions relate specifically to priorities in education in England but are almost certainly of wider significance. The following analysis follows the key themes in each question.

4.1.1. *The extent to which textbooks reflect or are shaped by current requirements and initiatives.* The most prominent national "initiatives" at the time of the research were agreed syllabuses, the Framework, schemes of work published by the Qualifications and Curriculum Authority, and public examination requirements. The RE professional reviewers found that books for younger children generally took little notice of these initiatives and focused on content, giving factual information about religions. Reviewers also noted the practice of publishing a series of books, one on each of the six religions regarded as "principal," but under the same headings (e.g., in one series each book was structured under the headings "principal teachings, scriptures, leaders, events, festivals, places of worship, community life, belief and practice across the world"). Books for upper secondary students concentrated on examination requirements, particularly those related to "learning about religion." The more interesting publications were directed at Key Stage 3 (lower secondary), where books took note of the Framework. In particular a balance was achieved between the two attainment targets. At Key Stages 1, 2 and 4 textbooks provided information but relating it to attainment target 2 was the teacher's role. None of this should cause surprise. The differing nature of books for different ages reflects teachers' priorities. In primary schools most teachers are not RE specialists and many are without basic knowledge of the religions they teach. They also favour teaching and learning strategies that involve active involvement from the children; such as researching a religion. Therefore factual books are in demand. At Key Stage 4 teachers' priority is examination success. Only at Key Stage 3 therefore do many teachers have the subject expertise and freedom to require more of their resources than factual information.

4.1.2. *The extent to which textbooks balance understanding and appreciation of religion(s) with a concern for pupils' personal development?* Like other school subjects, RE contributes to the rounded development of the pupil. The reviewers considered the contribution the books made/might make in five areas: pupils' personal and moral development; community cohesion; social and cultural awareness; global understanding; and spiritual development. Again, books for Key Stage 3 were most likely to contribute to these areas by examining a wide range of ethical and moral issues and philosophical approaches to such issues. Books for this age group also consider the moral frameworks offered by religions and the ideals they represent; the social and cultural aspects of religions; and the relation of faith to lifestyle and the contribution of faith to community life. These issues lend themselves well to attainment target 2, explaining in part why the balance between the two attainment targets was particularly strong at Key Stage 3.

4.1.3. *Approaches to learning.* The reviewers found that books for primary children which provided information about religions generally promoted empathy and appreciation of religion. These books particularly supported approaches to learning based on acquiring information and developing conceptual understanding but also reflected common primary school practice by promoting independent learning, developing skills and answering questions. In contrast only one of the 37 lower secondary books reviewed was simply an information book. Of the remainder most textbooks asked questions of pupils, including questions on ultimate issues; they raised questions of value and meaning, developed skills and concepts and promoted empathy and appreciations of religions. However, the reviewers found that tasks for pupils in Key Stage 3 books were often undemanding and unimaginative and that these books were not well suited to supporting independent learning. Rather they tended to be of the "textbook" type; packaged schemes that could be used in the classroom and would be particularly welcomed by non-specialist teachers. This was disappointing given the author's paper some years earlier expressing concern at the low level of tasks set for this age group.[19]

4.1.4. *Inclusivity.* The RE professional reviewers were asked to consider whether textbooks were suitable for use by their target age group. Most of the books claiming to be for primary school children were judged by the reviewers as unsuitable for this age group because of the complexity of language and conceptual understanding required, although they could be used by teachers in developing their subject knowledge. Some books were commended for their helpful glossaries, notes for teachers and pointers to additional material in books or websites. The main criticisms were of the size of fonts, complexity of text, and the treatment of controversial issues in and between religions. Books for 14–16 year olds were generally criticized for their extensive comprehension exercises and limited opportunities for the application of knowledge and understanding.[20]

4.1.5. *Community cohesion.* Periodically the Department devises new initiatives to which schools are expected to respond and which Ofsted inspects. One such initiative was *Community Cohesion.* This was defined as:

> Working towards a society in which there is a common vision and sense of belonging by all communities; a society in which the diversity of people's backgrounds and circumstances is appreciated and valued; a society in which similar life opportunities are available to all; and a society in which strong and positive relationships exist and continue to be developed in the workplace, in schools and the wider community.[21]

The concept of community cohesion was not new but the official requirement for schools to promote it became of particular interest to all concerned with RE because of the major contribution the subject could make. Most of the books reviewed pre-dated the requirement on schools to promote community cohesion. Nevertheless the reviewers commented on some topics relevant to community cohesion, notably the treatment of controversial issues. The reviewers found that Key Stage 3 books were most likely to deepen students' understanding of other cultures by explaining how faith relates to lifestyle, and how faiths contribute to community life. Topics selected for study in just over half of the books reviewed were considered relevant to community cohesion.

5. FAITH CONSULTANTS' AND ACADEMIC EXPERTS' PERSPECTIVES

A strength of the Warwick research was the evaluation of textbooks by two groups of experts; those with expertise in religious education and those with expertise in a specific religion, either from a professional or personal perspective and sometimes both. This dual approach produced a rounded evaluation which considered each book from a range of perspectives that may not have been available from a single reviewer. The 13 reviewers in group of faith experts evaluated two kinds of books, some dealing with their religion and others dealing with their religion in the context of a thematic publication that covered as many as six religions alongside each other.

5.1. The faith consultants' template
The review templates used by the faith consultants and academic experts drew on their specific knowledge and experience. The main purpose of their review was to identify those elements in commonly-used textbooks that help or hinder the development of pupils' understanding of and positive attitudes towards the six religions being considered. Each reviewer answered the following questions for their own religion or the religion that is the subject of their expertise.

(i)   How accurate are the materials regarding historical information, statistics and central/doctrinal teachings? Are there significant omissions?

(ii) To what extent do the materials represent the inner diversity, and the coherence, of the religion?

(iii) What sources of knowledge about the religion are used in the materials and is there clarity about the status of these?

(iv) How appropriate and helpful are the illustrations and activities for studying the religion?

(v)   What messages, positive or negative, do the materials convey about the religion and people of that religion?

(vi) In what ways do the materials contribute to community cohesion? Are any aspects of the materials unhelpful in this respect?

The analysis of the faith experts' reviews involved grounded analysis to identify key categories for each reviewer and then comparison of the categories across the reviewers to find headings for a combined analysis. The resulting report is presented under headings that reflect the reviewers' categories. Inevitably the reviewers from six different faiths had different priorities and interests and their findings are summarized in two sections. The first deals with common themes and concerns across the 13 reviewers and the second with issues specific to each religion.

5.2. Common themes and concerns

5.2.1. *Accuracy.* Several books were praised for their accuracy, notably those on Islam and in cases where publishers had consulted with experts and adherents. However, overall the largest category of complaints from faith experts concerned the widespread errors noted in textbooks. They identified factual inaccuracies, some causing offence, in books on all six religions concerning dates, figures, spellings and translations. They noted confusion in explanations of the theological and philosophical tenets of the religion and over the internal divisions and interrelationships of religious traditions. Omissions were as damaging as errors in their ability to fuel misconceptions; for example, a textbook on Judaism omitted reference to any moral dimension of the faith leaving students with the impression that Judaism was all about God and worship. The reviewers recognized the need to simplify explanations, especially for younger children, but found that some simplifications were inaccurate and misleading, for example describing Shabbat as "a day off." One trend that affected accuracy was a tendency in some texts to present one religion through the "lens" of another tradition. There was a particular tendency for textbooks to "view Judaism through the perspective of the Christian history of salvation and the significance of the Old Testament to that."[22] Concepts in one religion were sometimes interpreted through the lens of another, for example in one book on Buddhism, the concept of karma was treated as "synonymous with Hindu usage."[23] Equally misleading were some attempts to help pupils understand a religion by comparing it to another, usually Christianity; for example, suggesting that Sikh leaders were similar to Christian priests. Most worryingly, the source of many of these problems was seen to be the lack of expertise on the part of some authors and their failure to keep up-to-date with scholarship or practice. Reviewers suggested that these problems could be overcome by consultation with authoritative figures from the faith community concerned, and they praised textbooks whose authors had consulted in this way.

5.2.2. *Integrity and balance.* Reviewers expected to find rounded presentations of religions, without undue emphasis on some aspects to the detriment of others. They praised textbooks that gave balanced presentations of, for example, belief, practice, moral values, identity, aspects of culture and relevance to the contemporary world. Three reasons were identified for the skewing of the representation of religions in some textbooks. School syllabus and examination requirements might dictate a particular structure, especially when thematic approaches were adopted.

5.2.3. *Diversity.* "The reviewers appreciated books that represented the diversity of their tradition both in the variations of its denominations, schools or movements, and in the variations of individual practice and interpretations."[24] They found these qualities particularly in some books about Christianity, Judaism and Buddhism. They also praised books that reflected the cultural diversity, for example those that portrayed Islam as an eastern, western and African religion, or Christianity as a world religion rather than English. In other books this diversity was found to be lacking. For example, the presentation of Islam in one book was found to be "too exotic" (p. 105) while another was criticized for its over-concentration on Buddhism as a "white, British" religion. The representation of the diverse nature of religions is a particularly important feature of books for 11–14 year olds who are generally expected to reach Level 5. This requires them to "understand that similarities and differences illustrate distinctive beliefs within and between religions and suggest possible reasons for this."[25] It is therefore important that textbooks do not give the impression that *all* Christians or *all* Hindus, for example, share identical beliefs and values, worship in the same way or uphold the same traditions. It is equally important that textbooks do not present a religion from the perspective of one group within it. Several textbooks were found wanting in this respect.

5.2.4. *Depth versus superficiality.* Some of the most positive comments in the reviews overall were for the challenge to young people's thinking in several books, with particular praise for some books on Buddhism and Judaism. But reviewers of books on Christianity and Islam found a lack of challenge in books that avoided controversial issues in those that gave students challenging questions without enough detailed information for them to give high quality answers. For example, one textbook asked students "why doesn't God heal all who go to Lourdes?" without providing information on Christian perspectives on natural evil or free will. "What these comments from the reviewers and several others in the same vein show is that textbooks should not just require students to think as part of their learning, but should also inform and challenge that thinking. There is a direct link between these concerns and the question of the depth of the content of the resources."[26] Reviewers were interested in the extent to which textbooks conveyed what religions are and what being a follower and member of a religion entails and they praised books that took readers beyond external manifestations of religions to include something of religions' ongoing power for effecting change in people's lives and society. But other books omitted the personal, relational, numinous, inspirational, emotional or spiritual aspects of religious life and did not convey, for example, how it might *feel* to be a pilgrim or to experience a holy place or how belonging to a faith might change a person. This was seen as a particular issue for Sikhism where there were several comments along the lines that "connections were not made between outward elements of the faith—turban, kirpan, khanda—and the underlying values and principles associated with them that "we must 'rule' our own minds and the world around us with dignity, spiritual wisdom and spiritual qualities."[27]

5.2.5. *Selection of texts and examples.* Reviewers praised those textbooks that included a variety of texts from different periods and with different degrees of authority; for example, biblical, rabbinic, medieval and modern Jewish texts, and in books on Islam, texts from the Qur'an, hadith, Islamic stories and contemporary voices. Other books were criticized for selecting texts to match an educational agenda rather than their importance to the tradition. Reviewers of books on Judaism and Islam were particularly critical of the authors' failure to include more contemporary texts that would show the development of "religious thought." A long-standing feature of British textbooks has been the use of "exemplars" of the faith as illustrations of faith in action in the contemporary world. While the lives of the great might be more accessible to students than the theological and moral theories illustrated through their works, reviewers expressed a number of concerns. In particular a reviewer of Christian textbooks criticized the over-use of Mother Teresa and Martin Luther King, who have been the standard "representatives" of Christianity for many decades. It was not always clear why certain people had been chosen and both Muslim and Sikh reviewers were critical of the selection of controversial figures associated with conflict and violence.

5.2.6. *Contemporary relevance.* Reviewers wanted their religions to be portrayed as contemporary, as part of British society while also giving a realistic portrayal of their international dimensions. Books were welcomed that made "Buddhism seem normal...rather than strange and exotic," showed that "Hinduism is part of British society," or made "Islam and Muslims accessible as citizens of western and global societies." It was seen as important that students should be able to relate to people of the faith as people like themselves. Many resources for older students relate religions to ethical and global issues relevant to today, such as war and peace, capital punishment and human rights. While generally welcoming this approach, some reviewers were critical of over-generalizations (e.g., Christians believe that...) and a confusion between what is taught by authoritative voices and statements of personal opinion. Some textbooks were praised for their sensitive treatment of recent or live issues such as the Balkans wars, the Israel/Palestinian conflict, and Islamaphobia. Others were found to play down the role of religion in situations of conflict in order to promote the right attitudes for community cohesion.

5.2.7. *Other religions and traditions.* In their analysis of the texts, the faith consultants and academic experts were sensitive to the viewpoints of people from religious traditions other than their own focus, and were thus aware of elements in the materials specific to their religion that might be troubling or offensive to those of other traditions. The reviewers also praised a story book for primary children which presented a "model of friendship and sharing between faiths". Other books were written in a way that could cause offence. Reviewers were particularly concerned about the implied hierarchy of religions with Christianity as the "default religion" to which others were compared (see below). Occasionally the activities suggested for students were seen as insensitive to some traditions. In particular reviewers were concerned that some students would not feel comfortable drawing pictures of, or dressing up as, Hindu deities, making a replica of a Hindu shrine and acting out a puja ceremony. A few books were found to be confessional and evangelizing in their approach, such as a book which compared Buddhism as a "peaceful religion" with the conflicts between Catholics and Protestants in Northern Ireland and Sunnis and Shiites in Iraq.

6. RELIGION–SPECIFIC ISSUES

The previous section identified general issues with the representation of religions in textbooks raised by the Warwick report. The report also identifies specific issues which are of more concern to certain religions than they are to the others.

6.1. Concerns about the representation of Islam
Muslim reviewers were inevitably concerned with the public image of Islam. Generally they responded positively to the textbooks reviewed. They felt that these books presented a positive picture of Islam that occupied a place in British society and the wider world. But the reviewers found that some books on Islam tended to be simplistic and they would have liked students to have been given the opportunity to engage with Islam at a deeper level.

6.2. Concerns about the representation of Hinduism
Reviewers found a large number of inaccuracies in textbooks on Hinduism. Books for younger children were often colourful and attractive but authors were sometimes careless over details and set out confused explanations of Hindu beliefs and teachings. There were few texts for secondary pupils as such as existed, often in thematic books, were rather meagre. Few resources dealt adequately with the complex but fundamental issue of diversity in Hinduism.

6.3. Concerns about the representation of Sikhism
The key complaint about textbooks on Sikhism was that they tended to be superficial, focusing on descriptions of the external observable features of the religion rather than on their deeper significance or the religion's power to transform the lives of the individual or its contribution to wider society.

6.4. Concerns about the representation of Buddhism
Reviewers were particularly concerned about representations of the Buddhist community; especially those that made the tradition appear exotic and foreign or those that did not convey an appropriate balance between white British and migrant Buddhist communities, or the distinctive perspectives and experiences of each group.

6.5. Concerns about the representation of Judaism
Reviewers found textbooks on Judaism to be particularly problematic and found inadequacies in thematic texts and those dealing with Judaism alone. A key criticism was the presentation of Judaism as "the Old Testament religion that preceded Christianity," ignoring the development of Jewish thought over the last 2000 years and often failing to present Judaism as a contemporary religion in its own right. For example, in one thematic book "holy people" were identified as Christian monks/nuns, Hindu sadhus, Muslim imams and Jewish prophets. Another issue was the over-concentration on the Holocaust and anti-Semitism rather than a presentation of Judaism as a living religion "making the suffering of the Jewish people the focus rather than more positive aspects of Jewish life".

6.6. Concerns about the representation of Christianity
Reviewers raised more concerns about representations of Christianity than any other religion. Some textbooks appeared to assume that their student readership was Christian. As noted above, too often Christianity was presented as the default religion and other religions were often presented through a Christian lens or in comparison with Christianity rather than in their own terms. This was particularly the case with a thematic series, which began each chapter (on holy books, worship, etc.) with the Christian focus, then the Jewish and then the other four, suggesting a hierarchy of religions beginning with Christianity and Judaism. Constant reference to non-Christian faiths as "a religion other than Christianity," further confirmed the impression that Christianity was the default or baseline religions. Problems were also identified in the attempts of some authors to present Christianity in a way that would not give offence to others. This sometime led to a "sanitised, incomplete presentation of Christianity in some texts that was in turn unfair to that tradition." Hence central tenets of Christianity such as belief in Jesus as God incarnate, the salvation brought about through his death and resurrection, were sometimes avoided because they might give offence to others. Instead of engaging with the real core of the Christian faith, these books represented Christianity simply as an ethical system based on the life and teachings of Jesus, whose message was "one of compassion and encouraging care for others." Another issue, also arising from a concern not to cause offence, was the sanitization of Christianity in comparison to other religions by the removal of truth claims. This inconsistency was observed particularly in the frequent phrase "Christians believe that..." Reviewers found that similar phrases were found less in connection with other religions. For example, "Christians believe that" the Bible is the Word of God, but the Qur'an "is the word of Allah." Similarly the

Arabic colophon frequently appears after the name of Muhammad out of respect to Islam, while Jesus is rarely referred to as "Jesus Christ."

7. FACTORS CONTRIBUTING TO THE REPRESENTATION OF RELIGIONS IN TEXTBOOKS

The factors contributing to the nature of RE text books are complex and not always obvious. Three have been identified in particular.

7.1. Market forces expressed through the preferences of teachers
Publishers in the UK regularly send representatives into schools to discover teachers' priorities when buying textbooks. These priorities are reflected in the Warwick report and six broad themes emerged, one of which, examination requirements, will be considered separately.

Some teachers wanted resources that included challenging tasks and activities designed to make pupils think and to develop their thinking skills. Others looked for resources that could be used to support different learning styles or that encouraged creativity. They needed books that were written for different reading ages. To meet these diverse needs many teachers produced their own resources rather than purchase textbooks. A key factor that created a need for textbooks was the expertise of staff. Many pupils in secondary schools and most in primary schools are taught RE by teachers with no formal qualifications or training in the subject. Heads of department in the case study schools reported that non-specialist teachers felt safer with a textbook, even though pupils generally do not like them. "When confronted by the management of a team of non-specialists, many heads of department turn to a textbook to provide a basic level of content and structure."[28]

7.2. Syllabus and examination requirements
Public examinations for 16 year olds present publishers with a significant market. Several reviewers noted the close relationship between examination boards and publishers, resulting in books for Key Stage 4 students (aged 14–16) that gave good support to students in preparing for the exam but, in their representation of religions, mirrored the requirements of examination syllabuses rather than the internal logic of the religion, thus influencing the emphasis and balance. One example referred to the requirement in many examination syllabuses (and agreed syllabuses) that students should be able to give a balanced argument for and against the existence of God. A book on Christianity was found to refer to these arguments but not to explain "the distinctive Christian understanding of the nature of God, affected by incarnation and Trinity."

Concern was expressed particularly for the "fashionable" Key Stage 4 courses that focused on religious responses to social and moral issues. One textbook was found to concentrate too much on the social issues and too little on the religious perspectives. Religions were seen as "subservient" to other agenda, such as moral issues, and were used as "information fodder for debate."

The power and influence of examination requirements were felt by teachers in their selection of textbooks and some felt constrained to purchase sets of the "official book" written by the chief examiner, in spite of questioning its quality: *"He's the chief examiner. He writes the syllabus and writes the questions, and edits the textbooks. It is therefore sensible to buy it and use it... However, it doesn't allow for creativity—it's functional but not inspiring..."*[29]

The requirements of agreed syllabuses were also found to influence the representations of religions, especially where they promoted a thematic curriculum. Reviewers found that finding parallels across the six religions in relation to themes such as "religious leaders" and "places of worship" could lead to a too hierarchical and institutionalized understanding of religion. The comparison between Jesus, Muhammad and Abraham/Moses as "religious leaders" or "founders" could foster misunderstanding because the understandings of these people in their religious traditions were quite different. A reviewer of the Hinduism books was concerned at the primarily graphic presentation of the sacred syllable Om whereas in the tradition it was primarily a sound. 'This seems to be for the sake of the modern practice of giving every religion a logo in order to fit into the pattern dictated by RE.'"

7.3. The Non-Statutory National Framework for Religious Education
The National Framework (QCA 2004), commissioned by the DCFS (now the DfE), received the approval of all the professional associations and faith communities.[30] Its purpose is to provide guidance to those writing agreed syllabuses by clarifying standards in religious education and promoting high quality teaching and learning. The National Framework's purpose of achieving greater consistency in RE across the country has largely been fulfilled and most agreed syllabuses now incorporate elements of the framework. It was hoped that the widespread adoption of the National Framework would facilitate publishers' task of resourcing RE.

Two aspects of the National Framework that have influenced textbooks have been the focus on six religions and the inclusion of two attainment targets; "learning about religion" and "learning from religion." As we have seen, the Warwick review focuses on the six religions which are the subject of most RE publications. The influence of the attainment targets has been mixed. Textbooks were found to give more attention to "learning about religion," although a minority addressed "learning from" mainly through activities, which invited students to "reflect, respond, or discuss" or to "question or ponder."

8. CONCLUSIONS

In spite of the numerous concerns raised by the Warwick report, it is important to note that overall the team of reviewers praised many of the qualities in the textbooks they viewed, for example their approach, tone and quality of production. Many books, they found, were designed to broaden students' knowledge of religions, promote positive attitudes towards religions, and to support community cohesion by emphasizing the possibilities for peaceful existence between religions. In several cases where reviewers were critical of details in a book they nevertheless praised its overall value.

8.1. Key problems in English RE textbooks
However, the extent and seriousness of the criticisms of many books is worrying, to the extent that the report claims that, "the lack of attention to detail and accuracy...was in danger of undermining the credibility of religious education as an academic subject."[31] In particular, reviewers identified the following concerns:

- The content of books was often insufficient in quantity or depth to enable students to complete the activities set and set a poor example of scholarship for students to emulate.
- External influences, particularly syllabus and examination requirements and national agenda rather than the internal logic of religions, influenced the representation of religions. These factors were responsible for changing the emphasis of religions or underplaying important aspects.
- Students' understanding of world religions would be impaired by the inaccuracies, distortions and omissions in some textbooks.
- Few books conveyed any real sense of the deeper significance of religions and their power as motivating forces in the lives of adherents and the wider society in which they are present. "The community cohesion agenda...is predicated on the assumption that such understanding is a condition for positive and fruitful relations between people with different religions and worldviews in the future."

8.2. Useful qualities in religious education materials
In phase 3 of the Warwick project the co-ordinators of the review group used the analysis and distinctive perspectives of the faith consultants, academic and professional experts, to identify and discuss issues that emerged from the review of the materials and to make recommendations. From the reviewers' comments, it is possible to identify a number of qualities that they valued in religious education materials and on this basis to construct a list of recommendations for publishers of RE textbooks.

Textbooks should be:

- accurate—they do not need to include every detail but to be accurate in every detail that is included
- coherent—content should be selected according to internal logic of the religion rather than on other principles which could give a distorted and unbalanced picture

- comprehensive—a variety of aspects of religions should be presented including practice and belief, moral values, identity and aspects of culture
- authentic—the religion is to be understood in own terms, through its own voices, (including the voices of its authoritative texts) either directly or through consultation and the knowledge of experts
- internally diverse—the portrayal should not be dominated by one viewpoint unless that viewpoint is made explicit and becomes part of the learning
- numinous and transformative—the power of religion in people's lives and in society should be recognized and also the transcendent power that religious people discern in their narratives and in the cosmos
- living—the religion should be portrayed as active, relevant and contemporary with contributions to make to present society
- challenging—the complexities of religious traditions and religious lives should not be downplayed or used as an excuse to ignore them but rather should become the content of stimulating and challenging learning
- valued—well produced, attractive materials demonstrate respect for the religion in their quality and attention to detail
- fairly represented—care should be taken to do justice to the different religious traditions in religious education teaching and give due time and attention to each
- in relationship—emphasis should be given to the relationship between religions and between people of different religions and non-religious.

BIBLIOGRAPHY

Cooling, T. "The Stapleford Project: Theology as the Basis for Religious Education." In *Pedagogies of Religious Education: Case Studies in the Research and Development of Good Pedogogic Practice in RE*, ed. M. H. Grimmitt, 153–69. Great Wakering: McCrimmons, 2000.

DCSF. *Guidance on the Duty to Promote Community Cohesion*. London: Department of Children Schools and Families, 2007.

Falaturi, A. *Islam in Religious Education Textbooks in Europe*. Köln: The Islamic Scientific Academy, 1988. Trans. H. Schultze, 1990.

Falaturi, A., and U. Tworuschka. *CSIS Papers, Europe, no. 8: A Guide to the Presentation of Islam in School Textbooks*. Cologne: Centre for the Study of Islam and Christian-Muslim Relations for The Islamic Scientific Academy, 1992.

Gates, B. "Editorial." *British Journal of Religious Education* 27(2), 2005, 99–102.

Hayward, M. "Teaching Christianity: Process and Purpose." In *Teaching Christianity: A World Religions Approach*, ed. C. Erricker. Cambridge: Lutterworth Press, 1987; 2nd edn, 1995.

Hayward, M., and P. Hopkins. *Resources for Teaching about World Religions in Schools in England: An Audit*. London: DCSF, 2010.

Hull, J. M. "Religion in the Service of the Child Project: The Gift Approach to Religious Education." In *Pedagogies of Religious Education: Case Studies in the Research and Development of Good Pedogogic Practice in RE*, ed. M. H. Grimmitt, 112–29. Great Wakering: McCrimmons, 2000.

Jackson, R. "The Warwick Religious Education Project: The Interpretive Approach to Religious Education." In *Pedagogies of Religious Education: Case Studies in the Research and Development of Good Pedogogic Practice in RE*, ed. M. H. Grimmitt, 130–52. Great Wakering: McCrimmons, 2000.

Jackson, R., J. Ipgrave, M. Hayward, P. Hopkins, N. Fancourt, M. Robbins, L. Francis and U. McKenna. *Materials Used to Teach about World Religions in Schools in England: Appendices*. London: DCSF, 2010.

Office for Standards in Education. *Making Sense of Religion*. London: Ofsted, 2007.

Qualifications & Curriculum Authority (QCA). *Religious Education: The Non-Statutory National Framework*. London: Qualifications & Curriculum Authority. 2004. Available online: http://www.qca.org.uk/6163.html

Rudge, J. "The Westhill Project: Religious Education as Maturing Pupils' Patterns of Belief and Behaviour." In *Pedagogies of Religious Education: Case Studies in the Research and Development of Good Pedagogic Practice in RE*, ed. M. H. Grimmitt, 88–111. Great Wakering: McCrimmons, 2000.

UK Parliament Education Reform Act 1988. London, Her Majesty's Stationery Office.

Wintersgill, B. "Task Setting in Religious Education at Key Stage 3: A Comparison with History." *Resource* 22(3), 2000, 9–17.

Endnotes

1. The countries of the United Kingdom each have individual education systems. This report concerns England only.
2. Now the Department for Education (DfE).
3. R. Jackson, *et al.*, *Materials used to Teach about World Religions in Schools in England: Appendices* (London: DCSF, 2010).
4. A. Falaturi, *Islam in Religious Education Textbooks in Europe* (trans. H. Schultze, 1990; Köln: The Islamic Scientific Academy, 1988).
5. A. Falaturi and U. Tworuschka, *CSIS Papers, Europe, no. 8: A Guide to the Presentation of Islam in School Textbooks* (Cologne: Centre for the Study of Islam and Christian-Muslim relations for The Islamic Scientific Academy, 1992).
6. M. Hayward, "Teaching Christianity: Process and Purpose," in C. Erricker (ed.), *Teaching Christianity: A World Religions Approach* (Cambridge: Lutterworth Press, 1987 [2nd edn, 1995]).
7. J. Rudge, "The Westhill Project: Religious Education as Maturing Pupils' Patterns of Belief and Behaviour," in M. Grimmitt (ed.), *Pedagogies of Religious Education: Case Studies in the Research and Development of Good Pedogogic Practice in RE* (Great Wakering: McCrimmons, 2000), 88–111.
8. J. M. Hull, "Religion in the Service of the Child Project: The Gift Approach to Religious Education", in Grimmitt (ed.), *Pedagogies of Religious Education*, 112–29.
9. R. Jackson, "The Warwick Religious Education Project: The Interpretive Approach to Religious Education," in Grimmitt (ed.), *Pedagogies of Religious Education*, 130–52.
10. T. Cooling, "The Stapleford Project: Theology as the Basis for Religious Education," in Grimmitt (ed.), *Pedagogies of Religious Education*, 153–69.
11. Jackson, *et al.*, *Materials used to Teach*, 28.

12. M. Hayward and P. Hopkins, *Resources for Teaching about World Religions in Schools in England: An Audit* (London: DCSF, 2010).
13. In England primary schools are for children aged 5–11 and secondary schools for students aged 11–18.
14. UK Parliament (1988) Education Reform Act 1988 (London, HMSO).
15. Qualifications & Curriculum Authority (QCA) (2004) *Religious Education: The Non-Statutory National Framework* (London: Qualifications & Curriculum Authority). Available online: http://www.qca.org.uk/6163.html.
16. Office for Standards in Education, *Making Sense of Religion* (London: Ofsted, 2007), 35.
17. Key Stage 1 (5–7 year olds); Key Stage 2 (7–11 year olds); Key Stage 3 (11–16 year olds).
18. The sixth form is a traditional term for the 16–18 phase.
19. B. Wintersgill, "Task Setting in Religious Education at Key Stage 3: A Comparison with History," *Resource* 22(3) (2000), 9–17.
20. Wintersgill, "Task Setting," 9–17.
21. DCSF (2007) *Guidance on the Duty to Promote Community Cohesion* (London: Department of Children Schools and Families).
22. Jackson, *et al.*, *Materials used to Teach*, 99.
23. Jackson, *et al.*, *Materials used to Teach*, 99.
24. Jackson, *et al.*, *Materials used to Teach*, 97.
25. QCA (2004).
26. Jackson, *et al.*, *Materials used to Teach*, 107.
27. Jackson, *et al.*, *Materials used to Teach*, 107.
28. Jackson, *et al.*, *Materials used to Teach*, 160.
29. Jackson, *et al.*, *Materials used to Teach*, 15.
30. B. Gates, "Editorial," *British Journal of Religious Education* 27(2) (2005), 99–102.
31. Jackson, *et al.*, *Materials used to Teach*, 119.

6. REPRESENTATIONS OF INDIGENOUS AUSTRALIAN RELIGIONS IN NEW SOUTH WALES (NSW) HIGHER SCHOOL CERTIFICATE STUDIES OF RELIGION TEXTBOOKS[1]

*Carole M. Cusack**

INTRODUCTION

Among practitioners of the academic study of religion at the university level it has been acknowledged since approximately 1990 that the theoretical models of religion that have dominated the field since its inception in the mid-nineteenth century were in the main uncritically derived from Christianity and frequently produced caricatures or seriously misleading renditions of religions other than Christianity. This has led some scholars to call for the deconstruction of "Religious Studies" as a discipline and the abandonment of the category "religion" (McCutcheon 1997; Dubuisson 2003). Further, these models often resulted in the denial of the status of "religion" to many spiritual traditions. The case of Indigenous Australian religion is particularly poignant. From the time of the arrival of Arthur Phillip and the First Fleet in 1788, which signalled the beginning of

* Carole M. Cusack is Professor of Religious Studies at the University of Sydney. Her research interests include religious conversion, northern European mythology and religion, medieval Christianity, secularization and contemporary religious trends. She is the author of *Conversion among the Germanic Peoples* (Cassell, 1998), *The Essence of Buddhism* (Lansdowne, 2001), *Invented Religions: Imagination, Fiction and Faith* (Ashgate, 2010), and *The Sacred Tree: Ancient and Medieval Manifestations* (Cambridge Scholars Publishing, 2011). She has co-edited several volumes, including *Religion and Retributive Logic: Essays in Honour of Professor Garry W. Trompf* (Brill, 2010) with Christopher Hartney and *New Religions and Cultural Production* (Brill, 2012) with Alex Norman. She has published widely in academic journals and edited collections. With Christopher Hartney (University of Sydney) she is Editor of the *Journal of Religious History* (published by Wiley) and with Liselotte Frisk (Dalarna University, Sweden) she was foundation Editor of the *International Journal for the Study of New Religions* (published by Equinox), 2010–2013.

British colonial occupation, to the publication of pioneer anthropologist Edward Burnett Tylor's *Primitive Culture* in 1871, white settlers in Australia failed to recognize the existence of Aboriginal Australian religions, having classified them as merely "traditions" and "customs" (Swain 1985: 30). This was because the model of "religion" these Europeans employed was based on Christianity, and as Aboriginal people had no written texts, dedicated priesthood, religious buildings, or supreme being, colonizers assumed they had no religion. For example, in 1864 F. W. Farrar proclaimed Aboriginal Australians had "nothing whatever in the shape of religion to distinguish them from the beasts" (Farrar 1964: ccxvii–ccxxii). Tylor's landmark study proposed a minimum definition of religion, "belief in spirit beings," which was a radical change in the understanding of religion that enabled whites to recognize that the Ancestors of Indigenous culture were religious, after eight decades of ignorance and denigration of Aboriginal spirituality (Swain and Trompf 1997: 11).

Aboriginal Australians were granted citizenship in 1967, almost two centuries after white settlement, and since then a significant percentage of white Australians have developed an interest in Indigenous religions (Peterson and Sanders 1998: 17). The history of racism and exclusion of Aboriginal people under the White Australia Policy has given way to a more inclusive, though still troubled, relationship between white and black Australians (Habel 1999: 65–87, 150–63). The broader "New Age" fascination with First Nations and Indigenous wisdom contributed to white interest in Aboriginal culture, and resulted in similarly faulty representations of Indigenous Australian religions, which were deeply imbricated with clichéd images of Native Americans, African tribes, and the Maori of New Zealand. While the university-based discipline of Religious Studies has embraced the critique of its past, insights generated by this process have been slow to penetrate the teaching of Studies of Religion in schools. This chapter examines the presentation of Indigenous Australian religions in current textbooks used in Australian secondary schools in the New South Wales Higher School Certificate (matriculation) course Studies of Religion. These include Peter Mudge *et al.*, *Living Religion* (1993), Janet Morrissey *et al.*, *Living Religion* (2005), Christopher Hartney, *Cambridge Studies of Religion, Stage 6* (2008), and Rosemary King *et al.*, *Oxford Studies of Religion, Preliminary and HSC Course* (2010). It is argued that the majority of these textbooks, and the subject syllabus they reflect, continue to manifest the dominance of the "world religions" paradigm and the normative status of Christianity as defining religion. It is noteworthy, however, that Aboriginal religion is generally treated cautiously and with respect, reflecting the aura of "political correctness" surrounding discourses about Indigenous Australians in the twenty-first century.

STUDIES OF RELIGION AND THE NSW HIGHER SCHOOL CERTIFICATE

In 2010 more than 71,000 students sat for the NSW Higher School Certificate, a state matriculation examination. Australia is divided into six states and two territories, and there is no national secondary education curriculum or matriculation requirement. NSW Higher School Certificate students usually will be examined in six subject areas, which are chosen from over 100 courses on offer. English is the only mandatory course, and in 2010 Studies of Religion was the sixth most popular choice, with over 14,000 students enrolled (Anon 2010). Studies of Religion is a relatively new course that was first taught in 1992. However, this late introduction in New South Wales was anomalous in the Australian context, in that similar courses had been available in the other states since the 1970s. Section 116 of the Act to Constitute the Commonwealth of Australia (Australian Constitution) of 1900 states that:

> [t]he Commonwealth shall not make any law [i] for establishing any religion, or [ii] for imposing any religious observance, or [iii] for prohibiting the free exercise of any religion, and [iv] no religious test shall be required as a qualification for any office or public trust under the Commonwealth. (McLeish 1992: 208)

However, the 1980 publication of the Rawlinson Report on religion in NSW government schools recommended that, due to the shift from a mono-cultural to a multi-cultural and multi-faith Australia since the 1960s, students should be required to receive "general education in religion" in state schools (Rossiter 1981: 11).

The introduction of Studies in Religion followed a review of school education conducted in 1989, which resulted in the Education Act, passed by the NSW State Government in 1990. The Studies of Religion course is classified as "General Religious Education" (in contradistinction to confessional "Special Religious Education" courses taught in religious schools). Studies of Religion is offered in both a two-unit (standard) and a one-unit (exceptional) mode, the latter so that religious schools can combine it with one-unit Special Religious Education to reach the desired number of units to qualify for matriculation (Beck 1998). When Studies of Religion was introduced there were concerns expressed about a range of issues: the vast breadth of the curriculum; the course being taught primarily in religious schools; the fact that Studies of Religion teachers had not been trained in the academic study of religion and often had faith commitments; and finally, that students may acquire only superficial and atomized information about religion as a result of these problems with the development and delivery of the course (Taylor 1995: 53-71). Numbers of students taking the course were healthy from the beginning, with approximately four thousand (out of sixty thousand) students enrolled in 1994.

The first textbook to be available for students and teachers of Studies in Religion was Peter Mudge *et al.*, *Living Religion* (1993). The syllabus was divided into Foundation Studies, Religious Tradition Depth Studies, Cross-Religion Depth Studies and Interest Study Project. *Living Religion* devoted Part 1, chapters 2–4 to Foundation Studies (Origin and Nature of Religion, The Expression of Religion in

Australia, Aboriginal Religion) and Part 2, chapters 5–14 to Religious Traditions and cross-religion features (rites of passage and so on). The book fits the description of "world religions textbook" described by Mark MacWilliams:

> [w]orld religions textbooks are generally cut from the same cloth. They usually cover the same "big six"—Christianity, Judaism, Islam, Buddhism, Hinduism, and East Asian traditions—plus, occasionally, what Kay Read refers to...as the other religions in the "miscellaneous category." They rely on a world religions model that sees each of these traditions as a synthetic whole that can be coherently summarized through a set of sub-categories; founders, sacred scriptures, fixed doctrines, ritual practices, festivals and so on. (MacWilliams *et al.* 2005: 2)

The underlying world religions model has been found wanting because of its Western bias, Christian origins, and false promise of pluralism that masks a universalist stance (Masuzawa 2005). In *Living Religion* the total number of pages devoted to particular traditions is telling: Judaism receives 49 pages; Buddhism is treated in 48; Hinduism in 50. Christianity, the normative religion against which all others are compared, receives a total of 126 pages dedicated pages and, in fact, a far greater percentage of the book as it is the principal topic of the section on Australian religious history and expressions. Interestingly, there is a two-page chart at the end of the book which compares the syllabi for Studies of Religion across the Australian education system, and what emerges is that New South Wales has by far the most diverse curriculum in the country; other states have far narrower and more Christian-centred curricula (though South Australia does have a module on Aboriginal religion, the particular focus of this chapter) (Mudge *et al.* 1993: x–xi).

Indigenous religions are a prominent victim of the "world religions" paradigm, in that they are generally small traditions from a vast range of geographical locations, which are grouped together without regard to their cultural, linguistic, or indeed any other, particulars. This miscellaneous grouping is justified on the grounds that such religions (which may include Native American, Inuit, African, Maori and Aboriginal Australian religions) are primal, local, ethnic, non-literate, non-proselytizing and a variety of other terms that indicate their "difference" from the normative world religions (MacWilliams *et al.* 2005: 11). *Living Religion* calls these "ethnic religious traditions," and states that they are:

> typically small-scale religions that are found only in the context of a specific natural environment or culture. They are historically to be found among societies that traditionally did not have a written language, such as many tribal societies. Ethnic religious traditions do not have any written sacred texts, nor a specific founder. They are so closely intermeshed with the culture in which they are found that their people do not distinguish between religions and the rest of life the way modern Western societies tend to. (Mudge *et al.* 1993: 6)

This statement is found in the book's opening chapter, "Living Religion," in which are descriptions of various "types" of religions. Aboriginal Australian religion is offered as an instance of ethnic religion, and it is noted that the survival of such religions is gravely endangered by upheavals such as the conquest of their land. The bias toward world religions is revealed on the next page, where it is asserted that Judaism, Christianity, Islam, Hinduism and Buddhism "had a rigour and universality abut them that has seen them adapt to the demands of the variety of cultures to which they have spread" (Mudge *et al.* 2005: 7). Aboriginal religion is fragile and becomes imperilled when challenged by change, whereas Christianity and the other world religions are flexible, strong, and able to meet the challenges of change.

Chapter 2, "The Origins and Nature of Religion," deals with Aboriginal traditions briefly (reproducing the inherently racist notion that Aboriginal religion can be grouped with prehistoric religious expressions from the non-literate Palaeolithic era), and these are presented in greater detail in Chapter 3, "Aboriginal Belief Systems and Spirituality," which is 25 pages long (Cusack 1996: 44). The information provided is accurate in the main: readers are told that Aboriginal religions are not homogeneous but have certain common features; the legal definition of Indigenous status is provided—"an Aborigine or Torres Strait Islander, is a person of Aboriginal or Torres Strait Islander descent, who identifies with and is accepted as such by the community with whom he or she is associated" (Mudge *et al.* 1993: 35)[2]—and the core spiritual concept of the Dreaming (Aranda *alcheringa ngambukala*, Pitjantjatara *tjukurpa*) is adequately defined as "a complex concept of fundamental importance to Aboriginal culture, embracing the creative era long past (when Ancestral Beings roamed and instituted Aboriginal society) as well as the present and the future" (Mudge *et al.* 1993: 37), and meaningfully linked to ceremonies, kinship systems, and the centrality of the land for Indigenous Australians. The materiality and intimate relationship of Aboriginal religion with the whole of lived experience is well-expressed, with discussions of sacred objects, rites of passage involving physical transformations (such as birth, initiation for boys involving circumcision and scarification, initiation for girls at the *menarche*, marriage and death).

The chapter is frank about certain practices from the past that are now regarded with disfavour, such as the marriage of very young girls to middle-aged men, polygamy, and the forced removal of Aboriginal people to Christian missions, which were often little better than prisons. However, the majority of late-twentieth century Indigenous Australians identify as Christians, and while *Living Religions* does not present this in a triumphalist fashion, it is possible to read certain statements as building on the idea that Aboriginal Australian religion was poorly-equipped to develop and change, and thus the adaptable religion of Christianity offered a viable alternative belief system.

Theirs was a multitude of faiths based on places and events and wisdom and rights [that] were definitely *not* open to all people. For Christians there is a single source of sacred power, and authority pervades humanity and the world as a whole, universally. The tensions between "oneness" (Christianity) and plurality (Aboriginal religion), between the universal and that determined by place, was at the heart of the conflict between traditional Aboriginal and mission world views. (Mudge *et al.* 1993: 51)

The chapter then briefly considers the campaign for Land Rights by Indigenous people, the emergence of an Aboriginal flag, Aboriginal boycotts of the 1970 celebration of James Cook's "discovery" of Australia, and of the 1988 commemoration of the First Fleet's arrival on 26 January (which Indigenous Australians call "Invasion Day"), bodies dedicated to improving Indigenous conditions, such as the Council for Aboriginal Reconciliation, and landmark governmental reports including the National Report on the Royal Commission into Aboriginal Deaths in Custody (1991).

The final remarks on contemporary Aboriginal spirituality are, however, somewhat problematic, in that the authors repeat the statistic that 70% of Indigenous Australians are Christians and cite approvingly the development of the "Two Laws" movement, Aboriginal Christianity that incorporates aspects of traditional law. There is a distinct move away from the earlier expression of Christianity's suitability as the religion of the future for Aboriginal people; for example, the growth of both Evangelical and Pentecostal Christianity among Aboriginals is criticized by Indigenous and white commentators who have argued that "insofar as the evangelical movements do not contribute to tradition, they have in fact stepped in as Aboriginal neo-colonialists" (Mudge *et al.* 1993: 56). This seems to argue that, despite the late twentieth century context of Western societies in which individualism and religious choice are the norm, there is something not quite right if an Indigenous person chooses to convert to a non-Indigenous religion. Further, there is discussion of Tony Swain's contention that modern Aboriginals have developed a new mythology of Mother Earth (which provides a bridge from Indigenous understandings of the land and Western discourses of environment and conservation), that has been integrated with Aboriginal Christian beliefs (Swain 1991: 2–26). Here again, the suspicion of Christianity raises its head, with the authors cautioning readers that the Christian Sky God "breathed life into the Dreaming, yet also allowed the destructive processes of invasion. The idea of Mother Earth sits comfortably with the Aboriginal view of land" (Mudge *et al.* 1993: 57). The conclusion reached is unclear, but seems to indicate that Mother Earth functions as an effective metaphor for the environment *and* the dispossessed, for the land and the Indigenous people who are interconnected with it. In this formulation Christianity and colonial oppression are briefly conjoined, and the world religions paradigm is questioned, albeit inexplicitly.

The third edition of *Living Religion* (Morrissey *et al.* 2005) addresses the revised syllabus, which is directly quoted throughout, for the NSW Higher School Certificate course, and this more closely resembles the Oxford and Cambridge textbooks discussed in the next section. Some of the material from the earlier version is re-used in a different format, with the now-outmoded term "Aborigine" replaced by "Aboriginal" and the total number of pages dedicated to Aboriginal religion expanded to 43 or thereabouts. The textbook's format is more sophisticated, with increased illustrations, some topical material included in the student activities (for example, debating the creative tension between those who wish to harmonize and those who wish to separate Christianity and Aboriginal religion) and a more nuanced understanding of the diversity of Indigenous religions. Dreaming is here defined as:

> [a] complex concept of fundamental importance to Aboriginal culture, embracing the creative era long past of the Ancestral Beings as well as the present and the future. Shark Dreaming, or Honey Ant, Yam, and the hundreds of other Dreamings known across Australia are part of the spiritual identities of those Aboriginal peoples who claim them as their Ancestral Beings or totems. To falsely claim the Dreaming of another group is a serious infringement of Aboriginal law. (Morrissey *et al.* 2005: 12)

In contrast with the *Oxford Studies of Religion, Preliminary and HSC Course*, there is no attempt to describe Aboriginal religion in terms borrowed from Christianity (there is no mention of creation or a creator god, for example).

Chapter 9, "Religion and Belief Systems in Australia Post-1945," features discussion of critical issues, such as the pre-1960s policy of assimilation, which is defined as "a nineteenth century idea that Aboriginal peoples should be 'improved' by being 'civilised' and Christianised. From the 1930s assimilation was government policy and in the 1950s legislation was introduced to enforce it" (Morrissey *et al.* 2005: 249). There is also frank discussion of the "stolen generations," those Aboriginal children who were taken from their parents in pursuit of assimilationist policies. This new emphasis in *Living Religion* was the result of the impact of *Bringing Them Home: Report of the National Enquiry into the Separation of Aboriginal and Torres Strait Islander Children from their Families* (Australian Human Rights Commission 1997). The discussion of the stolen generations contains statements of responsibility and regret from churches and other Christian organizations. Perhaps significantly, these are all Roman Catholic; for example, the Catholic Diocese of Darwin and the Australian Catholic Social Welfare Commission (Morrissey *et al.* 2005: 252–53). At the close of this section, the interesting but rather unclear Sky Father-Earth Mother material is omitted, though strong opposition to the absorption of Aboriginal religion by Christian churches is expressed. Indigenous spokesman Chick Dixon, quoted on the Australia Broadcasting Commission (ABC) religious programme *Compass*, states that for the Christian churches;

> to try to absorb Aboriginal culture is genocidal. We will lose our traditional ways if they try to continue to marry our beliefs into their religious beliefs. It will be one more loss to a ravaged culture—it's the rape of our religion. (Morrissey *et al.* 2005: 274)

Despite this dire warning, the conclusion is tentatively positive, concentrating on the "creative tension" between those who want to revitalize Christianity with

Aboriginal influences and those who believe this to be a colonialist exercise. It is suggested that in the face of increasing secularism and the erosion of religion in Australian society, there is a desire for increased interfaith dialogue and ecumenical ventures, and that Indigenous spirituality may be what the West and its religion, Christianity, need. It remains to be noted that this depiction of Aboriginal religion, along with the sections of the first and third editions of *Living Religion* that dealt with the relationship of Aboriginal people to the land, is a positive, rather than a negative stereotype. Yet, as Hawai'ian scholar Julie Kaomea has shown with regard to her own indigenous culture, these positive stereotypes are often fuelled by political correctness, which, rather than building a new and authentic interpretative structure, simply overlay the old and politically incorrect structure with "cosmetic add-ons" that restrict the "potential for change" (Kaomea 2000: 331).

OXFORD AND CAMBRIDGE ENTER THE NSW STUDIES OF RELIGION MARKET

Christopher Hartney's *Cambridge Studies of Religion*, Stage 6 (2008) and Rosemary King *et al.*'s *Oxford Studies of Religion, Preliminary and HSC Course* (2010) were commissioned during a time of rapid expansion in the numbers of students studying Studies of Religion for the NSW Higher School Certificate. This growth justified the publishing giants Cambridge University Press and Oxford University Press entering the Australian textbook market. The two textbooks are quite different, for a variety of reasons (though they have certain common features, such as a large A4 format, with double column text broken up into accessible sections through the use of shaded blocks and charts, and a multitude of colourful illustrations); Hartney is 366 pages long, whereas King *et al.* is 460 pages, resulting in more detailed coverage of most topics. Because the NSW Higher School Certificate syllabus is the underlying structure, the backbone of the presentation of content in both the Oxford and Cambridge textbooks, it determines the delineation of certain subject areas, particularly Aboriginal Australian religion, which does not receive a chapter in and of itself, but is treated in the first section "The Nature of Religion" (which reflects the world religions paradigm in that it is treated as a methodological case, rather than as a world religion).

The syllabus support material recommends that Aboriginal people be consulted as sources for the study of Indigenous religion, and protocols for such interactions are laid out in the document *Working with Aboriginal Communities*. The agenda of political correctness is clear in statements such as "[o]nly by inviting Aboriginal people to speak about their spirituality can students gain an understanding of what the Dreaming truly means to Aboriginal people today" and "[i]t is important to acknowledge the existence of women's business and men's business within Aboriginal communities—particular knowledge that is owned only by certain people" (Board of Studies, New South Wales 2005). This emphasis is taken up in both the Cambridge and Oxford books. However, it is clear that, despite this sensitivity to Indigenous traditions, the world religions are expounded in a different way to Aboriginal religions, emphasizing an historical framework, in which the examination of origins, founders, principal beliefs, texts and ethics are located. This is unsurprising, as these are the core elements of the world religions paradigm (Tishken 2000).

This chapter will now consider the Cambridge and Oxford textbooks in detail. Christopher Hartney is a Lecturer in Studies in Religion at the University of Sydney (where he has been employed since 2003), with a doctorate on Caodaism, a twentieth-century Vietnamese new religion with a diasporic presence in Australia (Hartney 2002; Hartney 2007). The other credit on the textbook is "contributing editor" Jonathan Noble, but Hartney is the effective authorial voice *Cambridge Studies of Religion, Stage 6*.[3] This text is clearly informed by the methodological agnosticism of the academic study of religion, and determinedly gives no quarter to any particular religious tradition. The textbook has had a chequered history, partly because of the author's fearlessness in presenting non-politically correct aspects of religions. When it was published there were vociferous protests by the Australian Jewish community that Hartney's portrayal of Judaism was racist and anti-Semitic (Wilson 2009) and the book was temporarily withdrawn from sale.

However, *Cambridge Studies of Religion, Stage 6* was obviously rated very highly by other constituencies, in that it was the recipient of an Australian Award for Excellence in Educational Publishing in 2009, when it was named the winner in the Secondary Single Title Category (Australian Publishers Association 2009). In fact, while chapters 12–13 on Judaism do make some claims that may offend members of the Jewish community, these can nevertheless be supported by evidence or viewed as valid interpretations. For example, the two contentious statements that were most frequently cited in news coverage were first, that "much modern conflict in the world is related to the reactions of other groups to the Jewish people" and second, that "polygamy is commonly practised in Israel today" (Hartney 2008: 243, 277). The first of these statements could be interpreted as a relatively neutral way to allude to the Islamic world's problematic interactions with the state of Israel. In support of the second statement, the 2010 media coverage of the trial of Goel Ratzon, who lived with 17 women and had fathered more than 40 children, drew (possibly unwelcome) attention to the issue of polygamous Jews in Israel (Kershner 2010), suggesting that Hartney's observation, while possibly unwise, was not unfounded. As this chapter focuses on the treatment of Aboriginal Australian religions in school textbooks, attention will now turn to the rival Oxford textbook.

By contrast to the individualist voice of Christopher Hartney's textbook, Rosemary King *et al.*'s *Oxford Studies of Religion* is a book written by a committee, in that there are nine authors, only three of whom have doctorates, Aboriginal academic Anne Pattel-Gray, retired Professor of Asian Studies at the Australian National University, Tony Johns, and Kelvin McQueen (University of New England). The other six authors are high school teachers, some with Masters degrees in relevant fields (Theology, Religious Education), but none with academic training in the secular scholarly study of religion. The tone of the Oxford textbook is generally more open to theology and respectful of Christianity than that of the Cambridge textbook. This is clear from the opening chapter, "The Nature of Religion and Beliefs," in which it is argued that:

> [f]or a phenomenon to be called a religion, it must have all of the charac-teristics that distinguish a religion from other phenomena. Though it is often said that a large gathering of people that is held regularly and that has the same structure and operations each time it meets (for example, a football game or a Wimbledon tennis match) might be called a "religion," if such a gathering does not have all of the characteristics of a religion then it cannot correctly be called a religion. (King *et al.* 2010: 8)

Scholars employing contemporary approaches to the sacred in university-level Religious Studies would take issue with that statement, particularly given that the qualities of religion are stated to be beliefs and believers, sacred texts and writings, ethics, rituals and ceremonies (all of which are present in sports and other civil religious phenomena, and in the individualistic "sacred," which is uncoupled from official religion) (Demerath 2000).

With regard to the presentation of Indigenous religion both books cover the topics of the syllabus. These include the Dreaming and Aboriginal tribal tradi-tions, Ancestor stories, a historical sketch of the colonial period, the effect of Christian missions, and the implications of the separation of Aboriginal people from the land. Key twentieth century phenomena, such as the stolen genera-tions, land rights and native title campaigns to regain ancestral ground, citizen-ship and reconciliation, a process that operates both in spiritual terms, and as a civil religious programme for all Australians, bring the story of Indigenous reli-gion up to the present (Board of Studies, New South Wales 2005). Hartney's Cam-bridge book is notable for treating Indigenous religion more academically than the Oxford text. Dreaming stories are described as complex and layered in mean-ing, and referring to a specific class of events in which Ancestors shape the land (not to a time in the past). Here Hartney rejects the older terminology, "Dream-time," and uses the specifically academic understanding of Dreaming. An exam-ple of a Dreaming story is provided (the creation of the Darling River, told by Aunty Beryl Carmichael), and it is noted that Aboriginal songs and dances re-enact (Hartney 2009: 24–26). Dreaming, land and identity are connected in a dis-cussion of law and animal totems. The initial failure of missionaries to convert Aboriginals and the inappropriateness of the white response to Indigenous reli-gion are acknowledged:

> [t]hese days many Aboriginal people are Christians but, when Christians first arrived in Australia, many of them failed to recognize Aboriginal spir-ituality as a religion. They thought the best way to help Indigenous Aus-tralians was to make them Christian, to force them to forget about their

Dreaming stories.... Aboriginal people, when they first heard of Jesus, thought it was the white person's Dreaming story. They didn't understand why they had to believe it as well. White people couldn't understand why the Aboriginal people did not have a supreme god. (Hartney 2009: 19)

The negative consequences of being forced off the land (in terms of loss of language and kin-groups, as well as loss of traditional homelands) are presented unambiguously in plain language. Hartney argues that in direct contrast to the Western mindset, in which people own land, in the Indigenous mindset the land owns people, thus by losing the land "Aboriginal people were unable to draw effectively on the spiritual power of the Dreaming and the ancestor spirits. They were also restricted in their access to sacred sites and much tribal lore and law was lost" (Hartney 2009: 59). His portrayal of the stolen generation, the *Bringing Them Home* (1997) report's recommendation of a formal apology, and the effect of Labour Prime Minister Kevin Rudd's apology to Aboriginal people after the Liberal Prime Minister John Howard had refused for a decade to deliver one, are forcefully described.

However, it could be argued that Hartney's presentation of Aboriginal religion is informed by political correctness. For example, when students are recommended films that illuminate Aboriginal religion they include serious artworks such as Rolf de Heer's *Ten Canoes* (2006), in which Aboriginal elder, Minygululu, tells an Ancestral story about the disruption of marriage and society to his younger brother Dayindi, whom he suspects of intending to steal his third and youngest wife. This is a complex film that operates on several levels but ultimately teaches the importance of story in Aboriginal culture (Bradshaw 2007). By contrast, the irreverent comedy, *Life of Brian* (1979), is recommended as a resource for Christianity. Similarly, the student activities for the study of Christianity and Islam include Exercise 6.3, 2: "The Catholic Church is the true Church. Discuss"; and Activity 10.6, 3: "Collect examples from the media of the way the word *jihad* is used. Which *jihad* is being spoken about? Analyse the way it is discussed" (Hartney 2009: 129, 218). By contrast, the activities for the study of Aboriginal religion include the more neutral Exercise 1.7, 3: "Explain the Aboriginal concept of the land"; and Activity 1.7, 2: "Investigate some Indigenous art and write a report on a particular work that you feel demonstrates the Dreaming" (Hartney 2009: 28).

The coverage of Indigenous religion in King *et al.*'s *Oxford Studies of Religion, Preliminary and HSC Course* is more extensive than the Cambridge textbook, and it is presented in a significantly different way. Although particular sections are not credited to specific authors, it is clear that the section on Aboriginal religion was written by Dr Anne Pattel-Gray, a well-known Indigenous theologian and activist, who at the time of publication was described as "the Chair of Adelaide North TAFE [Technical and Further Education], President of the Aboriginal Advancement League SA Incorporated...and a member of the International Association of Black Religions and Spiritualities" (King *et al.* 2010: xi). The tone of the mate-

rial is subjective and theological ideas are prominent, which contrasts with Hartney's secular language. Certain academic understandings are rejected in favour
of "insider" interpretations. Emphasis is placed on Aboriginal religion and spirituality being "secret-sacred," only for the initiated, and the Dreaming (which is
also referred to as the Dreamtime and Dream Time) is said to hold:

> the essence of truth of Aboriginal religious beliefs...the Dreaming holds the
> Aboriginal view of creation: it is the beginning of everything—the begin-
> ning of time, the creation of life, the birth of humanity and the ordering of
> all things. It is the remote past of the Spirit Ancestors or Spirit Beings or
> Ancestral Beings; it is the period, long ago, when Spirit Beings interacted
> with Aboriginal people. (King *et al.* 2010: 17)

Coupled with this explicit rejection of the scholarly formulation of Dreaming as
atemporal is an emphasis on the Creator, a monotheistic overlay upon the Ancestor spirits, and a strongly ideological portrayal of Indigenous attitudes to the land
as environmentally responsible and morally superior to Western attitudes to the
land.

Paralleling the Cambridge textbook there are examples of Dreaming stories
provided (for example, the story of Nguthunanga Mai Ambatanha [The Dream-
time Spirit cooking of the damper] retold by Denise Champion), and there is
a strong focus on the role of Aboriginal women, who are presented as being
"the 'backbone' of Aboriginal society...a fact not often recognized or taken into
account by Euro-Australians" and as opposed to "white patriarchal values" (King
et al. 2010: 24). There are, however, internal contradictions in this depiction of
Indigenous Australian religion, in that it is stated that:

> [t]he narratives belonging to Aboriginal mythology have been passed on
> from time immemorial and are the eternal link between the Ancestral
> Spirits and the past, present and future generations. Aboriginal mythol-
> ogy is truth; its authenticity is never questioned. Aboriginal mythology
> is not written in a book; the environment contains the markings and
> narratives of the Ancestral Beings found in the Dreaming. (King *et al.*
> 2010: 20)

This contradicts the definition of religion provided earlier in the chapter "The
Nature of Religion and Beliefs," discussed above, which mandates sacred texts
and writings. This may, however, be no more than the authors of different sections of the Oxford textbook not communicating properly with each other, or the
failure of the world religions paradigm to adequately account for the "miscellaneous" religions that make up the Indigenous category (MacWilliams *et al.* 2005).

The coverage of Aboriginal religion covers essentially the same material as
Hartney, which is in accordance with the syllabus. The discussion of land is interesting, in that where Hartney argues that the land "owns" Aboriginal people, the

Oxford book argues that "the Ancestral bestowal of land on Aboriginal people gave them ownership, which includes control of all of the land's resources as well as the maintenance of its territorial integrity" (King *et al.* 2010: 27). This contrast in interpretation can be viewed as the result of two very different people approaching a sensitive topic; that a white Australian male and an Aboriginal Australian woman would reach varying conclusions on a subject as politically-charged as whether Indigenous people "owned" the land (which has implications for land rights and native title claims) is unsurprising. As Susanne V. Knudsen remarks in her study of portrayals of the Sami (formerly known as Lapps, a pejorative term) in Norwegian school texts has noted, it is important to be aware of "power and power relations...[and] procedures of ex- and inclusion" that are the result of the textbook format (Knudsen 2006: 70).

Chapter 9, "Religion and Religious Belief Systems in Australia Post-1945," brings the story of Aboriginal religion into the present. Here the period of Aboriginal occupation of Australia is given as 40,000 years, whereas in chapter 1 it is given as one 140,000 years (which might simply be a typographical error). Aboriginal rites of passage are described and the history of colonization and mission sketched. The subjects of lands rights and native title are treated positively, but the malign influence of white Australia is emphasized. The 1961 Native Welfare Conference promoted the policy of forcing Aboriginal people to assimilate to white society:

> all Aborigines and part-Aborigines are expected eventually to attain the same manner of living as other Australians and to life as members of a single Australia community, enjoying the same rights and privileges, accepting the same responsibilities, observing the same customs and influenced by the same beliefs and hopes as other Australians. (King *et al.* 2010: 212)

Aboriginal people are portrayed as having survived and transcended white oppression (which includes patronizing programmes directing Aboriginal self-determination and Indigenous welfare) through their strength and the "continuity of their beliefs" (King *et al.* 2010: 212). This chapter concludes with a section on the diversity of Aboriginal theologies in contemporary Australia, a topic largely absent from *Cambridge Studies of Religion, Stage 6*. Pattel-Gray's explanation of these theologies is problematic, in that she argues that "it is important to know that Aboriginals have never been given the critical tools to understand the Christian Bible fully. From the very first mission...the Australian churches 'read-out' the meaning of the text of the Bible in a way that distorted more than just the words" (King *et al.* 2010: 232). This enables her to dismiss Aboriginal conservative Christians as rejecting "their own Aboriginal identity, culture and languages...[and] betray[ing] a direct, interventionist, white, European 'missionised' theology" (King *et al.* 2010: 234). She then valorizes radical Aboriginal theology, which is characterized as autonomous, post-Western and post-denominational, keeping traditional practices important and looking to traditional religion as the divine grounding for contemporary faith. The subjective and politically correct tone of this chapter is reinforced by the student Activity 1, "Outline the position of the Aboriginal contributor to this section of this chapter in regard to the impact of religious traditions on Aboriginal people" (King *et al.* 2010: 233).

CONCLUSION

The NSW Higher School Certificate Studies of Religion syllabus deals, *inter alia*, with the problems of relationship between Indigenous and white Australians, through the lens of religion (Aboriginal traditional religion and colonial Christianity). The teaching of religion in a non-confessional manner to school students tends to be a fraught exercise in Australia, a notably secular country in which church attendance is approximately 9% of the population of 22 million. The Rawlinson Report's rationale in 1980 for offering such "general religious education" was framed in terms of cultural change rather than the specific religious needs of a multi-faith community. In fact, the percentage of the Australian population that are adherents of non-Christian religions was a mere 5.6% in the 2006 Census (Cusack 2011: 298). Thus the political correctness apparent in the portrayal of Aboriginal religion and culture in *Cambridge Studies of Religion, Stage 6* and Oxford *Studies of Religion Preliminary and HSC Course* has more to do with the troubled history of colonialism, forced Christianization, denial of citizenship, and exclusion from national politics that Indigenous Australians suffered at the hands of whites until the 1960s.

In the twenty-first century, the living conditions, health and life expectancy of Indigenous Australians are radically different to those of middle-class whites, with disease, substance abuse, suicide, domestic violence, alcoholism and other negative conditions contributing to radically reduced socio-economic status and life-expectancy. Viewed in this light, the politically correct presentation of a sanitized Aboriginal culture through the lens of traditional Indigenous religion is an attempt to induce in the Australian school students a positive image of, and respect for, Aboriginal people. From the point of view of the academic study of religion, however, such a portrayal draws on the world religions paradigm, which tends to marginalize indigenous religion, and contributes an essentialized (and partially theologized) image of Aboriginal culture. The textbooks reviewed in this chapter convey the portrayal of Aboriginal religion quite successfully, in that there are very few factual errors though there are variations in interpretation, yet the authors all accept that it is an exceptional case, not to be treated in the same way as the "named" religions (Judaism, Christianity, Buddhism and so on) but as a methodological curiosity and as an exotic and "other" element of the religious landscape of Australia.

REFERENCES

Anon. 2009. "The Australian Awards for Excellence in Educational Publishing 2009." *Australian Publishers Association*. At http://www.publishers.asn.au/emplibrary/2009_Education_Awards_Winners.pdf (accessed 19 August 2011).

Anon. 2010. "Media Guide 2010—Higher School Certificate and School Certificate." *Educational Resources, Board of Studies NSW Government*. At http://www.boardofstudies.nsw.edu.au/bos_stats/media-guide-2010.html (accessed 19 August 2011).

Australian Human Rights Commission. 1997. *Bringing Them Home: Report of the National Enquiry into the Separation of Aboriginal and Torres Strait Islander Children from their Families*. At http://www.hreoc.gov.au/social_justice/bth_report/report/index.html (accessed 19 August 2011).

Beck, Margie. 1998. "Implications of Research in Implementation of the Higher School Certificate Studies of Religion Course in New South Wales." *Australian Association for Research in Education*. At http://www.aare.edu.au/98pap/bec98362.htm (accessed 19 August 2011).

Board of Studies, New South Wales. 2005. "Studies of Religion Stage 6 Syllabus." At http://www.boardofstudies.nsw.edu.au/syllabus_hsc/studies-religion.html (accessed 19 August 2011).

Bradshaw, Peter. 2007. "Ten Canoes." *The Guardian*. At http://www.guardian.co.uk/film/2007/jun/01/drama.worldcinema (accessed 19 August 2011).

Cusack, Carole M. 1996. "Canon Fodder: General Religious Studies Textbooks and Educational Culture." *Intersections: The Journal of the Association for Studies of Religion* 2(1): 42–50.

Cusack, Carole M. 2011. "'Celticity' in Australian Alternative Spiritualities." In *Ireland's New Religious Movements*, ed. Olivia Cosgrove, Laurence Cox *et al.*, 281–99. Newcastle: Cambridge Scholars Press.

Demerath III, N. J. 2000. "The Varieties of Sacred Experience: Finding the Sacred in a Secular Grove." *Journal for the Scientific Study of Religion* 39(1): 1–11.

Dubuisson, Daniel. 2003. *The Western Construction of Religion: Myths, Knowledge and Ideology*, trans. William Sayers. Baltimore: Johns Hopkins University Press.

Farrar, F. W. 1864. "On the Universality of Belief in God." *Journal of the Royal Anthropological Society of London* 2: ccxvii–ccxxii

Habel, Norman C. 1999. *Reconciliation: Searching for Australia's Soul*. Sydney: HarperCollins.

Hartney, Christopher. 2002. "Caodaism." In *Religions of the World: A Comprehensive Encyclopedia of Beliefs and Practices*, 4 vols, ed. J. Gordon Melton and Martin Baumann. Santa Barbara, CA: ABC-CLIO.

Hartney, Christopher. 2007. "Spiritism and Charisma: Caodaism from its Infancy." *Australian Religion Studies Review* 20(3): 334–56.

Hartney, Christopher. 2008. *Cambridge Studies of Religion, Stage 6*, with Jonathan Noble. Cambridge: Cambridge University Press.

Kaomea, Julie. 2000. "A Curriculum of Aloha? Colonialism and Tourism in Hawai'i's Elementary Textbooks." *Curriculum Inquiry* 30(3): 319–44.

Kershner, Isabel. 2010. "Israel Raids Polygamist Compound." *New York Times*, 15 January. At http://www.nytimes.com/2010/01/15/world/middleeast/15harem.html (accessed 18 August 2011).

King, Rosemary, John Mooney, Elizabeth Carnegie, Helen Smith, Anthony Johns, David Johns, Anne Pattel-Gray, Sandy Hollis and Kelvin McQueen. 2010. *Oxford Studies of Religion, Preliminary and HSC Course*. Oxford: Oxford University Press.

Knudsen, Susanne V. 2006. "Intersectionality—a Theoretical Inspiration in the Analysis of

Minority Cultures and Identities in Textbooks." In *Caught in the Web or Lost in the Textbook*, ed. Eric Bruillard, Bengt Armotsbakken, Susanne V. Knudsen and Mike Horsely, 61–76. Caen: IAERTEM.

MacWilliams, Mark, Joanne Punzo Waghorne, Deborah Sommer, Cybelle Shattuck, Kay A. Read, Salva J. Raj, Khaled Keshk, Deborah Halter, James Egge, Robert M. Baum, Carol S. Anderson and Russell T. McCutcheon. 2005. "Religion/s between Covers: Dilemmas of the World Religions Textbook." *Religion Studies Review* 31(1–2): 1–35.

Masuzawa, Tomoko. 2005. *The Invention of World Religions, or, How European Universalism was Preserved in the Language of Pluralism*. Chicago: University of Chicago Press.

McLeish, Stephen. 1992. "Making Sense of Religion and the Constitution: A Fresh Start for Section 116." *Monash University Law Review* 18(2): 207–36.

McCutcheon, Russell T. 1997. *Manufacturing Religion: The Discourse of Sui Generis Religion and the Politics of Nostalgia*. Oxford: Oxford University Press.

Morrissey, Janet, Peter Mudge, Adam Taylor, Greg Bailey and Paul Rule. 2005. *Living Religion*. 3rd edn. Melbourne: Pearson Education.

Mudge, Peter, Adam Taylor, Janet Morrissey, Greg Bailey, Hamish Gregor, Penelope Magee, Laurence Mills and Jocelyn Sheerin. 1993. *Living Religion: Studies of Religion for Senior Students*. Melbourne: Longman Cheshire.

Peterson, Nicolas, and Will Sanders. 1998. "Introduction." In *Citizenship and Indigenous Australians: Changing Conceptions and Possibilities*, ed. Nicolas Peterson and Will Sanders, 1–32. Cambridge: Cambridge University Press.

Rossiter, Graham. 1981. *Religious Education in Australian Schools*. Canberra: Curriculum Development Centre.

Swain, Tony. 1985. *Interpreting Aboriginal Religion: An Historical Account*. Adelaide: Australian Association for the Study of Religion.

Swain, Tony. 1991. "The Mother Earth Conspiracy: An Australian Episode." *Numen* 38(1): 3–26.

Swain, Tony, and Garry Trompf. 1997. *Religions of Oceania*. London and New York: Routledge.

Taylor. Adam. 1995. "The Quiet RE volution: The Impact of Studies of Religion in Religiously Affiliated Schools." *Intersections: The Journal of the Association for Studies of Religion* 1: 53–71.

Tishken, Joel. 2000. "Ethnic vs. Evangelical Religions: Beyond Teaching the World Religions Approach." *The History Teacher* 33(3): 303–20.

Wilson, James. 2009. "University Press Pulls Textbook which 'Fuels Anti-Semitism.'" *Varsity*. 30 October. At http://www.varsity.co.uk/news/1397 (accessed 19 August 2011).

Endnotes
1. I am grateful to my research assistant Venetia Robertson for her skill in locating relevant materials and meticulous note-taking. My thanks are also due to Don Barrett for his sympathetic interest in my researches and assistance in clarifying my thoughts during the researching and writing of this chapter.
2. The use of the term "Aborigine," while appropriate for the early 1990s, gives the first edition of *Living Religion* a fusty, antiquated feel. Despite the fact that "Aborigine" is a noun and "Aboriginal" an adjective, in twenty-first century Australia the accepted English usage is to refer to Australian Aboriginals, as this is the term used by Indigenous Australians to refer to themselves (as a general term, rather than specific regional designators like "Koori" or "Murri").

3. Christopher Hartney has informed me that the greatest areas of contention were the two chapters, 6 and 7, that dealt with Christianity. He wrote what he considered to be a sober and scholarly account, which did not find favour because the vast majority of schools that teach Studies of Religion in NSW are Christian schools (chiefly Roman Catholic, but also Anglican, and other denominations). His dispassionate and non-confessional representation of Christianity was deemed problematic and he was compelled to make amendments, which were substantially suggested by Jonathan Noble.

7. VISUAL ENGAGEMENT: TEXTBOOKS AND THE MATERIALITY OF RELIGION

*Mary Hayward**

"Seeing" is not only the goal and prerogative of the "seers" but it is part of all our learning and knowing. (Eck 1985: 1)

"Seeing" and "looking" are rich words in English; their polysemic character particularly suits their use in the fields of religious studies and religious education. As metaphor, activity and experience they may belong to the adherent; as process and method they are expressive of the observer's or student's task. For both parties they may resonate with the relational, in the sense that the perceptions of the seer—and expectations too—may colour what is seen, whilst the "seen" may itself transform or at least change the seer's perspective. Diana Eck's exploration of the Indian concept of *darśan* alerts readers to the places where a devotee may seek *darśan*— in the presence of the image, in locations deemed sacred—mountains, the confluence of rivers, sites associated with particular gods, for example—and in the activity of pilgrimage. There is a "visual text" to be read by the student, and like written texts this is demanding (Eck 1985: 2).

1. RELIGION AND THE "MATERIAL"

Eck's short study of *darśan* necessarily draws our attention to the material world of religion; yet it is surprising how little attention this receives in introductions to the study of religion. Smart seems to have added his "material dimension" (Smart

*   Dr Mary Hayward is Associate Fellow, Warwick Religions and Education Research Unit (WRERU), University of Warwick UK, where she completed doctoral studies on the representation of Christianity in Religious Education in England. She has held RE related posts in the Universities of Leeds, Warwick and—earlier in her career—Lancaster and was for 13 years Deputy Director of York Religious Education Centre. She is a member of the International Seminar on Religion and Values (ISREV); has served on the Executive Committee of the Association of University Lecturers in Religion and Education, and is Reviews Editor of the *British Journal of Religious Education*.

1989), or "material or artistic dimension" (Smart 1996) almost as an afterthought to his earlier expositions of the dimensions of religion (Smart 1968, 1969). His later work points to the breadth of this dimension. It comprises

> ...buildings for worship and ritual, statuary and paintings, the dress and vestments of priests and so forth, books, amulets and the like, graves, burning ghats and so on, and sacrificial animals and the like. (Smart 1996: 227)

Smart does not however offer readers the detailed exposition which the other dimensions receive, although his exploration of different religions' buildings alerts readers to ways in which they are expressive of doctrine, ideology, ritual and power (Smart 1996: 277–84). Such expression points to the interconnectedness of Smart's dimensions, an important point for discussion of the materiality of religion, but important also for religious education (RE) in view of their too frequent misappropriation as discrete categories in curriculum planning.

Hinnells, addressing "Religion and the Arts," also draws attention to religions' material expression, as well as to the place he believes the Arts should have in Religious Studies:

> We cannot I suggest, gain an insight into a religion without a feeling for the forms in which it is experienced by its followers. Those forms such as music, dance, the inspiration of sacred architecture and the visual arts are the media through which many experience what is beyond words. (Hinnells 1990: 271)

More recently, a developing interest in "material religion" and its interpretation, its roots in museum studies, anthropology and sociology, and related also to a wider academic interest in material culture which cuts across traditional disciplinary boundaries,[1] suggests shifts in perspective regarding the material forms and expression of religion. In 2005 the Editorial of the new journal *Material Religion* had indicated the nature of this approach, as recalled here:

> ...it sets out to consider religion through the lens of its material forms and their use in religious practice. (Meyer, Morgan, Paine and Plate 2011: 6)

And five years later,

> Materialising the study of religion means asking how religion happens materially, which is not to be confused with asking the much less helpful question of how religion is expressed in material form. A materialised study of religion begins with the assumption that things are not something added to a religion, but rather inextricable from it. (Meyer, Morgan, Paine and Plate 2010: 209, cited in 2011: 6).

This gives rise to a vocabulary for conceptualizing religions, a vocabulary correlating with newer perspectives in social sciences, and offering new lenses through which to view religion.[2] Discussion of the insights which may be gained for RE from this kind of approach lies largely beyond the scope of this chapter, but points to an agenda for future consideration.

As I shall indicate below, RE in England has not been blind to the material dimension of religion; but it has perhaps been short-sighted. It does not always "see." Its historical embeddedness was in a Protestant tradition which prioritized word and speech, but without appreciating the materiality of either. A case can also be argued in the present that RE in England is showing a marked drift towards the verbal and cerebral in religion. Consequently, before turning to RE, I want to briefly consider "belief" and "thought" in relation to materiality drawing on two books. Published in the same year as the first issue of *Material Religion* of which the author is an Editor, Morgan's book *The Sacred Gaze* offers insights into his approach and epistemological stance. His comments on belief are pertinent to my concerns

> Belief happens in what people say, but also in what they do. It is embodied in various practices and actions, in the stories and testaments people tell, in their uses of buildings, pictures, in the taste of food, the smell of fragrances, in the way people treat children, one another, and strangers. Belief in other words does not exist in an abstract discursive space, in an empyrean realm of pure proclamation "I believe". Belief happens in and through things and what people do with them. (Morgan 2005: 8)

And

> ...images and how people look at them are evidence for understanding belief, which should not reduced to doctrines or creeds of a propositional nature. Belief is an embodied practice no less than a cerebral one. (Morgan 2005: 20)[3]

In this respect belief may be seen as lived and experienced in physical and sensory ways which may be prior to and more fundamental than its articulation in propositions and credal formulae.[4] My second text, a history of Christian thought (Miles 2005), opens with *Prelude: Flesh and Word*. This reminder of Christianity as an "embodied" religion—of Word made flesh—provides the conceptual frame for Miles' book. Thought is not here an abstraction but shaped and reshaped, amongst diverse people in different times, places and circumstances, preferencing some voices and excluding others—perspective is all important; by some thought is expressed in words, but its currency is varied:

> Relatively few Christians read theological treatises, but all participated
> in the community's artistic repertoire. Images and architecture inter-

preted Christian beliefs and practices, communicating theological, religious and social messages. Music was used in a variety of ways to unify liturgy and practice across wide geographical distances, shape religious sensibilities, create community, communicate theology and inspire gratitude and praise. The arts of Christian movements show how the religion of the "Word made flesh" was expressed in the world of bodies and senses, revealing what it meant to Christians to worship an incarnate God. (Miles 2005: 4)

Such expression is for Margaret Miles a primary source, not simply illustration—and is suggestive of how RE might approach religions' materiality. My purpose in this brief introduction has been to highlight interest and engagement with materiality[5] in the study of religions. Whilst the focus and perspective of each example I have given differs and could perhaps be placed on a continuum moving from "material expression" through "material dimension" to Morgan's interest in "how religion happens materially," each focuses our attention on the fact that religion is encountered materially and points to the hermeneutic horizons of seeing.

2. RELIGIOUS EDUCATION AND MATERIALITY

RE in England over many decades has espoused the illustrated textbook; then came the use of the "visual aid" and later the "audio-visual aid," and in the present a range of new technologies.[6] Teachers have also long arranged visits and visitors, used artefacts and sometimes simulations to offer their students a more immediate encounter with religion. Materiality has been communicated by all these means—but with the textbook as the constant factor.

2.1. A historical perspective

A recent study (Northcote 2010) examines how in the early nineteenth century the National Society—one of the prime actors in a gradual move towards universal education in England—used colour reproductions of the works of Italian Renaissance artists in the books they published for children's religious education.[7] Whilst such pictures might be embedded in a tightly structured exercise moving into an exposition of doctrine, they were especially valued for their close correspondence with biblical narrative. Northcote observes that the symbolism of the pictures belonged to a pre-reformation Catholicism and was thus most probably unfamiliar to those who met it, a point which serves as a reminder of contextual shifts which occlude our capacity to make sense of what is seen, or change the way of looking at particular *things*. From an educational perspective, the selected pictures were deemed to be of the highest quality, but then the sacred nature of their subject also called for this.

2.2. A personal recollection

With hindsight, we can see the capacity of pictures to shape the perspective of the viewer or form their understanding of religions. From my own recollection of secondary school the books we encountered in the first three years there were by today's standards rather dreary in appearance. I remember their flexible cloth covers, a different colour—brown, red and blue—for each school year; they had a dense text in two columns, but were quite extensively illustrated with maps and grainy black and white photographs. As I recall many of these were of places in Palestine, including archaeological sites—some in adjacent regions. At a basic level these pictures were intended to illustrate the text: you haven't been to Bethlehem but here is what it looks like. More subtly they endorsed an appropriation of this land by Christians—a significant geographical and thus material space—it was the Holy Land. Alongside this archaeological discoveries, places and objects, of the late nineteenth and early twentieth centuries served as evidence for biblical veracity or historicity; material not of religious significance *per se* was brought into the service of the tradition—in this case Christianity. I don't recall that the books demanded anything of the reader in relation to these pictures, but I am fascinated that I can recall them quite clearly several decades later.

2.3. Some observations and implications

Each of the above cameos belongs to RE's past and to earlier understandings of its purposes; but the two examples, and my introductory observations on religion and the "material" serve to highlight some important matters, among them questions about:

- boundaries—when we speak of the materiality of religion where are they to be drawn? The question takes us back to Morgan's comments on the shift in thinking about material religion (see above);
- contexts—diachronically, as well as in the present; in meeting religions' materiality what are the effects of its representation in the context of a book? This question cuts across book design as well as representation.
- the reception by the "seer" of the representations they meet; what is needed—in terms of skills, knowledge, background to interpret what is seen? This question is related to the previous one and is further sharpened where students' encounter unfamiliar cultural contexts;
- the relation of the "visual text" (in Eck's sense) to its place and purpose in the textbook, for example in relation to learning outcomes;
- latent messages in what is included and in what is visually represented in books;
- how does "quality" function as a criterion in selecting what will be portrayed? Is it a relevant concept here?

2.4. Student engagement: a challenge to books

Engaging students in the study of religion has taken RE outside of the school. Teachers who have been able to arrange a visit to a mandir when puja is taking place know that this will be a living and a multi-sensory experience for students; an occasion for exploring a range of concepts in RE—place, image, symbol and *darśan*; the relation of devotee and deities expressed through sound, offerings, gesture and bodily movement; an opportunity for questions and conversation. Where this is not possible, schools may have contact with members of different religions who are willing to speak to and talk with students, allowing them to hear an authentic voice from the tradition they are studying and to ask the questions they wish to ask. But for most schools most of the time, students will not be able to draw on the immediacy of such a visit or visitors. Perhaps, then, the teacher feels comfortable in offering a simulation—of puja at a home shrine for example;[8] or maybe there is film footage on DVD which can be used alongside a selection of related artefacts and posters which students carefully handle, question and research using a range of websites. But for some there may "just" be the textbook.

In the previous paragraph I have somewhat artificially suggested a hierarchy of experiences and media to which students may have access in RE; setting them out in this way serves to highlight the expectations we might bring to textbook pictures and illustrations with regard to clarity, content, "ambience" and authenticity; about the way textbooks may engage students through their presentation and representation of religions. Of equal importance is the opportunity textbooks offer for developing discernment about what is seen and "cultivating a listening eye."[9]

3. AN EXPLORATORY STUDY

Against the above background I set out to conduct a small qualitative study for this chapter, which would give particular attention to the visuals used in selected textbooks and to their representation of material aspects of religion. The steps in this study may be summarized as follows:

3.1. Textbook sample

Four series of books each from a different publisher were selected; each series included separate books on the six "principal religious traditions."[10] A decision was taken to focus on books on Christianity and Hinduism; each offers many opportunities for encountering materiality and whilst Christianity is taught at each key stage[11] in RE, evidence suggests that Hinduism is most likely to be taught at Key Stage 3, the stage selected for this study. The date from first publication to the present of some of the books spans ten years—school textbooks tend to have a long lifespan. Each of the series selected is in its publisher's catalogue for 2011. The series' titles tell their own stories: *Seeking Religion; Modern World Religions; Religious Belief and Practice; Beliefs and Issues.* Within the first two series, books on Christianity and Hinduism are of equal length; this is not so in the other two, where the books on Christianity are, in an unspecified way, deemed foundation texts and are twice as long as those on Hinduism.

Each series is intended for use with students aged 11–14; it is at this stage that students are most likely to study specific religious traditions, although some newer textbooks adopt a thematic approach, sometimes reflecting the organizing categories of the non-statutory National Framework for RE (QCA 2004),[12] providing a book for each of the first three years of secondary school. I had intended to include one such series in my sample but close inspection of it revealed much attention to page design, but few visuals directly relating to specific religious traditions. The effect of this on such books' capacity to develop students' sensitivity and skills in interpreting religions' materiality seems likely to be detrimental.

3.2. Focus

My research suggests that more attention has been paid to the analysis of the written text than visuals in textbooks, whilst some suggest that image-based research has low status (David 2000: 228). In England, RE textbooks have until recently received little research attention,[13] and I have found no study specifically concerned with their visual content. Focusing on the visual text of the book recognizes the primacy of the visual over the written word in memory and recall[14] as well as its initial impact in shaping "impressions" of the subject—here Christianity and Hinduism respectively.

It is useful at this point to draw attention to the potential complexity of the textbook page. Slater's report on Choppin (1992: 89–93) summarizes his concept of the paratext; this recognizes the complexity of textbook design and the need to move beyond a narrow focus on text: the

> …"proto-text" [paratext?] encompasses pictures, diagrams, maps, layout, colour scheme, typography etc. All contribute to pupil learning, some contain hidden messages, none can be separated from the written text. (Slater 1992: 14)

My methodology outlined below quickly drew attention to this range of features in textbooks, leading me to restrict my study to photographs. Additionally photographs potentially constituted primary evidence for students to consider.[15]

3.3. Method

3.3.1. A grounded approach was taken to each of the books. Basic data was tabulated in three columns: in the first the main subject of each visual was noted; the second recorded the type of visual—artist's impression, spidergram, speech or thought bubble, painting, advertisement, logo, computer generated image, photograph and so on. The third recorded the presence, or not, of a title or other text specifically accompanying a visual, prompting questions about how these functioned. At this first stage it became clear that the visual field revealed by the second column was too extensive for this small study and also related closely to the concept of the "paratext" referred to above. Moreover, many of the visual types functioned as conveyors of text in manageable "bytes." Consequently each book was re-visited to check the initial tabulation of data, but now restricting the scope of the study to photographs; the second column now came to record the material composition of each photograph; put another way, it recorded responses to the question, "In what ways did the photographs use and represent the materiality of Christianity and Hinduism?" Whilst focusing on photographs alone is a selective exercise, its importance is underwritten by popular understanding of this medium as most closely corresponding with the "real" world—a perspective which masks both their complexity and the skills required to interpret them.[16]

This initial tabulation of the data facilitated examination of the following matters:

- the emphases of the photographs overall in portraying a religion in a particular book.
- the possibility of comparison of religions with other books in the series or across different series and in each case with different religions.
- assessing the dependence of photographs on the materiality of religion.

3.3.2. The next stage was to examine the relation of photographs and text; this took further the examination of captions assigned to photographs and the relation of the photographs to the author's narrative (including the chapter, unit or spread title). Recognition that textbooks often fail to use photographs to promote student learning,[17] led to looking for evidence of their use. These steps in the process facilitated

- clarification of the purposes of the pictures in the textbook and the ways in which photographs function;
- discussion of what kind of "seeing" was encouraged by the juxtaposition of text and photographs;
- reflection on whether the presence of the photographs and accompanying text help to develop students' interpretive skills in relation to the material aspects of the two religions, or construct obstacles to understanding.

3.4. Reflexivity

3.4.1. Throughout this process I was mindful of the importance of reflexivity in interpretive approaches to the study of religions; here I use it relation to my own perception of the images I have been examining. I am aware I come to them with my own convictions about RE; with an understanding of Hinduism acquired from academic study and from multiple sources, primary and secondary. Academic study of different aspects of Christianity and personal experience of the Anglican Church, as well as growing up in a society culturally shaped by the Christian tradition colour and inform my understanding of Christianity. In examining the photographs in the selected textbooks, I have tried to bring a descriptive and a "listening eye" to them, not least to be able to describe them here in words.

3.4.2. It is also important to be aware of the number of filters photographs pass through before reaching the page of the textbook: the photographer's eye and that of the camera; the eyes of author and publisher; their reproduction and context in the book, where the purposes they must serve may be distant from those of the original photograph. There is already a remoteness, a detachment from the moment shown in the photograph—and "moment" itself points to the limitations of photographs, although paradoxically a really good photograph potentially opens up new horizons and new ways of "seeing." A further problem arises in textbooks' persistent use of photographs out of time and place—decontextualized. Add to these matters a class of 30 young people each bringing their own perspectives and responses to the visuals in a textbook, and we can see some of the complexity involved in seeing, as well as the need for careful thought when selecting textbook photographs.

3.5. Findings of the exploratory study

I have already indicated the nature of the books selected for this study and the method I chose to employ. A single chapter does not allow for a book by book analysis and the following sections will therefore report on the books with reference first to the representation of Christianity and then to Hinduism. In each case I provide a brief overview of the emphases which emerged from the photographs used to represent each religion, and then offer selected case studies arising from these emphases.

The books selected represent changing approaches to religions in RE as well as changing styles in books. Approaches which have moved to an emphasis on "beliefs" or "issues" contain a greater number of visuals relating to "life issues" which could constitute a detailed study in their own right; for the purposes of this study I focused only on those which might be labelled or popularly recognized as having "religious" content.

For brevity I shall refer to the books by denoting the series with the letters A, B, C and D and the religion by X (Christianity) and H (Hinduism). AX is thus the earliest of the four series and is about Christianity. I also hope that this will ensure a measure of impartiality about the series. My intention is to focus on photographs used in the representation of two religious traditions, not to expose the particular books selected for this exercise.

4. CHRISTIANITY

4.1. Overview

Tabulation and subsequent categorization of the photographs in each book pointed to their particular emphases. Whilst the list of contents of a book might cover a range of subjects, its visual field examined *in its own right* may emerge as narrower or other than anticipated. This was so particularly in AX where pictures of *Religious officiants*[18]—bishops, priests, ministers—mainly in vestments and in varied liturgical contexts achieved visual dominance. In terms of gender (not our key concern in this study, but of interest) this led to imbalance, with the only image of a woman in a clerical role being the "Vicar of Dibley"—a comedy series on television about an Anglican "vicar" in an idiosyncratic rural parish. Elsewhere two nuns were shown working in a soup kitchen, and the face of Mother Theresa appeared in a section on Monks and Nuns. Other photographs in AX fell under a broad category of *Worship*, individual and communal, including baptism, confirmation, marriage and death; there was interplay here with those showing clergy. *Place* emerged as a smaller category, visually represented through buildings— churches and shrines. As with the other books, there was some reference to *Jesus*, and a scattered selection of representations of him.

Whilst diagrams were outside the limits set for this study, BX included a spidergram which caught my attention: its centre was labelled "Christianity has an impact on..." and its many "legs" (most ending in a little illustrative drawing) were labelled: Literature, Entertainment, The Calender (*sic.*), Buildings, Places, Jewellery, Name, The Arts, Rites of Passage, Food, Carnivals, YMCA/YWCA, Charities, Business, Vocabulary and speech, Sport, Flags, Laws. This diagram and its associated pictures demonstrated a material tradition, but simultaneously failed to see it as such; rather "Christianity" is essentialized and "other." A shift of perspective is needed here to allow students some insight into "how religion happens materially." BX does not make a strong visual impact, although tabulation of its visuals reveals a larger number than one anticipates. This serves to highlight size; some photographs are very small and presented in a collage to make their impact in that way—to point to a range of Christian symbols for example, thereby signalling the subject matter of one unit. In this book, on the whole, photographs matched the subject of the unit in which they were placed. Viewed in their own right the photographs in BX fall into broad categories of *Place and buildings*; *Liturgy, Rites and ritual*; *People*—largely related to the former category and as in AX some *representations of Jesus* or events in his life are used.

Although DX is a later publication than CX, in design and approach it occupies a place somewhere between the style of the two earlier books and that of CX; AX and BX gave only a little attention to "issues," the intention of DX is to bring together belief and issues, but in effect its photographs (excluding life issues) fall into categories comparable to those we have already identified: *Buildings*, with interiors and aspects of these featuring quite prominently; *People* variously engaged—a child praying, a man meditating (we are told), a woman reading a Bible, a person receiving communion, for example—appear frequently. And as in the other books *pictures of Jesus* in varying contexts and presented through differing media are included.

Visually CX is a very different book from the others; almost twice as long as its companion volume on Hinduism it is able to give extensive treatment to "issues" and the "religion" element is treated according to a distinctive conceptual framework—"Looking for Meaning"—subdivided into four sub units: Beliefs and Concepts; Expressions of Spirituality; Authority and Science, and Religion. Relatively few pictures are of explicitly religious subjects. The rather staid pictures of churches are gone—in favour of just three: a church being built "in the 21st century"; St Peter's Rome with a crowded square; a photograph of the twentieth century martyrs on the west front of Westminster Abbey. All point to a living and relevant tradition in the present. Pictures of people include a police chaplain at work, an army chaplain celebrating Eucharist whilst in a field situation (accompanied by an extract in which he reflects on his work) and a "cut out" picture of a young man working as a missioner in a new town. These are very different images of those in clerical or official roles than those presented in the other texts. Some use is made of art and there are a few pictures depicting services, as in the other books. The whole impression of this book however is of montage, use of a large range of resources, but not specific engagement with "seeing" in relation to most of the photographs, although a few, of pamphlets for example, are used to promote student engagement.

This brief overview of the books on Christianity points clearly to the materiality of this tradition; not only does the tradition promote this or generate it, but it is arguably a—if not *the* key medium through which it is commonly encountered. Whilst particular aspects of Christianity emerge in varying "strength" across the books, there remains a piecemeal effect in these texts; none offers an ongoing visual text which might be possible if books provided the opportunity for students to study the particular, rather than the generalised.

4.2. Case studies
I now turn to a number of short descriptive case studies[19] which are drawn from the categories identified in 4.1; in doing this I shall comment also on the contexts the selected pictures were given within the authors' narrative, on their integration with any learning process or activities, and on their relation to accompanying captions.

4.2.1. Religious officiants. The "officiants" in AX are men—and it may be assumed those ordained or otherwise recognized by their respective churches. They appear in differing contexts which comprise some of the book's key concerns: baptism; confirmation; marriage; funerals; Easter Vigil and so on. Overall the male figure dominates—even where captions may signal another message. Care has been taken to present different traditions: Baptist; Roman Catholic; Church of England; Methodist; "Orthodox"; Armenian orthodox; Coptic; African. If we were asking a question about showing Christian diversity this book might score highly. But students are given little to help them interpret this diversity—simply the names of probably unfamiliar churches. Furthermore even to be told what is happening may confirm the strangeness of a picture to a student. A picture captioned "An Orthodox girl receives communion on a spoon" directs one to look at this practice; but the dominant figure visually remains the priest, with long hair and beard and wearing purple and gold vestments. Adjacent to this is a photograph of a Coptic priest with long hair and bearded, robed in white and with head covered by a white veil. He is accompanied by a server in white robe carrying flat bread; the scene is in a darkened building lit by candles. A woman can be seen at one side, kneeling and receiving the bread from the priest. The eye takes in the whole at a glance, perhaps before the directional caption is noted; this reads "A Coptic communion service. Notice the flat, Eastern style bread." Whilst captions direct attention photographs may pull in other directions—What of the dress of the priests? Why their long hair and beards? What of their role in the scene we can see? What do these pictures say of the role and relation of the priest to others in the pictures? And a caption may itself distract despite the information it conveys—Who are the Copts? The text doesn't mention them at all, although it does elaborate on Orthodox practice, adding that they receive "bread and wine on a spoon mixed together." In fact the narrative seems to have a preoccupation with the type of bread used in different communities and the manner of receiving bread and wine—even to the extent of speaking about the digestibility of the unleavened bread used by Roman Catholics and Anglicans. A related task suggests that students look at these pictures and "Describe any two methods of receiving communion that different Christians have. What do these different methods suggest?" In this case study, visuals, captions, narrative and activities are in tension and arguably run counter to each other.

4.2.2. *Church buildings—interiors.* Across the selected textbooks church interiors are placed in various contexts—worship, symbols, places of worship, the authority of God, and divisions and denominations for example. Few photographs of churches were of sufficient quality to really command interest, but for anyone prepared to look, here are material expressions of Christian belief and practice. This was particularly so in the case of the interior of a Roman Catholic Church in DX, placed in a unit on "places of worship."

A Roman Catholic church
The church is shown empty, but this photograph offers a lot of detail, especially of the sanctuary (although this word is not introduced or explored) and its arrangement: a central raised altar and tabernacle, a baldaccino with Latin inscription over the altar, candles, sanctuary lights, lectern with linen fall embroidered with symbols of wheat, and a font with an adjacent paschal candle. The pews can be seen in the foreground of the photograph, set back from but facing the "theatrical" setting of the sanctuary, where something clearly happens or is enacted. One is very aware of space in this picture and how it is used for a purpose.

The caption reads: "This Catholic church contains an altar and statues of the Virgin Mary." The presence of an altar (in Catholic, Orthodox and Anglican churches) is reinforced in the author's narrative, with an indication of where the priest may stand in relation to it (although no reasons are given); there is no other reference to statues here. None of the tasks related to places of worship require any specific engagement with this visual resource. The tasks do try to encourage students to think about the importance a church might have for worship for some Christians, whilst others may "prefer the open air surrounded by nature," but the concept of "place" or "sacred space" is not explored here, despite passing uses of "holy" and "holiness" in relation to churches. There is little here to help students make sense of the picture, to "read" what is there, nor any serious attention to concepts.

An Anglican church

This photograph, also in DX, shows a service in progress; the photograph has been taken from a raised position behind the congregation. We look down on the greying hair and balding heads of a sparse congregation, standing and with open books in their hands. But one's eye is directed beyond them to the chancel and altar; if it was not cut off in this photograph the chancel arch would further align our eyes to the centre of this scene. Robed clergy mark a boundary line between nave and chancel. This is a picture for a time capsule—perhaps of 30 years ago, not for 11–14 year olds students in the twenty-first century. But this is not here to explore an Anglican church, nor what is seen here of worship, but in the words of its caption:

> Most Christians believe that it is important to meet with other believers to worship God. In this way they come to know the will of God.

The author's narrative confirms that for Christians this is one of the ways of knowing the will of God, a dominant theme in this unit on "The Authority of God" where this picture is placed. This is textbook illustration by word association and as a hook for another issue; it demonstrates the secondary importance apparently given to visuals in students' learning by publisher and author alike.

4.2.3. *Jesus*. In representing Jesus books draw on a range of media: paintings; tapestry; sculpture; fresco; icon. Consequently, in seeing these, another perspective comes in, that of the artist. Occasionally we are told who this was, or when the work was produced. The place or person it was commissioned for (if this was the case), the work's dimensions and (where appropriate) its present location are often absent—even in the photo credits. The first example below is unusual in providing some of this contextual evidence.

A painting of Jesus on the underground

This small picture in CX sits on a left-hand page, with its right edge caught in the binding, leaving one uncertain as to whether the whole scene is shown. As shown, Jesus, in scarlet cloak and striped robe sits upright with arms folded; he is dark haired and bearded, with large golden nimbus. His eyes, open, look steadily and fixedly forward. On his right sits a young woman, legs crossed, eyes closed; she is brightly and trendily dressed. On his left a striped suited business man, newspaper wide open and head and eyes averted from Jesus, looking in the opposite direction; on the man's left, an older woman—obscured by the book binding noted above. The London underground sign visible through the window of the carriage indicates "Knightsbridge." The author's immediate narrative asks the question, Who is Jesus? (as part of a unit on the Authority of Jesus), exploring his historicity, his human and divine nature, and claiming a substitutional interpretation of the cross for Christians. The narrative would require a theologically literate teenager to link it with the picture. The caption however begins in a promising way

> The artist Antonia Rolls said the inspiration for her unusual painting was that Jesus could well be sitting next to you right now.

This information and the picture itself offer in my view excellent material for exploration with the intended age group. Note however that the caption continues with a second sentence:

> In the rush of daily life, we don't stop to notice the person squashed next to us or give them a second thought.

The activities do not include further consideration of this picture, but adjacent to it is another, whose subject and artist are unspecified for the reader.[20] Students are instructed to

> Compare this traditional picture of Jesus with the one on page 32 [that described above]. Which do you prefer?

Space doesn't permit a full description of the "traditional picture" here, but it is a dark scene (in this reproduction at least) showing Jesus with long hair and robe, standing with Peter who holds an oversized set of keys.[21] One might ask in what sense this is "traditional" and for whom? Is it so for the particular period in which it was painted; is this the author's view of what is "traditional" or of what she thinks students, or Christians regard as traditional? And precisely what is one to compare? Can this task be other than very superficial in the absence of necessary background? What is appropriate material for comparison? And how does this example serve this particular unit? What insights and skills might students develop here? Such questions shout for answers here.

4.2.4. *Icons.* Three of the books included an icon as illustration, but only CX made icons the subject of a unit: "The Code breakers," with the objective "to look at the use of art to convey a spiritual idea." This is a unit full of good intentions, but tends to present conflicting messages. A further issue which immediately hits the eye is the priority of design over sensitivity towards the image shown. On a right hand page and filling most of it is a reproduction of an icon of the Virgin and Child,[22] but this is partly obscured by a an overlaid panel of 7cms width giving the "key to the code," comprising ten points set out in some detail (though not all relevant in the case of the icon shown); an activity panel, and a reference letter for the icon also impinge. Moreover as a consequence part of the symbolism of this icon of the Theotokos (Mother of God) of the Passion is lost[23]—but then the icon is not named for students, and so its subject and the particularity of its symbolism are missed.[24]

The unit begins with students invited to describe the cut out photograph of a smiling and attractive looking young man—and to suggest evidence for character, and what he would be like as a friend. It moves to an analogy of icons on a computer screen—which open up to a bigger picture "and then the possibilities are endless"—with painted icons as "windows into heaven," an analogy which inevitably breaks down if pushed too far. A brief account is offered of Orthodox devotion before an icon and compared with having a photograph of a loved person, which signifies "the real person they are thinking of."

An activity invites students to use the "key to the code" to read the icon, and

Then write a brief description of what the artist has done to show worshippers what heaven is like.

and

Do you think the icon...conveys more information than a photograph would? Why?

Students are next given a quotation to explain:

What does the modern British icon painter Brother Aidan mean when he says icons are intended to "introduce you to reality, not to imitate nature. It is to show you not what you see, but what is real." (*Faith in Conservation*, 2003)

In this case study one empathizes with the author who is working hard on the one hand to convey something of the significance icons may hold for Orthodox Christians, but on the other is concerned with "code breaking," whilst the fundamental objective is to look at the "use of art to convey a spiritual idea." Regrettably despite the potential "attraction" of code breaking to some students, and analogies with photographs, somehow the objective is not realized. Perhaps a different starting point was needed—one rooted in the spirituality of the icon painter, the process and natural materials which are themselves transformed in the painting of an icon, a process of which Brother Aidan (quoted above) has written simply and eloquently and with theological depth (Brother Aidan 1991: 3–10).

5. HINDUISM

5.1. Overview

A comparison of the list of contents in books which belong to one series but cover different religions indicates that in the main publishers try to adopt a common framework across the series; this demands authors who are able to ensure that the particularity of a religion speaks through such frameworks which often derive from implicitly Christian perspectives. When analysed through photographs alone it is interesting to note the respective emergent categories for Christianity and Hinduism. Most prevalent in the Hindu texts were photographs of the gods or deities. This had no real parallel in the books on Christianity; at one level this may be expected—Christianity has a strong anionic tradition in relation to "God." Yet portrayal of Jesus (and Mary and the Saints) is prolific—though not in these textbooks.[25] The visual dominance of "religious officiants" appears peculiar to the Christian texts, whilst those on Hinduism show a number of famous Hindus. The focus on the deities—whether in murtis, popular colourful posters, paintings, miniatures or illustrations from popular books—was common to all the books on Hinduism and particularly evident in BH which devotes four of its chapters to the concept of "God" and uses images of the deities in other sections too; whilst these are occasionally supported by simple comments from (fictional?) Hindu voices, the absence of sources or context may give the feel of a visit to a museum with "dead" exhibits. CH has an opening page (5) to its first major section (Looking for Meaning: One God in many forms) showing six poster images (Kali, Lakshmi, Durga, Rama and Sita, Shiva and Parvati with Ganesh and Radha and Krishna—all un-named in the text) whilst a small inset of four pictures depicting flowers, water, sun and moon is placed alongside these. The text asks, and then takes up the question

> What is God? Power, nature, love, human, animal, male, female, creator, carer or destroyer?

Analysis of DH pointed to the use of pictures showing people variously involved in *ritual actions* linked also to space and place, whilst *place* emerged as a category from AH, sometimes also showing people. Echoing a concern with life's stages in the books on Christianity, *Samskaras* relating to birth, upanaya (sacred thread ceremony), marriage and death figure in series A, B and C. *Symbol* also occurs in these in its own right, as well as in relation to the depiction of various deities. I also became aware of a succession of *named people* pictured *across* these books: Chaitanya; Gandhi; Indira Gandhi; Sai Baba; Swami Vivekananda; A. C. Bhaktivedanta; Pramukh Swami Maharaj, or of people identified by status in pictures: two shaktas; a Brahmin priest; dalit/"Untouchables"; a Vaishnavite priest; a sadhu; a "Hindu holy man." Sometimes such figures in posture, dress and symbol may relate to the text, but they are rarely present on the page as more than illustration of a word used in the text; for many students the unfamiliarity of such pictures and the absence of any contexualization is likely to prove alienating.

As with Christianity, the case studies which follow are selected from some of the dominant visual categories found in the books.

5.2. Case studies

5.2.1. Sacred trees: two examples. Each of the books analysed tries to convey something of a Hindu respect for nature. One of the best photographs in AH in terms of clarity and size (half a page), shows and is captioned: "A tree offering in Calcutta." The photograph shows the gnarled roots of a tree, suggestive of great age; around it there is a low raised platform, painted red. On this are placed a number of oval shaped almost black stones; a garland of yellow and pink flowers weaves through the stones which are also scattered with fresh green leaves. The picture is in a section headed *Hindus show respect to all nature* one of a number of statements explored in a chapter on "What Hindus believe." The authors' narrative employs words from the Mahabharata, which support the picture

> ...even if there is only one tree full of flowers and fruits in a village, that place becomes worthy of worship and respect.

Whilst the related tasks do not explore the picture, one stems from it, implicitly inviting students to reflect on the picture and the words from the Mahabharata:

> Work out a ceremony for either planting a new tree or encouraging respect for a very old tree.

Note here that the task arises from what students have met of a Hindu respect for nature; I draw attention to this since it illustrates the possibility of extending student experience by introducing something new and unfamiliar and then reflecting on and engaging personally with what has been encountered.

In a unit on the Mandir, DH includes a picture with the caption "A wayside shrine in India. Many of them are tiny." The author's narrative helpfully relates that "there are many shrines alongside the roads and in the villages of India."

Although its size and clarity is not good for use with students, close inspection of the photograph reveals a lot of detail: a low platform surrounds the base of a tree which is central to the photograph; on the platform can be seen a number of small stone images and lingas. Offerings are being made by a small group of very dark skinned women seemingly dressed in black, with heads covered; a young barefooted boy stands with them. One of the women holds a small clay pot, and offerings of flowers can just be seen before some of the images. Around the trunk of the tree are tied numerous coloured threads. This tree stands not far from what may be the entrance to a small mandir, painted white—with ubiquitous Pepsi-Cola signs on adjacent walls. Readers are not directed to the picture, nor does the text directly speak of the tree. In fact the picture seems to have little purpose here, despite its caption; and the narrative noted above does not after all seem to include such trees at all. The narrative continues, speaking of mandir and shrine:

> Both kinds of *building* [my italics] express the belief that Brahman, the Supreme Spirit, is to be found everywhere and takes on many forms.

In the next paragraph "shrine" features again, now identified as the place housing a murti in the mandir. Not only is this photograph unused, it is also redundant as illustration since the narrative runs counter to what is seen, and is also in itself somewhat confusing.

5.2.2. *A Mandir interior.* Below the picture of the wayside shrine referred to above DH includes a larger picture, "Inside a Hindu Temple." No clues are given at all to the interpretation of the scene. Facing the viewer a framed picture of the head of Shiva is central; to the left of this is a large framed picture of Shirdi Sai Baba, to the right a picture of Sathya Sai Baba; a smaller picture of the latter is also in front of Shiva but at a lower level, with a small golden murti of Ganesh placed on either side. On the wall high above this arrangement of garlanded pictures are four plaques each showing a symbol representative of others' traditions: Muslim, Parsee, Christian and Buddhist. Beyond these key features there are many other details to notice. As far as I can see there is no reference at all in DH to Sathya Sai Baba, or to the place of the guru in Hindu tradition; moreover there is actually little in this picture which correlates with an adjacent eight-legged spidergram which indicates "Symbols found in the mandir" and which becomes the focus of a task for students. The picture also raises the question of whether this is a mandir, or a centre for those who are followers of Sathya Sai Baba. Again it is important to ask what is communicated through visuals when students have no information which is genuinely relevant to their interpretation.

5.2.3. *The Ganges—two examples.* Photographs of the Ganges appear in three of the books, but in different contexts: Pilgrimage AH; Symbols (Water); Pilgrimage BH; Dealing with death; Ahimsa DH. Images are either of bathing in the Ganges or of funeral pyres by the Ganges—very small and incidental photographs in the case of AH and BH. DH offers two very clear and large photographs. That under "Ahimsa" is across two pages and offers a close up of men washing in the river; one stands in water to the waist with his hands together and eyes closed. The feel here is of a somewhat intrusive zoom lens. And to what purpose? The author's narrative makes no reference to the Ganges or pilgrimage, nor to the men we see. Not so the caption, which claims

> These Hindu pilgrims are washing on the banks of the Ganges. They all share a strong belief in the doctrine of ahimsa.

In the second picture of the Ganges, a half-page picture, the viewer joins the back of a crowd of men and women, some are sitting on the ghats on "this" side of the river, some standing—all looking to the opposite side where funeral pyres burn or are being prepared. Behind these, on what appears to be a raised promenade, others look down to the pyres or simply pass by. The river itself is quite narrow here—and silted, not one of the expansive views which linger in the mind. The author's narrative refers to the subsequent scattering of ashes on rivers, especially the Ganges and of escaping rebirth; a caption tells the reader that what is shown is a common sight by rivers, and that this is the Ganges. Although the narrative of the Unit has taken the reader through details of rituals at death, this picture conveys much about attitudes to death and would I think prompt many questions from young people. It exemplifies the power the visual may have beyond the written text.

5.2.4. *Deities: Krishna and Arjun.* Reference was made above to the colourful posters of the gods with which CH opens. A colourful poster placed within the author's opening narrative depicts Vishvarupa, multi-armed and face flanked by the faces of many deities; he is richly dressed and bejewelled; at his feet we see the awed figure of Arjun in his chariot, and the figure of Krishna instructing him on the field of Kurukshetra, its tents forming a backcloth against a glowing sky. Within the context of the narrative this is used as an illustration of "how Bhagwan can take endless forms" and it is explained that his many arms show strength. The comment is appropriate, and subsequent tasks encourage students to think of ways of expressing the multiple ideas people may have of God. But the picture also poses the question of the amount of information which students need to make sense of visuals of this kind, as well as consideration of the cultural gulf many will need to navigate.

Some books offer many details about the visual symbols associated with particular murtis—Siva Nataraj is a popular subject in this respect, others simply give a name and provide no help with interpretation. Books might suggest approaches to this type of visual, an example of interpretation and then perhaps an opportunity for students to apply what they have learnt to a further picture. Access to some data about the provenance of the visuals would also be particularly helpful where photographs draw on different types of material—poster, painting, miniature, and sculpture for example—as in BH. That these media are overlaid in textbooks by their presentation in photographic form brings further complexity to interpretation. Furthermore textbooks give no guidance to students in relation to interpreting these different kinds of visual materials.

6. CONCLUSION

This chapter opened with a short reflection on religion and materiality, noting a shift from thinking of a "material dimension" or "material expression" of religion to understanding materiality as a "given," appropriated, shaped and reshaped by religions in a multiplicity of ways; and, in turn, moulding, changing and challenging those belonging to them—and sometimes those outside too. As Eck reminds us the seer both sees and is seen.

I next suggested that RE has pedagogically drawn on such materiality—by various means—to encourage student engagement and that the richness and immediacy of experience students may have had presents a challenge to textbooks. In the light of my subsequent study of selected textbooks, this challenge lies in two directions. First, the quality and nature of the photographs used (individually and collectively) to represent religions and second, the opportunities textbooks offer for students to develop interpretive skills and insight in relation to what they see. What is *seen* needs to be fundamental to the book, not just an adjunct to the text. The two belong together. My case studies (4.2 and 5.2 above) demonstrated that this is rarely the case; the studies have pointed to a range of problems which need not be repeated here, but call for research and resolution.

If students are to learn to interpret what they *see* of religion in textbooks, then more attention needs to be given to the use of the photographs as evidence, but also as offering insight into and empathy for others' beliefs and spirituality. Knowing the provenance of the visuals is important here, and this in turn might sharpen decisions about what is included and the context it is given. Developing skills and insight also calls for attention to students' visual literacy. Interpreting what is seen is a multi-layered task; different images require different kinds of question and varied pathways of research. RE has given too little attention to this.

Students live in a world of fleeting visual images. The textbook belongs to a more static world—yet it is perhaps just this that suggests its potential for offering students space to develop a reflective approach to what they *see* of religion materially—not only in textbooks but in the communities in which they live.[26]

REFERENCES

Bourdillon, Hilary, ed. 1992. *History and Social Studies—Methodologies of Textbook Analysis.* Report of the Educational Research Workshop held in Braunschweig (Germany), 11-14 September 1990. European Meetings on Educational Research 27. Amsterdam: Swets & Zeitlinger.

Brother Aidan. 1991. *Sacred Icons Paradise Regained.* An Oriel 31 Touring Exhibition of 17th 18th 19th Early 20th Century and Contemporary Icons. Oriel 31, Davies Memorial Gallery: Newtown, Powys, Wales.

Choppin, Alain. 1992. "Aspects of Design." In *History and Social Studies—Methodologies of Textbook Analysis,* ed. Hilary Bourdillon, 85–95. Report of the Educational Research Workshop held in Braunschweig (Germany), 11-14 September 1990. European Meetings on Educational Research 27. Amsterdam: Swets & Zeitlinger.

David, Robert G. 2000. "Imagining the Past: The Use of Archive Pictures in Secondary School History Textbooks." *Curriculum Journal* 11(2): 225–46.

Eck, Diana L. 1985. *Darśan: Seeing the Divine Image in India.* Chambersburg, PA: Anima Books, 2nd edn.

Erricker, Clive, with Alan Brown, Mary Hayward, Dilip Kadodwala and Paul Williams, eds. 1993. *Teaching World Religions: A Teachers' Handbook produced by the Shap Working Party on World Religions in Education.* Oxford: Heinemann Educational.

Hayward, Mary, and Paul Hopkins. 2010. *Resources for Teaching about World Religions in English Schools: An Audit.* Department for Children, Schools and Families. London.

Hinnells, John, R. 1990. "Religion and the Arts." In *Turning Points in Religious Studies: Essays in Honour of Geoffrey Parrinder,* ed. Ursula King, 257–74. Edinburgh: T&T Clark.

Hirst, Jacqueline.1993: "Learning How to look: Teaching Hinduism in the Secondary School." In *Teaching World Religions: A Teachers' Handbook produced by the Shap Working Party on World*

Religions in Education, ed. Clive Erricker, with Alan Brown, Mary Hayward, Dilip Kadodwala, and Paul Williams, 94–98. Oxford: Heinemann Educational.

Horrigan, Norah, E. 1981. "Reflections on a Synagogue Visit." *British Journal of Religious Education* 3(4): 165–66.

Jackson, Robert, Julia Ipgrave, Mary Hayward, Paul Hopkins, Nigel Fancourt, Mandy Robbins, Leslie Francis and Ursula McKenna. 2010. *Materials Used to Teach about World Religions in Schools in England.* Research Report DCSF—RR197. London: Department for Children, Schools and Families.

King, Ursula, ed. 1990. *Turning Points in Religious Studies: Essays in Honour of Geoffrey Parrinder.* Edinburgh: T&T Clark.

Marsden, William E. 2001. *The School Textbook: Geography, History and Social Studies.* London: Woburn Press.

Miles, Margaret R. 2005. *The Word Made Flesh: A History of Christian Thought.* Oxford: Blackwell.

Morgan, David. 2005. *The Sacred Gaze: Religious Visual Culture in Theory and Practice.* Berkeley/Los Angeles/London: University of California Press.

Morgan, David, ed. 2010. *Religion and Material Culture: The Matter of Belief.* Abingdon: Oxford/New York: Routledge.

Meyer, Birgit, David Morgan, Crispin Paine and S. Brent Plate. 2010. "The Origin and Mission of Material Religion." *Religion* 40: 207–11.

Meyer, Birgit, David Morgan, Crispin Paine and S. Brent Plate. 2011. "Introduction: Key Words in Material Religion." *Material Religion* 7(1): 4–9.

Northcote, Vivien Hornby. 2010. *The Use of Italian Renaissance Art in Victorian Religious Education.* Lampeter, Wales: Edward Mellen Press.

Pingel, Falk. 2010. *UNESCO Guidebook on Textbook Research and Textbook Revision.* Paris/Braunschweig: UNESCO/George Eckert Institute for International Textbook Research, 2nd revised and updated edn.

Qualifications and Curriculum Authority. 2004. *Religious Education: The Non-Statutory National Framework.* London: QCA/Department for Education and Skills.

Slater, John. 1992. "Report." In *History and Social Studies—Methodologies of Textbook Analysis*, ed. Hilary Bourdillon, 11–20. Report of the Educational Research Workshop held in Braunschweig (Germany), 11-14 September 1990. European Meetings on Educational Research 27. Amsterdam: Swets & Zeitlinger.

Smart, Ninian. 1968. *Secular Education and the Logic of Religion.* London: Faber & Faber.

Smart, Ninian. 1969. *The Religious Experience of Mankind.* New York: Charles Scribner's Sons.

Smart, Ninian. 1989/1992. *The World's Religions.* Cambridge: Cambridge University Press.

Smart, Ninian. 1996. *Dimensions of the Sacred: An Anatomy of the World's Beliefs.* London: Harper Collins.

Unsworth, Len. 2001. *Teaching Multiliteracies across the Curriculum.* Buckingham: Open University Press.

Woodward, Ian. 2007. *Understanding Material Culture.* London: SAGE.

Source material for the study was drawn from the following student texts:

Christianity

Aylett, J. F., and K. O'Donnell. 2000. *The Christian Experience.* Seeking Religion Series. London: Hodder Murray, 2nd edn.

Gibson, Lynne. 2002. *Christianity.* Modern World Religions Series. Oxford: Heinemann.

Taylor, Ina. 2006. *Christianity*. Religions and Beliefs Series. Cheltenham: Nelson Thornes.
Keene, Michael. 2007. *Christian Beliefs and Issues*. Badger KS3 RE Series. Stevenage: Badger Publishing.

Hinduism

Aylett, Liz, and Kevin O'Donnell. 2011. *The Hindu Experience*. Seeking Religion Series. London: Hodder Murray, 2nd edn.
Gibson, Lynne. 2002: *Hinduism*. Modern World Religions Series. Oxford: Heinemann.
Vyas, Neera. 2006. *Hinduism*. Religions and Beliefs Series. Cheltenham: Nelson Thornes.
Keene, Michael. 2007. *Hindu Beliefs and Issues*. Badger KS3 RE Series. Stevenage: Badger Publishing.

Endnotes

1. See, e.g., Woodward (2007: ch. 2).
2. See Meyer, Morgan, Paine and Plate (2011).
3. Contextually this statement comes at the end of an exposition of "seeing" in relation to Jan Gossaert's "St. Luke Drawing the Virgin."
4. Unfortunately whilst preparing this chapter I did not have access to Morgan (2010), which develops this theme more fully.
5. For the purposes of this chapter, I shall from this point use "materiality" to point to those aspects of religion which are encountered through sight, sound, touch, taste and smell. But because our concern is textbooks we are limited to meeting these through sight.
6. See, e.g., Hayward and Hopkins (2010) for an overview of the range of media available to teachers and students.
7. What we would now more properly call "instruction."
8. For an example of this see Hirst (1993: 94–98).
9. A memorable phrase used originally in relation to visits in RE (Horrigan 1981: 165).
10. Since its use in legislation for RE, this terminology has become widely used in England, referring to Christianity + Buddhism, Hinduism, Islam, Judaism, Sikhism.
11. The basic curriculum (RE+National Curriculum) in maintained schools in England is structured in four key stages, corresponding to the age groups: 5–7; 7–11; 11–14 and 14–16.
12. The series *Framework RE* (Hodder Murray 2005/2006) particularly demonstrates this point.
13. Jackson *et al.* (2010) is the first major national study. I note also that RE textbooks appear to lie outside the remit of the Georg-Eckert International Institute for Textbook Research at Braunschweig. For perspectives on issues in textbook research the RE researcher often has to turn to work undertaken in History, Social Studies or Geography. See, e.g., Marsden (2001).
14. Pingel (2010: 49) and David (2000: 243) make passing reference to this.
15. There is of course a discussion to be had about the use of "primary" here—as my observations at 3.4.2 imply.
16. Space here does not permit a visual analysis of photographs, but see, e.g., Unsworth where this is introduced in his chapter "Describing Visual Literacies" (2001: 71–112).
17. See Jackson *et al.* (2010: 51f, 63f).
18. I use "religious officiants" to reflect the photographic evidence, but also as a more inclusive term than "clergy."

19. Writing about the photographs necessitates describing them; I am *not* suggesting that this is how they should be approached in RE. Rather I hope that the case studies will prompt thought about the relation of photographs and text and about the function of photographs in textbooks.

20. A search in the Acknowledgements indicates that it is Jesus Returning the Keys to Peter, 1820 (oil on canvas), Jean Auguste Dominique (1780–1867) and to be found in the Musée Ingres in France. CX stands out from the other series in providing this kind of detail in Acknowledgements.

21. An image which might have contributed appropriately to the theme of the unit—the Authority of Jesus.

22. The Acknowledgements simply indicate that this icon is from the sixteenth century, of the Greek school and to be found in the Church of San Martino in Venice. Further research indicated that the icon is the Theotokos of the Passion; a good quality reproduction of this subject can be seen online at http://www.institutoellenico.org/museo/12.html (accessed 4.08.11).

23. Specifically, one of the two angels holding symbols of the Passion.

24. Presumably because the author was concerned with "icons" in general rather than their subjects—although these would seem to be fundamental to understanding icons as "windows into heaven."

25. Interestingly this visual reticence in the Christian books is matched by a verbal reticence about God which is not there in the textbooks on Hinduism. This deserves further exploration, but lies outside the scope of this chapter.

26. Readers may care to reflect how frequently it is religion "happening materially" which triggers conflict and debate.

8. CARTOGRAPHIC REPRESENTATIONS OF RELIGION(S) IN NORWEGIAN TEXTBOOKS

*Suzanne Anett Thobro**

Since the 1970s, world maps have been used in Norwegian textbooks to visualize the spread of religions across the world. In this chapter I examine cartographic representations of religions in textbooks for Norwegian upper secondary schools in the period from 1970 to the present. Thematic maps that seek to demonstrate the prevalence of religions "translate" abstract categories into two-dimensional surfaces, and in this "translation" a series of choices are made. These choices are determined by the discourse(s) the textbooks utilize. I wish to shed light on this usage of maps by means of discourse analysis and critical cartography. In addition to giving an overview of which religions have been given a place on maps, the chapter also focuses on how religions are "spatialized" through cartographic representations.

AN OFFICIAL DISCOURSE ON RELIGION

What is religion? The answer to this question is not solely given by religious institutions and religious peoples themselves. Our everyday conception of religion is also shaped by secular institutions like the public school system.[1] Sociologist Peter Beyer (2003: 154–57) distinguishes three main systemic perspectives—what I would call primary discourses—on religion: theological, academic and "official." In these three discourses the understanding of what religion is differs. The "official" discourse is, according to Beyer, formed by the institutional systems of politics, law, education and mass media, and in its own domain this discourse constructs what we perceive as religion in a more or less different way than do the other two discourses. Textbooks, though they incorporate both theological and scientific perspectives, are a part of this official discourse and by studying how religion and religions are represented in them, one can get a look into how reli-

* Suzanne Anett Thobro is a PhD student at the Department of History and Religious Studies, University of Tromsø. Thobro is currently writing her PhD thesis on the topic of cartographic representations of religions in textbooks used by the Norwegian upper secondary school system.

gion, as it is conventionally conceived, is constructed. This chapter, then, is not an attempt to provide an answer to the question "what is religion?", but rather to shed light on what textbooks represent for their readers as religion. I will do this, as I said, through critical cartography—looking at *maps*.

CRITICAL CARTOGRAPHY AND MAPS ON RELIGION

According to Jeremy Crampton (2010: 17), there are four basic principles of critical cartography, three of which I adopt in this chapter. The first principle is that critical cartography examines how maps organize and produce knowledge, and how this knowledge is limited by conventional ways of thinking about the world around us. In the present chapter, this means the highlighting of how religion(s) are presented on textbooks maps and what kind of conventional assumptions about religion can be deduced from them. The second principle is that one examines the knowledge produced in maps by placing them in time and space. All of the maps considered in this article are produced in different historical periods, and they are all produced in Norway. Therefore, the knowledge about religion(s) in these maps is from a Norwegian point of view—this is the world (of religion) seen from Norway at specific points in time. The third principle is that knowledge exists in different power relations. As Crampton formulates it: "geographic knowledge is shaped by a whole array of social, economic, and historical forces..." (2010: 17). Crampton's fourth principle is that critical cartography is emancipatory, meaning that it tries to overthrow or dismantle official forms of knowledge. This last principle I see as problematic, and I am not sure it is more than a theoretical possibility. This is not the time or place to discuss it, so here I will just state that the present chapter stops with the critical examination, and does not seek alternative knowledge or alternative ways of representing.

WHY MAPS?

Maps can be defined as "graphic representations that facilitate a spatial understanding of things, concepts, conditions, processes, or events in the human world" (Harley and Woodward 1987: xvi, cited in Crampton 2010: 21).[2] The maps I seek to examine in this article are thus *graphic representations that facilitate a spatial understanding of religion*. The four principles for critical cartography mentioned above are shared with other critical theories, and I see critical cartography as a subcategory of discourse theory. Placing myself in a foucauldian tradition, I use Parker's definition of a discourse: "a system of statements which constructs an object" (1989: 61).[3] In maps, statements about religion are cartographic, a visual representation that seeks to represent religion geographically. To develop my definition of textbook maps on religion: *Maps, being a system of graphic representations that facilitate a spatial understanding (statements), constructs religion and religions as spatial objects.* This "spatialization" of religions is also present in metageographical terms such as "world religion," which is a widely used term both in academic and official discourses on religion.

In textbooks there seems to be a general tendency towards an ideal of describing religions as abstract objects, with no relations to time or space.[4] The moment one visualizes religion(s) cartographically, spatialization occurs, albeit still as abstract object(s). Depending on the map view and on where the different religions (or adherents) are placed on the map, the different religions are made into local, regional or world religions, and more or less affixed to specific areas. The term "local religion" is used to some extent in academic discourse on religion, but "regional religion" is seldom employed. As I will show in this chapter, in textbooks—though not used as a textual expression—"regional religion" is often used as a representational and cartographical statement about religion(s).

According to discourse theory any cultural or social product, including maps, can be analysed as text, and that is what critical cartography does. This however does not mean that maps do not differ from written texts in certain important aspects, and it is this difference that makes maps, in my view, even more exiting as an object for analysis. A map is a kind of medium that, more than written text, invokes objectivity. Although "map is not territory" is a well-known expression, our expectation for a map is that it represents the territory in a truthful way. The reason for this lies in the history of cartography as a discipline developed as a (seemingly) more and more accurate science (Harley 2001 [1990]: 35). Only recently in that history—beginning in the 80s—has the discursive function of maps has come under critical examination.[5]

But how can a map make a statement about what religion is? A map does not give us a definition of religion, but the choices made in a map construct what counts as religion and, more accurately, what counts as important enough to be shown on a map visualizing the geographical spread of religions across the world. There are some basic principles in mapmaking that are useful to have in mind while analysing maps: downscaling, generalization and selection of information (Karrow 2007: 3-6). These are more or less intuitive, but because maps tend to be treated as non-fictional (Karrow 2007: 4-5), it is easy to forget that they all constitute choices. In textbooks, when thematic maps are used (which they mainly are), this means that the diversity of religions in the world has to be cut down to a "sensible" number that can be translated into visually coherent areas on the world map. All of these choices, which a mapmaker is bound to do, results in some features being left in, others left out—the latter category, because of a map's nature, are always bigger than the former. The choices a constructor of a world map visualizing religion will have to make are not just which religions to leave in and which to leave out, but also what constitutes a religion and in what kind of detail level the different religions should be shown. Should one for example visualize "Christianity" with or without distinguishing between different denominations?

MAPS IN TEXTBOOKS

The textbooks in question are all from the upper secondary school, from the many-named subject on religion.[6] I have examined a number of books from the period 1935–2010.[7] In 1935 a new Education Act came into force, and with this, history of religions (i.e., religions other than Christianity), were made mandatory for the subject on religion in the upper secondary school (Møvig 1998: 35).

Textbooks can be described as a conglomerate of information which is collected and put together as a book. By this I mean that there are a number of people involved in the making of a textbook, not just writers. Often there are editors for each aspect of the layout of the book, so that the person(s) making the maps are not the same as the ones choosing the maps or the persons writing the body of the text. In several instances maps, pictures and other illustrations were not explicitly made for the textbooks, but are chosen from, for example, an international picture database. Because of this, the maps I analyse must be understood as *cotext*,[8] as something that is chosen—often not by the author—to be juxtaposed with other kinds of information to make a complete whole. The choices made by the original mapmakers are thus sometimes less interesting than the choice of maps that are combined with the other information in textbooks.[9]

A NOTE ON TERMINOLOGY

I will use abbreviations for four terms that I utilize frequently throughout this chapter: these are *multiple religions world map* (MRWmap), *single religion world map* (SRWmap), *multiple religions regional map* (MRRmap) and *single religion regional map* (SRRmap). Though they are probably self-explanatory, these four terms denote whether the map in question represents one or more religion categories,[10] and whether it shows the whole world or just a part of it (large and small). But there is a problem, namely how do I decide what counts as a religion? Can I, for example, term a map visualizing the spread of Theravada and Mahayana as a single religion map, or should it be a multiple religions map? I will try to solve this in a pragmatic way, staying as close to the textbooks' ways of categorizing them as possible. In the Theravada-Mahayana example, I will term such a map a single religion map, because every map in the textbooks referring to these two are placed in chapters named Buddhism. So, as my readers will see below, I *do* sort and place smaller categories in larger categories, letting some terms trump others. And because this is impossible to avoid, I hope the categorization carried out in my analysis will be more clarifying than confusing.

THE HUMBLE START

Prior to 1970, maps were rarely used to illustrate religion(s) in textbooks. Sporadically, some maps showing historical sites considered relevant to the history of Christianity were used in textbooks at all school levels. Maps were, however, never used to visualize other religions, and were never about the contemporary situation. Even though *geography of religion* was taken as an entry into the curriculum for the subject on religion in upper secondary school from 1935 onwards, it was not until 1970 that cartography was taken in and used in this way.

Throughout the 1950s and 1960s, there had been an ongoing debate about, and revising of, both the school system and the subject of religion, which resulted in a fairly radical change in pedagogy (Skrunes 2001: 26–29). A new curriculum for the subject, which until then had been called *Kristendomskunnskap* (Knowledge about Christianity), but now changed to *Religion*, appeared in 1976. As early as 1970, however, trial versions of new types of textbooks came into circulation, anticipating the changes in the 1976 curriculum.

The first textbook maps in my material appeared in books published in 1970 by Aschehoug and Dreyer.[11] In the Dreyer book there are two maps: one of Africa and one of Latin America. The map in the book from Aschehoug is a *multiple religions world map* (MRWmap). All three maps seek to visualize the contemporary situation.[12] From about 1970 onwards, there was, as mentioned, a shift in religious education, in which the focus on so called non-Christian religions (religions different from Christianity) changed from "historical" to "living" religions.[13] Before this there was probably, because of the historical focus, no reason for the use of contemporary maps, but this new use of maps can also be seen as a consequence of new approaches to teaching.

In this early period map use seems to be more or less random, with no general expectation that maps should be a part of a textbook or that a particular kind of map should be employed when cartography was used. Books published in the 1970s by publishers other than the two mentioned above did not employ maps at all.

Only two single religion maps were included in publications in the 70s. These, printed in Aschehoug's 1976 book, are an historical map of Jerusalem in a chapter on Judaism, and a contemporary map of Christendom in Europe.

A discourse of primitivism
From the 1930s until the introduction of the new curriculum in 1976, primitivism was an explicitly used explanatory model for the development and spread of religion(s). From 1970 and onwards there is evident an overarching discursive struggle, where the new type of textbooks denounced primitivism at the same time as the old type of books were reprinted in new circulations. Despite denouncing primitivism in the body of the text, this theory of religious evolution is evident in the *multiple religions world map* in the 1970 book from Aschehoug. Religions covered by this first map are, in the map's own order: Protestantism, Catholicism, Communism, Islam, Shintoism, Buddhism, Hinduism, Confucianism and Taosim, and the category "Uninhabited or inhabited by *naturfolk*" (nature people). On the map in question, symbols on white/blank background are used to show the qualitative differences between religions, except when it comes to the

"Uninhabited or inhabited by *naturfolk*." Quite large areas of the world are left blank on this map, and these areas are "Uninhabited or inhabited by *naturfolk*." That this category is only white/blank seems to indicate areas not filled with the other religions mentioned on the map.[14] That *naturfolk* are represented as being in the same category as uninhabited areas is a colonial and primitivistic view, reflecting an understanding of "primitive" people as neither proper people, nor their religion as proper religion. In the body of the text of the 1970 book, however, primitivism is denounced: "The fact is that every *naturfolk* has its own distinctive religion, although there may be a certain mutual resemblance between them."[15] Later on in the text, however, the description of *naturfolk* is very similar to that found in earlier textbooks, where primitivism is explicitly claimed as perspective. As mentioned, textbooks of the earlier type, where primitivism was explicit, were still in circulation and use in the early 1970s. Both pro-primitivism and anti-primitivism books, even some written by the same author, were thus in circulation at the same time. Use of the map category "Uninhabited or inhabited by *naturfolk*" continued to be used in books from 1976 and 1982, even when primitivism ceased to be a hot topic.[16] There is clearly a discursive struggle about primitivism here, not just between books, but also inside the same book.

Mission discourse on Africa

Despite little consensus on the use of maps in the 1970s and the early 1980s, the most widely used maps in this period were *multiple religions regional maps* (MRR-maps) of Africa, which ceased to appear after the end of the 1980s. There are eight books[17] that employ a separate map for representing what is called "religions in Africa" or "African religions." The oldest of these books are from 1970, the youngest from 1989.[18] Among publishers, only Aschehoug and Dreyer/Gyldendal[19] use such maps. It is clear that all of the maps are drawn from the same source, or from each other, since all of them are similar in design.[20] Only Aschehoug's map from 1987 uses colours; the others are black and white in style, with white/blank denoting "tribal religions"/"religions of *naturfolk*" ("nature people"), and symbols on top of white areas denoting other categories.

On the Africa maps religions are regionalized on quite a large area; the continent of Africa. In all of these books, there are six categories on the map and in the map legend, with some differences in category name (depending on the time period):

1. Tribal religions/Religions of nature people[21]
2. Islam
3. Tribal religions and Muhammadan mission/Religions of nature people and Islamic mission.
4. Protestantism and Catholicism/Protestant and Catholic Christianity
5. Tribal religions and Christian Mission/Religions of nature people and Christian mission.
6. Coptic/Coptic Christianity/Ethiopian Christianity

As with the multiple religions world map described above, in these Africa maps "nature religions"/"tribal religions" has been given the colour white or blank, while Christianity and Islam are denoted by symbols or colours added on top of the white/blank colour. The focus on Africa as a continent, through cartographic spatialization makes a discursive statement about "religions of *naturfolk*"/"tribal religions" as being the same as long as they all occur in Africa. All of the MRR-maps with a view of Africa were used to visualize the position of Christian and Muslim mission in relation to "religion of *naturfolk*"/"tribal religion" ("*stammereligion*"), and the continent is represented as a blank sheet for missionizing activities by these two major religions.

Because the maps do not distinguish between Protestant and Catholic Christianity, the six categories listed above can be grouped into four: Islam (Islam and Islamic/Muhammedan mission), Christianity (Protestant and Catholic, Christian mission), religions of tribes/nature people and Coptic/Ethiopian Christianity. The map colours indicate that Protestantism and Catholicism are considered to be more similar to each other than to Coptic/Ethiopian Christianity. Lisbeth Mikaelsson (2003: 195), in her study on mission biographies, shows how Orthodox Christianity was understood by some missionaries as being heathenism. The use of a different colour for Ethiopan/Coptic Christianity might be a reflection of such an attitude.

Using cartographic representations of Africa, where the intention is to highlight the mission's work, is not new in the Scandinavian context. Pellervo Kokkonen (1993) shows in his article, "Religious and Colonial Realities: Cartography of the Finnish Mission in Ovamboland, Namibia," how the use of maps was adopted by the mission early in the second half of the 1800s:

> The most notable use of cartography in missionary work was to support distribution of information among supporters in the homeland. Missionary cartography communicated highly ideologically charged images of the fairly utopian "stage" of missionary activity using authoritative and objective-looking cartographic language. These maps supplemented information of mostly religious content that was otherwise textual and pictorial. (Kokkonen 1993: 162)

Maps thus functioned in the same way as photos, film and textual narratives from the mission field (Gullestad 2007). A focus on missionary work is also evident in the text of these books, so that in this instance the maps speak with the text, not against it.

Religions as mutually exclusive categories
A common feature of the early maps is the use of symbols instead of coherently coloured areas, which are more common in later books. This, at first glance, seems to enable a more detailed representation of multiple religions present in one area at the same time. For example, on a MRWmap from 1976, published by

Aschehoug, one can find small enclaves of Roman Catholics and Muslims in a bigger, mainly Greek Orthodox, Eastern European area. In later books, from the 1980s and 1990s, this kind of representation of diversity disappears when shifting from the use of symbols to coherently coloured areas. However, both kinds of cartographic techniques are subcategories of what has been called the *chorochromatic map type*. Chorochromatic maps visualize qualitative variables. The term originates from the Greek (choros = area, chroma = colour), and through sectioning the map into different colours/shades/marked areas, the reader should be able to acquire an understanding of qualitative differences between the various entities (Rød 2009: 144–46). In the textbooks, chorochromatic maps are used to show where religions and/or directions within religions should be separated from each other. The principle behind the use of this map type is thus to emphasize and highlight the differences between religions/ideologies; Islam is unlike Christianity, Christianity is different from Buddhism, and so on. It varies from textbook to textbook whether the MRWmaps differentiate between movements within the various religions, or if only religions as primary categories are indicated as units. In the books that distinguish between directions within the same religion, it even varies whether the selection is qualitatively different (for example, lines of Protestantism, crosses for Catholicism), or if the directions are marked with different shades of the same colour/symbol (for example dark green for Sunni Islam, light green of Shia Islam, black cross for Protestantism, red for Catholicism).

THE EXPERIMENTAL PERIOD

The period from the end of the 1980s into the 1990s can be called an experimental period, where centrifugal forces were present in textbook map discourse, especially when it came to the *multiple religion world maps* (MRWmaps). This seems to be the peak period with regard to the number of religion categories being represented on these maps. In this period there also seems to have been an expectation that religion(s) should be visualized cartographically, and, especially, that MRWmaps should be included.

Apart from Communism, all religion categories found on the first MRWmap from 1970 are continuously in use throughout the 1980s and into the beginning of the 1990s: Protestantism, Catholicism, Islam, Shintoism, Buddhism, Hinduism, and Confucianism and Taosim. These categories, however, do not stay constant/static, in that, for example, there are differences if the map categories denote religions or adherents (for example, Hinduism versus Hindus). The formerly-used category "Uninhabited or inhabited by *naturfolk*" ("nature people") now splits in two, as in Aschehoug's 1987, 1991 and 1996 editions: "Religion(s) of *naturfolk*" ("nature people") and "Areas of low population."[22] Often each of the religions visualized on the maps are also represented in their own chapters of the textbooks.

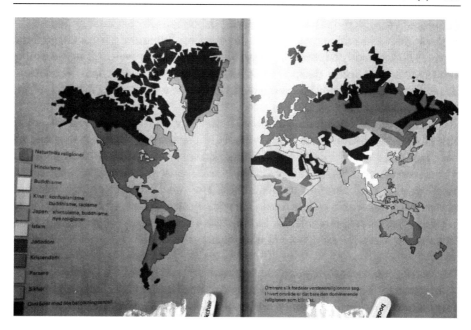

MRWmap. Elseth (1996: inside of cover).

The centrifugal forces in the textbook map discourse in this period is clearly evident on the map in Aschehoug's 1987 edition, repeated in 1991 and 1996. On this map all of the religion categories but two are also visualized in earlier books. In addition to the religions mentioned above, the categories "Parsis" and "Sikhs" are prevalent. Parsism and Sikhism are not described under separate headlines or emphasized anywhere in the texts of the books, so here is an apparent difference between what the maps communicate about existing religions and what the body of the text communicates. In later books, a listing of quite large numbers of religions in addition to the ones represented on maps or in chapters are often printed either on the same page as the MRWmap or in the same chapter. In the books from the 1970s and 1980s, and from the first part of the 1990s, this seldom occurs, with the result that a discourse giving space to a very small number of existing religions/religious practices are formed.

In this period the national categories Chinese religion(s) and Japanese religion(s) also begin to be used. On the map from Aschehoug shown above, China and Japan form separate categories, with the former specified as Confucianism, Buddhism and Taoism, and the latter as Shintoism, Buddhism and "New religions." In the majority of other textbooks employing national categories, however, this specification is not prevalent and the categories are named only "Religion(s) in/of China" and "Religion(s) in/of Japan." This use of national categories "spatializes" religion into local/regional objects textually as well as cartographical, and it corresponds to a common way of sorting religion(s) into chapters in the textbooks, which was seen in books as far back as the 1930s. The majority of books from the 1930s had chapters on "Religion(s) in/of China," and from 1970 onwards chapters on Japan were common as well. After the end of the 1990s such chapters disappeared from textbooks, though these two national categories can be found on some maps in the first years after the turn of the millennium as well.

The important change in the maps, from the earliest to the more recent, is therefore not the transition from symbols to colourizing, but that enclaves on the maps disappear from Europe, and that national categories are taken into use. The consequence is that each area of the world seems as coherent when it comes to religion, as the colour on the map itself. The small enclaves on the 1976 map represented Islam and Roman Catholicism as local religions, embedded in larger regions of other religion entities. In the 1980s small enclaves representing Sikhism and Parsism appeared, only to disappear again.

"World religions" made cartographically regional

As mentioned above, single religion maps occurred in the 1970s, but only in chapters on Judaism and Christianity, and only the former showed the contemporary situation. Buddhism and Islam were the two next religions to be visualized on *single religion maps*, both in a book from Gyldendal in 1984.[23] From this point single religion maps become fairly common in textbooks.

Both the 1984 maps mentioned are regional: the map on Buddhism with a view of East and South-East Asia, and the one on Islam with a view of a larger region, covering a distance from North-Africa to South-East Asia.

The map on Islam is one of a kind, being a dot map. By combining dots and coloured areas this map represents both the contemporary and an historical situation; the coloured areas "Muhammedan conquests in the seventh and eight century CE" and the dots "Muhammedan population today."[24] Dot maps usually employ symbols that are used to place a phenomenon geographically, and the size of the dots represents a specified value (Rød 2009: 144–46). On this map the dots are primarily used to place religious followers geographically, and the density of dots provides an indication of number of adherents. Here, then, the contemporary focus is on people and not on "religion" as a unit. This somewhat contrasts with the text body, where the formulation "Islam spread to..." is used several times. Another contradiction, reflecting a general discursive struggle in the discourse on Islam, is the simultaneously used terms Islam/Muslim and Muhammedanism/Muhammedan. It is only on the map that the latter are used in this book, but in earlier textbooks this was a frequently used term. Some discursive elements seem to stick longer to the map discourse than to the general textbook discourse, and this is one example.

The Buddhism map in the same book visualizes only the historical situation, by using arrows to show where Mahayana and Theravada spread from India at different points in time, but no later than 1400 CE. This map is reused by the same publisher in 1989.

An interesting aspect when it comes to these two religions is that, together with Christianity, they were the earliest religions given the term "world religion" in the textbooks, as early as the 1940s (possibly earlier). Cartographically, in contrast, they start out as regional religions on the single religion maps, and although Islam is portrayed on a world map as early as 1992 in a book published by Samlaget, the single religion maps on Buddhism are never anything other than regional (SRRmaps).

The first single religion map visualizing the spread of Hinduism is a regional map centring on South and South-East Asia, printed in a book from Aschehoug in 1987. Until 2002 (Cappelen Damm) all Hinduism maps are regional. These regional maps showing the spread of adherents include a view of South and South-East Asia, but additionally some books make use of map views of India, visualizing "sacred places in India."[25]

In 1987 the first *single religion world map* (SRWmap) visualizing the contemporary spread of Christianity is employed in a book from Aschehoug. After this point, no regional maps are used to show the contemporary situation only for Christianity. Before this there were both regional maps of Europe, as mentioned above, and historical maps. Here it is important to recall that earlier, before approximately 1980, the subject on religion was usually separated into several books. Christianity was represented in separate books. However, because of the use of only one binding instead of several in the subject on religion from the 1980s and onwards, these textbooks include representation of Christianity from that point forward. I have therefore included comments on maps in these chapters as well. As far I know, however, no maps visualizing the contemporary situation of Christianity were used in older books, only historical, regional maps.

All of the religions called "world religions" in the textbooks in this period, apart from Christianity, then, are made cartographically regional or local by the use of single religion regional maps (SRRmaps).

STABILIZATION AND LEGITIMATION

The last period, from the end of the 1990s until 2008 (when the last books in my material were published), is a period where the centripetal forces are most prevalent in the map discourse. At the end of the 1990s there was an "explosion" in use of maps, largely because of an increased use of single religion maps, both regional and world maps (SRR- and SRWmaps.) The new curriculum in 1996 seems to be the turning point, and in the books published in 1997 there are a large number of maps.

The MRWmap type is now obviously functioning as the main map type that is expected to occur in all textbooks. Often the MRWmaps are placed either before or in the first chapter. In this period there is in the textbooks prevalent an interesting intertextuality, where both the choice of religions visualized on the MRWmaps and what religions are termed world religions, are made an object for discussion and explicit legitimation. Especially Judaism's status as world religion is thematized in a way that seems to presuppose a critique focusing on a contradiction between its status as world religion (also in the cartographic sense) and the low number of adherents compared to other religions. Despite of this presupposed critique, Judaism continues to be represented cartographically as a world religion on MRWmap, even when it is no longer represented in an own chapter, as in one of the latest books published in 2008.

At the end of the period, only five main categories remain at the MRWmaps:

1. Christianity/Christians/(Roman) Catholics/(Greek) Orthodox/Protest-ants
2. Buddhism/Buddhists/Mahayana/Theravada/Tibetan Buddhism
3. Hinduism/Hindus
4. Islam/Muslims/Sunni/Shia
5. Judaism/Jews/Jewish believers

After Judaism appeared on a MRWmap in 1976, these five categories are the only main categories prevalent on all MRWmaps from then to 2008. In the late 1990s and early after year 2000, there still is prevalent on the MRWmaps both national categories ("religion in Japan," "religion in China") and the category of religion(s) of *naturfolk*/primal religions. I nevertheless include these textbooks in the centripetal period, because there is a clear tendency, not just in the maps but also in terms of chapter themes, towards a smaller and smaller number of religion categories being represented. In the former period, from the end of the 1980s, there were a growing number of categories, both on maps and in the text bodies of the books.

Multiple religion regional maps (MRRmaps) are, during the whole period, seldom used, with the exception of Africa maps (see above). In this last period only one publisher makes use of this type. In 1997 Gyldendal prints a map view of Europe, similar to maps used previously to envision "Christian churches." In 1997 this map, however, which is given the title "Religious conditions in today's Europe,"[26] Muslims are also represented. This can be seen as a reflection of a higher awareness of Muslim presence in Europe, which is also prevalent in the book's text bodies in this last period.[27] The enclaves seen on the 1976 MRWmap from Aschehoug (see above), are on this map from Gyldendal reintroduced in Europe. In this period there is also several MRWmaps combining coherently coloured areas with symbols, allowing local enclaves, but with no other categories than can be put into the five main categories mentioned above.

In this last period Christianity continues to be the religion most often represented on single religion world maps. Historical maps, with different views of the Middle East, are also often employed in chapters on Christianity. A use of historical maps that shows for example "important places in the Gospels" (Gaarder *et al.* 1997: 153) or "the journeys of Paul" (Heiene *et al.* 1997: 185), have a long history in textbooks that stretches back beyond the books I have examined.

MRRmap Europe. Hellern (1997: 25).

Christianity is the religion which maps most frequently show spreading through choroplethic maps. The choroplethic maps (Greek choros = area, plethos = volume) visualize quantitative variation within the same variable. Differences in hue indicate that there is more or less of something in one area than in another (Rød 2009: 148). The textbooks use choroplethic maps when the prevalence of one religion is made visible by showing how many adherents the particular religion has. For example, dark colour tone is used in areas where the religion has many and light where it has fewer.

There is a tendency in the textbooks to show that Christianity, in contrast to others, is a religion less confined to specific areas of the world. This is achieved in three ways. Firstly, as mentioned, world maps are more frequently used when portraying the spread of this religion. Secondly, choroplethic maps with categories showing percentages of adherents instead of religion as an abstract category are used more frequently with Christianity, and, thirdly, when percentages of adherents are the basis for the map, there is a tendency—more often than with members of other religions—to indicate that Christians can be present all over the world.

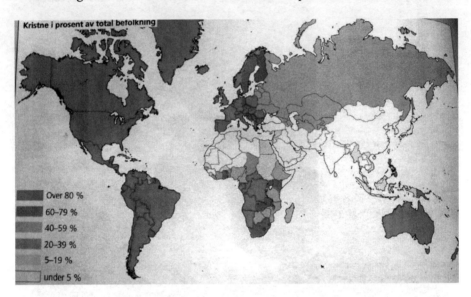

SRWmap Christianity. Heiene, Gunnar *et al.* Mening og mangfold: religion og etikk for den videregående skolen. Oslo: Aschehoug, 1997 (p. 258).

Judaism, in the textbooks which include a chapter on this religion, is also represented several times on SRWmaps. The contemporary maps on Judaism are, however, never either chorocromatic or choroplethic. Maps with bar graphs or dot maps are used, where the dots mark big cities. Because of this, Judaism is cartographically represented as a city phenomenon. An interesting aspect of the dotted SRWmaps on Judaism is that no dots occur farther east than the Caspian Sea. There therefore seems to be a contradiction between the use of world maps when representing Judaism, and regional maps representing Islam and Hinduism, where information on prevalence of these religions outside the map are often given. It is likely that the discourses on the different religions construct them as being local, regional or worldwide, more or less independent of their factual distribution. The common equation between Islam and the Arab world, and between Hinduism and India, is reflected by the use of regional maps when picturing these religions cartographically, whereas a focus on Judaism as a religion of diasporas results in the use of world maps to visualize the contemporary situation.

CONLUSION

The representations of religion(s) on the textbook maps analysed here results in different kinds of spatialization for each religion. The *multiple religions world maps* (MRWmap) constructs religions as local, regional and world religions. Throughout the period, MRWmaps function more and more in the textbooks as the main map type for representing religion. That a religion is represented on a MRWmap constructs it as a world religion, or at least as an important enough religion to be represented on a primary map. The number of what I have called primary religion categories being present on all MRW maps are only five: Buddhism, Christianity, Hinduism, Islam and Judaism. Because of the chorochormatic technique, the religion categories on the MRWmaps have to be confined to certain areas, and inherently they are also constructed as regional, though maps in later books also uses symbols in the coloured areas to visualize how religions can be prevalent in areas where the population majority adheres to a different religion. In those cases, and in earlier books where enclaves appear on the maps, the religions in question are made local by the representation of enclaves.

The regionalization of religions is reinforced by the increasing employment of single religion regional maps (SRRmaps). Buddhism, which never occurs on a single religion *world* map (SRWmap), is confined to East Asia. Hinduism is mostly equated with India/South Asia, although some newer books represent it on SRWmaps. The SRRmaps on Islam centre on the Middle East and North Africa, but as with Hinduism, world maps have been used in newer books. Judaism is the religion most often constructed cartographically as a *local* religion. On the one hand, the use of single religion world maps constructs it as a world religion, but on the other hand since, apart from Israel, cities are marked on both the SRWmaps and the MRWmaps, Judaism is constructed as local. Christianity is the religion that is earliest and most often constructed cartographically as a *world* religion.

The textbook maps form a separate discourse, despite being closely connected to both *cotext* (the surrounding book) and *context* (which embraces everything from other textbooks to cultural and political movements). This is evident primarily in three ways, where the maps "speak" differently from both the text and from other illustrations in the books: (1) when the same maps are used in books from different publishers, and in subsequent books from the same publishers but with significant changes in the texts; (2) When religion categories prevalent on the maps are not mentioned or discussed in the text or in other illustrations, and; (3) when theoretical perspectives which are prevalent on the maps are denounced or not discussed in the body of the text. That the cartographic discourse differs from the textual discourse can be viewed as a struggle in an overarching discursive field on religion. Because of constant changes, either in maps or in texts, discursive struggle can be said to be evident in the textbook genre at all times. That there are lengthy phases of struggle is also evident when it comes to the primitivism and mission discourses, where the struggles start in the beginning of the 1970s and continue until the end of the 1980s.

SOURCE MATERIAL (BY PUBLISHER)

Aschehoug

Ribsskog, R. 1942. *Religionshistorie for gymnaset.* Oslo: Aschehoug.

Strøm, H. 1970. *Religionskunnskap og religionshistorie.* Oslo: Aschehoug.

Strøm, H. 1973. *Religionskunnskap og religionshistorie.* Oslo: Aschehoug.

Strøm, H. 1976. *Hinduismen, buddhismen, religioner i Kina og Japan: religion for videregående skoler.* Oslo: Aschehoug.

Strøm, H. 1976. *Jødedommen, kristendommen, islam: religion for vidaregåande skolar.* Oslo: Aschehoug.

Strøm, H. 1976. *Religionskunnskap: Afrikanske naturfolks religioner: religion for videregående skoler.* Oslo: Aschehoug.

Strøm, H. 1976. *Religionskunnskap: religionar i dag: religion for vidaregåande skolar.* Oslo: Aschehoug.

Strøm, H. 1982. *Religioner i dag: religionskunnskap for den videregående skolen.* Oslo: Aschehoug.

Strøm, H. 1987. *Religioner i dag.* Oslo: Aschehoug.

Elseth, E., B. Myhre, L. Akslen, J. Opsal, T. B. Pettersen and A. Østnor. 1991. *Veier og visjoner: Levende religioner, Kristendommen, Etikk/Livssyn.* Oslo: Aschehoug.

Elseth, E., B. Myhre, L. Akslen, J. Opsal, T. B. Pettersen and A. Østnor. 1996. *Veier og visjoner: Levende religioner, Kristendommen, Etikk/Livssyn.* Oslo: Aschehoug.

Heiene, G., B. Myhre, J. Opsal, H. Skottene and A. Østnor. 1997. *Mening og mangfold: religion og etikk for den videregående skolen.* Oslo: Aschehoug.

Heiene, G., B. Myhre, J. Opsal, H. Skottene and A. Østnor. 2006. *Mening og mangfold: religion og etikk for den videregående skolen.* Oslo: Aschehoug.

Heiene, G., B. Myhre, J. Opsal, H. Skottene and A. Østnor. 2008. *Tro og tanke: religion og etikk for den videregående skolen.* Oslo: Aschehoug.

Cappelen/Cappelen Damm

Strøm, H. 1947. *Religionshistorie for gymnaset.* Oslo: Cappelen.

Strøm, H. 1948. *Religionshistorie for gymnasiet.* Oslo: Cappelen.

Strøm, H. 1956. *Religionshistorie for gymnaset.* Oslo: Cappelen.

Strøm, H. 1960. *Religionshistorie for gymnaset.* Oslo: Cappelen.

Strøm, H. 1968. *Religionshistorie for gymnaset.* Oslo: Cappelen.

Strøm, H. 1971. *Religionshistorie for gymnaset.* Oslo: Cappelen.

Grande, S. Ø., and J. F. Myklebust. 1992. *Logos: religion—livssyn—etikk.* Oslo: Cappelen.

Grande, S. Ø., and J. F. Myklebust. 1997. *Logos: religion—livssyn—etikk.* Oslo: Cappelen.

Kvamme, O. A., A. R. Hauge, E. M. Lindhart and A. E. Steineger. 2002. *I samme verden.* Oslo: Cappelen Damm.

Kvamme, O. A., A. R. Hauge, E. M. Lindhart and A. E. Steineger. 2008. *I samme verden.* Oslo: Cappelen Damm.

Dreyer

Hellern, V., H. Notaker and U. H. Stubbraaten. 1970. *Verdens religioner: kristendomskunnskap for gymnaset.* Lærebok 1. Oslo: Dreyer.

Hellern, V., H. Notaker and U. H. Stubbraaten. 1972. *Verdens religioner: lærebok med tekstsamling for videregående skoler.* Oslo: Dreyer.

Hellern, V., H. Notaker and U. H. Stubbraaten. 1975. *Verdens religioner: lærebok og tekstsamling.* Oslo: Dreyer.

Hellern, V., H. Notaker and U. H. Stubbraaten. 1976. *Religionane i verda: lærebok og tekstsamling.* Oslo: Dreyer.

Fabritius
Aasland, R. 1941. *Religionshistorie for gymnasiet.* Oslo: Fabritius.
Aasland, R. 1953. *Religionshistorie for gymnaset.* Oslo: Fabritius.
Aasland, R. 1956. *Religionshistorie for gymnaset.* Oslo: Fabritius.
Aasland, R. 1961. *Religionshistorie for gymnaset.* Oslo: Fabritius.
Aasland, R. 1966. *Religionshistorie for gymnaset.* Oslo: Fabritius.
Aasland, R. 1967. *Religionshistorie for gymnaset.* Oslo: Fabritius.
Aasland, R. 1971. *Religionshistorie for gymnaset.* Oslo: Fabritius.

Gyldendal
Jor, F. 1976. *Dei store spørsmål og dei store svar: religionskunnskap.* Oslo: Gyldendal.
Hellern, V., H. Notaker and J. Gaarder. 1984. *Verdens religioner.* Oslo: Gyldendal.
Hellern, V., H. Notaker and J. Gaarder. 1989. *Religionsboka.* Oslo: Gyldendal.
Gaarder, J., V. Hellern and H. Notaker. 1997. *Religionsboka.* Oslo: Gyldendal.
Hellern, V., H. Notaker and J. Gaarder. 1997. *Religionsboka: religion—livssyn—eEtikk.* Oslo: Gyldendal.
Gaarder, J., V. Hellern and H. Notaker. 2000. *Religion og etikk: for den videregående skolen.* Oslo: Gyldendal.
Aronsen, C. F., L. Bomann-Larsen and H. Notaker. 2008. *Eksistens: religion, etikk, livssyn, filosofi.* Oslo: Gyldendal undervisning.

Nomi/Luther
Skjerpe, O. 1973. *Religionskunnskap for videregående skoler.* Oslo: Nomi.
Skjerpe, O. 1974. *Religionskunnskap for vidaregåande skolar.* Oslo: Nomi (Luther).
Skjerpe, O. 1980. *Religionskunnskap for videregående skoler.* Oslo: Luther.

Samlaget
Christoffersen, S. A., T. Rasmussen and N. R. Thelle. 1992. *Mennesket og mysteriet.* Oslo: Samlaget.
Christoffersen, S. A., T. Rasmussen and N. R. Thelle. 1997. *Mennesket og mysteriet: religion og etikk VK 2.* Oslo: Samlaget.

Tanum
Jansen, H. L. 1941. *Religionshistorie for gymnasiet.* Oslo: Tanum.
Jansen, H. L. 1948. *Religionshistorie for gymnaset.* Oslo: Tanum.
Jansen, H. L. 1965. *Fremmede religioner.* Oslo: Tanum.
Jansen, H. L. 1968. *Fremmede religioner.* Oslo: Tanum.
Jansen, H. L. 1971. *Fremmede religioner.* Oslo: Tanum.

REFERENCES

Beyer, P. 2003. "Conceptions of Religion: On Distinguishing Scientific, Theological and 'Official' Meanings." *Social Compass* 2(50): 141–60.
Crampton, J. W. 2010. *Mapping: A Critical Introduction to Cartography and Gis.* Chichester, UK: Wiley-Blackwell.
Gullestad, M. 2007. *Misjonsbilder: bidrag til norsk selvforståelse.* Oslo: Universitetsforlaget.

Harley, J. B. 2001. "The New Nature of Maps: Essays in the History of Cartography." In *The New Nature of Maps: Essays in the History of Cartography*, ed. P. Laxton, introduction by J. H. Andrews. 1–18. Baltimore: Johns Hopkins University Press.

Harley, J. B. 2001 (1990). "Text and Context in the Interpretation of Early Maps." In *The New Nature of Maps: Essays in the History of Cartography*, ed. P. Laxton, introduction by J. H. Andrews. 33–50. Baltimore: Johns Hopkins University Press.

Harley, J. B., and D. Woodward. 1987. *The History of Cartography. Vol. 1*. Chicago: University of Chicago Press.

Karrow, R. W. 2007. "Introduction." In *Maps: Finding our Place in the World*, ed. J. R. Akerman and R. W. Karrow. Chicago: University of Chicago Press.

Kokkonen, P. 1993. "Religious and Colonial Realities: Cartography of the Finnish Mission in Ovamboland, Namibia." *History in Africa* 20: 155–71.

Mikaelsson, L. 2003. *Kallets ekko: studier i misjon og selvbiografi*. Kristiansand: Høyskoleforlaget.

Møvig, A. 1998. *Religionsfaget i videregående opplæring: utvikling, mål, basis*. Oslo: Hovedfagsoppgave i religionshistorie, Universitetet i Oslo.

Parker, I. 1989. *The Crisis in Modern Social Psychology and How to End It*. London: Routledge.

Parrinder, G. 1969. *Religion in Africa*. London: Pall Mall.

Rød, J. K. 2009. *Verktøy for å beskrive verden: statistikk, kart og bilder*. Trondheim: Tapir akademisk.

Skrunes, N. 2001. *Religionsfaget i videregående skole: historie, planinnhold og didaktikk*. Bergen: NLA-Forlaget.

Thobro, S. A. 2008. "Representasjoner av buddhisme og hinduisme: en diskursanalyse i postkolonialt perspektiv av lærebøker i religionsfaget for gymnas/videregående skole." Master thesis, Universitetet i Bergen.

Thobro, S. A. 2009. "Endringer i representasjoner av buddhisme: en analyse av norske lærebøker i perioden 1948–2006." *Din: Tidsskrift for religion og kultur* 4: 4–29.

Endnotes

1. The Confession Article was taken from the Education Act for Norwegian Upper Secondary schools in 1974. This is much earlier than for Primary schools, where a Confession Article continued until 2008.
2. Although a map, according to this definition, can vary from the conventional to the more abstract and artistic, all maps in the textbooks belong to the former type.
3. See also Thobro (2009).
4. Although it seems to be the ideal, this is never achieved fully, and it varies from one religious representation to another. See Thobro (2008).
5. J. B. Harley's essays, collected in Harley (2001), give an insight into the early start of critical cartography.
6. The subject has been called *Kristendomskunnskap* in the period 1935–1974/76 (Knowledge of Christianity), *Religion* (Religion) in the period 1974/76–1997, and *Religion og etikk* (Religion and ethics) from 1997 onwards.
7. Taken together all editions and circulations in this period, from all publishers, counts to almost 90 books. Because textbooks are books that "expire" with each new curriculum, older ones are not always easy to obtain. Some holes therefore appear in my source material, but from analogy it is likely that my findings can be transferred to the missing books. My project, however, is not dependent on looking at every book. I am looking for discursive patterns, and will therefore not comment on the details in each book. Mistakes and mis-

prints, or elements that are possibly just that, are in the larger picture insignificant. This, however, does not mean that I will ignore every detail—it is the details that together make the pattern. Please see the list of source material for books included in this study.

8. *Cotext* denotes the map's surrounding text in the book, which I extend to include illustrations as well as written text.

9. When in this chapter I choose to study maps to highlight how textbooks construct "religion," it is because of the apparent objectivity of maps. It is likely that the maps used to demonstrate the prevalence of religion to a greater extent are "slipping through" the critical view of a reader, and simultaneously highly influencing the reader's conception of what counts as religion. This is not to say that the general reader of textbooks will be more influenced by the maps then by the written text or other book illustrations—maps are only a small part of a textbook as a whole—but this is the presumption that makes me choose maps as objects of study.

10. I call it this because I am not trying to establish what religion is or not, independent of the textbooks. Though at this point I can say that the religion categories—names of religion entities—in the textbooks are quite conventional.

11. It is probable that Dreyer had already published a textbook of the new type in 1969. I have not been able to get hold of this book.

12. The Dreyer map of Latin-America combines historical and contemporary situations.

13. The early years of the 1970s were a period of overlap, where books of both the "old" and "new" kind were in circulation. The reason for this was that this was a period of experimentation, leading up to a new curriculum in 1976. See Thobro (2008: 21–22).

14. It is likely that the blank spaces indicate that these areas of the world are like a blank canvas for missionaries; I will return to this theme later when analysing maps of Africa.

15. My translation. Norwegian text: "Faktum er at hvert eneste naturfolk har sin særegne religion, selv om det kan være en viss innbyrdes likhet mellom dem" (p. 12).

16. Primitivism is mentioned in these two later books, but does not have the same focus as in the 1970 book. Also in 1973 a map that employs forms of the same categories are used, where "Uninhabited or inhabited by naturfolk" are replaced by "*Naturfolk* or desert" ("Naturfolk eller ørken").

17. Dreyer 1970, 1975, 1982, Gyldendal 1984 (revised version of Dreyer 1982), 1989, and Aschehoug 1976, 1982, 1987.

18. As previously mentioned there is a possibility that Dreyer published a book in 1969, and there is a chance that this book contains this type of Africa map as well.

19. Dreyer's textbook publishing was taken over by Gyldendal in the 1980s.

20. The majority of the books state that Geoffrey Parrinder's *Religion in Africa* (1969) was the source. In several of the books an explicit intertextuality is thus present, where information on the source of the map is given. In this examination of the map discourse in textbooks, however, what is the most interesting is not the source, but that this particular map is used in the textbooks.

21. Norwegian: "Stammereligioner/naturfolks religioner."

22. My translation. Norwegian text: "Områder med lite befolkningsantall."

23. I have only been able to get the 1984 print of the 1982 edition, but it is likely that all maps occurring in 1984 also were prevalent in the 1982 printing.

24. My translation. Norwegian text: "Muhammedanske erobringer i det 7. og 8. århundre e.kr," "Muhammedansk befolkning i dag."

25. My translation. Norwegian text: "Hellige steder i India."
26. My translation. Norwegian text: "Religiøse forhold i dagens Europa."
27. The map places Muslims in South-East Europe. Since Muslims have lived there as majority for much longer than the textbook maps have represented them as being there, the Muslim presence on the map has to do with discourse, choice and/or awareness.

9. A RESERVOIR OF SYMBOLS: ON THE CONCEPTUALIZATION OF "RELIGION" IN INTRODUCTORY BOOKS FOR RE IN TEACHER EDUCATION IN NORWAY

*Bengt-Ove Andreassen**

This chapter focuses on Norwegian introductory books for didactics in the study of religions and how these textbooks communicate an understanding of "religion." The principal argument is that "religion" is primarily understood and conceptualized as a resource for human development and spiritual growth. The textbooks present religion through well-known but vague concepts such as "the Holy" or as "a mystery one cannot perceive." The vagueness of these concepts makes it possible to apply them to any religion, thus making every religion a reservoir of symbols which students can choose from and make use of in their spiritual and human development. This implies that religion is primarily treated as a solely good or positive phenomenon—what might be described as an empathetic conceptualization of religion. A main argument in the presentation of the textbooks is that the perspectives and conceptualization of religion are clearly rooted in liberal theology and the phenomenological tradition.

The textbooks referred to here are designed and written for students in Norwegian teacher education. This means that the textbooks also reflect recent developments in primary and secondary education, as textbook authors present what, from their vantage point, is the correct or the most constructive way of under-

* Bengt-Ove Andreassen has a PhD in the study of religions and is Associate Professor in the Department of Education at the University of Tromsø—The Arctic University of Norway. One of his areas for research is themes related to religion in education and how perspectives from the academic study of religion(s) can be applied to develop religion education (RE) in public schools. His recent publications include, "On Ethics and Religious Culture (ERC) in Québec: Comments and Comparative Perspectives from a Norwegian and European Context," in *Religion & Education* 38(3) (2011); *Religionsdidaktikk. En innføring* (Oslo: Universitetsforlaget, 2012), and "Religion Education in Norway: Tension or Harmony between Human Rights and Christian Cultural Heritage?" in *Temenos* 49(2) (2013: 137–64).

standing religion for teachers teaching religion education in the public school—in Norway labelled RLE.[1] However, I will argue that the empathetic understanding of religion, and religion as a means for human development, is an ideological and normative approach to religion which cannot be accepted as a basic understanding and conceptualization of religion, especially when it comes to religion education in non-confessional public schools in a secular state. The last part of the article will point to the academic study of religion as providing the important principles to didactics for religion, as in accordance with recent developments in the RLE subject.

RELIGION EDUCATION, DIDACTICS OF RELIGION AND RELIGION IN TEACHER EDUCATION

The term "didactics of religion" (Norwegian, *religionsdidaktikk*) refers here to an academic discipline which focuses on factors related to the teaching of religion. "Didactics" is a term which can be placed in the German educational tradition of *didaktik*. It is not a term commonly used in English, where it can also have negative connotations. However, it has also found use in English by researchers with reference to a German educational tradition (cf. Hudson and Meyer 2011). Didactics in this article will be used to describe different factors with respect to the teaching of religion in secondary and primary school, as well as in teacher education.

In Norwegian four-year general teacher education, didactics is a topic in all of the subjects that student teachers can choose from as part of their specialization. Related to different school subjects, didactics is commonly referred to as "subject didactics" (Norwegian, *fagdidaktikk*). Hence, in RLE in teacher education, didactics of religion is a subject area aimed at preparing students for teaching RLE in primary and/or secondary school.

Until 2010, RLE was a mandatory subject (of 20 ECTS)[2] for students in the general four-year teacher education programme. A reform has since made RLE optional. Because student teachers now specialize in three or four subjects (depending on specialization for teaching in secondary or primary school), the subjects have been expanded to a minimum of 30 ECTS each.

Although the books to which I refer were primarily written for students in general teacher education in Norway before the last reform in 2010,[3] they are still presented as relevant for general teacher education by the publishers.

All of the books I originally analysed (Andreassen 2008) were published in the wake of a reform in primary and secondary education in 1997. In that year a new religion education subject was introduced, which replaced the former subject of Christian knowledge. The Norwegian school system thus went from organizing religion education as a *separative religious education* to an *integrative religious education*, to use concepts developed by Wanda Alberts (2008). The new school subject (initially named KRL,[4] and from 2008 RLE) now includes world religions (Christianity, Judaism, Islam, Hinduism and Buddhism), secular world-views and philosophy and ethics. The didactics of religion in teacher education now had to include material on religions other than Christianity. This challenged religion education specialists to deal with religion as an analytical category and as a theoretical concept to a much larger extent than before. The need for new introductory books for teacher education was apparent.

Since 1997, when KRL (Christianity, Religion and Life Stances) was made a compulsory subject in primary and secondary schools, a new curriculum has been presented no less than four times (in 1997, 2002, 2005 and 2008). In 2004 and 2007 the Norwegian state was criticized by the UN's Human Rights Council and the European Court for Human Rights (ECHR) in Strasbourg. The UN's Human Rights Council issued a statement in November 2004 which made it clear that KRL and the limited right to exemption could be a violation of basic human rights in accordance with the right to freedom of religion. The UN's criticism led to a new and adjusted curriculum for KRL which was implemented in August 2005. In June 2007, the ECHR in Strasbourg also ruled in favour of the parents and HEF[5] in the "Case of Folgerø and others vs. Norway." The ruling from the ECHR resulted in yet another curriculum, which was implemented in August 2008 along with a new name for the school subject: RLE (cf. Lied 2009). The many revisions in the curricula have been directed towards ensuring that RLE is in accordance with basic human rights and secured as a secular subject and not as a subject for religious instruction. It now clearly reads, in the Education Act and in the curriculum, that teaching in RLE shall present world religions and views of life in an "objective, critical and pluralistic manner." The teaching should be *about* religions.

This has of course also challenged RLE in teacher education and introductory books for teacher education. However, surprisingly little effort has been made by scholars and publishers to update and revise textbooks. Instead, the introductory books, to some extent, represent enduring and stable forces that have continued to shape RE in the face of the educational system's reforms and structural changes. In discourse analysis, the term *longue durée* is used to describe how discourses are difficult to change, but tend, rather, to be maintained even in the face of a world that is constantly changing (Murray 2001: xv). Introductory books seem to represent such a force. Hence, I find it crucial to raise the question of whether the understanding and conceptualization of religion offered in textbooks in the didactics of religion for teacher education can be applied in a didactics of religion for teaching a subject like RLE as part of integrative religion education in the public school system.

Still, at the risk of being unfair to the authors of the introductory books, one might argue that some of them have not had the chance or opportunity (or found it relevant) to make changes in accordance with every new curriculum or new criticism. Nevertheless, publishers present as the same books in new editions to students as the authoritative introductory books in the didactics of religion. This is why such books constitute an interesting and valuable source in the investigation and analysis of how "religion" is conceptualized in Norwegian didactics of religion.

INTRODUCTORY BOOKS IN DIDACTICS OF RELIGION

As part of my PhD project, a thorough investigation of literature for teacher education found only five books that were presented and defined as introductory books for didactics of religion in teacher education. This count did not include the many introductory books to specific religions. I only included books which were explicitly defined by their authors as introductions to the didactics of religion.

My principles for identifying criteria for a general understanding of "didactics of religion" were three-fold. They had to include perspectives on (1) the students in the schools (pupils), (2) the RE teacher, and (3) religion education as a school subject (KRL/RLE). The relations between subject, teacher and student are often described as the core elements in didactics (Künzli 1998). The analysis displayed interesting findings in terms of how some of the introductory books conceptualized religion, and how this conceptualization was presented as universal or general, and thus relevant for all students. In this chapter I will develop and further discuss the findings in the two textbooks which in 2013 are still available for purchase and promoted as textbooks in didactics of religion.

The five books that were my starting point for the analysis were:

Author/Authors	Title in Norwegian	Title in English	First published	Analysed edition	In the text referred to as
Geir Afdal, Elisabet Haakedal and Heid Leganger-Krogstads	*Tro, livstolkning og tradisjon*	Faith, life interpretation and tradition	1997	2nd edn 2001	Afdal *et al.* 2001
Sverre Dag Mogstads	*Fag, identitet og fortelling. Didaktikk til Kristendomsskunnskap med religions- og livssynsorientering*	Subject, identity and narrative. Didactics for KRL	1997	2nd edn 2004	Mogstad 2004
Njål Skrunes	*Religionspedagogikk for grunnskolen*	Religious education for primary schools	1999	2nd edn 2004	Skrunes 2004
Arnt Stabell-Kulø	*Religioner i klasserommet. Innføring i religionsdidaktikk*	Religions in the classroom Introduction to didactics of religion	2005	2005	Stabell-Kulø 2005
Helje Kringlebotn-Sødal, ed.	*Religions- og livssynsdidaktikk. En innføring*	Didactics of religions and life stances	2001	4th edn 2009	Sødal *et al.* 2009

My analysis of these books found they were not unanimous in how either "didactics of religion" or religion was presented. Three out of five presented similar understandings in their presentation of the didactics of religion (Afdal *et al.* 2001, Mogstad 2004; Sødal *et al.* 2009), while the other two presented diametrically different perspectives. Skrunes (2004) clearly had an explicitly conservative Christian and theocentric viewpoint, while Stabell-Kulø (2005) had what could be described as a secular and religious studies-based understanding of the didactics of religion and religion.

In addition to analysing these five books, I collected reading lists from 15 teacher education institutions in Norway to see which of the books were used the most (Andreassen 2008). The three books that were unanimous in their understanding of the didactics of religion completely dominated, particularly Sødal *et al.* (2009). This book was often supplemented with excerpts from one of the other books, Afdal *et al.* (2001).

I also investigated which books were recommended at the official website for RE teachers (www.krlnett.no).[6] This website is financially supported by the Directorate for Education and Training (DET).[7] The same three books that dominated the reading lists at the teacher education institutions were also the ones recommended for RE teachers and for teacher education at the official website. The other two books (Skrunes 2004 and Stabell-Kulø 2005), were not in the official list of recommended books. Neither were they used at any of the teacher institutions where I collected reading lists. However, it has been brought to my attention that Stabell-Kulø (2005) has been used in excerpts in some teacher education institutions.

Based on these findings, I will argue that the understanding of the "didactics of religion" found in Afdal, Mogstad and Sødal is a powerful force in the construction of the "didactics of religion" in Norway. These three books have dominated the discourse on didactics of religion in teacher education and have been the textbooks that students in teacher education are encouraged and obliged to read. As these are also the three books recommended at official websites financed by the Norwegian government, their position as textbooks of special significance is obvious. Mogstad's book is now out of print and no longer available. I will therefore put the main focus on Afdal *et al.* (2001) and Sødal *et al.* (2009).

From a discourse analysis perspective, the fact that some books are always present, while others appear to be in the dark, so to speak, can be illustrated via the distinction between *centripetal* and *centrifugal* forces (Maybin 2001: 65). The three books that are unanimous in their presentation of the didactics of religion in my study represent centripetal forces. Being the books recommended at the official websites with financial support from the executive agency for the Ministry of Education, they produce the authoritative, fixed, inflexible discourse on the didactics of religion. The authoritative understanding in these books can be associated with strategic centralization and a unified cultural canon. These centripetal forces are in constant tension with, and sometimes challenged by, centrifugal forces. In the centrifugal forces lies the understanding of a didactics for religion that is in opposition to authoritative centripetal forces. This simple distinction illustrates clearly that there seems to be an authoritative understanding, which also implies that there is an authoritative understanding on how "religion" is understood and treated. On the basis of the distinction between centripetal and centrifugal forces in the discourse on RE and the didactics of religion in Norway, I will focus on these three books.

It is first necessary to make a few remarks about analysing introductory books in the didactics of religion. Introductory books can be defined in different ways: as pedagogical texts, prose, or as the voices of the disciplines, and as a key mechanism for the production and reproduction of ideas within the field (cf. Baumfield 2006; Issitt 2004; Olsson 2010). Educational textbooks offer rich but complex material for analysis as they are embedded in other discourses. Some of the introductory books I analysed were clearly examples of this. The so-called "whole child discourse" (Fendler 2001; Krejsler 2006) in pedagogy seems important for the didactics of religion in Norway, because within this discourse religion is regarded as an important factor in the development of the "whole child." This discourse is based on premises which communicate that a child without religion or some sort of spirituality is not a "whole child," so to speak. In this way, the "whole child discourse" gives importance to religion for the sake of the spiritual growth of children. This also influences the way "religion" is understood; the understanding of "religion" is adjusted in accordance with the whole child discourse and presented as an important factor for the child's growth into a fully developed human being.

TO DEFINE OR NOT TO DEFINE RELIGION?

In the textbooks there are quite different strategies regarding the question of defining religion. It is stated in Sødal *et al.* (2009) that defining religion should not be part of the didactics of religion, and that the question about defining religion belongs to "other parts of the subject": "A thorough discussion about what religion and life views really are should be discussed in other parts of RLE"[8] (Sødal *et al.* 2009: 14, my translation). Although it does not specify which other parts of RLE, it clearly indicates that defining religion is not regarded as being of great importance for the didactics of religion. However, later in the book when religion is discussed, the text reads:

> Det religiøse er dypest sett et mysterium tanken alene ikke kan fatte. (Sødal *et al.* 2009: 62)

> The religious is deeply a mystery which thoughts alone cannot perceive. (Sødal *et al.* 2009: 62, my translation)

Despite the lack of explicit reference to any scholars or traditions in relation to this statement, the formulation about the religious as "a mystery which thoughts alone cannot perceive" is closely related to the famous phrase "*mysterium tremendum et fascinans*" by Rudolf Otto (1926: 12–13). In religious studies, this is a well-known perspective which communicates a conceptualization of religion developed within the phenomenology of religion and rooted in theories developed in liberal theology in the early 1900s (Cox 2006: 220; Wiebe 1999: 57). As noted above, there is no explicit reference to Otto in the textbook. Still, the statement can be related to a long phenomenological tradition in the study of religions, which communicates a perspective on religion as inexplicable and impossible for humans to understand intellectually. In Sødal *et al.* (2009), religion and the religious is rather something which can be reached and understood through experience and emotions, and not intellectually. Hence, the question of an explicit definition of religion in the didactics of religion is refused in Sødal.

In Afdal *et al.* (2001), the problem of defining religion is dealt with explicitly. Different conceptualizations or definitions of religion are presented in the first part of the book. A distinction is made between a "wide functionalist" and a "narrow substantial" understanding of religion (2001: 44–45). It is indicated that both understandings are important in RE. The wide functionalist understanding is compared and interlinked with the term "life interpretation" (Norwegian: *livstolkning*). The narrow substantial understanding of religion is compared with faith or belief (Norwegian: *tro*). The wide functionalist is presented as a student-orientated or student-centered understanding of religion. The narrow substantial understanding, on the other hand, is presented as "subject orientated."[9] In the first part of the book, it is argued that both understandings should be part of teaching in RE and in the didactics of religion. However, in the second half of the book, emphasis is placed on "the Holy" as the "central nerve" of RE (2001: 205–206, 211). Here it reads that the substantial understanding of religion refers to a "transcendent reality":

> Det substansielle eller materielle religionsbegrepet refererer til en transcendent virkelighet, som vi—med teologen Rudolf Otto—vil kalle "det hellige", eller det som er fullstendig annerledes. I ideen om og opplevelsen av det hellige mener vi å finne et ytre, objektivt fenomen som er tilstrekkelig udefinerbart—og likevel samlende—til at det kan vise til det spesifikke og særegne ved religionsfaget i en skole for et pluralistisk samfunn. En annen nærliggende tanke å gripe fatt i er gudsbegrepet (se Gravem 1992a og 1992b). Vi foretrekker likevel hellighetsfenomenet fordi det kan oppfattes som videre og kanskje litt mer allment tilgjengelig enn gudsbegrepet. Hellighetsbegrepet har både religiøse og moralske aspekter. Til hellighetsfenomenet svarer menneskets hellighetslengsel—også det moderne menneskets lengsel (se Thelle 1994).[10] (Afdal *et al.* 2001: 206)

The substantial or material understanding of religion refers to a transcendent reality, which we—like the theologian Rudolf Otto—refer to as "the Holy," or that which is completely different. In the idea and the experience of the Holy we find an objective (neutral) phenomenon which is inexplicable—and yet common—which brings the characteristics of RE in education in a pluralistic society to the surface. Closely related is the concept of God... However, we prefer the Holy because it might be considered as a wider and more common concept compared to the concept of God. The concept of the Holy has religious as well as moral aspects. The phenomenon of the Holy answers the human longing for the Holy— as well as modern man's longing [for the Holy]. (Afdal *et al.* 2001: 206, my translation)

The emphasis on the Holy as a transcendent and objective (neutral) phenomenon, which is common and inexplicable, clearly puts this introductory book into a phenomenological tradition. As the Holy is also described as "the central nerve" in RE, it is even more explicit in its phenomenological approach than Sødal *et al.* (2009). Defining the Holy as the subject's "central nerve," even if the Holy cannot be defined, yet at the same time can be considered as a common phenomenon, clearly communicates that religion should be treated with awe. An interesting but rather unclear perspective is that the Holy is in some respect related to God, but, as the excerpt reads, the Holy is preferred because it is "wider and more common" compared to God. Additionally, one might add, it is obviously easier to argue for the rather unclear concept of the Holy as the central nerve of RE in a non-confessional public multi-cultural school than for God. The confessional orientation in this perspective becomes clearer when it is stated that the Holy, despite the difficulties in defining it, has "religious and moral aspects." This clearly shows that the book understands the concepts of "the Holy" and "God" as being more or less synonymous. Without this connection between the Holy and God, it is unclear how the Holy—which in the book is underlined as inexplicable— can serve as the central nerve in RE as well as have moral aspects.

Christian evangelical perspectives in Afdal *et al.* (2001) come to the surface in other parts of the book where a "prophetic voice" in Christian faith is referred to. In the "prophetic voice" lie values which, according to the authors, prevent the book's perspective from being relativistic.

Det kristne verdi- og trosgrunnlaget rommer en "profetisk røst" som vil kunne hindre kulturkonservering på den vestlige materialismens og selvgodhetens grunnlag. (Afdal *et al.* 2001: 293)

Christianity's faith and values contain a "prophetic voice" that might prevent a cultural preservation on the grounds of Western materialism and conceit [selfishness]. (Afdal *et al.* 2001: 293, my translation)

Seeing the perspective of the "prophetic voice" in relation to the emphasis of the Holy, this "prophetic voice" is directed towards experiences of a particular religion: Christianity. And through emotions and experience children in school can learn to get in touch or communicate with the Holy:

Vi vil argumentere for at elevene best gis anledning til et møte med det hellige når det åpnes for å gjøre erfaringer gjennom sansene så vel som intellektet. Derfor vil vi framheve de dimensjonene som tydelig viser til

det synlige, hørbare, følbare osv., altså den praktiske og rituelle, den narrative eller mytiske, og ikke minst den materielle dimensjonen. Fortel-
linger, ritualer, gjenstander, lukter og tonesvingninger kan alle gi impulser
til elevenes hellighetslengsel og begynnende livstolkningsprosess. (Afdal
et al. 2001: 208)

Our argument is that the best way for students to encounter the Holy is
when one is open to experiences through senses as well as through intellect.
Thus, we will emphasize the dimensions [presented by Smart] as clearly connected to the visual, to listening, and to what you can feel etc., which are the
practical and ritual, the narrative and the mythical, and last but not least the
material dimension. Stories, rituals, physical objects, smells and sounds can
all give impulses to the student's longing for the Holy and start the process
of life interpretation. (Afdal *et al.* 2001: 208, my translation)

The "prophetic voice" of Christian faith and values seemingly secures the understanding of religion from being relativistic, while emotions and experience are
the way in which students should encounter religion. The approach presupposes
that every student has a longing for the Holy and that teaching religion in school
should help students deal with this longing. The transcendental serves the function of a guide or inspiration for human beings, and for human growth. A key
point is therefore the question regarding communication with this transcendental sphere. In this process, learning a "religious language" and "life interpretation" is of great importance.

The two textbooks reflect an understanding of religion in their use of concepts and terms such as "the transcendent," "the Holy," "a prophetic voice" and
"God." God, the Holy, religion and the prophetic voice appear as more or less
synonymous concepts. The conceptualization of religion in the textbooks can
therefore be characterized as religious, and maybe even confessional, when it is
related to a "prophetic voice" and God, especially in Afdal *et al.* (2001). This book
clearly displays a conceptualization of religion which seems to be an admixture
of Evangelical-Christian beliefs and the phenomenology of religion. In Sødal *et al.*
(2009), despite the reluctance to define religion, a phenomenological perspective
comes to the surface when religion is explained as "a mystery which thoughts
alone cannot perceive." Drawing on a phenomenological understanding of religion, both textbooks promote a conceptualization of religion which belongs to
a paradigm or era which is often described as closed within religious studies
(McCutcheon 2003). And drawing on a confessional Christian Evangelical tradition, Afdal *et al.* (2001) also promote a confessional Christian perspective, which
in 2013 is in conflict with the national curricula in the Norwegian educational
system. The religiousness in these perspectives becomes even clearer when they
are related to an understanding of RE as an existential subject and to perspectives
on the student's spiritual growth.

THE SIGNIFICANT CHARACTER OF RE: THE EXISTENTIAL DIMENSION

The introductory books are unanimous when they point to the existential dimension of RE being its significant character. This means that religion in RE, in some way or another, is, or has to be, related to the students' present lives. There is, in other words, a basic understanding in the introductory books that RE in school, and religion in itself, has an existential dimension for every human being. In terms of this existential dimension lies the possibility for RE teachers to facilitate the student's learning of religion through experiencing religion via the Holy, a transcendent sphere, God, hope or religious symbols. Such experience is intended to contribute to the student's personal and existential growth, which also displays how this discourse is embedded in the "whole child discourse." Some examples:
In Sødal *et al.*—

Det eksistensielle aspektet finnes neppe i samme grad i andre skolefag. For i religionsundervisningen handler det gjennomgående om hvordan livet kan forstås og tolkes—i enkeltstående hverdagssituasjoner, og på et mer grunnleggende nivå som er forankret i bestemte trostradisjoner. Det ligger i religionsundervisningens vesen at den må komme i kontakt med livsforståelsen til mennesker. (Sødal *et al.* 2009: 13)

The existential aspect [of RE] is hardly present in other subjects in school. RE is about interpretation and understanding of life—in everyday life and in a basic level which is based in distinct traditions of faith. It is in the nature of RE that it has to be connected with human beings' understanding of life. (Sødal *et al.* 2009: 13, my translation)

Det eksistensielle aspektet i religionsundervisningen knytter den i særlig grad opp mot skolens overordnede mål om å stimulere og utvikle "det meningssøkende mennesket." (Sødal *et al.* 2009: 13)

The existential aspect of RE relates it to the general aim of stimulating and developing "the spiritual human being."[11] (Sødal *et al.* 2009: 13, my translation)

In Afdal *et al.*—

Å anta at eleven er et meningssøkende vesen, at menneskene pr. definisjon søker en livstolkning, er et nødvendig og fruktbart perspektiv på faget. (Afdal *et al.* 2001: 206)

To presume that the student is a spiritual human being, [and] that human beings by definition are seeking a life interpretation, is a necessary and fruitful perspective on the subject [RE]. (Afdal *et al.* 2001: 206, my translation)

The excerpts offer just a few examples of how the introductory books understand RE in school as a subject with existential dimension as its significant character. The existential dimension is a way of relating RE to the students' lives here and now. This is clearly regarded as the best, and only, way to make RE interesting for the students. In all the books it is explicitly written that RE is of great importance for every human being, regardless of religious beliefs (or not) or age.

The introductory books' writings on such perspectives are to some extent inspired by Ninian Smart's experiential and emotional dimension of religion (Smart 1989: 13–14). Smart's dimension model helps provide a basis for understanding RE as a subject orientated towards an understanding of the students as spiritual human beings, with a longing for the Holy. Smart's dimensions even provide the basis and primary argument for making experience and feelings essential to understanding religion, and to conceptualizing religion in reference to the Holy. As part of his well-known model, Smart writes: "And it is obvious that the emotions and experiences of men and women are the food on which the other dimensions feed: ritual without feeling is cold, doctrines without awe or compassion are dry, and myths which do not move hearers are feeble" (Smart 1989: 13). Therefore, according to Smart, it is important to enter the feelings which religions generate, and to "feel the sacred awe, the calm peace, the rousing inner dynamism," and so on (Smart 1989: 13).

Smart is given quite a bit of importance when introductory books underline the significance of experience and feelings. Afdal *et al.* writes:

Smart har lagt ned et stort arbeid i å vise at et religionsstudium ikke kan nøye seg med det rent deskriptive, slik mye empirisk-historisk religions-vitenskap har gjort. (Afdal *et al.* 2001: 207)

Smart has made great effort to show that religious studies cannot be limited to description only, like a great deal of empirical-historical comparative religion has done. (Afdal *et al.* 2001: 207, my translation)

Smart's understanding is adopted when the introductory books unanimously argue that if RE does not take into account the experiential and emotional aspect of religion, it might, according to Afdal *et al.* (2001), be labelled as "limited," "intellectualized" and "distant" (Andreassen 2008: 92–97, 122). The academic study of religions, religious studies, is clearly the addressee of what is referred to as limited, intellectualized and distant.

The works of Ninian Smart have experienced quite a renaissance in Norwegian RE. His seven-dimension model presented in *The World's Religions* (1989) is frequently cited. Among experts in the didactics of religion, special emphasis is often placed on the dimension of experience and emotions. Smart himself writes that "the emotions and experiences of men and women are the food on which the other dimensions of religion feed," and further makes it clear that "If our seven-dimensional portrait of religions is adequate, then we do not need to worry greatly about further definitions of religion" (1989: 13, 21). This offers an opportunity for the phenomenologically- and theologically-inspired RE experts to maintain their orientation towards emotions and experience, and it allows them to avoid the problem of defining religion in their textbooks. From my point of view, there has been a strategic use of Smart's work to legitimize established theological perspectives as if they corresponded with religious studies (Andreassen 2010).

AN EMPATHETIC CONCEPTUALIZATION OF RELIGION

So far I have argued that the introductory books that dominate reading lists for teacher education present an understanding of religion through the Holy and as a transcendent sphere, which can be experienced through emotions and experiences. It presupposes that students have a longing for the Holy and, in facilitating experiences of the Holy, students might relate religion to their own spiritual growth and development as human beings. Thus, RE in school is clearly understood as an existential subject, and religion in RE is understood as a highly valuable existential resource for students.

Religion, as the Holy, is regarded as a common human phenomenon and therefore ought to be connected to the student's existence. Making this connection is the way in which the student's supposed longing for the Holy can be satisfied. Accordingly, it is argued in the textbooks, students should also learn something *from* religion—not simply gaining knowledge *about* religions. An understanding of religion has to be acquired via experiences and feelings. In this process empathy is important. A clear distinction is made between an empathetic understanding of religion, which is characterized as an approach in which experience and emotions are important, and, on the other hand, a more cognitive and analytical approach, which is regarded as limited in terms of understanding religion. Some examples of how this is formulated in the texts follow:

> Reform 94's fagplan for Religion og etikk synes enda mer intellektualisert og distansert i forhold til erfaringslæring enn fagplanen for KRLs ungdomstrinn. Når målet i første rekke er rasjonell fagkunnskap, kan en spørre seg om ikke allmenndannelsen er kjørt ut i en grøft den har problemer med å komme seg opp av. Tross en slik kritisk hovedinnvending, må den enkelte religionslærer ut fra planens rammefaktorer i det minste et par ganger i løpet av skoleåret kunne stoppe opp ved egnede emner og skape et rom for stillhet og hellighet. [...] Det må etter hvert bli utviklet blant annet audiovisuelle læremidler som kan skape kanaler for hellighetserfaringer. (Afdal *et al.* 2001: 216)

> The curriculum for RE in upper-secondary school seems even more intellectualized and distant to learning through experience than the curriculum for RE in secondary school. When the main aim is to achieve rational [technical]

knowledge, one might ask if the general education ["Bildung"] is run into a ditch and stuck there. Despite this critical objection, every single RE teacher must, within the curriculum's limits, at least a couple of times during the school year, stop whenever appropriate, and create a room for silence and holiness... Audiovisual aids also have to be developed which can create channels for experiencing the Holy. (Afdal *et al.* 2001: 216, my translation)

Med personlighetskunnskap siktes det her til at bilder kan kommunisere på andre nivåer enn det intellektuelle eller analytiske. De kan gi opplevelser, følelser, stemninger og fornemmelser som er dypt personlige, og som derfor ikke kan formaliseres i undervisningen. Slik personlig kunnskap er likevel viktig, og en bør gi rom for både faglige og ikke-faglige reaksjoner på bildene. (Sødal *et al.* 2009: 129)

By "knowledge of the person" (personal knowledge)[12] we here refer to pictures[13] which might communicate on other levels than the intellectual or the analytical. Pictures might give experiences, feelings, moods or intuitions which are highly personal, and therefore cannot be formalized in the teaching. Such personal knowledge is still important, and one ought to create room for different reactions when using pictures. (Sødal *et al.* 2009: 129, my translation)

Selv om barna ikke kognitivt skjønner trosinnholdet fullt ut, kan de delta i et religiøst fellesskap. De kan utføre ritualer og ha religiøse opplevelser. Barn har med andre ord forutsetning for religion, også før de har valgt selv og forstår intellektuelt... Det religiøse er dypest sett et mysterium tanken alene ikke kan fatte. (Sødal *et al.* 2009: 62)

Even if the children do not fully have a cognitive understanding of the content of faith, they nevertheless might participate in a religious community. They can take part in rituals and have religious experiences. Children have, in other words, a disposition for religion even before they have made a choice themselves or before they understand intellectually... The religious is deeply a mystery which thoughts alone cannot perceive. (Sødal *et al.* 2009: 62, my translation)

These excerpts illustrate how experience and emotions are emphasized. Religion in RE has to be interlinked with student experiences and emotions, while a more cognitive approach is evaluated as "limited." Only an empathetic attitude can secure good learning in RE, and, according to the introductory books, good learning is, of course, learning *from* religion and relating it to the student's existence.

Religion can thus only be understood through the proper degree of empathy, emotions and experience. For students to learn something in RE, empathy and awe seem to be the important skills.

RELIGION AS A RESERVOIR OF SYMBOLS

The empathetic understanding of religion and a student-oriented conceptualization of knowledge have a long tradition in Norwegian didactics of religion. It is
also closely related to the concept of learning *from* religions in RE. A part of this
perspective is the concept of "*livstolkning*," usually translated in English as "life
interpretation." This concept of "life interpretation" seems, in my understanding of the concept, to be a didactical strategy in which experience, emotions and
the content of each religion can be related to each student's "life world." Again,
the basic assumption in the textbooks is that everyone can learn something *from*
every religion, not only *about* religions. Religion is in itself something good for
human beings. It is universal. As a consequence, religions appear to be a "reservoir of symbols," which can and should be used in the student's process of "life
interpretation." Independent of cultural context, behind religion lies the Holy,
which is universal and for which human beings long. This is especially clear in the
"contextual approach" presented in Afdal *et al.* (2001), in which the "contextual
approach" is anchored in contextual theology.

Learning *from* religions is also related to the introductory books' promotion
of so-called "aesthetic teaching." In Norwegian didactics of religion, aesthetics
has been of great importance since KRL was introduced in 1997. The "aesthetic
dimension" includes pictures, art, architecture, music, drama and literature. In
the introductory books aesthetics seems to be understood as a way of creating
and stimulating the student's emotions, empathy and experiences. Hence, aesthetics is a means within RE of making sure that RE teaching involves more than
technical knowledge and learning *about* religions.

The aesthetic dimension displays religious symbols in various ways. Through
religious stories, music and pictures (and audio-visual aids) symbols appear in
various shapes and meanings, and may be interpreted and treated in different
ways. As a result, religions appear as reservoirs of symbols, which are available
for students to use in their spiritual growth. This applies to all students and all
religions, and is probably why Afdal *et al.* (2001) point to the importance of developing audio-visual aids which can help lead students to experience the Holy. In
Sødal *et al.* (2009), aesthetics in general are promoted as a means to learn *from*
religions:

> Hvis en for raskt identifiserer denne fortellinga[14] som ei buddhistisk for-
> telling, risikerer en å snevre den inn slik at den får eksistensiell gyldighet
> bare for buddhister. Da kan den som ikke er buddhist, i høyden lære noe
> *om* buddhismen av denne fortellinga. Men det bør være åpenbart at dette
> er ei fortelling som alle kan ha noe å lære *av*, uavhengig av trostilhørighet
> og alder. (Sødal *et al.* 2009: 120)

If one too quickly identifies this story[15] as a story from Buddhism, one risks
limiting it to only having relevance for Buddhists. In that case, those who

are not Buddhists can only learn something about Buddhism. But it should be obvious that this is a story which everybody can learn something from, regardless of faith and age. (Sødal *et al.* 2009: 120)

Regarding the use of religious pictures and art, other more nuanced perspectives are also expressed in Sødal—for example, where it says that the specific religious tradition must not be devaluated (Sødal *et al.* 2009: 130). On the same page it also reads that religious stories have two dimensions: a "common human dimension" (Norwegian: *allmennmenneskelig*) and a "religious dimension" (Norwegian: *religionsspesifikk*). The basic assumption seems to be, in reference to this distinction, that religious aesthetics have a common human dimension as well as a religious dimension. It is the first of these two dimensions which makes it possible to use different aesthetic approaches and then relate them to an existential dimension when teaching RE.

RELIGION AS AN EXISTENTIAL RESOURCE

A conceptualization of religion which gives weight to learning *from* religions can be described as a resource perspective. Sociologist James A. Beckford (1992: 171) argues that religion in modern societies appears to be a cultural resource. Beckford claims that traditional religion has lost some of its significance in modern society, as a result of secularization and globalization. Still, Beckford argues, religion and religions "retain the capacity to symbolize, for example, ultimate meaning, infinite power, supreme indignation and sublime compassion" (1992: 171). From this perspective, borders between religions are diminished with the result that doctrines and religious leaders lose their status. The partial freeing of religion from its points of anchorage in communities and natural social groupings has also turned religion into a resource which may be invested with highly diverse meanings and used for a variety of purposes. As the introductory books put emphasis on the student's longing for the Holy, a transcendental sphere, and the importance of learning *from* religions, it is of no relevance whether it is a Hindu or Christian symbol, as long as the students can relate it to their own existence and spiritual growth. According to the textbooks, teaching RE should help provide opportunities for spiritual growth by making students aware of all religions as rivers of symbols, which it is possible to pick from and use.

As it is conceptualized in introductory books, religion as an existential resource seems to be a way of understanding religion which is not uncommon in a postmodern, "liquid" society (Bauman 2000). In many ways the textbooks develop what can be described as a "liquid school religion" without doctrines and rituals, but which can be applied to stimulate students' existential growth. The vagueness in this conceptualization of religion makes it possible to use religion in modern multicultural societies and educational systems. The rather loose conception of religion as a cultural resource provides a great degree of flexibility and unpredictability to religion. As an existential resource, and not as an old-fashioned dogmatic religion, it can be made relevant to students with little or no connection to formal religious organizations or groups. There is no escape, so to speak. Everybody can, and must, learn something *from* religions, according to the textbooks. In the textbooks a conceptualization of religion that is *not* open for use as a cultural resource is pushed away and characterized as an intellectualized and "distant" teaching.

There is not an academic consistent and explicit way of defining or understanding religion in these books. However, there are clearly influences from phenomenology of religion and liberal theology. These influences are used to promote what I have described as an *empathetic understanding* of religion. In addition it might be characterized as an *existential-functionalist* understanding of religion, in terms of the orientation towards the individual student and the way religions should be approached and applied.

In the existential-functionalist conceptualization of religion in introductory books there is no focus whatsoever on doctrines, rituals, organized communities—on what is usually characterized as traditional religion (Beckford 1992; Bauman 2000). As a result, or maybe because of it, religion and religious traditions can be regarded as traditions of holiness and transcendent spheres, and thus an opportunity to provide resources for spiritual growth. The reference made in Afdal *et al.* (2001) to the Holy or a transcendent sphere are of course the most explicit references to religion as a transcendent reality which human beings should try to contact. To learn *from* religion, or to experience the Holy, is, in the end, a subjective experience. To make learning *from* religions a valid perspective in a pluralistic society, religions have to be understood as a transcendent reality, and this transcendent reality as a reservoir of symbols. It does not matter whether it is Buddhism or Christianity—religion in either form represents a resource for spiritual growth.

FROM THE VANTAGE POINT OF AN RS-BASED RE

The existential-functionalist conceptualization of religion in the introductory books discussed here is clearly a part of a long tradition within phenomenologically- and theologically-based didactics of religions in Norway. The close relation between RE and the student's spiritual and personal growth has a long tradition in confessional RE and still represents a major perspective in Norwegian didactics of religion (Andreassen 2009). However, in confessional RE the main purpose is to ensure personal growth in accordance with Christianity. Today the curriculum and the Education Act in Norway make clear that teaching in RE must be non-confessional.

From the vantage point of the academic study of religions (Religious Studies), it is interesting how the textbooks describe this approach to religions. It is descriptive-empirical, distant, intellectualized and limited as an approach to understand religions, and thus, according to the textbook authors, irrelevant for RE. This seems to be mainly because religious studies has no place for experience and emotions and does not take the student's spiritual growth as a primary goal. There seems to be a major concern that an RS-based RE would drain religion of its potential as a resource for spiritual growth.

This of course provides a challenge for RS-based RE (cf. Jensen 2008, 2011), how to make this approach relevant in teacher education in general, and particularly in Norway. An attempt to deal with this challenge is the book in Norwegian *Religionsdidaktikk. En innføring*, published in 2012 (Andreassen 2012). In this book, I argue that if one turns to the official curriculum for RLE, perspectives from religious studies should be of obvious relevance for teacher education. Then it also becomes clear that the importance of learning *from* religions promoted by the textbooks is based on a rather challenging interpretation of the curriculum for RE. In all curricula for KRL and RLE since 1997 it has been made clear that the teaching should provide knowledge *about* religions and not be "*opplæring i religion*" [training in religion]. In the KRL curriculum from 1997:

> Faget skal gi kunnskaper om, ikke opplæring til, en bestemt tro! (KRL97: 89).

> The course will provide knowledge, not training in a particular faith! (my translation)

And in the curriculum for KRL in 2002 and 2005:

> Faget skal gi kunnskap og forståelse, ikke opplæring til en bestemt religion eller et bestemt livssyn..." (KRL-boka 2002: 12; KRL-boka 2005: 9)

> The teaching [in KRL] shall provide knowledge and understanding, not training for a particular religion or a particular belief. (my translation)

And in RLE in 2008:

> The subject shall teach knowledge of Christianity, other world religions and philosophies of life, and ethical and philosophical themes... Classroom teaching shall not include preaching, proselytising or religious practice. (RLE08, 1, official translation by DET)

As the curriculum so clearly expresses that the subject should provide students with knowledge and that RE is not an arena for religious practices, there should be no doubt that RE in Norway is a non-confessional school subject. After criticism from the UN in 2004 and the ECHR in 2007, it has been pointed out quite clearly—and even more clearly for each new curriculum—that religion education is supposed to provide information *about* religions.[16] In the 2008 curriculum, an additional formulation now reads that teachers should be careful when choosing pedagogical approaches:

> Care must be used when selecting working methods. The careful choice of working methods is especially important when considering parents, guardians and pupils so that they feel their own religion or philosophy of life is respected and that the subject be experienced without seeming to exercise another religion or forming an affiliation to another philosophy of life. Respect for the views of individuals and local communities should be paramount. (RLE08, 1, official translation by DET)

A similar remark and warning was originally included in the 2005 curriculum. The textbooks in didactics of religion clearly challenge some parts of the curriculum in RLE. This is especially the case in the promotion of the importance of religious language in relation to "life interpretation," where reference is made to the Holy or to a transcendent sphere, and where it is stated that every human being has a longing for the transcendent. When the curriculum underlines teaching *about* religions, the textbooks point to the importance of learning *from* religions.

The two textbooks in the didactics of religion which I have focused on here, and which represent the authoritative, official understanding of religion, are in fact out of step with the official curriculum for public education. They are still put forward and presented as relevant, which is possible because of the vague and empathetic conceptualization of religion, which had a positive goal interlinked with the pedagogical discourse on the whole child. Even if the conceptualization of religion is religious and closely related to Christian and liberal theological perspectives, and even if it is out of step with the official curriculum, the strategic alliance with whole child discourse makes this, the official, authoritative understanding of religion in teacher education, a powerful impetus that is difficult to change.

REFERENCES

Afdal, G., E. Haakedal and H. Leganger-Krogstad. 2001. *Tro, livstolkning og tradisjon. Innføring i kontekstuell religionsdidaktikk.* Oslo: Universitetsforlaget, 2nd edn.

Alberts, W. 2008. "Didactics of the Study of Religions." *Numen* 55(2-3): 300–34.

Andreassen, B.-O. 2008. "'Et ordinært fag i særklasse.' En analyse av fagdidaktiske perspektiver i innføringsbøker i religionsdidaktikk." PhD thesis. Tromsø: University of Tromsø.

Andreassen, B.-O. 2009. "Seige strukturer—perspektiver på endring og diskursivt arbeid i norsk religionsdidaktikk." *Din. Tidsskrift for religion og kultur* 1: 5–29.

Andreassen, B.-O. 2010. "Ninian Smarts dimensjonsmodell i tilnærmingen til religion i norsk religionsdidaktikk." *Religionsvidenskabeligt tidsskrift* 55: 55–73.

Andreassen, B.-O. 2012. *Religionsdidaktikk. En innføring.* Oslo: Universitetsforlaget.

Bauman, Z. 2000. *Liquid Modernity.* Cambridge: Polity Press.

Baumfield, V. 2006. "Textbooks and RE—Empowering or Restricting?" *British Journal of Religious Education* 28(3): 223–24.

Beckford, J. A. 1992. *Religion and Advanced Industrial Society*. London/New York: Routledge.

Cox, J. L. 2006. *A Guide to the Phenomenology of Religion*. London: T&T Clark International.

Fendler, L. 2001. "Educating Flexible Souls: The Construction of Subjectivity through Developmentality and Interaction." In *Governing the Child in the New Millennium*, ed. K. Hultqvist and G. Dahlberg, 119–42. London: RoutledgeFalmer.

Hudson, B., and M. A. Meyer. 2011. *Beyond Fragmentation: Didactics, Learning and Teaching in Europe*. Opladen: Barbara Budrich.

Issitt, J. 2004. "Reflections on the Study of Textbooks." *History of Education. Journal of the History of Education Society* 33(6): 683–96.

Jensen, T. 2008. "RS Based RE in Public School: A Must for a Secular State." *Numen* 55(2-3): 123–50.

Jensen, T. 2011. "Why Religion Education, as a Matter of Course, Ought to be a Part of the Public School Curriculum." In *Religious Education in a Plural, Secularised Society: A Paradigm Shift*, ed. L. Franken and P. Loobuyck, 131–49. Münster: Waxmann verlag.

Krejsler, J. 2006. "Education as Individualizing Technology: Exploring New Conditions for Producing Individuality." In *"The Future is not what It Appears to be." Pedagogy, Genealogy and Political Epistemology. In Honor and in Memory of Kenneth Hultqvist*, ed. T. S. Popkewitz, K. Petersson, U. Olsson and J. Kowalczyk, 193–212. Stockholm: HLS Förlag.

Künzli, R. 1998. "The Common Frame and the Places of Didaktik." In *Didaktik and/or Curriculum: An International Dialogue*, ed. B. Gundem and S. Hopmann, 29–45. New York: Peter Lang.

Lied, S. 2009. "The Norwegian Christianity, Religion and Philosophy Subject KRL in Strasbourg." *British Journal of Religious Education* 31(3): 263–75.

Maybin, J. 2001. "Language, Struggle and Voice: The Bakhtin/Volosinov Writings." In *Discourse Theory and Practice: A Reader*, ed. M. Wetherell, S. Taylor and S. Yates, 64–71. London: Sage.

McCutcheon, R. T. 2003. *The Discipline of Religion: Structure, Meaning, Rhetoric*. New York: Routledge.

Mogstad, S. D. 2004. *Fag, identitet og fortelling. Didaktikk til Kristendomskunnskap med religions- og livssynsorientering*. Oslo: Gyldendal akademisk, 2nd edn.

Murray, O. 2001. "Introduction." In F. Braudel, *Memory and the Mediterranean*, ix–xx. New York: Vintage Books.

Olsson, S. 2010. "*Our* View on the *Other*: Issues Regarding School Textbooks." *British Journal of Religious Education* 32(1): 41–48.

Otto, R. 1926. *The Idea of the Holy: An Inquiry into the Non Rational Factor in the Idea of the Divine*. London: Oxford University Press.

Rasmussen, T., and E. Thomassen. 1999. *Kildesamling til KRL. Bind 1-2*. Oslo: Nasjonalt læremiddelsenter.

Smart, N. 1989. *The World's Religions*. Cambridge: Cambridge University Press.

Skrunes, N. 2004. *Religionspedagogikk for grunnskolen: kristendomskunnskap med religions- og livssynsorientering*. Bergen: NLA-forlaget.

Sødal, H. K., R. Danielsen, L. G. Eidhamar, H. Hodne, S. Skeie and G. Winje. 2009. *Religions- og livssynsdidaktikk. En innføring*. Kristiansand: Høyskoleforlaget, 4th edn.

Stabell-Kulø, A. 2005. *Religioner i klasserommet. Innføring i religionsdidaktikk*. Bergen: Fagbokforlaget.

Wiebe, D. 1999. *The Politics of Religious Studies*. New York: Palgrave.

Endnotes

1. RLE is the abbreviation of the religious education subject in primary and secondary schools in Norway. The official English translation of the subject's name is Religion, Philosophy of Life and Ethics.
2. European Credit Transfer and Accumulation System (ECTS) is a standard for comparing the study attainment and performance of students of higher education across the European Union and other collaborating European countries. One academic year corresponds to 60 ECTS-credits that are equivalent to 1500–1800 hours of study.
3. There is only one book which has been written specifically for RLE and didactics of religion for teacher education since the last reform, and that is my own book which was published in Norwegian in 2012 (Andreassen 2012). A part of the work with analysing textbooks has also been to develop an alternative based on principles from the academic study of religion. My book is an attempt to present such an alternative. I will not discuss my own book in any further detail here.
4. In English, KRL is usually translated as Christianity, Religion and Life Stances.
5. HEF abbreviation for The Norwegian Humanist Association (in Norwegian, Human-Etisk forbund).
6. The site now has a new name and address: www.rlnett.no. The list of recommended books is still the same, http://www.rlnett.no/undermeny0302_bokliste.html (accessed 15.04.2011).
7. In Norwegian: *Utdanningsdirektoratet*. In the Directorate's website it reads: "The Norwegian Directorate for Education and Training is responsible for the development of primary and secondary education... The Directorate is the executive agency for the Ministry of Education and Research," http://www.utdanningsdirektoratet.no/templates/udir/TM_Artikkel.aspx?id=346 (accessed 15.04.2011).
8. In Norwegian: "*En grundig drøfting om hva religioner og livssyn er, hører primært hjemme i andre disipliner innen RLE-studiet*" (Sødal *et al.* 2009: 14). RLE in this context refers to the subject in the general teacher education in Norway.
9. In the book, what lies in the "subject oriented" understanding is not clearly explained any further, but the substantial definition of religions seems to be understood as more of a theoretical approach to religion, and therefore in contrast to the student-centred and functional understanding of religion.
10. The reference to the Norwegian theologian Notto Thelle (1994) is an article in Norwegian about the Holy published in a Norwegian journal.
11. "The Spiritual Human Being" is one of seven chapters of the *Core Curriculum* in Norway. The first six are "The Spiritual Human Being," "The Creative Human Being," "The Working Human Being," "The Liberally-Educated Human Being," "The Social Human Being" and "The Environmental Human Being." These six chapters are integrated in the final seventh chapter of the *Core Curriculum*, which is called "The Integrated Human Being."
12. The Norwegian word used here, "*personlighetskunnskap*," is difficult to translate. It could either be translated as "knowledge of the person" or "personal knowledge." I have chosen the latter alternative. The main point is that it is a kind of knowledge which should be made personal. This means that it is also individual and closely connected to emotions and personal experience.
13. The text here refers to actual pictures and how to use pictures in teaching, especially religious art. There is also a warning in the text: "The analytical approach should not be pre-

ferred to the student's immediate experience of the art. Still, a rational approach is also necessary when one is using art in teaching" (Sødal *et al.* 2009: 130–31).

14. Fortellingen det refereres til er fra Zen-buddhismen og handler om Shichiri Kojun og er hentet fra *Kildesamling til KRL. Bind 2* (Rasmussen and Thomassen 1999: 472).

15. The story discussed here is a Zen Buddhist story about Shichiri Kojun. The story is presented in a collection of textual sources from different religions as a teaching resource for RE teachers (Rasmussen and Thomassen 1999: 472).

16. At this point it is important to mention that the introductory books which I have analysed were mainly written in reference to the curriculum from 1997. Only Sødal *et al.* (2009) has been revised and printed in new editions as a result of changes in the curriculum. A great deal has happened in RE in Norway and, with a new curriculum every third year, it is of course difficult for authors of introductory books to keep track of every single change. And, of course, publishers are probably not too happy about the need for such rapid revisions. Still, Sødal *et al.* (2009) is the only book which is updated in accordance with changes made in the curriculum. Afdal *et al.* (2001) is still available for purchase but appears rather outdated with its reference only to the 1997 curriculum.

10. STONES AND BONES: INDIGENOUS AFRICAN RELIGIONS AND THE "EVOLUTION" OF WORLD RELIGIONS

James R. Lewis*

> At Lomé in Central Togo, a strange selection of stones, skulls and bones are on sale as fetishes. Spirits are believed to reside in the fetishes.
> (Illustration caption in Eerdman's *Handbook to the World's Religions*
> [Beaver *et al.* 1982: 130])

Over two decades ago, my article on "Images of Traditional African Religions in Surveys of World Religions" appeared in the well-regarded journal *Religion* (Lewis 1990). When I began to rewrite it as the basis for the current chapter, I found—as I assume other writers have discovered when they try to rewrite a prior composition—that the original piece exhibited an unexpected internal coherence that resisted modification. So rather than write an entirely new paper, what I eventually decided to do instead was to make some relatively minor changes in the original and add a new concluding section that would bring my analysis of the evolutionary pattern found in the majority of world religions textbooks up to date by examining the structures of the texts currently available for world religions survey courses.

I

Since at least the 1970s, academicians have invested increasing amounts of energy into analysing the scholarly discourse of previous eras, particularly the scholarship that was carried out by colonialist nations with respect to subject peoples. The focus of most of this work has been to point out how the images

* James R. Lewis is Professor at the University of Tromsø. His most recent books include *Sacred Schisms* (edited with Sarah Lewis; Cambridge University Press, 2009) and *Children of Jesus and Mary* (with Nicolas Levine; Oxford University Press, 2010). He is editor of *The Oxford Handbook of New Religious Movements*.

of non-European peoples presented in such discourse were shaped by the (usually unconscious) presuppositions of European scholars, as well as how this scholarship ultimately fed back into, and helped to legitimate, imperialist attitudes. With respect to Africa, the connection between colonialism and scholarship is especially clear because it was in Africa that the policy of "indirect rule" (i.e., leaving ground-level administration in the hands of "customary rulers") was implemented most fully. Anthropologists played an important role in this system by providing colonial administrators with information necessary to oversee the activities of traditional leaders. Such an orientation inevitably influenced the direction of anthropological theorizing.[1] Ethnologists also tended to legitimize colonialism by portraying conquered peoples as living in "static," or socially "unevolved" cultures from which the colonial system would eventually liberate them. And, while in recent decades the imperialist enterprise has been largely abandoned, residues of these older formations of scholarship continue to linger into the present.

As someone who has been professionally involved in the teaching of general courses on world religions, I became interested in examining how non-Western peoples were presented in contemporary survey treatments of world religions, especially the representations found in world religions textbooks. In line with the practice of other academic disciplines, most religious studies departments offer certain standard, introductory courses to undergraduate college students. Out of this standard offering, the only course in which one is likely to encounter traditional African religions is "world religions," or some similarly designated class—a fast-moving survey that leaves the student with a shallow and often confused impression of everything from sacred cows to the doctrine of vicarious atonement. While older textbooks for such courses dealt with the religions of traditional societies under the generic category "primitive," more recent texts have tended to replace chapters on "primitive" religions with chapters on the traditional religions of particular continents, chapters that often include treatments of specific ethnic groups. Because of the large number of people of African ancestry in the United States—where most world religions textbooks are produced and where most world religions courses are taught—as well as certain other factors, such as the large number of available sources, the religions utilized for such chapters are most often African religions, with Native American religions running a close second.

A lifelong exposure to the popular media has tended to implant crude, negative stereotypes about unfamiliar cultures in the minds of most Western students. In the words of one author of a world religions text:

Perhaps no religions have been so confused in the minds of Western audiences as the religions of Africa. The images of these religions as presented in films and popular literature depict the black African as a hopeless savage and African religion as ugly superstition. Most people associate African religions with the image of a missionary in the cannibal's pot about to be boiled and eaten. Or people remember the many, many motion pictures in which the evil witch doctor in a horrible mask tries to put a voodoo curse upon a victim. Even supposedly factual sources are likely to contain images of blood sacrifice, fetishes, shrunken heads, and babies sacrificed to crocodile gods. (Hopfe 1983: 57–58)

World religions courses provide one of the few institutionalized avenues through which these negative images can be overcome, though this potential is seldom realized in practice.

The present chapter arises, as I have already noted, directly out of this writer's experience of teaching world religions. My pedagogical goals for such courses have been comparatively modest; in addition to trying to convey a basic understanding of a select number of religions, I have also attempted to make a dent in the abysmal ethnocentrism that characterizes most students (particularly American students). With respect to this goal of breaking down the barrier between "us" and "them," my basic feeling is that the task is hindered rather than assisted by the majority of available world religions textbooks. While most contemporary writers have abandoned overtly prejudicial discourse, many of the old stereotypes continue to be expressed in subtle ways. The following pages will analyse the treatment of traditional African religions in these texts,[2] focusing on the tendency of authors to (1) emphasize sensationalistic items of information, (2) treat different religious traditions unevenly, and, especially, (3) arrange religions into implicit evolutionary hierarchies.

Before proceeding, it should be remarked that many of the points that I will be criticizing originate in faulty scholarship on African religions, especially the scholarship produced by earlier generations of Africanists, which textbook writers have merely reproduced. Contemporary authors are not, in other words, personally culpable for all of the faults found in their productions. However, once a faulty item of scholarship is incorporated into a popular textbook, it tends not to get corrected in subsequent editions—and some world religions textbooks are currently in their twelfth and thirteenth editions.

II

Before moving into the analysis proper, I will "unpack" an especially rich statement found in a world religions survey text that will provide us with a larger context for the present discussion. This exercise will also give the reader a sense of my general approach to such texts, which is a close reading that develops a critique by pulling out unstated implications and corollaries. The following passage is taken from the 1983 edition of Lewis M. Hopfe's *Religions of the World*:

African nations have become a vocal and active segment of the so-called Third World. Many of them control raw materials that are essential to the industrialized nations of the world. The leaders of today and of the future must learn to deal with Africans on both political and business levels if there is to be peace and prosperity in the world. Essential to understanding the leaders of black Africa is a knowledge of their culture. A major step in understanding customs and values is a basic knowledge of religion. (Hopfe 1983: 57)

The difference between the overt, "foreground" message of this citation and some of the author's underlying assumptions—which are just visible in the "background"—is symptomatic of a contrast that we find in many other survey texts. To the superficial reader, presumably a citizen of an "industrialized nation," Hopfe would appear to be saying that African peoples and their religions need to be understood in order to make the world a more peaceful place. I have little doubt that he consciously intended to convey this message. Hopfe presupposes, however, a certain view of the world as well as a certain view of the function of knowledge that cannot simply be taken for granted.

In the first place, the author emphasizes the distinction between "us" and "them" in language that suggests a qualitative difference. While not explicit in this particular passage, at least one aspect of his conceptualization of the us/them dichotomy can be uncovered by looking elsewhere in the book. Specifically, one finds that 32 pages earlier Hopfe had referred to societies in "less-developed areas of the world" as "primitive" (Hopfe 1983: 15), a designation which implies that industrialized societies are "civilized" (i.e., the term "primitive" is a polar notion that makes no sense without "civilized," its conceptual complement.)[3] And, because the primitive/civilized contrast is a value judgment rather than an empirical distinction,[4] he has thus subtly (and, to give Hopfe the benefit of the doubt, unconsciously) provided support for the reader's ethnocentrism.

The judgmental aspect of this distinction is reinforced by the author's apparent approval of the perpetuation of the colonial economics in the postcolonial world: "they" (in this case Africans) must continue to supply "us" (the industrialized West) with the raw materials necessary for our highly consumptive lifestyles in order to maintain "peace and prosperity in the world." This self-serving, "Westocentric" vision clearly implies that the material happiness of "civilized" peoples is such a desirable value that it can legitimate the continued exploitation of "primitive" peoples. As if this picture of the relationship between the industrialized West and Africa was not bad enough, Hopfe tops off his vision of the world with an imperialist view of knowledge: in order to maintain colonialist economics—in order to better manipulate the leaders of Black Africa, and, consequently, to obtain needed raw materials—politicians and businessmen must learn more about African culture and religion. This view of knowledge represents a new incarnation of the attitude of colonial anthropologists who willingly adopted the role of handmaidens to imperialism. Such a pragmatic, instrumentalist perspective, which reduces the understanding of other people's religious traditions to little more than a variable in a political-economic calculus, is clearly at odds with any kind of humanistic pedagogy.

III

Before looking closely at other contemporary authors, it should be said that almost any text published within the last 20 or 30 years represents a welcome change from comparable works published earlier in the preceding century. Previous generations of writers, even by the middle of the twentieth century, felt free to give expression to such demeaning remarks as "[t]he thought-life of these people is weak and covers a very limited range" (Soper 1951: 34), or, to cite a couple more examples,

> It is possible to get lightning-flash glimpses, sudden, fragmentary, of a primitive mind at work, with its slow stupidity and fear... Very primitive minds even now are unsure of the recurrences of nature, believing sun and season are whimsical. (Hawkridge 1970: 4)[5]

> [A]n estimated 40 percent of the world's people still live under extremely primitive conditions... The outward circumstances of their lives are, as a matter of course, reflected in their worship rites and religious practices... No "savages" have yet been found with a highly developed religion. (Ham 1966: 44–45)

However, as demeaning as such statements undoubtedly are, they constitute a considerable improvement over such nineteenth-century statements as,

> The religion of the Dahomans, like that of the neighboring kingdoms, consist of such a mass of superstition as can hardly be described... The Ashantees are, perhaps, the most polished nation of negroes to be met with in Western Africa. They are, however, gross idolaters, and most lavish of human blood sacrifices at their funerals and festivals. (Milner 1871: 494–95).

The one exception to the development of less evaluative discourse is that a few recent authors have continued to use the word "superstition," as when Geoffrey Parrinder says, in the context of a discussion of African religions, that "magical superstitions are more tenacious and will long remain" (Parrinder 1983: 68)[6] but, except for new editions of older books, even this term has dropped out of most current works.

While most present-day writers have set aside explicitly prejudicial discourse about traditional religions, there is still a lamentable tendency to call attention to sensationalistic (to the outsider) aspects of the cultural life of a few peoples. Allow me to illustrate what I mean with a couple of citations from two contemporary world religions texts:

Female circumcision is still practiced among some African peoples...
Sometimes this circumcision is clitoridectomy, while at other times the
labia is mutilated...there seems to be no clear reason for this practice.
(Hopfe 1983: 70)[7]

The birth of twins or triplets is an extraordinary event, frequently viewed
with superstitious fear. Some African societies expose or kill such children,
or even kill the mother. (Hutchinson 1981: 34)

Especially when stated in such an incautious manner, remarks like these tend to
prejudice students' impressions of African religion, particularly as these charac-
terizations reinforce the stereotypes that most students bring to the course in
the first place. It should also be pointed out that comparatively sensationalistic
practices in other religions, such as snake-handling in certain Christian sects,
somehow fail to be mentioned in these surveys, or, when they *are* mentioned, the
thrust of the discussion is to cast aspersions on both.[8]

Another, subtler way in which authors sometimes slight African traditional
religions is in their choice of illustrations. *Eerdman's Handbook to the World's Religions*, for example, contains a rather striking picture with the caption, "[a]t Lomé
in Central Togo, a strange selection of stones, skulls and bones are on sale as fetishes. Spirits are believed to reside in the fetishes" (Beaver 1982: 130). Or, to take
another example, in *The Religious World*, one finds a picture of a wooden stool that
has been carved into the shape of a half-naked woman (Nanji 1988: 46); not the
kind of image that would provoke positive associations in the minds of students,
particularly female students.

A more subtle but, to my way of thinking, more pernicious pattern is for
authors to call attention to such phenomena as possession and "black" magic
among traditional peoples while failing to mention that such practices are widespread among adherents of most major world religions. For example, in the African religions section of the multi-authored work, *The Religious World*, one learns
that, among the Akan, spirits "can often possess people and cause disease or mad-
ness" (Nanji 1988: 36). But in the Hinduism chapter, one does *not* learn that the
great majority of Hindus hold precisely the *same* belief, not to mention the members of most other world religions.

Another example of this one-sided approach is the tendency to note acts of
sacrifice in African religions without noting the same pattern in other world religions. For instance, in *Religions of the World*, Lewis Hopfe observes that "[o]ne of
the most common practices in all of the religions of the world is sacrifice," including the "relatively rare practice" of human sacrifice (Hopfe 1983: 28). However,
the only place in the text where he gives sacrifice more than a passing mention
is in his chapter on African religions, a chapter that includes several paragraphs
given over to an analysis of human sacrifice. While the majority of other contemporary texts are more balanced on this particular point, none that I have carefully
examined bother to bring up the rather obvious fact that the central redemptive

drama in Christianity represents a comparable form of human sacrifice. If this were pointed out in the right way, it might reduce the sense of alienation that students feel when they study the sacrificial practices of other religious traditions.

After reading about 20 textbooks, I concluded that the more authors concentrated on specific groups, the less they tended to bring up sensationalist details or to indulge in pejorative statements. In other words, the best treatments of traditional African religions were the ones that focused on the religious life of the Nuer or the Dogon or some other particular people. Poor surveys were most often those that lumped together diverse groups of people under such labels as "African Religion" or "Native American Religion," with the worst treatments tending to be those that placed every tradition that was not a major world religion in the generic category "Primitive Religion."[9] With respect to African religions, it was clear that the source of the skewed image presented in these surveys was that such a broad classification allowed authors to range over the diversity of traditions, pick out their most sensationalistic aspects, and present them together as if the composite image gave one a true picture of "African-religion-in-general," an image most of the relevant authors likely did not intend to create. The lesson to be learned here is that future world religion textbook authors should concentrate their efforts on specific traditions and not create broad categories for religions that share little more than a common geographical location, and, of course, the common traits shared by all religions universally.

IV

One final, major fault that can be found in almost all general surveys is the implicit evolutionary structure according to which the majority of world religion texts are organized. Most contemporary survey works that I have examined devote at least some space to a discussion of the religions of traditional societies. For reasons that have already been mentioned, African religions (sometimes specific ethnic groups, sometimes traditional African religions as a whole) are most often chosen to exemplify such religions. The implicit evolutionary structure comes through in two ways (1) the religions of traditional societies are almost always dealt with at the beginning of the book, with Semitic religions usually being treated last (while the majority of contemporary texts terminate in Islam because of its status as the most recent of the major world religions, early twentieth-century texts were more explicitly Eurocentric, as evidenced by their tendency to culminate in Christianity),[10] (2) more often than not, authors of survey texts group prehistoric and smaller contemporary religions together. The following are a few examples of this later tendency. Chapter 1 of the seventh edition of John B. Noss and Davis S. Noss's *Man's Religions* is entitled "Religion in Prehistoric and Primitive Cultures," a chapter that discusses the religions of Cro-Magnons as well as the religion of the Ba Venda of South Africa (Noss and Noss 1984). Part one of Denise Lardner Carmody and John Tully Carmody's *Ways to the Center* is entitled "Ancient

Religions," within which are subsections on both "Prehistoric Religion" and the traditional religions of contemporary Africans (Carmody and Carmody 1981). Chapter 2 of Ward J. Fellows' *Religions East and West* groups together "Some Prehistoric, Primitive, and Ancient Religions" (Fellows 1979). The subtitle of Robert Ellwood's second chapter in *Many Peoples, Many Faiths* is "Prehistoric and Tribal Religion" (Ellwood 1987). Only slightly less obvious are works like Lewis M. Hopfe's *Religions of the World* that, under the title "Basic Religions," discusses both the "Prehistoric Beginnings of Basic Religions" and "African Religions." Most revealing are such remarks as "[t]he Neur are a Neolithic people" (Fellows 1979: 21),[11] and explicit arguments for grouping together "Prehistoric and Primal Religions" (Smart 1984: 27–29).

An interesting variation on this pattern are books in which sections on African and Native American religions are located *prior to* surveys on the no longer extant religions of the ancient cited culture, such as the religions of classical Greece and Rome. Such an arrangement implies that the religions of contemporary traditional peoples represent an earlier developmental stage than the religions of the ancient world. Some current texts containing this structure are the Noss and Noss volume, which discusses "Religion in Pre-historic and Primitive Cultures" in chapter 1 and "Bygone Religions that Have Left their Mark on the West" in chapter 2, the Carmody and Carmody volume which places the "Religions of Oral Peoples" prior to the "Religions of Ancient Civilizations," John A. Hutchinson's *Paths of Faith* (1981) which discusses "African Traditional Religion" and "American Indian Religion" before "Mesopotamian Religion" and "Greek Religion," and Niels C. Nielsen *et al.*, *Religions of the World* (1983) which surveys "Religious Symbolism among the Dogon and Yoruba" in chapter 2 and the "Religions of the Ancient World" in chapter 3.

In close readings of contemporary world religion texts, it is sometimes possible to uncover tangible traces of the evaluative freight being carried by this kind of temporal discourse. For example, after grouping together "pre-historic, African traditional, and American Indian" religions, John Hutchinson goes on to discuss humanity's "breakthrough" to "civilization"—a kind of language that belies his earlier assertions that he is describing rather than evaluating "preliterate" societies (Hutchinson 1981: 23). Also, in *Many Peoples, Many Faiths*, Robert S. Ellwood goes so far as to observe that "the world of non-literate religions indeed seems childlike" (Ellwood 1987: 28)—a contemporary echo of the older evolutionary approach that characterized traditional peoples, both ancient and modern, as constituting the childhood of the human race.

A more subtle example of such normative discourse can be found in Ninian Smart's argument for utilizing contemporary traditional religions for understanding prehistoric religions, an argument which can be found in the third edition of his *The Religious Experience of Mankind*.[12] Smart asserts, for example, that "[b]ecause literate cultures tend to prize intellectual knowledge, the historical religions generally have a more developed doctrinal dimension than is the case in tribal and preliterate religions" (Smart 1984: 27). The obvious though unstated corollary of the first clause of this statement is that "tribal and preliterate religions" do *not* "prize intellectual knowledge," an assertion that is true only if one defines "intellectual knowledge" as written knowledge, in which case the statement becomes tautological, rather than an empirical observation. Another remarkable sentence that one finds on the same page is the statement that "for prehistoric men (*sic*), and for his contemporary counterpart, religion is part of the fabric of ordinary existence, of custom rather than of conscious choice." Once again the unstated corollary, which in this case is the assertion that for members of the major world faiths religion *is* a matter of conscious choice rather than custom, is simply untrue for the great bulk of the human race.

One of the reasons why I am subjecting to close scrutiny the tendency to conflate contemporary traditional peoples with prehistoric peoples is that some of the most derogatory remarks found in the productions of earlier scholars were articulated in the context of evolutionary discourse. If this kind of judgmental discourse continues, albeit unconsciously, to influence current academic productions, it is likely to reinforce the more consciously and explicitly held prejudices of undergraduate students. To cite at length one particularly revealing passage that well exemplifies the judgmental approach of our academic "ancestors," and which probably represents a close approximation of the attitude we often confront in our classrooms,

> A scientist may reconstruct a skull from a fragment, or even assume a race from a molar tooth, but how can he reshape ideas that used to be inside the broken skull? Two clues are the arts and tools left by the prehistoric men; and the customs of present-day primitive tribes, which often seem like living illustrations. For the savages are conservatives, who cling to basic routines in spite of change of place and time, and the superficial variations that time and place bring them. Their ways are amber, preserving little flies of old custom... The customs of the stone age can be matched in savage ritual today, sometimes in such striking likeness of detail that it gives an almost incredible sense of community and stubbornness... The conservatism is glacial. Modern savages may have their customs changed by contact with brighter races, but the study of their ways, their sense of values, gives a suggestion of the mentality of ancient man. (Hawkridge 1970: 6, 11)[13]

How the author knows that there is a "striking likeness of detail" between contemporary rituals and the customs of the stone age is unclear. Even more problematic is the characterization of members of "non-savage" nations as "brighter" races, an attribution which clearly implies that "modern savages," as well as ancient peoples, are and were "dumber" races.

Another important unstated corollary is that whereas "primitive" societies are static and unchanging, "civilized" societies are dynamic and progressive. The description of both prehistoric and present-day traditional religions as "unchanging" persisted in Western discourse, until very recently, in the face of much disconfirming evidence because the static-progressive contrast occupied a central place in the ideology of "civilization," an ideology which required that other groups of people play the role of regressive counter-images.[14] A more contemporary view is that so-called "primitive" religions are flexible traditions, quite capable of adapting to social and environmental changes.[15]

Although no contemporary author consciously intends to increase the felt distance between "us" and "them," any discourse that places traditional peoples in another time or in another stage of development will inevitably increase this distance by emphasizing these peoples" "otherness." In other words, the net effect of temporal distantiation is to reinforce further the sense of alienation that is promoted by the factors mentioned in section three. It thus seems to me that any author who wants to humanize the treatment of other groups of people will have to take seriously the project outlined by Johannes Fabian in *Time and the Other*, the goal of which is "[t]he radical contemporaneity of mankind" (Fabian 1983: xi).

V

My goals in this new postscript are modest. The most significant criticism levelled in my survey of world religion textbooks is the implicit evolutionary structure reflected in the order of chapters, so that smaller-scale traditional religions such as the aboriginal religions of sub-Saharan Africa are typically placed at the beginning of these texts as if to suggest that such religions represent an earlier level of religious development. Almost all relevant textbooks continue to reflect this structure, but not every survey text groups currently-existing peoples together with prehistoric peoples, and not every such book discusses the religions of contemporary indigenous peoples prior to discussing the dead religions of the classical world. So I decided to examine the tables of contents of a select number of contemporary world religion surveys.

To begin with, I was really rather shocked to find that certain older textbooks, such as the Hopfe and Noss volumes, had survived by reincarnating into twelfth editions (e.g., Hopfe and Woodward 2012) and thirteenth editions (e.g., Noss and Grangaard 2011). In these two cases, the original authors are dead, but publishers perpetuated their legacies by bringing in co-authors to revise the texts for new editions. The most recent edition of Lewis M. Hopfe and Mark R. Woodward's volume continues to include a chapter on generic African religions, which is one of the approaches I earlier identified as problematic. As with almost all recent textbooks, Hopfe and Woodward continue the tradition of placing African and Native American religions near the beginning of their volume and concluding with the Semitic traditions.

David S. Noss and Blake R. Grangaard's text continues to replicate the pattern of its earlier editions by grouping together "Primal and Prehistoric Cultures" (which include the BaVenda of Africa), and placing these prior to "Bygone Religions that Have Left their Mark on the West," such as ancient Mediterranean religions. Thus while the volume avoids the generic African religions issue found in Hopfe and Woodward, it constitutes the most egregious example of the temporal distancing of living peoples by simultaneously placing a living African religion alongside prehistoric religions, and by placing the BaVenda plus certain other contemporary peoples in a chapter that precedes the chapter on the no longer extant religions of classical Greece and Rome. Like Hopfe and Woodward, Noss and Grangaard begin with "Primal" religions and culminate with the Semitic traditions. In another example of this kind of temporal distancing, in the ninth edition of another older book that has picked up a co-editor, Robert S. Ellwood and Barbara A. McGraw's *Many People, Many Faiths* (2009), "The Religions of Prehistoric and Tribal Peoples" are grouped together under one heading.

Before some readers respond that it might seem "obvious" or "natural" to group traditional and prehistoric religions together, or that it somehow makes sense to place certain contemporary aboriginal religions in an earlier developmental stage than the religions of the ancient cited cultures, it should be noted that these patterns are *not* "obvious" to more recent textbook authors. Thus, to take one refreshing example, in Christopher Partridge's *Introduction to World Religions* (2005), the "Religions of Antiquity" are discussed in the second chapter, which is followed by the third chapter on "Indigenous Religions." I also liked the fact that Partridge placed his chapter on East Asian religions toward the end of his book, following chapters on Judaism, Christianity and Islam. Similarly, in Solomon A. Nigosian's *World Religions* (2008), chapters on African and American Indian religions follow a set of chapters on the "Religions of the Past." And in Roger Schmidt *et al. Patterns of Religion* (2004), "Ancient Religions" are examined prior to "Indigenous Religions."

I have noticed that some of the more recent entries in this field have switched the placements of the Asian religions and the Semitic religions, so that chapters on Judaism, Christianity and Islam are situated prior to the Hinduism, Buddhism and East Asian traditions chapters (e.g., Oxtoby and Segal 2011). However, even some of the better world religion textbooks continue to place African and other indigenous religions near the beginning of their volumes (e.g., Hexham 2011), which still implies that they are located at some sort of earlier developmental stage.

One remarkable exception to this pattern is John L. Esposito, Darrell J. Fasching, and Todd Lewis's *World Religions Today* (2011). These authors abandon the indigenous category altogether, begin their textbook with discussions of some of the major forces shaping contemporary religions—such as colonialism and modernism—and make Christianity the first religion they examine. *World Religions Today* thus completely avoids the problem of arranging different religions into developmental sequences, though it leaves instructors who want to cover some aspect of indigenous traditions in their courses on their own to find relevant supplemental reading material. I would, nevertheless, be more likely to adopt *World Religions Today* as my primary text over other options should I ever again be called upon to teach a world religions course.

REFERENCES

Beaver, R. Pierce *et al.*, eds. 1982. *Eerdman's Handbook to the World's Religions*. Grand Rapids, MI: Eerdmans.

Bradley, David G. 1963. *A Guide to the World's Religions*. Englewood Cliffs, NJ: Prentice-Hall.

Carmody, Denise L., and John T. Carmody. 1981. *Ways to the Centre: An Introduction to World Religions*. Belmont, CA: Wadsworth.

Ellwood, Robert S. 1987. *Many Peoples, Many Faiths: An Introduction to the Religious Life of Humankind*. Englewood Cliffs, NJ: Prentice-Hall, 3rd edn.

Ellwood, Robert S., and Barbara A. McGraw. 2009. *Many People, Many Faiths*. Upper Saddle River, NJ: Pearson, 9th edn.

Esposito, John L., Darrell J. Fasching and Todd Lewis. 2011. *World Religions Today*. New York: Oxford University Press, 4th edn.

Fabian, Johannes. 1983. *Time and the Other: How Anthropology Makes its Object*. New York: Columbia University Press.

Fellows, Ward J. 1979. *Religion East and West*. New York: Holt, Rinehart and Winston.

Fields, Karen E. 1985. *Revival and Rebellion in Colonial Central Africa*. Princeton, NJ: Princeton University Press.

Ham, Wayne. 1966. *Man's Living Religions*. Independence, Missouri: Herald.

Hawkridge, Emma. 1970 [1945]. *The Wisdom Tree*. Freeport, New York: Books for Libraries Press.

Hexham, Irving. 2011. *Understanding World Religions*. Grand Rapids: Zondervan.

Hopfe, Lewis M. 1983. *Religions of the World*. New York: Macmillan, 3rd edn.

Hopfe, Lewis M., and Mark R. Woodward. 2012. *Religions of the World*. Upper Saddle River, NJ: Pearson, 12th edn.

Hutchinson, John A. 1981. *Paths of Faith*. New York: McGraw-Hill, 3rd edn.

Lewis, James R. 1990. "Images of Traditional African Religions in Surveys of World Religions." *Religion* 20: 311–22.

Long, Charles H. 1986. *Significations: Signs, Symbols, and Images in the Interpretation of Religion*. Philadelphia: Fortress.

Ludwig, Theodore M. 1989. *The Sacred Paths: Understanding the Religions of the World*. New York: Macmillan.

Milner, Vincent L. 1871. *Religious Denominations of the World*. Philadelphia: William Garretson.

Nanji, Azim. 1988. "African Religion." In Kyle M. Yates, Jr, *The Religious World: Communities of Faith*. New York: Macmillan, 2nd edn.

Nielsen, Niels C., *et al.* 1983. *Religions of the World*. New York: St Martin's Press.

Nigosian, Solomon A. 2008. *World Religions: An Historical Approach*. New York: Bedford/St Martins.

Noss, David S., and Blake R. Grangaard. 2011. *A History of the World's Religions*. Upper Saddle River, New Jersey: Pearson, 13th edn.

Noss, John B., and David S. Noss. 1984. *Man's Religions*. New York: Macmillan.

Oxtoby, Willard G., and Alan F. Segal. 2011. *A Concise Introduction to World Religions*. New York: Oxford University Press, 2nd edn.

p'Bitek, Okot. 1970. *African Religions in Western Scholarship*. Kampala: East African Literature Bureau.

Parrinder, Geoffrey. 1983. *World Religions: From Ancient History to the Present*. New York: Facts on File.

Partridge, Christopher H. 2005. *Introduction to World Religions*. Minneapolis: Fortress.

Ranger, Terence O. 1988. "African Traditional Religion." In *The World's Religions*, ed. Stewart Sutherland, Leslie Houlden, Peter Clarke and Friedhelm Hardy, 864–72. Boston: G. K. Hall.

Ray, Benjamin C. 1976. *African Religions: Symbol, Ritual, and Community*. Englewood Cliffs, NJ: Prentice-Hall.

Reinach, Salomon. 1935. *Orpheus: A History of Religions*. New York: Liveright.

Ruland, Vernon. 1985. *Eight Sacred Horizons: The Religious Imagination East and West*. New York: Macmillan.

Schmidt, Roger, *et al.* 2004. *Patterns of Religion*. Stamford, CT: Wadsworth, 2nd edn.

Smart, Ninian. 1984. *The Religious Experience of Mankind*. New York: Charles Scribner's Sons, 1984, 3rd edn.

Smart, Ninian. 1989. *The World's Religions*. Englewood Cliffs, NJ: Prentice Hall.

Soper, Edmund Davidson. 1951. *The Religions of Mankind*. New York: Abingdon, 3rd edn.

Walls, Andrew. 1987. "Primal Religious Traditions in Today's World." In *Religion in Today's World: The Religious Situation of the World from 1945 to the Present Day*, ed. Frank Whaling, 250–78. Edinburgh: T & T Clark.

Endnotes

1. For example "the rule-governedness of human behaviour that is central to anthropological theorizing converged with the theoretical implications of indirect rule" (Fields 1985: 66).

2. For a more general, critical treatment of Western studies of traditional African religion, refer to Okot p'Bitek's *African Religions in Western Scholarship* (1970). This is an uneven work that fluctuates between solid insights and overheated polemics.

3. Terms "such as 'primitive,' 'nonliterate,' and 'premodern'...characterize Africa as the opposite of the West and thus reinforce a negative perspective" (Ray 1976: 5). Although less overly pejorative, there are similar problems with the term "primal." For a thoroughgoing critique of the term "tribal" to describe African religions, refer to p'Bitek (1970).

4. In this regard, refer to the analysis in Charles H. Long, "Primitive/Civilized: The Locus of a Problem" (Long 1986: 79–96).

5. Later the author observes that primitive man "reasoned foggily... He was as freighted with fancies as a poet or madman" (Hawkridge 1970: 9).

6. This statement follows the observation that "Much of African traditional religion is declining and disappearing before the advance of modern education and commerce," an assertion that places such religions in the past tense as "non-modern." It also evokes an image of the mists of savagery dissipating and vanishing before the advance of civilization—a kind of discourse that was more prevalent in earlier eras, as when Soper asserted that "this condition [of animism] must soon be exchanged for another as they come into more intimate contact with the commerce and education and religion of the Western world" (Soper 1951: 34). Echoes of this image also surface in such works as Ninian Smart's later survey of world religions, where he asserted that a particular ethnic group follows what is "no doubt a vanishing modes of life" (Smart 1989: 308).

7. There *is*, of course, a reason for this practice, which is, in at least some groups, the self-conscious purpose of transforming the individual into a complete female by eliminating that part of her which suggests maleness.

8. For example, "We talk glibly about the practice of magic and the worship of idols among African tribes, but we often overlook such low or uncivilized practices among Christians as snake handling [or] the outrages of the Ku Klux Klan" (Bradley 1963: 13).

9. On this particular point I should note that, although I am critical of his text, Robert Ellwood's *Many Peoples, Many Faiths* is not exceptionally bad in this regard.

10. For example, Reinach (1935). Later examples of this same tendency can be discovered, such as Ruland (1985).

11. In his discussion of the "religions of non-literate peoples," Theodore M. Ludwig somewhat more subtly groups together contemporary hunter-gatherers with "our ancestors" (Ludwig 1989: 39).

12. Before laying out my critique of Smart, it should be noted in passing that in his later survey of world religions, *The World's Religions*, he has, to his credit, abandoned this particular argument. However, Smart's treatment still leaves much to be desired, as when he briefly mentions the practice of clitoridectomy as a "widely practiced" African rite without offering any explanation or interpretation of the practice (Smart 1989: 302).

13. Another strong, explicit assertion of the static nature of contemporary traditional religions can be found in the mid-century edition of Soper's world religions survey: "These forms of religion, like the culture out of which they spring, have...no possibility of any significant and conscious progress... A traditional civilization is always stationary" (Soper 1951: 34).

14. With respect to this point as it bears on African religion, refer to the discussion in Ranger (1988). Most of Ranger's other writings have emphasized the need to study African religions in terms of historical change.

15. For example, refer to the discussion in Walls (1987).

11. "CHRISTIANITY" OR "*THE* CHRISTIANITY"—THAT IS THE QUESTION

*Annika Hvithamar**

Luther has not lived in vain. Not only is he responsible for one of the larger branches of Protestantism, but also the Lutheran insistence on *sola scriptura* has profoundly influenced the way religion is taught in Denmark. This heritage and the consequences thereof constitute the topic of the following chapter. After introducing the law and the history of teaching religion in the Danish educational system, I will discuss the Lutheran legacy in primary and secondary education, starting with the approach to the concept of "Christianity." The basis for the discussion will be the executive orders for the topic in the education system and examples from popular contemporary textbooks. Finally I will discuss textbook material for primary and secondary education, based on religious studies didactics: To what degree is it possible to produce educational material based on study-of-religion didactics in the existing system, and what challenges are connected with doing so?

1. *FOLKESKOLEN*—THE NATIONAL SCHOOL

Today, Denmark is considered a secular country. Since 1849, with the adoption of the country's first democratic constitution, freedom of religion has been granted to all citizens. But Denmark is also a country with an established church, the Lutheran Evangelical Church—in Danish, *Folkekirken* (a literal translation would be "The People's Church"). The name of the church is a result of nineteenth-century European nationalism, when former absolute monarchies and pietistic state churches developed into democracies. Thus the national church was supposed to be of the people,

*   Annika Hvithamar is Associate Professor at the Department of Cross-Cultural and Regional Studies, History of Religions Section, at the University of Copenhagen and a sociologist of religion, specializing in the Russian Orthodox Church and contemporary Christianity. She has published textbooks in Religious Studies for upper secondary school and articles (in Danish) on the dichotomy between how religion is studied at the university level compared with how it is taught in primary and secondary schools.

not of the state, hence the name *Folke*kirken. Other institutions that stem from the nineteenth century are named accordingly; the Danish parliament is called *folke*tinget, and the Danish primary and secondary school are termed *folke*skolen. The bond between the state and the church is displayed in the Education Act [Folkeskoleloven], in which §6 states, "The central area of knowledge for teaching the subject of Christianity is the Evangelical-Lutheran Christianity of the Danish *folkekirke*." Christianity is the only subject taught in the school that is specifically mentioned in the Education Act. The reason for this is historical as well.

When universal education for all citizens was first introduced in 1814, the aim of the law was to "educate [children] into good and upright people in accordance with the Evangelical-Christian faith" in order to make them "useful citizens of the state."[1] In accordance with the pedagogical view of the period, religious education was seen as necessary in order to bring up good citizens. Therefore, throughout this period, Lutheran Christianity was the backbone, not just of religious education, but also of the formation of the student. Church and school cooperated closely and the local priest supervised all teaching at local schools. However, the increasing secularization in the twentieth century led to public debates about the connection between school and church. As a consequence, churchly supervision of the school was limited to teaching the subject "religion" in 1933. In 1949 supervision by the vicar was abolished.[2]

By the second half of the twentieth century, the role of the church had become less visible in education. In the 1975 regulation of the Education Act, the connection between church and school was abolished. At the same time the name of the subject was changed from "Religion" (which in reality meant the Christian religion, as the content of the subject was exclusively Christianity) to "Knowledge of Christianity." The change of name implied that it is *knowledge about* the religion, not *upbringing in* the religion that is the intention of the subject. However, at the same time, a duality was introduced. Firstly, the connection to the national church was upheld, as the national church is responsible for religious education in either 7th or 8th grade (depending on which grade the students are preparing for Lutheran confirmation). Secondly, the abovementioned paragraph on the precedence of the national church was kept. Finally, §6,2 granting the right of exemption to parents who want to take care of the provision of religious knowledge for their child was not abolished.[3] Despite the supposedly non-confessional intention of the subject, it was still considered something that could be regarded as contrary to the worldview of some students.

The exemption-clause has been a point of discussion, both before the passing of the law and currently. In the present circular on exemption from the subject it is stressed that the principal of the school must guide parents who wish to have their child exempted. In the guidance information the non-confessional, Knowledge-providing character of the subject must be stated. The status of the subject is considered important enough to be brought up to the principal-level (and not just a matter for the religion-teacher). Having said that, very few students, an estimated 0.5%, are exempted from the subject.[4]

Today, Knowledge of Christianity is taught one lesson per week from 1st–10th grade (except for the above-mentioned 7/8 grade). Since 2007 the course is concluded with a final examination after 9th grade. This examination was introduced after a committee appointed by the Minister of Education had worked out new guidelines. The committee, called "The committee for strengthening of Knowledge of Christianity in the national school," was composed of representatives from university colleges and the primary and secondary schools, theologians and pedagogical experts and was headed by a vicar from the national church. No scholars from Religious Studies at Danish universities were invited to take part in the committee.

To sum up, Lutheran Christianity is, for historical reasons, closely connected to the Danish school system. The heritage of state pietism with a focus on the plight of state to make good Lutheran citizens by educating them into the faith is one reason. The national era, which coupled ethnicity with religious belonging, is a second. Both made the state-educated ministers of the Lutheran Church the natural alley of the state in terms of religious education. With the separation of church and school in 1975 the task of educating religion teachers was moved from the church to the secular education system. But the close connection between a theologically-based religious education and the school system was retained. This is discernible when we turn to the educational system in Denmark.

2. TEACHING RELIGION IN DENMARK

The education system in Denmark is, when it comes to teaching religion, divided in two. Teachers for primary and lower secondary school (*folkeskolen*) are educated at university colleges, whereas teachers for upper secondary school are educated at universities.[5]

2.1. Educating teachers for primary and secondary schools
At the university colleges a course in "Knowledge of Christianity/Life-enlightenment/Citizenship" is obligatory for all students.[6] In order to become a teacher, the student has to specialize. One of the non-obligatory options for specialization is "Christianity/religion." However, a survey by the Danish Ministry of Education in 2006 showed that only 14-22% of classes in Knowledge of Christianity are taught by specialized teachers.[7] Most teachers who are teaching the subject do not have higher qualifications than Christianity/Life Enlightenment/Citizenship. In the executive orders, central content in the topic regarding religion is:

Religion and Culture
The content is:

(a) The narratives of the* Christianity, fundamental concepts and historical impact with weight on Danish circumstances.
(b) Judaism and Islam as European minority religions.

(c) Religion and human rights in a culture meeting and school-perspective.

(d) The relationship between religion, culture and politics in contemporary perspective

(e) The significance of Evangelical Lutheran Christianity for democracy, welfare and school in Denmark.[8]

The citation points to two central topics. One is the wording. In Danish legislation as well as textbooks and public discourse "Christianity" is used with a definite article and in singular: *The Christianity*. It has to be mentioned that this is the common way of naming the Christian religion in the Danish language. However, if we regard the effect of this naming, it connotes, that Christianity is something, which can be described as a singular entity. This leads to the second topic: In Danish primary and secondary education Christianity is taught "with weight on Danish circumstances" and with focus on "the Significance of Evangelical Lutheran Christianity for democracy, welfare and school in Denmark." Thus an essentialist conception of Christianity as a singular entity is coupled with a focus on the Danish version of Lutheran Christianity as the primary example of *the* Christianity.

Furthermore a straightforward connection between the Evangelical Lutheran Church and such concepts as democracy, welfare and school is a topic, which, according to the national curriculum, should be taught to the future teachers.

In other words, comparative perspectives or notions of religion as fluid is not part of the departmental orders. Instead the idea of Christianity as a backbone for the *bildung* of the future teachers is in focus. In the education of teachers for primary and lower secondary schools a vital connection between Christianity, ethics and citizenship is stipulated. Bringing up children with Knowledge of Christianity and bringing up children with knowledge of ethics and citizenship are seen as two sides of the same subject. In short, in primary and secondary education, religious education is seen as part of educating the child as a citizen and as a human being.

2.2. Educating teachers for upper secondary schools

The teachers for upper secondary school are educated in Religious Studies departments at universities.[9] Historically, in Denmark, Religious Studies has been connected with the study of history, philology, sociology and anthropology. Denmark has had theological faculties since the founding of University of Copenhagen in 1475, and has educated ministers for the Lutheran-Evangelical Church since the Protestant Reformation in 1536. But when Religious Studies emerged in Denmark in the late nineteenth century, it broke away from Theology. Religious Studies advocates were interested in other religions and other methods of studying religion than the theological approach, with its focus on the development and maintaining of Lutheran Christianity. Today, in the educational debate, Religious Studies is often contrasted with Theology. Religious studies in Denmark are non-confessional and taught by historians, sociologists, philosophers and, sometimes, theologians of religion. At the universities and thus in upper secondary school in Denmark the religious education, as a result, is viewed as a subject which educates the student in historical, sociological and philosophical phenomena. There may be more focus on historical and sociological aspects of the Christian religion in the basic education and more time is dedicated to topics of local and hence Lutheran origin, but all religions are treated on a comparative basis. Religious Studies departments at the Universities work out their study plans independently, but the approach is reflected in the national curriculum: executive orders for the upper secondary school. Here the "identity" of the subject is identified as:

> The world religions are central to subject religion, and of these Christianity is mandatory.
>
> On a scientific, non-confessional background the religions and their central phenomena are described and understood in relation to individuals, group, society, culture and nature.
>
> The subject covers the origin of religions, their historical development, their contemporary form and their impact on history. The subject's perspective is global. The role of religions in European and Danish history of ideas and identity is given special attention.
>
> Working with texts is mandatory. Also included is other documentary material.[10]

In the objects clause it is noticeable that the subject in its outset is seen as something which treats religion *per se*, not any one religion. The outreach is global, explicitly non-confessional, the primary method is the historical and comparative approach—and the singular, definite form of Christianity is absent.

Thus, in the education system two approaches to religious education are represented. In *folkeskolen* and at university colleges, religious education is described in terms of *bildung*—a way to enlighten and qualify the student as a human being and as a citizen. At universities and in upper secondary school religious education is described in terms of a historical and sociological discipline, where the personal attitude to religion is seen as irrelevant. In the public debate there has been little discussion concerning the content of the education in religion in upper secondary school, but an ongoing debate concerning the content of the education in religion in primary and (lower) secondary school. Therefore, in the following I will concentrate on the latter.

3. RELIGIOUS EDUCATION IN PRIMARY AND SECONDARY SCHOOLS

In current religious education for the primary and secondary school, the *bildung*-aspect of teaching religion is stressed. According to the objects clause for Knowledge of Christianity:

The purpose of teaching Knowledge of Christianity is that students acquire knowledge in order to understand the meaning of the religious dimension for the individual's life perception and for his relationship to others.

Paragraph 2
The subject's central knowledge area is the* Christianity, as it appears in historical and contemporary context. Students should gain knowledge of biblical narratives and their significance for the values of our culture. Additionally, students must gain knowledge about non-Christian religions and philosophies.

Paragraph 3
Through the meeting with various forms of life questions and answers found in the* Christianity and other religions and conceptions of life, the lessons must give students a foundation for personal decisions and responsibility in a democratic society.[11]

In the common objectives for Knowledge of Christianity the same characteristics as in the objects clause for university colleges repeats themselves: Christianity has a dominant position; other religions (and non-religious attitudes) to religion are represented, but with little room and Christianity is seen as a singular entity, which is helpful for the *bildung* of the student.

Today, the subject Knowledge of Christianity is publicly debated. Advocates for the subject see it as a bulwark against fragmentation. A common canon should be taught to the students in order to provide coherence. In this position Christianity is primarily regarded as culture. The prominent position of Christianity is seen as exemplary: even though Christianity is seen as one of several religions, Christianity is used as an example to provide the students with tools to deal with the religious dimension of the human being. In this position Christianity is seen as a philosophical system. Even though the subject should not be confessional, another dimension is added to the subject.[12] Apart from teaching the student the above-mentioned *knowledge about* the religion, the student should also learn *from* the religion.

3.1 Lutheran Christianity as a paradigmatic example
Critics of the subject point to the need to broaden the subject and incorporate religions other than Christianity. One point of criticism is that Denmark is developing into a multicultural society and that it is the task of the national school to educate young citizens to this reality.[13] Another point of criticism is the essentialization of Lutheran Christianity, exemplified above with the use of the definite article as *the Christianity*, where the rather particular Scandinavian variant of Lutheranism is described as a paradigmatic example. One effect of this in textbook material is that mainstream Danish Lutheran positions such as a liberal attitude to female and homosexual ministers, same-sex marriages, second marriages and so on, are described as exemplary characteristics for Christianity.[14] Because

the diversity of Christianity is overlooked by this approach, "the Christianity" is equated with contemporary Western liberal values, whereas conservative "maximalist" versions of Christianity, as well as contemporary Orthodox and Catholic positions are largely ignored.[15]

This becomes particularly visible in the parts of the textbooks which deal with "Philosophy of life." In the textbooks, topics like "love," "suffering" and so forth are thematized. This is difficult to do without compromising one of the basic tenants of comparative religious studies: not to compare the ideals of one religion with the actual practices of another. For example, the above-mentioned textbook-system *Liv & Religion* for 9th grade, when dealing with the "love and Christianity" will include such statements as:

> The* Christianity is special by being the only religion that directly defines its God as love. It happens in the first letter of John, chap. 4, v. 8, where it is directly stated: "God is love"[16]

Or, when dealing with religion and food: "In the* Christianity in contrast to the other four world religions, there is no ban on food."[17] Another bias can be found in this textbook's illustrations; 8 out of 12 illustrations dealing with Islam show show aggressive Islamists, veiled women, pictures taken from the palace of Saddam Hussein and Osama Bin Laden.[18] This teaching material has been criticized for being covertly confessional, implicitly preaching the superiority of Lutheran Christianity.[19]

3.2. Sola Scriptura

Another bias, which also could be described as a consequence of Lutheran heritage is stressing the importance of scripture over tradition. In the departmental orders for the National School four "central knowledge and proficiency-areas" have to be covered at all levels of the teaching: "Life-philosophy and ethics," "Biblical Narratives," "The* Christianity and its various expressions in a historical or contemporary connection" and "Non-Christian religions and other philosophies of life." How "Biblical narratives" should be taught is explained as:

> The main aim of this knowledge area is that students gain an understanding of the fundamental Christian narrative in an Evangelical Lutheran perspective as a process built on a triad of life (creation), death (doom/sin) and new beginnings (hope/forgiveness)—including the relationship between biblical chronology and historical chronology and biblical interpretations and biblical genres.

> The principal issues in this knowledge area are:

> What fundamental human life issues are the narratives about?

> How do the biblical narratives illustrate the Christian triad of life?

The interpretation of the knowledge and proficiency-area is focused on how the Bible is existentially relevant for contemporary people. The teaching should not primarily treat the Bible as an ancient document, which should be analysed and interpreted in a historical setting (as would be the logical choice seen from the perspective of Religious Studies), but as a text, which informs the students of "fundamental human life issues."

Knowledge of Christianity is, in this understanding, best acquired by going back to the sources and applying the biblical texts to a contemporary setting instead of seeing the narratives of the Bible as something dependent on historical circumstances. Thus, the instruction is based on an existential, theological[20] understanding, where a notion of *ad fontes* is applied, not Religious Studies-didactics.

In the textbook material this approach is used by applying biblical narratives to a contemporary context. A theme such as "trust and doubting" is applied to questions about trust in modern technology, jealousy, and trust as a "sovereign expression of life" (see note 6), existential doubts shown in, for example, Pablo Picasso's Guernica and Edvard Munch's life and art. These themes are coupled with the binding of Isaac, trust and doubt among the disciples of Jesus, narratives of Jesus trusting God and doubting God.[21] As such the biblical texts are brought into contemporary contexts, making the narratives meaningful and relevant for the student. A more graphic use of this style of didactics is the use of illustrations. The system *Liv og Religion* (Life and Religion) is well-illustrated with art, photos and other illustrations. However, the illustrations are the same as if they were depicting biblical myths, historical developments or contemporary situations. In this way mythic lore and contemporary situations are given equal standing.

3.3. Lutheran Christianity as the Christianity

A third Lutheran bias is connected with the weighting of Lutheran Christianity. Other branches of Christianity are mentioned as a part of an historical development of the Christian religion, but contemporary examples of Catholic or Orthodox Christianity are downplayed. For example, the above-mentioned system *Liv og Religion* for 9th grade contains a theme on "The Church in contemporary society," where the whole chapter is devoted to the National Church—with the consequential use of the term "The* Christianity."[22] In the serial *Tre religioner* (Three Religions), where Islam, Judaism and Christianity are compared, headlines like "The two sacraments of the* Christianity,"[23] conclusions like "In the* Christianity there are no precepts of ritual cleansing in connection with religious acts" and "in the* Christianity there are no food prescriptions" are concurrent.[24]

It is important to stress that all of the above-mentioned textbooks incorporate a comparative method. All of the above include numerous examples of texts, pictures and descriptions of other religions and thorough approaches to ethical issues. However, the Lutheran-Evangelical version of Christianity as it is practised in the Danish National Church is the starting point and this essentialized version of "The Christianity" is the basis for how ethical issues are approached.

Thus, even though religious education in Denmark is allegedly non-confessional, the long-standing link between state and church and school and church clothes the subject Knowledge of Christianity with a confessional bias—not so much due to deliberate choice, but more as a consequence of popular understanding of what religion is about and of a theological teaching didactic, focused on ethical and existential questions—in a Lutheran interpretation. Also, even though the discussion asks whether the subject should be concentrated on knowledge or *bildung*, in practice it is also a question about which didactics are employed. Historically, it has been a theologically-based didactic which has dominated at seminars and in primary and secondary school. Scholars of religion and hence Religious Studies didactics have also been absent from committees working out departmental orders as authors of textbooks aimed at primary and secondary school.

Finally, the essentialist approach in textbooks is closely connected to the departmental orders and their directions regarding the subject Knowledge of Christianity. Any textbook has to accommodate these directions, so as long as the national curriculum: executive orders are written without the participation of people educated in Religious Studies, the orders are unlikely to change.

4. A Religious Studies-approach

In 2011/12 a textbook and an accompanying teacher's guide, *Tror du det?* (*Do you think so?*),[25] were published. The book was the result of a co-authorship between two sociologists of religion and a historian of religion. The aim of the book was to create a Religious Studies based textbook for primary and secondary schools—a textbook that would be acceptable to the departmental orders for primary and secondary schools in the subject Knowledge of Christianity.[26] The considerations and challenges of working out this system is the topic of the balance of the present chapter.

4.1. Adapting theories and methods from Religious Studies.

Firstly, there is a question of the extent of the material. In the Danish system Knowledge of Christianity is one lesson per week, which puts a natural limit to how much material could be included in a textbook.

Secondly, teachers in primary and secondary schools are not educated in Religious Studies. As mentioned above all teachers have a general course in the subject Christianity, Life-enlightenment, Citizenship. Only a small percentage of the classes are taught by teachers with a specialized degree. Hence education in other religions and confessions than Lutheran Christianity (and, lately, Islam) is limited. If dealing with "non-world religions" or antique religions, it cannot be assumed that teachers have prior knowledge.

One of the tools for assisting teachers is the teaching guides that are produced along with the textbook. Not only in subjects like Knowledge of Christianity, but in all subjects for primary and secondary school, teacher's guides accompany textbooks—the publishing houses do not typically publish textbooks without them.

Furthermore, as mentioned previously, teachers are schooled in a theological didactical tradition. Hence there is a focus on ethics, both in departmental orders and in the experience of most teachers. One cannot assume that either student or teacher is familiar with technical terms, basic concepts/theories/names, and theories and methods that are part of Religious Studies.

Accordingly the 143 page-long textbook was accompanied by a 199 page-long teacher's guide, in which the body of the text, assignments, primary sources and textbook illustrations were explained along with basic Religious Studies concepts/theories and so on. It is, however, not certain how useful this type of information is for the teacher—even detailed information and practical guides can be quite limited, and a more through treatment of subjects must be sought elsewhere. On the other hand, individual teachers can quickly become overloaded with information.

The textbook is organized from a comparative perspective, and thus opens with a chapter on "when something is sacred" and "creation myths." To provide a framework for a comparative perspective, we introduce two characters who appear in boxes throughout the volume, *The caveman* and *Thea*.

The caveman is a religion scholar. The reason why he was pictured as a caveman was because we wanted a phenomenologist—a figure who could describe common features of all religions. In his boxes concepts from Religious Studies (e.g., "syncretism," or "holy and profane"), phenomenological features (e.g., creeds or food prescriptions) or other general notions are explained.

Thea, a girl who ages along with the students, is our "case." In contrast to the caveman, she contemplates the religions at eye level. She witnesses religious events, conflicts and problems. She watches rituals and contemplates experiences. She is an example of how religion may be approached from a lived religion perspective. The aim of the figure is to see the religions from an individual level. She is curious, inquiring, and far from always clear concerning her own opinion—as most people are. Because she engages in dialogues with representatives from various religious traditions she finds that religion is often impossible to essentialize into categories like "Islam" or "the* Christianity," but rather has to be contextualized. Although Thea is probably more interested in religion than the average student, the point of including her is so that the students may recognize themselves in her, and that the boxes with the cases may stimulate class discussion.

To further facilitate class discussion, a number of working questions are part of the book. The questions encourage students to reflect on their own experiences with others and/or their own religious traditions and to analyse religion as a cultural phenomenon—for example, by comparing religious phenomena with non-religious historical and sociological features. One example is that we ask the students to reflect upon "signs on the body" and compare circumcisions with norms for dressing, tattoos and piercing, or to compare food regulations with food preferences.

For illustrations, we used productions stemming from the religious tradition described, be it artefacts, architecture or art. Hence, the examples of religious art, which are part of the chapter on Judaism, are artwork made by artists from a Jewish cultural sphere. Works of art that are part of the chapter on Christianity are made by artists from a Christian cultural sphere, and so on. Furthermore an illustrator, the artist Helle-Vibeke Jensen, decorated the book. She did so by using objects from the various religions to show their material side—in order to stress that any religion also has a physical, everyday, and sometimes a kitschy dimension. Lastly the book was organized so that primary sources were marked in one colour, captions in another and the body of the text in a third, to emphasize the different genres.

So the aim of *Tror du det?* was to apply religious studies didactics to a primary and secondary school level text, by using such contemporary didactics as case based teaching and student engaged learning methods.

4.2. The art of lawmaking.
Historically, representatives for Religious Studies have not participated in the composition of executive orders. Hence the statuary aims are focused on topics (such as ethics and [Lutheran-evangelical] Christianity) which are only a tiny part of the Religious Studies approach. But since it is the teachers who are responsible for the fulfilment of executive orders, any textbook must live up to the format presented in the law. To put it bluntly, publishing houses do not want to publish books that are not in compliance with departmental orders. They do not sell. Consequently, "Life-philosophy and ethics," "Biblical Narratives," "The* Christianity and its various expressions in a historical or contemporary connection" have to be utilized. In order to do so as authors, we often had the feeling that we were fulfilling the word but not the spirit of the law. One example is the use of hymns. Danish Protestant-Lutheran tradition hymns, created to be sung during services and collected in the official Danish hymnbook, are part of the executive orders. Hymns are an integral part of services in *Folkekirken*, but are also part of national culture and many of the hymns are sung at other occasions than services, for example, at national holiday-celebrations. However, in the departmental orders the teaching of hymns is described as: "the students sing and converse about hymns." Note the verbs. Hymns are not considered something to be analysed or discussed, but are something that should be acquired, and thus a part of the *bildung* in Christianity, not part of knowledge about the religion. In *Tror du det?* we incorporated hymns, but treated them as sources for understanding a particular historical period—as knowledge, not as formation, as objects for analysis, not as religion productions.

The use of hymns in religion education highlights the fuzziness of Knowledge of Christianity. Hymns are part of the departmental orders in several subjects at the National School. In the subject Danish they are studied as poetry, in Music as genre (where it is also more obvious that they should be sung) and in Knowledge of Christianity as religion.

4.3. Reception of Study-of Religions based textbooks
Most text-book material for primary and secondary education in Denmark is written by teachers of primary and secondary education. There are many good rea-

sons for this: intimate knowledge of the target group; personal experience with teaching the subject; knowledge of areas of overlap with other subjects; knowledge of the tradition of the subject, and pedagogic training aimed at children and young people. On the other hand, there are also pitfalls. Even though there are excellent examples of to-the-point textbooks, teachers of primary and secondary education do not have the same opportunity and access to current developments in the field. New discoveries, critiques of former authorities, professional discussions of trends in the field are all topics to which university employees have better access. When dealing with textbooks for primary and secondary school a close co-operation between university-scholars and teachers are both desirable and necessary.

But in the field of religion the above-mentioned difference between Theology based didactics and Religious Studies based didactics is influencing the reception of RE based material. This applies for both primary and secondary education. When in 1997 the historian of religion Dorthe Refslund Christensen published the textbook *Scientology—a New Religion,* aimed at upper secondary schools, the book was heavily criticized in Danish media: how could a "money-machine" like Scientology be seriously portrayed as a religion, without spending a substantial portion of the book criticizing the controversial aspects of this religious movement. In the Danish Parliament the Minister of Education Ole Vig Jensen was called into consultation and afterwards stated that if the textbook was used in upper secondary school it had to be presented together with texts criticizing the Scientology-movement.[27]

Ten years later I authored a textbook for upper secondary schools, *World Religions in Denmark—Christianity.* The book included a chapter on Jehovah's Witnesses as an example of minority religion in Denmark. This gave rise to a discussion in the Christian press, such as in the journal for high school teachers of religion, about the appropriateness of including a religious movement that was not recognized as Christian by most branches of Christianity.[28]

There was a milder version of the same reaction to *Tror du det?* A critical review in the journal for teachers of Knowledge of Christianity in the National School led to an article in the newspaper *Kristeligt Dagblad* (Christian Daily), criticizing the sociological approach taken by the book: the chairman of the association for religion-teachers in the National School attacked the textbook for presenting questions that "are close to students personal beliefs and convictions"[29]—the examples were questions where students were asked to compare their own religious traditions or to compare piercings and circumcisions. However, there was a response to the article which stated that engaging students to reflect on religious beliefs, traditions and the like must be part of the teaching, and later reviews have been positive.

The reception of the above-mentioned books highlights a problem with Religious Studies didactics: they are not familiar to the public. The neutral approach to a given religious movement or phenomenon is interpreted as lack of reflection or as an uncritical approach. The focus on minorities as methodological examples of religious dynamics are seen as irrelevant, and approaches where religion is described as a comparable cultural phenomenon is considered controversial.

On the other hand, at universities the authoring of textbook material for other sectors of the educational system has traditionally not been regarded as prestigious and the debate on which didactics should be applied in the primary and secondary schools are seen as a political more than a methodological question. However, if we as scholars of religion are in any way interested in disseminating the insights from Religious Studies, we need to engage in writing textbooks ourselves. And if we are convinced that Religious Studies provides theories and methods for studying religion that are more adequate than the theological approach, these theories and methods ought to be available for students in the educational system.

Summing up, the subject of religion in primary and secondary school has by way of tradition primarily been taught by, and with influence from, representatives of a theological approach to the field. This is evident in executive orders and, as an effect of this, in textbooks for the subject, which are focused on essentialized versions of especially Lutheran Christianity with a focus on biblical themes and ethical questions. If we, as scholars of religion, wish to disseminate the insights from Religious Studies, we do not only need to write textbooks. We also need to be part of the committees that work out executive orders and national curricula. Finally, it should be pointed out that if we as scholars of religion wish to enlighten groups other than our students and peers—textbooks for primary and secondary school are probably one of the more effective methods.

BIBLIOGRAPHY

Buchardt, Mette. 2006. "'Store forventninger.' Konstruktion af identitet i multikulturalistisk religionsundervisning." In *Religion, skole og kulturel integration i Danmark og Sverige*, ed. Peter B. Andersen, Curt Dahlgren, Steffen Johannessen and Jonas Otterbeck, 263–91. København: Museum Tusculanums Forlag.

Buchardt, Mette. 2006. "Kristendoms status i kristendomskundskab. Norm eller indholdsområde." In *Religionsdidaktik*, ed. Mette Buchard, 216–28. København: Gyldendal.

Böwadt, Pia. 2005. "Den lille livsfilosof." *Religionslæreren* 1, 4–6.

Engel, Merete. 2007. *Tre religioner 2. Tro og Traditioner.* København: Haase.

Hvithamar, Annika, and Morten Warmind. 2012. *Tror du det—Teacher's guide.* København: Alinea.

Hvithamar, Annika, Mikael Rothstein and Morten Warmind. 2011. *Tror du det 9.* København: Alinea.

Hvithamar, Annika. 2007. *Verdensreligioner i Danmark—Kristendom.* København: Gyldendal.

Hvithamar, Annika, and Morten Warmind. 2006. "Det religionsvidenskabelige grundvilkår. Religionsvidenskaben i religionsundervisningen." *Religionspædagogisk Forum* 1, 63–78.

Jensen, Jesper Juul. 1997. "Ole Vig: Scientology-bog må ikke stå alene." *Information*, 06-12-1997.

Jensen, Tim. 2009. "Hvordan bliver man religionslærer i Danmark? 'Religion' og 'kultur' som viden og social klassifikation i klasserummet." *Din* 1, 50–73.

Jensen, Tim. 2000. "Objektivt, kritisk og pluralistisk—folkeskolens religionsfag." *Religionslær-eren* 6, 11–13.

Juul, Henrik. 2006. "Religionsundervisningens historie i Danmark." In *Religionsdidaktik*, ed. Mette Buchardt. København: Gyldendal.

Jørgensen, Tobias Stern. 2011. "Kritik af lærebog for at udfritte elever om tro". *Kristeligt Dagblad*, 05-11-2011.

Lilleør, Kathrine. 2006. *Rapport fra Udvalget til styrkelse af kristendomskundskab.* Department of Education.

Mortensen, Carsten Bo, John Rydahl and Mette Tunebjerg. 2009. *Liv og Religion, 7/8.* København: Gyldendal.

Mortensen, Carsten Bo, John Rydahl and Mette Tunebjerg. 2009. *Liv og Religion, 9.* København: Gyldendal.

Pedersen, René Dybdahl. 2008. *Religion i øjenhøjde.* København Gyldendal.

Reeh, Niels. 2006. "Debatten om afviklingen af det gejstlige tilsyn i folkeskolen uden for København fra 1901 til 1949—en skitse." In *Religion, skole og kulturel integration i Danmark og Sverige*, ed. Peter B. Andersen, Curt Dahlgren, Steffen Johannessen and Jonas Otterbeck, 165–82. København: Museum Tusculanums Forlag.

Schnabel, Laura Elisabeth. 2007. "Skarp kritik af ny lærebog." *Kristeligt Dagblad* 22-03-2007.

[n.a.] Executive Order for Christianity/Life Enlightment/Citizenship. http://www.emu.dk/sem/fag/klm/studerende/bekendtgoerelse_klm.html

[n.a.] Executive Order for Knowledge of Christianity. http://www.uvm.dk/Service/Publikationer/Publikationer/Folkeskolen/2009/Faelles-Maal-2009-Kristendomskundskab

[n.a.] Executive Order for Religion at Upper Secondary Education. https://www.retsinformation.dk/Forms/R0710.aspx?id=132647#B47

[n.a.] *The Education Act.* https://www.retsinformation.dk/Forms/R0710.aspx?id=133039#K1

Endnotes

1. Henrik Juul, "Religionsundervisningens historie i Danmark," in Mette Buchardt (ed.), *Religionsdidaktik* (København: Gyldendal, 2006), 75.

2. Niels Reeh, "Debatten om afviklingen af det gejstlige tilsyn i folkeskolen uden for København fra 1901 til 1949—en skitse," in Peter B. Andersen, Curt Dahlgren, Steffen Johannessen and Jonas Otterbeck (eds), *Religion, skole og kulturel integration i Danmark og Sverige* (København: Museum Tusculanums Forlag 2006), 165.

3. In the 1975 version of the Education Act, the above-mentioned paragraphs were §5 and §5,2: https://www.retsinformation.dk/Forms/R0710.aspx?id=133039#K1

4. Report by the *Commission for Strengthening of Knowledge of Christianity in the National School*: 18.

5. The distinction between full universities and lower-ranked university colleges is quite common in northern Europe. For a discussion of the education of teachers for the subject religion in the Danish educational system see Tim Jensen, "Hvordan bliver man religionslærer i Danmark? 'Religion' og 'kultur' som viden og social klassifikation i klasserummet," *Din* 1 (2009), 50–73.

6. The term "Life-enlightenment" describes ethics inspired by the philosophy of the Danish theologians F. S. Grundtvig and his ideas of *bildung* as conversation and and reflection, and K. E. Løgstrup, and this ideas that, "sovereign manifestations of life," like trust, love, charity, open speech, are common to all humankind. This philosophy has had a crucial influence on "kristendomskundskab" in *folkeskolen*.

7. Kathrine Lilleør, Rapport *fra Udvalget til styrkelse af Kristendomskundskab i folkeskolen* (Undervisningsministerie, 2006), 15.

8. National curriculum: executive orders for Christianity/Life Enlightment/Citizenship: http://www.emu.dk/sem/fag/klm/studerende/bekendtgoerelse_klm.html

9. In Denmark three universities out of a total of five have Religious Studies departments: The University of Copenhagen, The University of Århus and the University of Southern Denmark. Two of these, Copenhagen and Århus also have departments/faculties for the study of theology.

10. Executive orders for religion in upper secondary school (gymnasium): https://www.retsinformation.dk/Forms/R0710.aspx?id=132647#B47

11. Ministry of Education. Common objectives for the subject Knowledge of Christianity: http://www.uvm.dk/Service/Publikationer/Publikationer/Folkeskolen/2009/Faelles-Maal-2009-Kristendomskundskab/Formaal-for-faget-kristendomskundskab

12. Mette Buchardt, "Kristendoms status i kristendomskundskab: norm eller indholdsområde," in Buchard (ed.), *Religionsdidaktik*, 220–21.

13. Mette Buchardt, "'Store forventninger.' Konstruktion af identitet i multikulturalistisk religionsundervisning," in Peter B. Andersen, Curt Dahlgren, Steffen Johannessen and Jonas Otterbeck (eds), *Religion, skole og kulturel integration i Danmark og Sverige* (København: Museum Tusculanums Forlag, 2006), 263.

14. For example, *Liv & Religion*: 82–83, *Tre Religioner*: 22. Teaching material in Denmark is not regulated by the state. Each school decides which teaching material it wants to use.

15. Annika Hvithamar and Morten Warmind, "Det religionsvidenskabelige grundvilkår. Religionsvidenskaben i religionsundervisningen," *Religionspædagogisk Forum* 1 (2006): 63–78.

16. Carsten Bo Mortensen *et al.*, *Liv og Religion* (København: Gyldendal 2009), 112.

17. Mortensen *et al.*, *Liv og Religion*, 128.

18. Mortensen *et al.*, *Liv og Religion*, 15, 45, 50, 55, 59, 61, 112.

19. Pia Böwadt, "Den lille livsfilosof," *Religionslæreren* 1 (2005), 6; Tim Jensen, "Objektivt, kritisk og pluralistisk—folkeskolens religionsfag," *Religionslæreren* 6 (2000), 11–13.

20. I use the notion of "theological" broadly, meaning that the interpretations are given from inside a given religion and that a given biblical text is interpreted as how it may give religious meaning. Theological research in church history and exegesis at Danish Universities is based on historical-critical methods.

21. Mortensen *et al.*, *Liv og Religion* 7/8 (2009), 110–31.

22. Mortensen *et al.*, *Liv og Religion* 9 (2009), 80–95.

23. Merete Engel, *Tre religioner 2. Tro og traditioner* (København: Haase & Søns Forlag 2007), 86.

24. Engel, *Tre religioner 2*, 93.

25. In Danish "at tro" has the double meaning of "to think" and "to believe."

26. *Tror du det?* was not the first book for primary and secondary school based on study-of-religion didactics in Denmark. In 2008 *Religion i øjenhøjde* (Religion at eye level) based on the Warwick RE approach appeared. But only one textbook, for 8th/9th grade was published.

27. See, e.g., Jesper Juul Jensen, "Ole Vig: Scientology-bog må ikke stå alene," *Information*, 06-12-1997.

28. See, e.g., Laura Elisabeth Schnabel, "Skarp kritik af ny lærebog," *Kristeligt Dagblad* 22-03-2007.

29. Tobias Stern Jørgensen, "Kritik af lærebog for at udfritte elever om tro," *Kristeligt Dagblad*, 05-11-2011.

12. SCHOOL BIBLE IN THE SERVICE OF THE DANISH NATIONAL CHURCH—A CASE STUDY

*Jens-André P. Herbener**

1. INTRODUCTION

In 2011 the Danish Bible Society published a huge work called *The School Bible* (*Skolebibelen*). It includes the following sections: A *Bible Guide* and a *Bible Dictionary* composed by Inger Røgild, the authorized 1992 Danish translation of the Bible and *The New Agreement—the New Testament in present-day Danish* from 2007, for which the Danish Bible Society itself is responsible. All together it is a work of 1.5 kilo and 2016 pages.

The Danish Bible Society is a non-profit church organization. Its purpose is "making the Bible and biblical material available internationally as well as in Denmark,"[1] and it is affiliated with the international organization the United Bible Societies. Inger Røgild was educated as a school teacher and Master of Education (religion and life interpretation), and today works as a school consultant in the School Service of the Danish National Church (Kristeligt Dagblad 2011c).

The contents and structure of *The School Bible* in greater details are as follows: The first part is the *Bible Guide*. It describes the composition, contents, background and "key" subjects of the Bible; introduces fundamentalist, historical critical, existential and literary ways of reading the Bible; it informs readers about differences and connections between the Hebrew Bible and the New Testament, and about the historical period of Jesus' birth.

* Jens-André P. Herbener is Assistant Professor of the History of Religions at the University of Southern Denmark. Previously he has worked as a project manager and editor at the Department of Oriental and Judaica Collections, the Royal Library of Denmark. His research and teaching cover especially monotheism, ancient Israelite religion, Judaism, classical Hebrew and Bible translation. He has published extensively on Bible translation from a non-confessional perspective. His publications include, for example, "Ny bibeloversættelse på videnskabeligt grundlag: Introduktion" (ed., 2001) and "Bibeloversættelse mellem konfession og videnskab" (2004). Currently he is working on a two-volume monograph on monotheism and its historical consequences.

The second part contains the authorized Danish translation of the Bible (1992), which the vast majority of churches in Denmark use. This is followed by *The New Agreement* (2007) which is a translation of the New Testament into idiomatic, present-day Danish. Following the Bible translations, the *Bible Guide* continues by referring to narratives that the Bible and the Qur'an have in common, and then it provides information about Christian festivals.

The last part of *The School Bible* includes the *Bible Dictionary* which refers to a number of "key texts" and "key subjects" in the Hebrew Bible and the New Testament. This part also includes chapters such as "The Bible Gallery of Characters," "Explanation of Words," "Symbols in the Bible" and "Biblical Sayings." Then there is a section that contains references to books and web sites where schoolchildren and school teachers can "read more." Finally, *The School Bible* contains maps of the countries mentioned in the Bible. All in all, the *Bible Guide* and the *Bible Dictionary* consist of only 144 pages; the rest of *The School Bible* consists of the two Bible translations.

As the title suggests, the primary target group of *The School Bible* is the Folkeskole[2] in Denmark, more precisely the subject referred to as *Christian studies*[3] in the lower secondary school (Kristeligt Dagblad 2011c); this is a subject in which "biblical narratives" should play a key role according to the so-called *Common Objectives 2009* of the Ministry of Education. With the assistance of the Danish church, *The School Bible* has quickly gained a foothold in the Folkeskole. Some time ago the vicar Poul Joachim Stender suggested that parochial church councils should "buy the new school Bible of the Danish Bible Society and give it out as class sets to the schools" (Kristeligt Dagblad 2011b). In fact, this has happened—even before *The School Bible* was published, more than half of the initial print run of 3000 copies was sold in this way (Kristeligt Dagblad 2011a).

The Danish Bible Society itself has launched *The School Bible* as "the new basic material for Christian studies" in Denmark (Bibelselskabet 2011a) and as "Denmark's new teaching Bible" (Bibelselskabet 2011b). Furthermore, in light of the separation of church and school in Denmark in 1975, the general secretary of the Danish Bible Society has emphasized that the contents of *The School Bible* are non-confessional, and that it agrees with the *Common Objectives 2009* of the Ministry of Education (Højsgaard 2011b).

Inger Røgild has also stressed that the purpose of *The School Bible* is not Christian preaching but the communication of knowledge:

> I have done a great deal to live up to that. Accordingly, I do not, for instance, write about what "we Christians" do or think, but about what "the Christians" think and do, so that the text meets the Folkeskole's requirement for Christian studies as a subject of knowledge. In that way, it also takes into account that a school class today can be composed of Christians, atheists, Hindus or Muslims (Kristeligt Dagblad 2011c).

Furthermore, in an interview with the *Jyllands-Posten* newspaper a month earlier, Røgild pointed out that it is essential "that *The School Bible* can be used as a non-preaching tool... We must not preach Christianity in the classes in the Folkeskole. It is a subject where the schoolchildren gain knowledge" (Jyllands-Posten 2011).

In other words, both the author and the publisher present *The School Bible* exclusively as an academic[4] publication that is tailor-made for Christian studies in the Folkeskole in Denmark. As the following review will show, this is a truth with many modifications. In fact, from an academic point of view, *The School Bible* is quite problematic and raises questions about the use of textbooks and translations published by religious organizations in the Folkeskole.

2. REVIEW

The communicative side of school textbooks is obviously of great importance, and in this respect Røgild has done well. *The School Bible* is written in an easily accessible and natural language, and it includes fact boxes, illustrations and images. Therefore, schoolchildren should have fine opportunities to acquire the contents.

However, the importance of the communicative aspect—and the simplification of complex issues which it implies in a school context[5]—does not exclude or diminish the requirements for academic rigour. If a textbook be characterized as academic, it should as far as possible be correct, updated, secular, critical, comprehensive, historical and comparative (Jensen 1999, 2008; Hvithamar and Warmind 2007; Rothstein 1997), and if a Bible translation similarly be characterized as academic, it should not have considered elements alien to the text such as the church tradition and modern church politics. In the following paragraphs, at first the *Bible Guide* and the *Bible Dictionary*, and then the Bible translations will be reviewed from an academic point of view.

2.1. Review of the Bible Guide *and the* Bible Dictionary

In principle, *The School Bible* published by the Danish Bible Society is a good idea. In one book, it brings together the biblical texts and different types of materials that can contribute to our understanding of them. Two birds hit with one stone. In fact, there are also several good elements that can be noted: In addition to providing a basic introduction to the Bible's background, origin, contents, structure, many of its main characters and so on, *The School Bible* points to the lack of external evidence that may confirm the existence of the patriarchs, Moses, David and Solomon (pp. 34, 36–37, 75, 99). One of the chapters deals with the historical, political, social and religious background of the New Testament (pp. 62–70). A paragraph informs the reader about some of the problems associated with the use of the Gospels as historical sources (pp. 40–42). Entries about "salvation" and "blessing" inform one about the different meaning which these concepts have in the Hebrew Bible and the New Testament (pp. 112 and 125–26). A chapter is devoted to narratives that recur in Judaism, Christianity and Islam in different ways, and in that way one's attention is drawn to similarities and differences between the three monotheistic religions. Another chapter talks about the Christian festivals and their background, including the Jewish and pagan festivals of which they, in some cases, represent a transformation (pp. 77–79).

More fine elements could be mentioned, but the good sides of *The School Bible* are marred by a large number of errors, misleading formulations and shortcomings as well as other problematic aspects. In the following paragraphs, we will take a look at some of these.[6]

Mistakes and misleading formulations. First, a few critical remarks about the different *reading strategies* which *The School Bible* presents. In the introduction to the paragraph about this subject it describes the academic language that characterizes academic literature as "brain language." Here you can read "about things that can be true or false. Right or wrong" (p. 16). The scholarly literature is contrasted with the biblical texts, which deal with "values and emotions such as faith, doubt, suffering, hope and love" (p. 16). They are "poetic texts such as hymns, myths, legends, etc., and they are written in something that might be called *heart language*" (p. 18). Therefore, the biblical texts may not be used as sources of the origin of the world and man, nor in all areas as sources of the history of ancient Israel (pp. 18–19). *The School Bible* describes a literal reading of the Bible as "fundamentalistic" (pp. 18–19; cf. 48–49).

The School Bible fails, however, to inform readers that its distinction between "brain language" and "heart language" is a modern invention which is a result of the breakthroughs of science and biblical criticism in the last 200–300 years. The distinction does not exist in the Bible itself, which in large sections pretends to be historiography. And even though a literal reading of the biblical texts has rarely stood alone,[7] it has played an important role in church history, not least with Martin Luther. Why does *The School Bible* take it for granted that the Bible consists of "poetic texts" written in a "heart language"? A likely answer could be that it wants to *immunize* its "message" to the criticism from natural science and historical research—at least that will be one *consequence* of this procedure.

The reading strategy that *The School Bible* uses the most space to describe is a so-called "existential" reading (pp. 19–22). Its purpose is to,

...read the Bible in the way that you look at the issues it is dealing with—and then relate them to your own world. Here, it is not so much the text, but your own life as you live it every day that is the main point of the reading... You focus on things that you can use in relation to your own existence (p. 20).

The "existential" reading strategy of *The School Bible* is probably warranted by *Common Objectives 2009* (The Ministry of Education 2009: 4–9). From a strictly non-confessional perspective, however, the question is why it should be included in a school context. It overlaps in many ways with traditional religious Bible reading, and it is obvious that the "existential" approach to the Bible is a relic of the Christian preaching that characterized religious studies in the Folkeskole until 1975. The main difference is in the name, and that the approach is less explicitly Christian. As Inger Røgild herself has put it:

> After all, the biblical texts are the foundation of ethics and culture in the Western world, and if you don't know them, there is a lot that you cannot understand in our society. It is important that we still get the answer to life that the Bible can give. Other answers can then be retrieved in science or philosophy, but there will be a vacuum if we forget the message and thinking of the biblical texts. (Kristeligt Dagblad 2011c).

In other words, after *the Folkeskole Act* closed the front door in 1975, with the "existential" reading of the Bible a backdoor has been opened for a Christian-philosophical approach where the purpose is to learn *from* the Bible instead of *about* the Bible, Christian preaching "in a new dress" (Böwadt 2001; 2007; cf. Andreassen 2008).[8] The lack of critical analysis and distance it implies is reprehensible from an academic perspective, and should be avoided in textbooks about the Bible in the future.

On page 24 *The School Bible* informs us that the name of the ancient Hebrew god Yahweh can be translated "I am the one I am," page 57 informs us that Yahweh means "I am," while page 97 informs us that Yahweh means the "the one who is." Apart from the problematic inconsistencies in the translations, we know nothing with certainty about the etymology of Yahweh, but morphologically it cannot be a verb in the first person singular, only in the third person singular. Therefore, the first two translations are erroneous. Apparently, Røgild has based them on "the folk etymologies" in Exodus 3:14, both of which are in the first person singular, but these should not be confused with modern philological research. The etymology of Yahweh can be a form of the verb "to be" (and thus the third translation may approach the meaning), but there are also other options (see *DDD*, 913–19; *ABD* 4, 1011).

We also find an insufficient understanding of Hebrew in an entry on page 113, according to which the Hebrew expression "Hallelujah" means "*praise* God." It does not, but "praise Yah(weh)," with "Yah" being a short form of Yahweh.

On pages 28 and 35 *The School Bible* says that after Israel was divided into two parts, it was later conquered by the Neo-Babylonian Empire. The statement is misleading. It was only the *southern* part of the country called Judah, which was conquered by the Babylonians (2 Kgs 24–25). The *northern* part of the country, which carried on the name of the former complete country, Israel, was conquered by the Neo-Assyrian Empire (2 Kgs 17).[9]

On pages 35 and 111 *The School Bible* states that "the Babylonian exile," which plays an important role in the Hebrew Bible, "lasted from 587 to 539 BC and is confirmed by Babylonian sources." The fact is, however: According to the Hebrew Bible, the Babylonians conquered Jerusalem both in 597 and 587 BCE, and in both conquests larger or smaller parts of the inhabitants were exiled to Babylon

(2 Kgs 24–25; Jer. 52:28-30). However, it is only the conquest in 597 BCE which is confirmed by Babylonian sources (*ANET*, 564). There are no sources from the Neo-Babylonian Empire mentioning the conquest in 587 BCE, nor the deportations of Jerusalem's population in 597 and 587 BCE (Lemche 2008: 142–43, 186–89). In addition, the Hebrew Bible tells us very little about the exile. The only thing we have from the Babylonians are a few administrative documents mentioning some Judeans, including Jehoiachin, "king of Judah," also according to 2 Kings 25:27-30 (see *ANET*, 308). They do not inform about *how* or *why* they got there. This could very well be a result of a forced exile as the Hebrew Bible claims, but there are no external sources confirming it.[10] Therefore, the statements in *The School Bible* regarding "the Babylonian exile" are misleading.

The following sentence from *The School Bible*'s summary of the Hebrew Bible is quite euphemistic or biased: "After struggling against some of those who already live in the country and against other nations around, the people settle in the land of Canaan" (p. 27; cf. p. 98). The term "struggling" may be based on the alternative conquest narrative found in Judges 1. According to accounts in Exodus–Deuteronomy, however, the Israelites either *drive out* the indigenous population or *eradicate* it completely, women, children and old people included. In fact, an outright genocide hit those people who came across the Israelites on their way to the land of Canaan (according to Deut. 2:26–3:7), as well as large parts of the indigenous people of the land of Canaan (Josh. 6; 8; 10–11), and it was carried out on the order of Yahweh himself (Deut. 20:16-17; 7:1-2, 23-24).

Moreover, *The School Bible* gives contradictory information about the establishment of the biblical canon. On page 32 it states: "Around 90 AD the Jews decided to assemble their holy scriptures." On page 33, however, *The School Bible* informs us, as part of an illustration: "The Old Testament assembled about 200 BCE." Immediately below this, *The School Bible* says: "Canon (binding collection for the Jews) was established in 90 A.D." What does the author of *The School Bible* mean?

We also find dating problems on pages 32-33: According to a timeline Israel was divided around 800 BCE, but this is wrong. It was about 930 BCE according to biblical chronology (see *GBL* 1, 441). The early dating of some of the prophetic scriptures at the same place (e.g., Hosea, Micah and parts of Isaiah, which are all placed in the eighth century BCE) is out of touch with influential parts of modern biblical research. Nor is it consistent with the fact that *The School Bible* elsewhere notes that the oldest parts of the Bible "were written around 600–400 BCE" (p. 30).

In *The School Bible*'s review of the New Testament, a Lutheran bias is reflected on several occasions. According to Paul, the textbook says on page 54, it is "a not a matter of observing laws and regulations to be saved, but of faith." On page 110 it says that according to Paul no man can be "acquitted by his actions but only by his faith." On page 112 this position is extended to the New Testament as a whole: "Here it is not the actions and observance of laws that save people, but the belief that Jesus is the Son of God..." On page 119 we learn that according to the New Testament, "God's grace" includes "all men" (cf. pp. 75, 103, 126).

This emphasis on "faith" and "grace" at the expense of "justification by deeds" is central to Lutheranism, but it is an anachronism to back read it into the New Testament, which is far more complex than *The School Bible* suggests. Paul exhorts his congregations to imitate him as he imitates Christ (1 Cor. 11:1; cf. Phil. 3:17-19; 2 Cor. 11:23-27; 2 Thess. 3:7-9), indeed, he ascribes great significance to *deeds* for the salvation of man: "For all of us must appear before the judgment seat of Christ, so that each may receive recompense for what has been done in the body, whether good or evil"[11] (2 Cor. 5:10; cf. Rom. 2:1-11; Phil. 1:29-30, 2:12). According to the Letter of James, "a person is justified by works and not by faith alone" (2:24). According to the Gospel of Mark, anyone who wishes to follow Jesus must "deny themselves and take up their cross" (8:34-35). According to Gospel of Luke, it is only the person who hates his own family and his own life and walks in Jesus' path that can be his disciple (14:26-27). In other texts, at Judgment Day everyone shall be judged according to their deeds (e.g., Matt. 16:27; Jn 5:28-29; Rev. 20:13). In the entry on "Judgment Day" (pp. 109–10), *The School Bible* also refers to this, but it stands in sharp and unexplained contrast to the recurring emphasis on faith/grace as the only key to salvation.

The School Bible is also characterized by a striking one-sidedness when, in light of Paul, it states that in "Christianity all humans have equal value" (p. 54). This statement is probably based on texts like Romans 3:22 and Galatians 3:26-28. According to some people, Paul thus lays one of the first foundation stones for what we call the human rights. But in fact, it is by no means a message of the equality of all human beings in the modern sense.

First, texts like Romans 3:22 and Galatians 3:26-28 do not rule out the fact that Paul elsewhere strongly condemns non-Christians (Rom. 1:18-32), "false" Christians (Gal. 1:6-9; 2 Cor. 11:12-15), homosexuals (Rom. 1:26-27; 1 Cor. 6:9-11; 1 Tim. 1:9-11) and Jews (1 Thess. 2:14-16), takes slavery for granted (Col. 3:22; Eph. 6:5; Titus 2:9-10) and discriminates against women (1 Cor. 11:6-7; 14:34-35; 1 Tim. 2:9-14).

Second, according to several texts only baptized, heterosexual and righteous Christians have access to "the kingdom of God." For idolaters, homosexuals and people who are guilty of adultery, alcoholism, theft, sorcery, enmity, envy, and so on, the door to paradise is closed (1 Cor. 6:9-11; Gal. 5:19-21; Rom. 1:18–2:11; 1 Tim. 1:10-11).

Finally, at Judgment Day "sinners" in general are abandoned to the Christian god's "wrath and fury," "flaming fire" and "eternal destruction" (Rom. 2:5, 8-9; 2 Thess. 1:3-9; cf. Matt. 25:41; Mk 9:42-48). Thus, neither in this nor in the coming world do people have equal value according to several texts in the New Testament.

The School Bible hardly mentions these elements in the New Testament. In turn, it includes a chapter titled "The time around the year 0." Here you can initially read that women during this *time* occupied a subordinate position, just as slavery was common (pp. 62-64). The chapter, however, fails to tell the reader that Paul also, and quite explicitly, endorses both, and thus one of the main purposes of the chapter seems to be apologetic: If the schoolchildren themselves subsequently run into the embarrassing passages of the New Testament, they can downplay them as "time-bound."[12] The fact is, however, that these elements are still part and parcel of the biblical canon of almost all Christian denominations, including the Danish National Church today.

According to Christian tradition, the prophecies in the Hebrew Bible of a "saviour" refer to Jesus Christ; but the Hebrew Bible itself does not once mention Jesus. In most cases *The School Bible* exclusively presents the Christian reinterpretation of this "saviour" (pp. 28–29, 46, 55–57, 60,[13] 94,[14] 95, 99, 101, 108, 118,[15] 124–25); only in approximately half as many cases do we find information about how Jews have interpreted the figure or what it means in its own context in the Hebrew Bible (pp. 39, 50, 52, 59–60,[16] 94, 118[17]). With this over-representation of the Christian reinterpretation of the prophecies, the author of *The School Bible* probably intends to equip the schoolchildren with Christian glasses when they subsequently read or think about the Hebrew Bible. And if not, why the difference?

Shortcomings and omissions. As suggested above and as will be elaborated below, *The School Bible* often gives a one-sided, uncritical and highly selective representation of the biblical texts. Of course, the subject-matter which a textbook for the school system can include is quite limited. A rigorous selection is required, and this will probably always be debatable. In any case, an academic textbook about the Bible should not only focus on important elements from a contemporary, but also from a historical point of view, and it should focus on both the light and dark sides of the biblical texts. In the following, I will comment on some of the shortcomings and omissions of *The School Bible*.

First, *The School Bible* is characterized by either a complete omission of or a minimum reference to elements in the Hebrew Bible which, from a modern perspective, is open to severe criticism. For instance, it does not mention that one can find numerous examples of holy war in the text, that is, wars in which Yahweh participates in one way or the other (e.g., Deut. 20:1-4; 3:22; 23:15; *GBL* 1, 436). Such information could have been relevant in order to introduce light and shade into the modern, often one-sided debate on Islam and *jihad*.[18] Nor does *The School Bible* inform one that Yahweh in several cases not only dictates systematic genocide, but that the Israelites, according to the main account of the conquest of Canaan, also commit systematic genocide on large parts of the indigenous population (Deut. 7:1-2, 23-24; 20:16-17; Josh. 6; 8; 10–11).[19]

Second, one looks in vain for information about the fact that the Hebrew Bible stipulates the death penalty for numerous offences, often by stoning.[20] For instance, "a sorceress" must be executed according to Exodus 22:17, a text that has been used to legitimize the witch burnings in early modern Europe. According to Leviticus 20:13, male homosexuals should also be executed, which is part of the reason why homosexuals were not allowed to marry in the Danish National Church until 2012. Additionally, blasphemers, "idolaters," indeed people who merely encourage "idolatry" should all be executed by stoning (Lev. 24:15-16; Deut. 17:2-7; 13:7-11). Information about this might contribute to a more (self-) critical debate about Islam, blasphemy, Muhammad caricatures and stoning.

Admittedly, *The School Bible* refers to the violent myths about the Flood and Sodom and Gomorrah (pp. 25, 47, 98–99, 124), and that Yahweh may punish his people with war when they are "disobedient" (p. 58). But this is usually done in an uncritical way as if it were part of a religious discourse or preaching.[21] For example: "When the people have endured the just punishment that he [God] has imposed on them, he liberates them again" (p. 58). Furthermore, when *The School Bible* mentions the story of the golden calf, which includes explicit carnage, it restricts itself to noting that the Israelites "forsake God" and worship "a golden calf instead of God himself" (p. 26). No further information here or elsewhere that a group of Levites mete out punishment by slaughtering about 3000 Israelites, more than 40 times as many as died at the massacre on Utøya in Norway in 2011. Nor does it mention that the Levites, as a reward for killing even their own sons and brothers, shall be honoured by serving Yahweh (Exod. 32:25-29; cf. Exod. 12:28-30; Num. 25; 1 Kgs 18; 2 Kgs 10:18-30). According to the American peace scholar Jack Nelson-Pallmeyer, violence—not least in relation to Yahweh—is one of the dominant themes in the Bible, and he calls it "the elephant in the room of which nobody speaks."[22] As demonstrated above, in important respects *The School Bible* is no exception.

When a religion is to be described from an academic point of view, comparisons with other religions are important. Comparisons may say what is exceptional in the religion, and what is typical, and it may talk about the influence of other religions, indeed, much more than that. In other words, it puts the religion in a crucial *perspective.*

As noted above, *The School Bible* includes comparisons between the three monotheistic religions, Judaism, Christianity and Islam, and that is very good. But it lacks comparisons with ancient Near Eastern religions. This is bad since the Hebrew Bible contains many examples of influence from these religions. For instance, something as familiar as the Flood myth has to a great extent been adopted from Mesopotamia (i.e., the myth of Atrahasis and the Gilgamesh epic), and *The School Bible* could easily have informed about this in a fact box. All in all, the historical background of the Hebrew texts is ignored, and therefore they appear as more unique than they actually are.

But the *new* and *exceptional* elements the texts include are missed as well. When you read *The School Bible*, you receive no impression about the dark side of the mono-Yahwism of the Hebrew Bible, a radical religious intolerance which was more or less unknown in contemporary, Near Eastern religions (see, e.g., Exod. 20:3-5; 22:19; 34:12-17; Deut. 7:5; 12:2-4; 13:6-18; 17:2-7; 2 Kgs 23).[23] They were characterized by polytheism—and sometimes also by henotheism and summodeism[24]—just as Palestine was before the second half of the first millennium BCE. Indeed, more than that: According to a couple of the most famous ancient Near Eastern inscriptions, Yahweh probably had a wife, the goddess Asherah.[25]

The School Bible says nothing about this, which would have been an obvious religio-historical contextualization in order to understand the innovations of the Hebrew Bible. It could have been included in a chapter about ancient Palestine and its Near Eastern neighbours in the first Millennium BCE, corresponding to the chapter "The time around the year 0," or at least in three to four fact boxes. In that way the historical background of the Hebrew Bible and the New Testament would have been highlighted in an even-handed way.

In the review of the Hebrew Bible (mainly pp. 23–28, 32–39, 46–49) the *Bible Guide* only once touches on the fact that there were gods other than Yahweh (p. 28). It does not at all communicate that the Israelite worship of them is the main explanation for the many calamities that hit them, including the fall of Israel and Judah, and the Babylonian exile (e.g., 2 Kgs 17; 21; 23; Ezek. 5–6; 8; 16). It restricts itself to saying that the Israelite people were "disobedient," that they did not "keep the covenant," that they were not "faithful" and the like (pp. 28, 35, 39, 48, 58); in *which* way it does not suggest.[26] Thus, the *Bible Guide* makes the Hebrew Bible far more monotheistic than it usually is (see *DDD*), but *also* compatible with the traditional monotheistic interpretations of the text anthology.[27] Probably a welcome side effect.

Many vicars today might give their seal of approval to *The School Bible*'s presentation of the New Testament (primarily pp. 28–30, 39–45, 50–55). In a paragraph titled "Key elements of the New Testament" (pp. 50–55) we read that Jesus preached "the kingdom of God" which is "all places where people are loved and forgiven" (p. 50), he spoke in parables, performed miracles and healings, preached forgiveness and love of "God" and "neighbour," and conquered death. Then, *The School Bible* refers to baptism and to Paul's conversion from a zealous Pharisee to the apostle of the Gentiles and his idea that Jesus died to "atone for the sin of man," that faith is crucial, not actions, and that all people have "equal value" (pp. 54–55). In other words, according to *The School Bible*'s presentation of the "key elements" of the New Testament, there is not much that is not compatible with the Danish National Church or similar kinds of modern (Protestant) Christianity.

But is this correct from a religio-historical point of view? There are similarities between the New Testament and the Danish National Church, sure, but there are also many significant differences. *The School Bible*, however, fails to mention them, or touches on them in only a peripheral or an indirect way. For instance, as already mentioned, that homosexuals qua homosexuals cannot enter "the kingdom of God," that women should occupy a submissive position, that slaves should remain slaves, that sinners will burn in hell forever, and whether you come into "the kingdom of God" or "hell," may well depend on your actions (see above). Indeed, in clear contrast to what *The School Bible* maintains (pp. 54, 110, 112), the New Testament may attribute great importance to actions. Think of the repeated requests to follow Jesus in self-abasement, self-denial and suffering, and to turn your back on the world and one's own family, often as a condition of salvation.[28] This was also the ideal and the ethics that underlay the Christian martyrs and various ascetic movements and organizations when the church became institutionalized (Bilde 2001: 464–85; 2011: 245–47; Allison 1998: 172–216).

Additionally, *The School Bible* does not say a word about the claim to universal monopoly on truth and salvation centred around Jesus, which might be one of the most important innovations of the New Testament (see, e.g., Jn 14:6; Matt. 12:30-32; 28:18-20; Acts 4:11-12; Phil. 2:9-11; 1 Tim. 2:3-6; 2 Jn 1:9). Historically, it has played a huge role as it has constituted a major part of the background of the worldwide mission of the Church and the intolerance which it has often demonstrated: Externally towards non-Christian religions, and internally towards "aberrant" forms of Christianity, the so-called "heresies" (Zagorin 2003; Assmann 2010).

Furthermore, *The School Bible* reveals nothing about the anti-Judaism that characterizes important parts of the New Testament. In 1 Thessalonians 2:14-16 Paul condemns the Jews as murderers of Jesus and of the prophets, in Matthew 27:20-26 the blame for Jesus' death is placed exclusively on the Jews, and in John 8:44 they are demonized as the Devil's offspring. According to a professor in early Christianity, Per Bilde, "the many hostile statements against the Jews in the New Testament are constitutive of the text as a whole. It seems that Christianity has just been established in a fundamental conflict with Judaism" (Bilde 1997). But more than that: Historically, the New Testament claims that the Jewish people are responsible for Jesus' death, have often legitimized or motivated discrimination and persecution of the Jews (see Lüdemann 1997: 76–127; Bilde 1997, 2001: 286–327). A discussion of the anti-Judaism and the spectacular truth claims of the New Testament could have contributed to the modern debate on religious freedom and tolerance and their historical roots.

In general, one of the biggest problems from a comparative, religio-historical point of view is that *The School Bible* does not inform one about the fact that substantial parts of the New Testament reflect a millenarian-apocalyptic movement that lived in the expectation of an imminent end of this world and the coming of "the kingdom of God."[29] *The School Bible* could also have drawn attention to the fact that the New Testament exhibits significant similarities with many recent millenarian movements, partly to put its many differences to the subsequent church organizations into a religio-historical perspective, and partly because the early Christian mythology has inspired many of the these millenarian movements (Allison 1998; Rothstein 2001: 218–29; Clair 1992). Finally, *The School Bible* could have included a small paragraph on the interesting similarities between parts of the New Testament and the mystery religions of the Hellenistic-Roman world where death and resurrection and life after death play a key role (*GBL* 2, 94-95).

As should be evident from the preceding discussion, *The School Bible* does not live up to its own purpose of becoming "the new basic material for Christian studies" in Denmark (Bibelselskabet 2011a). It is characterized by significant shortcomings and misleading emphases or information. One of the problems with the one-sided representation of the Bible is that significant parts of church history become unintelligible or may be brushed aside as mere "misunderstandings" or "abuse" of the Bible. It is of secondary importance whether this is a result of a deliberate choice, ignorance or the conventions according to which many of the textbooks about the Bible in the Folkeskole have been prepared so far. What matters is that it is academically unacceptable, because modern textbooks should give a multifaceted picture of the Bible and cover both the light and dark sides of the texts.[30]

Additionally, the religio-historical background of the Hebrew Bible should have been elucidated to a greater extent, just as the New Testament should have been described on its own religio-historical terms to a far greater extent. Of course, the scope of a textbook has significant limitations and simplifications are inevitable, as stressed above. But at least some of the above mentioned elements should have been included if the worst examples of anachronisms and one-sidedness were to have been avoided.

Christian-emic terminology. It should go without saying that textbooks for the education system should make use of a neutral, adequate and academic terminology, as far as possible. Looking at *The School Bible*, however, this is not so in many cases. Some examples:

Although it points out that Jews call the Hebrew Bible "Tanakh" (pp. 32 and 71[31]), it consistently uses the term "the Old Testament." Although there is an ancient tradition for that name, it is strictly speaking only legitimate from a retrospective, Christian frame of reference, and therefore the name should only be used when the text is being viewed from a Christian perspective. As a more neutral term, "the Hebrew Bible" is increasingly used in many countries. Explained in three or four lines at the beginning of the book, the schoolchildren should easily be able to understand the issue.

Another problem is the use of the word "God." Although *The School Bible* says that "Yahweh" is the name of the god of the Israelites (pp. 24 and 97), it consistently applies the name "God" as if the textbook was religious literature. It does not explain why. Quite apart from the fact that Christian conventions may unconsciously play a role, it can also be due to a deliberate choice. So when *The School Bible* uses the term "God" for Yahweh of the Hebrew Bible and "God the Father" of the New Testament, it supports a doctrine that is almost as old as the church itself: That the two text anthologies attest to the same god, the one, universal "God" of Christian monotheism. Based on the Christian understanding of the Hebrew Bible and the New Testament as a soteriological-historical unity, "God" as a common name is favourable, just as the term "the Old Testament" is. From the academic point of view of the study of religion, however, it reflects disrespect and disguises the differences. Just as historians of religion and Bible scholars call the main god of the Hebrew Bible "Yahweh," so should *The School Bible*.

A third example of religious terminology is the consistent use of "the Fall" or "the story of the Fall" about Genesis 3 (pp. 20, 25, 55, 72, 91, 93, 95, 110, 111, 116). The designation is Christian, and implies a Christian interpretation of Genesis 3 as the source of original sin (*GBL* 2, 328). From a religio-historical perspective, however, Genesis 3 is an origin myth about the human condition and culture (male and female relationships, painful childbirth, life as a farmer, death, etc.). *The School Bible* seems to be familiar with this distinction (pp. 21–22, 72), but nevertheless uses Christian terms, even in several cases where it does not imply a Christian interpretation of Genesis 3. Whether or not the terminology is due to old convention or reflects a deliberate choice, it is unacceptable from the point of view of the study of religion.[32] A term such as "origin myth" would clearly be preferable.

In short, the author of the *Bible Guide* and the *Bible Dictionary* often lacks a professional distance from her own tradition, so that it can be treated as terminologically adequate and on a par with other religious traditions. In a number of areas she uses an *emic* rather than an *etic* terminology. To be sure, problems of this kind in the Folkeskole are by no means restricted to *The School Bible* (Hvithamar and Warmind 2007), but as always: *Two wrongs don't make a right.*

Christian bias. Despite the fact that the Hebrew Bible is more than three times as large as the New Testament, *The School Bible* devotes just as much, or considerably more, space to the New Testament and church issues in general. Admittedly, there are a few excellent exceptions. In a chapter titled "The Bible—in brief" (pp. 23–30) and a chapter titled "The Bible gallery of characters" (pp. 93–105) the amount of the space *The School Bible* uses correlates with the different sizes of the Hebrew Bible and the New Testament. Additionally, one finds a fairly balanced presentation of common narratives in Judaism, Christianity and Islam (pp. 71–76).

In the rest of *The School Bible*, however, this is usually not the case: In the chapter "How was the Bible created, and what is where?" *The School Bible* refers to the Hebrew Bible on pages 32–39 and to the New Testament on pages 39–45. In the chapter "The key elements of the Bible," *The School Bible* refers to the Hebrew Bible on pages 46–49 and to the New Testament on pages 50–55. The chapter "Biblical sayings" includes 15 examples from the Hebrew Bible and 17 examples from the New Testament (pp. 130–36).

In a chapter titled "Key texts," *The School Bible* refers to 42 stories from the Hebrew Bible (pp. 82–83) and to 123 stories from the New Testament (pp. 83–87). In a chapter titled "Key subjects in the Bible" (pp. 88–92), there are 46 references to the Hebrew Bible and 152 references to the New Testament. In a chapter titled "Symbols in the Bible" (pp. 127–29), a number of symbols have been selected, which, in the words of *The School Bible* itself, "are especially important within Christianity" (p. 127).

Additionally, there is a separate chapter on the historical background of the New Testament (pp. 62–70), but, as mentioned above, there is no corresponding chapter on the historical background of the Hebrew Bible. Similarly, *The School Bible* includes a separate chapter on Christian festivals, but you look in vain for a corresponding chapter on Jewish festivals.

In other words, although everything cannot be measured in a quantitative manner, a Christian bias in the disposition and selection of the subject-matter is undeniable. From a religio-historical point of view, *The School Bible* should quite simply have given higher priority to the Hebrew Bible in order to ensure a balanced presentation.

Nor is the academic perspective on religion in focus when *The School Bible* recommends schoolchildren consult the web pages bibelselskabet.dk, religion.dk and kristendom.dk in order to learn more about the Bible (p. 137). The Danish Bible Society is above all a religious organization, not a research institute. Both religion.dk and kristendom.dk are run by *Kristeligt Dagblad* (*Christian Daily*), which in many ways serves as an influential advocate of and agenda-setting forum for the church in Denmark, and it is more often religious people than scholars of religion who write or are interviewed on these web portals (in particular on kristendom.dk). In other words, these web pages are in many cases a source of a religious approach to religion, not an academic approach. *The School Bible*, however, does not say a word about this.

2.2. Review of Bible translations

In addition to the *Bible Guide* and the *Bible Dictionary*, *The School Bible* also contains two Bible translations. The first includes both the Hebrew Bible and the New Testament, and is the authorized Danish Bible translation from 1992, which according to the Danish Bible Society is used by "all Christian churches in Denmark" (Bible Society 2011c). That is not entirely true. Jehovah's Witnesses, for instance, use their own Bible translation, the so-called *New World Translation of the Holy Scriptures*.

The second translation—*The New Agreement* from 2007—includes only the New Testament and is characterized by being written "in a modern and easily accessible language—a language that the schoolchildren understand!" (Bibelselskabet 2011c). In contrast, the language of the authorized Danish translation (hereafter DT92) is more traditional and influenced by church tradition.

The Danish Bible Society is responsible for the preparation and publication of both translations. Moreover, both of them are prepared with a Christian purpose—not only DT92 as we soon shall see, but also *The New Agreement* to a certain extent. Thanks to its modern usage "without the church codes," it is, according to the Danish Bible Society itself, "missionary work in the enlightened and popular terms of the 21st century" (Højsgaard and Raaberg 2011).

Confessional versus non-confessional translation of the Hebrew Bible. The following concerns the translation of the Hebrew Bible, since this is where one finds the greatest divergence between a confessional Christian and a non-confessional scholarly approach. The point is that Christians have always interpreted the Hebrew Bible as a prophecy of Christ, and the New Testament as the fulfilment of this prophecy. Therefore, they have read the two text anthologies as a soteriological-historical unity.

In many ways this has been reflected in the Bible translations of the church. Not only has it placed the two text anthologies in one book called "The Bible," it has also, through titles, headings, comments, illustrations, cross-references and so on, as well as through an often tendentious wording, tried to convey the impression that the Hebrew Bible is about Christ.

In different ways we see this in the first, official Luther Bibles in Denmark, Christian III's translation of the Bible in 1550 and its two revisions, Frederick II's Bible in1589, and Christian IV's Bible in 1633, and we see it in Bishop Resen's Bible in 1607 when the Bible was translated from the original languages for the first time in Denmark. This continues in Bishop Svane's revision in 1647 and in Christian VI's revision in 1740 (Ejrnæs 1995).

With the appearance of modern biblical research in the eighteenth and nineteenth centuries, however, the Christian interpretation of the Hebrew Bible became increasingly problematic. A boundary was set up between the Hebrew Bible and the New Testament. People began to study the text anthologies separately and in their own historical contexts. In short, many realized that the traditional Christian view of the Hebrew Bible as a prophecy of Christ was a result of Christian exegesis; the scholarly exegesis could not confirm it (Ejrnæs 1994).

In a Danish context one of the fruits of modern biblical research was professor Fr Buhl's privately funded, non-confessional translation of the Hebrew Bible in 1910. Here, the text anthology was translated and annotated on its own religio-historical terms. But this was not a translation for the church, and that made an important difference. When the Danish Bible Society in 1917 on the basis of Buhl's version launched a new, authorized translation of the Hebrew Bible, it was considered necessary to prepare an ecclesiastical revision. Thus, the task was, as a former employee of the Danish Bible Society has written, "to develop a translation acceptable to the church, a translation which considered the ecclesiastical understanding of the Old Testament Scriptures" (Kollerup 1994: 22). The result of the revision was the authorized Bible translation of 1931.

What characterizes DT92, which is the most recent, authorized Bible translation in Denmark? Although it is far from unaffected by modern biblical criticism, it continues the traditional Christian approach to Bible translation in important areas.[33] When the new translation of the Hebrew Bible was launched in 1975, it was primarily university theologians from the universities in Aarhus and Copenhagen who were in charge of the work, and although they partially took the church into account, the main emphasis was on a religio-historical approach to the text. Initially the translation work resulted in a number of *sample translations* (hereafter ST) that were published from 1977 to 1989. The purpose of the ST was to gather responses from the public, especially from Danish church people. The responses were to be included in a *revision* of the ST, a revision that would result in the final, authorized translation of the Bible.

The most comprehensive and critical reactions to the ST came from the Christian right (*den kristne højrefløj*) in Denmark. Its two education institutions, the Lutheran School of Theology in Aarhus and the Danish Bible Institute in Copenhagen, submitted a large number of amendments to the Danish Bible Society. In short, the Christian right wanted their own theologians to participate in the revision of the ST, and that the translation of a large number of texts and expressions that have played an important role in the Christian tradition should be changed.

The pressure from the Christian right as well as its numerous amendments had considerable consequences. From 1988 to 1992 several revision teams were established. A so-called *revision committee* was in charge, and it consisted of a mixture of university theologians and church representatives (including three from the Christian right). Its terms of reference were to "discuss and decide on the translation of parts of the Bible which play a crucial theological role in the church tradition, including texts in the Old Testament that are quoted in the New Testament" (Cappelørn 1988: 42–43). Its explicit goal was a "Church Bible" (Kollerup 1994: 57; Cappelørn 1990: 31–34).

This meant that the Hebrew Bible texts should not only be translated in the light of their historical context of composition, but also and especially in the light of their reception history in the New Testament, the church tradition, the Danish Bible and hymn tradition and the national church liturgy. The final result of the translation and revision work, which also included a new translation of the New Testament, was published in 1992.

Generally speaking, the translation can be characterized as a complex mixture of religio-historical and ecclesiastical considerations. The latter are reflected in a variety of areas. Basically, they appear in the placement of the Hebrew Bible next to the New Testament in one book with the common name "the Bible"; in a common table of contents in the beginning; in the continuous pagination between the Hebrew Bible and the New Testament; and in the placement of the prophetic scriptures at the end of the Hebrew Bible (unlike TaNaK, the Jewish Bible, which places them in the middle).

The ecclesiastical considerations in DT92 are also reflected in the use of the title "the Old Testament" as a name for the Hebrew Bible, and in the myriad of cross-references that tie the Hebrew Bible and the New Testament together. Overall, they construct the impression that there is an inextricable link between the two text anthologies. The cross-references are put into perspective by a marked *absence* of references to the religio-historical background and context of the Hebrew Bible. The above mentioned facts are all based upon—and carry on—the fundamental ecclesiastical notion that the Hebrew Bible and the New Testament constitute a continuous soteriological-historical unity (see Herbener 2006: 94–98).

An adaption to the Christian interpretation and use of the Hebrew Bible is to a great extent also reflected in the text itself. This includes, for instance, many of the so-called "scriptural proofs" of the church tradition. Some examples: Unlike the ST the DT92 rendering of Genesis 1:1 supports the ecclesiastical doctrine of *creatio ex nihilo*, and an omnipotent creator god; unlike the ST the DT92 rendering of Genesis 1:2 supports the old ecclesiastical notion that the Holy Spirit already appears here; unlike the ST the DT92 rendering of Genesis 3:15 supports the old Christological interpretation of the text (in the church called "the proto-gospel"); unlike the ST the DT92 rendering of Isaiah 7:14 supports the old Christian interpretation of the text as a prophecy of the Jesus-child; unlike the ST the DT92 rendering of Habakkuk 2:4 supports the Reformation doctrine of salvation by faith; unlike the ST the DT92 rendering of Psalm 22:17 supports the Christian interpretation of the text as a prophecy of Jesus' crucifixion; unlike the ST the DT92 rendering of Psalm 51:7 supports the Christian concept of original sin; unlike the ST the DT92 rendering of Daniel 7:13 supports the New Testament representation of Jesus as the "son of man" (see Herbener 2004a: 161–206; 2004b; 2006: 104–26).

Furthermore, the approximately 300 quotations from the Hebrew Bible in the New Testament, and the several thousand allusions in the New Testament to the Hebrew Bible have been thoroughly coordinated with the purpose, when possible, to establish conformity or recognizability. This revision work was also a result of the ecclesiastical notion that the two text anthologies constitute a soteriological-historical unity.

In addition, a number of old, soteriological theological expressions that had disappeared from the ST, were included in DT92. For example "favour" was corrected to "grace"; "help" was corrected to "salvation"; and "crime" was corrected to "guilt." Moreover, a number of terms in the ST, which the Christian right saw as "pagan," were expunged from DT92. For example "sons of gods" was corrected to "sons of God"; "oracle" was corrected to "answer"; "ecstasy" was corrected to "prophetic rapture"; and "amulet" was corrected to "mark" (see Herbener 2004a: 207–25).

Finally, ecclesiastical considerations are also reflected in the rendering of several god names. For example YHWH who DT92, with a few exceptions, has translated with "the Lord" (to "follow the meaningful tradition of the church"[34]), and *el shaddaj* that DT92 translated with "God Almighty," despite the fact that this meaning is not supported by the Semitic languages (see Herbener 2001: 187–208; 2004a: 225–27).

In other words, although it is less compared with translations in older Bible traditions in Denmark, DT92 still considers the church. The Hebrew Bible is presented in Christian clothing and is in many respects influenced by the interpretation and use of the church. In short, from the academic point of view of the study of religion, the adaptations to the church must be described as anachronistic: In itself, the Hebrew Bible is basically a non- and pre-Christian work, and in a non-confessional translation context, adaptations for the church must therefore be characterized as illegitimate.

As already mentioned, the point is that *The School Bible* includes DT92. Of course, it must be an internal affair of the church that the Danish Bible Society does not inform readers about the adaptations in the version used in the church. But it is unacceptable that it does not inform readers about them when DT92 with *The School Bible* is part of the education system.[35] Thus, the schoolchildren have no chance of discovering that the Hebrew Bible in key areas—including numerous places in the text itself—has been adapted to the ecclesiastical tradition, and most teachers will probably not be aware of this either. It is all the more reprehensible since DT92 has often been criticized for its many adaptations for the church,[36] and because there had been a good opportunity to draw attention to the issue in *The School Bible*.

Another problem is that the Hebrew Bible is not only part of the foundation of Christianity, but in different ways also of Judaism and Islam—which the Folkeskole teaches as well. For that reason as well, the Bible translation that is used should not be influenced by Christianity or any other post-biblical religion, but be academic as far as possible. If such an updated and complete Bible translation does not exist—and it does not in Danish—it is all the more important that the publisher of "the Church Bible" plays with open cards.

To keep the record straight, it should be emphasized that all translation also implies interpretation. There are sometimes several translation options from an academic perspective, and a completely "objective" translation is nothing more than a utopian vision. But there is a *difference* between *disregarding* one's religious preconceptions *as far as possible* and *deliberately putting* them *into* the text. It is the latter that characterizes confessional Bible translations, including DT92. All in all, the application of the DT92 translation of the Hebrew Bible to the subject Christian studies must be considered problematic. As *Common Objectives 2009* say:

> In relation to an academic understanding of religious texts, the historical-critical method plays a fundamental role because the school is engaged in the communication of knowledge. (The Ministry of Education 2009: 20)

Not only has the DT92-translation of the Hebrew Bible in many respects been prepared in accordance with the church tradition, the Danish Bible Society also fails to state so. And no, it is not obvious that the translation is as it is, for the majority hardly gives the issue of confessional versus non-confessional Bible translation any thought. Especially not schoolchildren.

Translations of the New Testament are a different situation. After all, the text anthology is inherently Christian. That does not mean, of course, that translations cannot be influenced by the church organizations which often stand behind them. But, at least, neither the DT92-version of the New Testament nor *The New Agreement* has been the subject of any particular criticism in this respect.

3. CONCLUSIONS

The extensive criticism provided by the present chapter should not belittle the fact that *The School Bible* contains a number of good elements. As already mentioned the book is easily accessible, reasonably structured, and there are several examples of a historical and historical-critical approach. Additionally, it sheds light on both similarities and differences between the Hebrew Bible and the New Testament and makes comparisons between the three monotheistic religions, Judaism, Christianity and Islam. In my opinion, these elements also belong in an academic textbook about the Bible.

As we have seen above, however, *The School Bible* is marred by numerous problems—and more could have been mentioned. The *Bible Guide* and the *Bible Dictionary* contain a number of factual errors, misleading formulations and inconsistencies. They are characterized by omissions or marginal references to elements in the Bible that are reprehensible from a modern, Western point of view. Furthermore, the discussion of the religious background and context of the Hebrew Bible can be placed on a postage stamp, and there is a Christian (especially Protestant) bias, for instance in its terminology, disposition and selection of subject-matter. In many cases, this contributes to a one-sided, uncritical picture of the Bible, and thus important parts of *The School Bible* may serve as a tool to promote the Bible and the church, especially the Danish National Church, in the Folkeskole.

Neither of the two Bible translations included in *The School Bible* are unproblematic. Neither of them are academic, religio-historical translations, but are each in their own way characterized by the fact that they have been prepared with a church/proselytizing purpose. Most problematic is the DT92-version of the Hebrew Bible, which is characterized by a diversity of Christian adaptations and considerations, despite the fact that it is itself a non-Christian work and despite the fact that the Danish Bible Society does not say a word about this.

Is all this an unavoidable consequence of the educational demand that the Folkeskole's textbooks about the Bible must be easily accessible, simplified and concise? No.

From an educational point of view, of course, it is unproblematic to communicate that according to ancient inscriptions Yahweh probably had a wife, and to explicitly state that the Bible among many other things *also* dictates stoning, genocide, religious intolerance, slavery, self-denial, patriarchal dominance, anti-Judaism, and deeds as a condition of salvation. From an educational perspective, it is equally unproblematic to treat the Hebrew Bible (including its religio-historical background) in far greater detail than is the case, just as nothing prevents the author from treating the New Testament on its own religio-historical terms to a far greater extent.

Finally, from an educational perspective, it is unproblematic to use a non-confessional Bible translation à la Semitic philologist Ellen Wulff's recent translation of the Qur'an[37] (if such a Bible translation had been available), or to inform schoolchildren that the authorized Danish translation of the Hebrew Bible is a Christian source text prepared in important respects in accordance with the church tradition. In other words, a textbook about the Bible could easily have been far more historically based, comprehensive and critical without sacrificing the educational aspect, and without requiring more than perhaps 20-25 extra pages.

The conclusion is that *The School Bible* in some respects lives up to a modern, academic approach to religion, but in many respects it does not. On the whole, it is marred by many mistakes and problems.[38]

Does the criticism imply that *The School Bible* also goes against the provisions of *the Folkeskole Act* regarding the subject of Christian studies? Yes, in some respects, but hardly in all. The objects clause of the subject emphasizes that the teaching must provide schoolchildren with "knowledge" about religion. The teaching guide explains that "instruction in ecclesiastical practice is not part of the school's activities," and as quoted above a historical-critical approach must underlie any dealings with religious texts (The Ministry of Education 2009: 3, 19–20).[39] This means that significant parts of *The School Bible* should rather be used as a source of an ecclesiastical understanding of the Bible than as an academic textbook about it.

In contrast, the reading strategy which *The School Bible* gives most space to describing[40] seems to correlate with the requirement that schoolchildren after 9th grade should have learned "to relate to the interpretation of basic issues of life which you find in the biblical narratives" (The Ministry of Education 2009: 4).

Some might argue that the parts of *The School Bible* characterized by an ecclesiastical bias are warranted by *the Folkeskole Act* §6, according to which "the key knowledge area of Christian studies is the Evangelical Lutheran Christianity of the Danish National Church" (Folkeskoleloven 2011). Even if this is the case, it is not tantamount to an *academic* approval of these parts, but that the law is *also* problematic from an academic perspective. As several scholars of religion have pointed out, the law and the end objectives' emphasis on an existential approach to the Bible is more a result of Protestant and theological preferences than of academic considerations (e.g., Jensen 1999, 2009; Rothstein 2002, 2009; Hvithamar and Warmind 2007).

If *The School Bible* is problematic in the Folkeskole, it is on the other hand well suited for confirmation classes[41] and study groups engaged in Christian Bible instruction on the terms of modernity (Højsgaard 2011a: 49–77). The question is whether this should surprise us? No. It is a church organization that is responsible for the publication of *The School Bible*, and it would be naive to imagine that it would publish truly critical textbooks about the Scriptures it tries to promote.[42] In that case the Danish Bible Society would contribute to cutting off the branch it is sitting on. In other words, using *The School Bible* as a textbook in the Folkeskole corresponds to using a textbook about a political party composed by the political party itself.

This does not imply that such a textbook cannot include self-critical elements, but only to a certain degree: When things begin to get dangerous and detrimental to the religious organization, it must be expected that self-criticism will end, and this is not acceptable to a modern education system. Religious considerations— directly or indirectly—should be just as illegitimate in the religious classes as in the biology classes.

Most people would probably be sceptical of a textbook about the Qur'an published by an Islamic organization called "the Danish Quran Society," or of a textbook about L. Ron Hubbard's texts published by a Scientology organization called "the Danish Dianetics Society." This is simply because religious organizations typically lack the distance to represent their sacred texts in a (sufficiently) critical, comprehensive and religio-historical way. As demonstrated, this is precisely the problem with *The School Bible*. The fact that many people are not aware of this is probably a result of having grown up in a society influenced by Protestant Christianity; in short, *habit* which has the power to make culture appear as nature. For the same reason, people do not "see" their own culture in the same way as they see other cultures.[43]

The point is that the school system should take care when using textbooks for which religious organizations are responsible.[44] A critical, secular distance is a necessity, and this cannot reasonably be required from religious organizations. Fortunately, there are more and more scholars of religion who prepare academically based textbooks on religion for the Folkeskole (see Pedersen 2008; Hvithamar, Rothstein and Warmind 2011; Hvithamar and Warmind 2007).[45] This development coincides with a growing interest among scholars of religion in studying and contributing to religious studies throughout the entire education system.[46]

REFERENCES

Allison, Dale. 1998. *Jesus of Nazareth: Millenarian Prophet*. Minneapolis: Fortress Press.

Andreassen, Bengt-Ove. 2008. "'Et ordinært fag i særklasse'. En analyse av fagdidaktiske perspektiver i innføringsbøker i religionsdidaktikk." Tromsø Universitet. Phd dissertation.

Assmann, Jan. 2006. *Monotheismus und die Sprache der Gewalt*. Wien: Picus Verlag.

Assmann, Jan. 2010. *The Price of Monotheism*. Stanford, CA: Stanford University Press.

Bibelselskabet. 2011a. Til omtale/anmeldelse: Skolebibelen—en klassiker er født!

Bibelselskabet. 2011b. http://www.bibelselskabet.dk/Boghandel/Varekatalog/978-87-7523-660-2.aspx.

Bibelselskabet. 2011c. http://www.bibelselskabet.dk/Aktuelt/Nyhedsoversigt/Arkiv%202011/~/media/Pressematerialer/Skolebibelen/SKOLEBIBELEN_tilbud.ashx.

Bilde, Per. 1997. "Jødefjendtlighed i Det Nye Testamente." *Jyllands-Posten* 23.3.1997.

Bilde, Per. 2001. *En religion bliver til. En undersøgelse af kristendommens forudsætninger og tilblivelse indtil år 110*. København: Anis.

Bilde, Per. 2011. "Kristendommens tilblivelse og ældste historie." In *Gyldendals religionshistorie. Ritualer, mytologi, ikonografi*, ed. Tim Jensen, Mikael Rothstein and Jørgen Podemann Sørensen, 227–48. København: Gyldendal, 2nd edn.

Böwadt, Pia. 2001. "Mod til livet—kristendommen i nye klæ'r." *Unge pædagoger*, 7: 19–29.

Böwadt, Pia. 2007. *Livets pædagogik. En kritik af livsfilosofien og dens pædagogisering*. København: Gyldendal.

Cappelørn, Niels Jørgen. 1988. "Den nye danske bibeloversættelse." *Det Danske Bibelselskabs Årbog*, 35–47. København: Det Danske Bibelselskab.

Cappelørn, Niels Jørgen. 1990. "Fra prøveoversættelse til kirkebibel." *Det Danske Bibelselskabs Årbog*, 15–35. København: Det Danske Bibelselskab.

Clair, Michael. 1992. *Millenarian Movements in Historical Context*. New York and London: Garland Publishing.

Ejrnæs, Bodil. 1994. "Det gamle Testamente som del af den kristne kanon i oversættelserne af 1931 og 1992." *Dansk Teologisk Tidsskrift* 57: 161–76.

Ejrnæs, Bodil. 1995. *Skriftsynet igennem den danske bibels historie.* København: Museum Tusculanum.

Folkekirkensskoletjenste.dk. 2011. *Folkekirkens Skoletjeneste—hvad er det?* http://www.folkekirkensskoletjeneste.dk/Baggrund.

Folkeskoleloven. 2011. *Bekendtgørelse af lov om folkeskolen.* https://www.retsinformation.dk/Forms/r0710.aspx?id=133039#K1.

Gearon, Liam. 2006. "Human Rights and Religious Education: Some Postcolonial Perspectives." In *International Handbook of the Religious, Moral and Spiritual Dimensions in Education*, ed. Marian de Souza *et al.*, 375–85. Springer: Dordrecht.

Hedenius, Ingemar. 1985. *Tro og viden.* København: Finn Jacobsens Forlag. Translation by Mogens Boisen.

Herbener, Jens-André P., ed. 2001. *Ny bibeloversættelse—på videnskabeligt grundlag. Introduktion.* København: Det Kongelige Bibliotek and C. A. Reitzel.

Herbener, Jens-André P. 2004a. *Bibeloversættelse mellem konfession og videnskab. Et bidrag til en religionshistorisk vurdering af Bent Melchiors oversættelse af de fem Mosebøger fra 1977-87, den autoriserede bibeloversættelse fra 1992 og Ny bibeloversættelse—på videnskabeligt grundlag fra 2001.* København: C. A. Reitzel. Prize dissertation awarded the gold medal by the University of Copenhagen.

Herbener, Jens-André P. 2004b. "1992-bibelen. Et præliminært bidrag til belysning af oversættelsens art og baggrund." *Chaos: Dansk-Norsk Tidsskrift for Religionshistoriske Studier* 42: 43–67.

Herbener, Jens-André P. 2006. *Teologi og magt. En debatbog om den autoriserede bibeloversættelse.* København: C. A. Reitzel.

Herbener, Jens-André P. 2012. "Summodeisme." *Den sammenklappelige tid. Festskrift til Jørgen Podemann Sørensen*, ed. Tim Jensen and Mikael Rothstein, 243–55. København: Forlaget Chaos.

Herbener, Jens-André P. 2013. "On the Concept of Monotheism." *Numen* 60(4). Forthcoming.

Herbener, Jens-André P., and Philippe Provençal, eds. 2001. *Ny bibeloversættelse—på videnskabeligt grundlag. Annoteret prøveoversættelse. Da Gud begyndte kap. 1-12, Jeshajahu kap. 1-12.* København: Det Kongelige Bibliotek and C. A. Reitzel.

Hjärpe, Jan. 2011. "Islam." In *Gyldendals religionshistorie. Ritualer, mytologi, ikonografi*, ed. Tim Jensen, Mikael Rothstein and Jørgen Podemann Sørensen, 329–83. København: Gyldendal. 2. udg.

Holt, Else, and Kirsten Nielsen. 1997. *Bibelkundskab. Introduktion til Det Gamle Testamente.* Århus: Århus Universitetsforlag.

Hvithamar, Annika, Mikael Rothstein and Morten Warmind. 2011. *Tror du det? 9, religion.* København: Alinea.

Hvithamar, Annika, and Morten Warmind. 2007. "Det religionsvidenskabelige grundvilkår: Religionsvidenskaben i religionsundervisningen." *Religionspædagogisk forum* 1: 63–78.

Højsgaard, Morten Thomsen. 2011a. *Den tredje reformation—fra statskristendom til google-buddhisme.* København: Kristeligt Dagblads Forlag.

Højsgaard, Morten Thomsen. 2011b. "Forfejlet kritik af Bibelselskabet." *Kristeligt Dagblad*, 26.4.2011.

Højsgaard, Morten Thomsen, and Cecilie Vestergaard Raaberg. 2011. "Det Nye Testamente—nu uden kirkekoderne." *Kristeligt Dagblad*, 14.4.2011.

Jensen, Tim. 1999. "Et religionskritisk religionsfag—En sekulær stats svar på den flerreligiøse udfordring." In *Visioner for religionsfrihed, demokrati og etnisk ligestilling*, ed. Lisbet Christoffersen and Jørgen Bæk Simonsen. København: Nævnet for Etnisk Ligestilling, 103–32.

Jensen, Tim. 2007. "The Study of Religions and *Religion* in Denmark." *Nederlands Theologisch Tijdschrift* 61(4): 329–42.

Jensen, Tim. 2008. "RS based RE in Public Schools: A Must for a Secular State." *Numen* 55(2-3): 123–50.

Jensen, Tim. 2009. "Hvordan bliver man religionslærer i Danmark?" *Din: Religionsvitenskapelig tidsskrift* 1: 72–105.

Jyllands-Posten. 2011. *Aktuelt portræt: Bibelguide anno 2011*. 16.3.2011.

Kollerup, Ove. 1994. *Hvem bestemmer over Bibelen? En historisk undersøgelse af retten til at oversætte og udgive autoriserede bibeludgaver i Danmark med særlig vægt på 1992—Bibelens tilblivelse—herunder de kirkelige retningers indflydelse*. Århus: Det Teologiske Fakultet, Århus Universitet. Upubliceret afhandling.

Kristeligt Dagblad. 2011a. *Skoler får ny bibel af menighedsråd*. 28.2.2011.

Kristeligt Dagblad. 2011b. *Slidte bibler kan nu skiftes ud*. 28.2.2011.

Kristeligt Dagblad. 2011c. *Bibelguide har Koranen med*. 6.4.2011.

Lemche, Niels Peter. 2008. *Det Gamle Testamente mellem teologi og historie*. København: Anis.

Lüdemann, Gerd. 1997. *The Unholy in Holy Scriptures: The Dark Side of the Bible*, trans. and with an Appendix by John Bowden. London: SCM Press.

Nelson-Pallmeyer, Jack. 2005. *Is Religion Killing us? Violence in the Bible and the Quran*. New York: Continuum.

Nielsen, Svend Aage. 1977. "Omkring udgivelsen af Davids Salmer." In *Det Danske Bibelselskabs Årbog*, 4–8. København: Det Danske Bibelselskab.

Pedersen, Rene Dybdal. 2008. *Religion i øjenhøjde*. København: Gyldendal.

Pye, Michael, Edith Franke *et al.*, eds. 2006. *Religious Harmony: Problems, Practice and Education*. Proceedings of the Regional Conference of the International Association for the History of Religions, Yogyakarta and Semarang, Indonesia. 27 September—3 October, 2004. Berlin/New York: W. de Gruyter.

Rothstein, Mikael, ed. 1997. *Humanistisk religionsforskning. En indføring i religionshistorie og religionssociologi*. København: Samleren.

Rothstein, Mikael. 2001. *Gud er (stadig) blå*. København: Aschehoug.

Rothstein, Mikael. 2002. "Kulturmødet—og dets betydning for formidling af viden om religion i skolen." In *Kristendomskundskab / Livsoplysning*, ed. John Rydahl, 113–49. København: Gyldendal Uddannelse.

Rothstein, Mikael. 2009. "Folkeskolens religionsfag?" *Unge pædagoger* 4: 11–17.

Skolebibelen. 2011. *Skolebibelen. Med bibelguide og leksikon af Inger Røgild*. København: Det Danske Bibelselskab.

The Ministry of Education. 2009. *Fælles Mål 2009: Kristendomskundskab*. http://www.uvm.dk/~/media/Publikationer/2009/Folke/Faelles%20Maal/Filer/Faghaefter/090707_kristen_08.ashx.

Wulff, Ellen. *Koranen*. København: Vandkunsten.

Zagorin, Perez. 2003. *How the Idea of Religious Tolerance Came to the West*. Princeton, NJ: Princeton University Press.

ABBREVIATIONS

ABD   *The Anchor Bible Dictionary*, 1–6, ed. D. N. Freedman. New York: Doubleday, 1992.

ANET   *Ancient Near Eastern Texts: Relating to the Old Testament*, ed. J. B. Pritchard. New Jersey: Princeton University Press, 1969, 3rd edn with Supplement.

COS   *The Context of Scripture*, ed. W. W. Hallo. I: *Canonical Compositions from the Biblical World*; II: *Monumental Inscriptions from the Biblical World*; III: *Archival Documents from the Biblical World*. Leiden: Brill, 1997–2002.

DDD   *Dictionary of Deities and Demons in the Bible*, ed. K. van der Toorn, B. Becking and P. W. van der Horst. Leiden: Brill, 1999, 2nd edn.

GBL   *Gads Bibelleksikon*, vols 1-2, ed. Gert Hallbäck and Hans Jørgen Lundager Jensen. København: Gads Forlag, 1998.

Endnotes

1. http://www.bibelselskabet.dk/Servicenavigation/OmBibelselskabet/AboutDBS.aspx.
2. The Folkeskole is the name of the municipal primary and lower secondary school (age 7-15) in Denmark.
3. In Danish *kristendomskundskab*; in German *Christentumskunde*.
4. With the word "academic" I refer in this article to a non-confessional, historical and critical perspective of religion.
5. But, of course, without being at the expense of a factual and comprehensive representation.
6. Because of the limited space, the criticism in the following pages does not reflect a systematic and exhaustive review, but only various examples of problematic aspects. In other words, more criticisms could have been mentioned.
7. Think, e.g., of the so-called fourfold method of interpretation (*Quadriga*).
8. Indeed, with *The School Bible*'s emphasis on the Bible as "poetic texts" and with its emphasis on an "existential" reading strategy, it is actually linked directly to the Danish National Church today. As the general secretary of the Danish Bible Society himself has pointed out, "the poetic-existential universe" occupies a key role in the modern National Church of Denmark (Højsgaard 2011a: 75–76).
9. There are other problems related to geography. For instance, the entry on "Judah" says that "the Books of Kings refer to Judah as the Southern Kingdom" (p. 116). This is wrong— "the Southern Kingdom" is a research designation and does not appear in the Bible (see *GBL* 2, 323).
10. The lack of external sources of "the Babylonian exile" has made professor of the Old Testament, Niels Peter Lemche, remark: "The scholar must ask himself whether this exile is much more than an ideological construct created in posterity in order to legitimize that the Jews had a right to Palestine, despite the fact that they were certainly not the only people living in the country" (Lemche 2008: 189).
11. The examples in this article of English translation of the Bible follow *The New Revised Standard Version* (NRSV).
12. See also Inger Røgild's opinion on this matter: "I think it's important to remember that a text has been created in a particular time. One should not believe that the biblical texts can be transferred to the present day without reservations, so I have written a paragraph about how society was around the year 0" (Jyllands-Posten 2011).

13. See at the bottom of the page.
14. See the second column at the middle of the page.
15. See the first column.
16. See at the top of the page.
17. See the second column.
18. A word, which moreover has a wider range of meaning than "holy war," namely "striving," "effort," "battle" and "conflict," depending on the context, see Hjärpe (2011: 375–78).
19. This happens as part of the so-called "ban" (*cherem*), see GBL (1, 67–68).
20. The only and, moreover, marginally placed exception is found at the end of the entry on "crucifixion" (p. 116).
21. As the former professor of practical philosophy at Uppsala University Ingemar Hedenius (1908–1982) has put it: "to present the teachings of a religion as one of the believers is tantamount to being a preacher of these teachings" (Hedenius 1985: 111).
22. Nelson-Pallmeyer (2005: xiv). The quotation in Nelson-Pallmeyer's book also includes the Qur'an; see also Lüdemann (1997); Assmann (2006, 2010).
23. Just as the exclusivism of the New Testament was atypical of the contemporary new religions, see below. It is true that the earliest known example of religious intolerance as a result of a monotheistic revolution is found with the Egyptian King Akhenaten in the fourteenth century BCE, but unlike Akhenaten's short-lived religion the Hebrew Bible had huge religious consequences, see Assmann (2010).
24. See Herbener (2012, 2013).
25. See COS (2, 171–73, 179); Lemche (2008: 298–300). Ashera also plays a remarkable role in the Hebrew Bible, but neither the *Bible Guide* nor the *Bible Dictionary* of *The School Bible* mentions her.
26. The *Bible Dictionary* compensates only poorly for the shortcomings of the *Bible Guide*. The only god in the Hebrew Bible it mentions in addition to Yahweh is Baal (pp. 94, 107).
27. See also the application of "God" in the paragraph *Christian-emic terminology* below.
28. E.g. Matt. 5:20, 27-30, 44-48; 6:19-21; 7:13-14, 17-21; 16:24-28; 19:21, 24, 27-29; Mk 8:34-38; 10:17, 21, 24-25; Lk. 14:7-11, 26-27; 18:18, 22-25; Jn 12:24-26; Rom. 2:6; 1 Cor. 11:1; 2 Cor. 5:10; Phil. 1:27–2:18; Jas. 4:4; 1 Jn 2:15-17; see also above.
29. These characteristics can by no means be restricted to the Book of Revelation, which *The School Bible* does (pp. 28, 30, 45, 115, 126); see, e.g., Matt. 4:17; 10:23; 16:28; 19:28; 24:32-44; Mk 1:15; 9:1; 13:28-36; Lk. 9:27; Rom. 13:11-12; 1 Cor. 7:29-31; 10:11; 15:51; Phil. 4:5; 1 Thess. 4:13-17; 5:2-3; Heb. 10:37; Jas. 5:8-9; 1 Pet. 4:7; 2 Pet. 3:3-14; 1 Jn 2:18; Rev. 1:3; Matt. 24-25; Mk 13; Lk. 21; Rev. 20-22; see also GBL (1, 136–37; 180–81); GBL (2, 123; 407).
30. To give the dark aspects of religions (violence, intolerance, conflict perspectives etc.) a lower priority in favour of a main focus on the light aspects, is a problem that is far from limited to *The School Bible* or a Danish school context, see, e.g., Andreassen (2008); Gearon (2006); Jensen (2008: 132–33).
31. On p. 71 *The School Bible* states that "Tanakh is the same as the Old Testament." It is only half the truth. It is true that they often include the same scriptures, but the *order* of them is different in important respects, see Lemche (2008: 19–23); Holt and Nielsen (1997: 24–26).
32. An example of how the misleading terminology can contribute to a hermeneutic mess is the entry on "Fall": "A biblical expression of the fact that the relationship between man and God is destroyed. For example at the Fall (Gen. 3)" (p. 111). The fact is, however, that we have to go to the New Testament to find a statement that Genesis 3 leads to a "fall" in

the sense of a "destruction" of the relationship between humans and the god (see Rom. 5). From the perspective of the Hebrew Bible itself, this is not the case. As already mentioned, Genesis 3 is most likely a myth about the emergence of culture and the human condition, and the goal is not to return to paradise as it is in countless Christian texts.

33. DT92 and its origin has been reviewed in a detailed and extensively documented way in other publications, see, e.g., Ejrnæs (1994; 1995); Herbener (2001; 2004a; 2004b; 2006). Therefore, only the most important aspects will be outlined here.

34. Nielsen (1977: 7–8).

35. *The School Bible* only says that DT92 is used by the vicar in the church (pp. 10, 13).

36. See Herbener (2004a; 2006).

37. Wulff (2006).

38. It should here be called into question that the Danish Bible Society has asked only one person to prepare both the *Bible Guide* and the *Bible Dictionary*. Given the present specialization and hyper-specialization both in the Hebrew Bible and the New Testament, it is impossible for one person to manage it all in an acceptable way—even at the level of primary and lower secondary school. At least two people should have been put on the job, and they should also have good language skills.

39. It should be noted that the emphasis on "knowledge" is of a fairly recent date and is related to the fact that Christian studies since 2007 has been an examination subject. It is not compulsory, however, but drawn at random, see Jensen (2009: 73–78).

40. I.e. the "existential."

41. Indeed, according to the Danish Bible Society it has *also* been prepared with confirmation classes in mind (Bibelselskabet 2011b).

42. For example, by informing that early Christianity represents one of history's cardinal examples of a millenarian-apocalyptic movement that failed. Contrary to what many of the scriptures of the New Testament predict will happen within a short time, this world has not come to an end. Jesus has not come again. Judgment Day has not taken place. The kingdom of God has not manifested itself. The *Bible Guide* and the *Bible Dictionary* do not mention a word on the failed prophecies of the New Testament.

43. As has been written about many of textbooks about Christianity in the Folkeskole: "Christianity is presented as the normal, natural, virtually non-religious, cultural phenomenon in Denmark—and is almost inevitably identified with the Danish National Church; that, however, is only one version of the multifaceted phenomenon that Christianity is" (Hvithamar and Warmind 2007: 66–67).

44. As well as people with close relations to religious organizations, in this case Inger Røgild who works in the School Service of the Danish National Church, which aims "to strengthen the cooperation between local churches and schools (vicars and teachers) on educational tasks" (Folkekirkensskoletjeneste.dk 2011).

45. In comparison, scholars of religion have for a long time prepared textbooks for *gymnasiet* (i.e., upper secondary school/high school), see Jensen (2007: 342).

46. See, e.g., the IAHR-conference report, *Religious Harmony: Problems, Practice and Education* (Pye, Franke *et al.* 2006) and especially the journal *Numen* 55 (2–3) that is dedicated to religious education.

INDEX

Østnor, A. 172
Otterbeck, J. 40–41, 224–26
Otto, R. 9, 22–23, 41, 66, 182–83, 195
Ox, J. L. 195

P
Paden, W. E. 41
Paine, C. 135, 154–55
Palestine 138, 235–36, 250
Parker, I. 174
Parrinder, Geoffrey 174, 209
Parsism 165–66
Partridge, C. H. 209
Parvati 149
Passion, the 148, 156
Paul 27, 37, 232–33, 237
P'Bitek. O. 209
Pedersen, R. D. 225, 247, 249
Peled-Elhanan, N. 5, 14
Persecution 49, 61, 237
Peterson, N. 132
Pettersen, T. B. 172
Phayakkharachasak, C. 60
Phenomenology of religion 9, 19–20, 182, 185, 192
Philosophy, contemporary 46
Philosophy of life 194, 196, 218
Pingel, F. 7, 14, 154–55
Plate, S. B. 135, 154–55
Plato 54–55
Pluralism 29, 120, 132
    religious 78, 86, 88
Political correctness 11, 118, 124, 127, 130
Polygamy 121
Power text 4–7
Practices
    everyday 92
    Jewish 91–92, 95
    religious 74, 84, 91, 135, 165, 193, 202
Prayer 26–27, 51, 83, 92–93
Prehistoric 12, 204–208
Primary school 15, 103–104, 111, 116, 174, 178, 180
Primitive 199, 201–202, 204–205, 210
Primitive religions 23, 199, 204, 207
Primitivism 161–62, 171, 175
Prophecies 234, 240–41, 243
Protestant/Protestantism 13, 24, 66, 87, 89, 109, 161–64, 212, 236, 245–47

Prothero, S. 6, 14
Public schools 10, 16, 44–45, 54, 60–62, 64, 74, 78, 177–78, 184, 194–95, 249
Publishers 6, 8, 43, 48, 53, 58, 61, 78, 89, 99–101, 106, 111–13, 139, 142, 146, 148, 161–62, 166, 168, 171–72, 174, 178–79, 197, 207, 229, 244
Puja 138–39

Q
QCA 101, 103, 112, 115–16, 140, 154
Qualitative research 72, 76
Quebec 10–11, 86–97, 177
    contemporary 88
Quebec Jewish community 86
Quebec Ministry of Education 11, 89, 97
Quebec Society 89–90, 95
Quebecers 86–87, 90, 95
Qur'an 25, 27, 30, 52, 72, 74, 93, 108, 110, 228, 245–46, 249, 251

R
Raaberg, C. V. 248
Racine, J. 96
Racism 17, 118
Radha 149
Raj, S. J. 132
Rama 149
Ramayana 69, 74
Ranger, T. 210–11
Rasmussen, T. 173, 195, 197
Ray, B. C. 210
Read, K. A. 132
Reeh, N. 225
Reinach, S. 210
Religio-historical approach 236–38, 240–41, 245
Religion, definitions of 23, 66, 183, 188
Religion education 11, 44, 62–64, 71, 74, 78–81, 177–80, 193, 195, 222
    Islamic 63
Religion/s in RE 132, 142, 186–90
Religion teachers 10, 16, 119, 213–14, 223
Religions
    aboriginal Australian 118, 120–21, 124–25, 130
    Africa maps 162
    American Indian 205, 208
    ancient 205, 208

Lightning Source UK Ltd.
Milton Keynes UK
UKOW04f2244210714

235535UK00001B/6/P